Ugo Rabbeno

The American commercial Policy

Three historical Essays

Ugo Rabbeno

The American commercial Policy
Three historical Essays

ISBN/EAN: 9783337188597

Printed in Europe, USA, Canada, Australia, Japan

Cover: Foto ©ninafisch / pixelio.de

More available books at **www.hansebooks.com**

THE AMERICAN COMMERCIAL POLICY

THE AMERICAN COMMERCIAL POLICY

THREE HISTORICAL ESSAYS

BY

UGO RABBENO

PROFESSOR OF POLITICAL ECONOMY IN THE UNIVERSITY OF MODENA

SECOND EDITION
PARTLY RE-WRITTEN AND ENTIRELY REVISED BY THE AUTHOR

TRANSLATED AT THE TRANSLATIONS BUREAU
LONDON, W.C.

London
MACMILLAN AND CO.
AND NEW YORK
1895

TO

MY MOTHER

LOST BUT STILL FONDLY CHERISHED

AS MY GUIDING STAR

TO

MY WIFE

WHOSE AFFECTIONATE ENCOURAGEMENT HAS TAUGHT ME

TO SEEK IN LABOUR

A SOLACE FOR EVERY AFFLICTION

PREFACE

THE student of the great question of international trade cannot but be struck by the strange contrast between economic science and the actual state of things: on the one hand, science, which during the whole of this century has been endeavouring to perfect and complete the doctrines of Adam Smith and Ricardo, and which has built up a theory of international trade, esteemed one of its greatest triumphs, proclaiming harmony and union of human interests; on the other hand, history, which lays before us the sad spectacle of animosities and cruelly persistent struggles. The theory of free-trade is held by economists almost as a dogma of faith; history shows us in reality the mercantile policy and the colonial system of past centuries, and the protectionist policy so widely diffused at the present day.

This divergency is rendered still more serious by the fact that the struggle which had been going on for so many years has so far influenced men's minds as to render a just and impartial judgment almost an impossibility; so that while one party holds that any deviation from the strict doctrine of free-trade, or any doubt or qualification, is an error to be condemned as a heresy, the other party maintains that the whole theory of free-trade is merely a Utopia, an abstract idea of absolutely no practical value.

And yet, as an illustrious economist once observed, it is

unreasonable to believe that any institutions based upon error can last for any length of time and reappear at different epochs and places; it is not possible that what has been a fact for centuries can only be the result of wandering minds; neither may we allow, on the other hand, that a theory, which has been so warmly and for so long a time approved by economists, and has also stood the test of prolonged experiments, can only prove to be some vague and abstract conception, far removed from the reality of facts.

In the meantime, however, both the student and the statesman, who, keeping aloof from partiality, desire to examine the question from a just point of view, find that in this variance between science and history, between logic and facts, they are left perplexed and doubtful, without a sure guide to lead them out of their uncertainty.

This unhappy condition of affairs is due, in my opinion, to the fault of scientific method; the abstract theory with regard to international trade is sound enough, but the concrete idea, that is to say, the historical interpretation given to each particular fact, is, I think, very defective. The former can to a certain extent be a guide to the latter, but of itself it is absolutely insufficient. Hitherto the science of economics has proceeded by the method of deduction; now, however, it must start afresh and take an inductive course. By the former method it has traced in theory the rules which, in certain abstract and uniform conditions, international trade should follow; but now by a course of inductive investigations it must point out the historical laws which it follows in each separate instance. To the abstract study of the laws regulating international trade we must now substitute a definite research of the causes which, at the different epochs of the economic existence of a nation, have determined the adoption of one or the other system of commercial policy. Such a research will certainly prove very difficult, requiring great impartiality of judgment, for it is no easy matter to discover the real causes of a number of social facts.

But if the course to pursue be a long and troublesome one, it is also productive of new and important results; it is the only one which can breathe new life into a question that seemed almost extinct, and after all it is the only method that remains to be tried, since, after so long a series of abstract researches, the result has certainly not proved entirely successful.

We have already some elements to start with in this new field of inductive investigation in the theory of international trade, and some light has already been thrown upon the subject by eminent writers. Still we are yet very far from the end that we are aiming at, and there is plenty of scope for further researches.

The present work purposes to be a modest contribution to this new order of investigations. It does not propose to trace out a new theory, but simply to explain certain facts which during a long period of time have been taking place in the United States; and from them to draw conclusions which, though they are as yet only referable to that country, may perhaps, after other researches, be also applicable to other nations.

The novelty of my researches, the difficulty of the method followed, the desire to maintain scrupulous accuracy and impartiality, and a certain natural hesitation that one cannot quite throw off when compelled by facts to question principles generally accepted by science, have perhaps rendered my conclusions not altogether clear and definite; and consequently I have not tried to disguise certain doubts and uncertainties that may yet remain in my mind. But these faults, which I frankly confess, and which have arisen chiefly from the fact of my desiring, above all, to avoid partiality, in order that my statements may prove independent and free from bias, these faults, I trust, will gradually disappear as I acquire greater experience in the method which I have followed, and as I continue my investigations on the commercial policy of other countries.

In the present English edition I have endeavoured to improve my work by several modifications which seemed opportune, omitting in some parts useless digressions, in other parts adding new statements of facts and observations, taking advantage of recent publications, and profiting by the various suggestions and criticisms of some of the most competent authors who have, generally in a favourable light, noticed my work in the scientific reviews.

The translator has in most instances been able to revise the quotations by comparing them with the English originals. In those cases, however, where this has not been possible, I must beg the indulgence of the authors from whose writings I have drawn, if they find their ideas, the sense of which has always been scrupulously adhered to, expressed in words different to those in which they were originally written.

My warmest thanks are due to all those who, either by their advice or by providing me with matter for my investigations, have been generous in their help. Among the Americans I particularly desire to thank Professors Seligman, Ely, and Patten, also Colonel Carroll D. Wright, the eminent Commissioner of Labour in Washington; and among my own countrymen, Comm. Luigi Bodio, ever ready to aid all students; Professor Luigi Cossa, for many useful suggestions; Professor Giuseppe Ricca Salerno, from whose excellent work on protectionism I have derived many of my ideas; and lastly, to my dear friend Professor Achille Loria, to whom I am so closely drawn by sympathy of ideas, and who with patient care and brotherly kindness revised the whole Italian edition of this work.

I have to tender my grateful thanks to Professor Edgeworth, of the University of Oxford, who, by so favourably

PREFACE

commending my work to Messrs. Macmillan, obtained for me the honour of an English translation; and also to Professor Taussig, of Harvard University (Mass.), so well versed in the history of American tariffs, who kindly accepted the task of revising the proof-sheets of this edition, and furnished me with many useful suggestions. And finally, I must express my sincere appreciation of the services of Mr. Leo Culleton, through whose Translations Bureau the translation has been carried out.

UGO RABBENO.

UNIVERSITY OF MODENA (ITALY),
November 1894.

SUMMARY OF CONTENTS

	PAGES
DEDICATION	v
PREFACE .	vii

FIRST ESSAY

The English Commercial Policy in the North American Colonies

CHAPTER I

FACTS RELATING TO THE COMMERCIAL POLICY OF ENGLAND IN THE NORTH AMERICAN COLONIES, FROM THEIR ORIGIN TO THE DECLARATION OF INDEPENDENCE (4TH JULY 1776)

1. Importance of the evolution of English commercial policy in the North American colonies. 2. Three distinct periods: from their origin to the Navigation Acts; the Navigation Acts; from these to the independence of the colonies. 3. Ideas of colonial monopoly in England prior to the foundation of the colonies. 4. Slight traces of commercial monopoly during the first period of the existence of the colonies, which enjoyed almost complete commercial liberty. 5. The Navigation Acts; traditions of protection to shipping in England. 6. Cromwell's Act; its objects and regulations; it only slightly restricted the commercial liberty of the colonies. 7. The Act of Charles II.; its stipulations; this Act monopolised not only the navigation, but also the commerce of the colonies, and tended to impoverish them to the sole advantage of the mother-country. 8. Third period of colonial policy; rise of the system of prohibitions against colonial manufactures. 9. Last years of English domination; the colonial system becomes still more oppressive. 10. Revolt and emancipation of the colonies 3-25

CHAPTER II

THE GENESIS OF THE ENGLISH COMMERCIAL POLICY IN THE NORTH AMERICAN COLONIES

                                                                PAGES
11. Practical and scientific elements in the origin of the English commercial policy: the first elements have already been noticed; the second are to be seen in the mercantilist system: characteristics of the latter; its policy. 12. Historical justification of mercantilism. 13. Historical evolution of the mercantilist theory; its successive transformations; first manifestations of a reaction in favour of free-trade, which, however, did not yet exercise any influence. 14. English colonial policy as treated by Adam Smith; he justifies the Navigation Acts and commercial monopoly, though not without criticism, but condemns the prohibitions of manufactures. 15. Ricardo admits colonial monopoly to be advantageous to England. 16. Historical justification of the English colonial monopoly. 17. Justification of Adam Smith's opinion of the English colonial policy 26-47

CHAPTER III

THE EFFECTS OF THE ENGLISH COMMERCIAL POLICY UPON THE NORTH AMERICAN COLONIES

18. Social and economic conditions of the American colonies before the Navigation Acts: their prosperity; their primitive economic life; agricultural predominance; small importance of commerce. 19. Effects of the Navigation Acts; Cromwell's Act did not injure the colonies, neither did the Act of Charles II. because of the condition of the colonies at the time. 20. Causes of increased severity of the colonial policy during the third period; prohibition of manufactures. 21. Condition of English manufactures in the eighteenth century; their progress and transformation; formation of the factory system; necessity of protection; this explains the colonial prohibitions. 22. Economic and social condition of the colonies during this period; increase of population; greater importance of international commerce and manufactures. 23. The industrial productiveness continued, however, to be extremely limited and non-progressive; the very conditions of the land contributed to this effect. 24. The economic condition and evolution of the colonies described by Franklin; causes that prevented the progress of manufactures in America during the first half of the eighteenth century; abundance of free lands and impossibility of hired labour. 25. In 1760 Franklin foresees the possibility of a transformation, and the development of manufactures; up till

SUMMARY OF CONTENTS

then, however, the manufactures being very scarce, the prohibitions were not burdensome. 26. Later on complaints begin to break out. 27. At length very energetic protests are made against the English prohibitions. 28. Although the prohibitions against manufactures began with the century, yet no complaints appeared before 1760, because the condition of the colonies rendered such prohibitions only slightly injurious; protests and resistance of the colonists during the last years, which, though caused by the colonial policy, at last really prejudicial, were more especially due to political reasons. 29. Conclusion: until Cromwell's time the colonies had enjoyed commercial freedom; the Navigation Acts caused less damage than is usually believed, owing to the economic condition of the colonies, and to the then small importance of international commerce; even the industrial prohibitions were not very injurious until towards the latter half of the eighteenth century, because no industrial development had yet been possible; the colonial policy was therefore both historically rational and practicable, and only towards the end did it begin to decline, and even then, if it co-operated to bring about the revolution, it was not the sole and essential cause of it 48-91

SECOND ESSAY

The Causes of the Commercial Policy of the United States

CHAPTER I

FROM THE DECLARATION OF INDEPENDENCE TO THE ESTABLISHMENT OF THE CONSTITUTION

1. Historical notes; the Confederation; weakness of its government. 2. The right of regulating commerce denied to the Confederation. 3. Two periods, from the beginning of the war to the Treaty of Paris, 1783; and from 1783 to 1789; interruption of the foreign trade of the colonies during the war, resulting in an impulse to the colonial manufactures; slight importance of the commercial policy through the suspension of commerce; the commercial policy of each State as distinguished from that of the Continental Congress. 4. Tendency towards monopoly and protection in the colonies during the English rule. 5. This tendency continued in the new independent States, which had the right of regulating their own commerce. 6. Free-trade proclaimed by Congress; an important step in itself, even if of no practical value; its political causes; free-trade, moreover, was the most suitable *régime* for the United States at this period. 7. The war, though giving impulse to

xvi   THE AMERICAN COMMERCIAL POLICY

PAGES

American manufactures, did not alter their character ; the peace and the resulting importation of foreign goods injured them considerably. 8. These circumstances naturally suggest the idea of protection in the country ; each State adopts protective measures. 9. The inefficiency of these measures through absence of co-ordination ; lack of authority in the Congress ; necessity of political and economic unity, and of a common commercial policy ; this latter need gives a great impulse towards the formation of the Federal Constitution 95-110

CHAPTER II

THE TARIFF OF 1789—THEORETICAL PROCLAMATION OF PROTECTION IN THE UNITED STATES AND ITS PRACTICAL IMPOSSIBILITY

10. Importance of the economic history of the United States ; our task limited to the examination of the factors that caused their commercial policy, and especially the reasons for adopting protection. 11. Three elements in the American commercial policy ; the productive condition of the country, wars, and the exigencies of Federal finance. 12. A preliminary view of the history of American commercial policy ; four great periods into which it is divided. 13. The first acts of American commercial policy ; the duties on tonnage ; the customs tariff of 1789 ; different opinions respecting it. 14. Arguments in favour of the thesis that the object of this tariff was protection. 15. Arguments in favour of the contrary thesis that its scope was only political and fiscal ; this idea, though in our opinion the correct one, is somewhat exaggerated ; the tariff of 1789 not protective, because the industrial conditions of the country neither demanded nor would have tolerated protection. 16. Condition of American industries in 1789 ; various sources of our information ; Hamilton's *Report* ; slight and primitive development of industries and means of transport. 17. Impossibility of protection under these conditions, and consequently free-trade a natural course for the country as satisfying the interests of all ; the capitalist origin of protection, then still premature 111-133

CHAPTER III

THE AMERICAN TARIFFS FROM 1789 TO 1807—FARTHER IMPRACTICABILITY OF PROTECTION

18. Successive increase of duties from 1789 to 1808, caused almost exclusively by financial difficulties. 19. Alexander Hamilton's *Report on Manufactures;* a most important document of these

SUMMARY OF CONTENTS xvii

times; its importance more scientific than practical. Hamilton's scheme of protection; moderate proposals made by Hamilton; even these not accepted; protection still premature. 20. Progress of protective ideas. 21. Political and industrial condition of the United States in this period; increase of American international commerce in consequence of political events; its effect upon the manufacturing industries, which were progressing very slowly; necessity for free-trade still continues 134-145

CHAPTER IV

THE FOUNDATION OF THE FACTORY SYSTEM AND THE PROTECTIVE POLICY

(From 1807 to 1832)

22. Historical notes; almost complete destruction of American international trade. 23. Impulse given to American manufactures; they undergo a transformation; Gallatin's report on manufactures; their condition; difficulties they met with; rapid progress in the formation of capitalism. 24. The peace of 1815 threatens the growing manufactures with inundation of foreign goods; demands for protection; the "American system" started; the tariff of 1816 in reality a protective one. 25. Growth of protective ideas in the country; supporters and adversaries of protection; increased protection in the tariffs of 1824 and 1828; reaction against protection; rebellion; diminution of the tariff in 1832; the Compromise Act of 1833 establishes a gradual reduction in duties. 26. Interpretation of the above facts; political events were only among the causes of the adoption of protection; the real cause to be found in the condition of industries, which were then in a state of transition during the period of the formation of the factory system; towards 1832 this period had ceased. 27. The idea of protecting the young industries especially favoured during this period; mentioned by Hamilton and List and accepted by Stuart Mill; this, however, not sufficient to explain the rise of protectionism in America; the protected industries were not infant industries. 28. The capitalist theory of protectionism; this can only arise together with capitalism; utility of protection during the foundation of capitalism; its object; the theories of Loria and Ricca Salerno; protection paralyses the effects of free land, forces the labourer to work for wages, and lowers the rate of wages; this fact is indirectly confirmed by Carey. Important observations of E. G. Wakefield. 29. The American land policy and its relation to capitalism and protection. 30. Effects of protection on the manufactures during this period; Taussig's researches; paucity of results; this, however, must not discourage further researches 146-183

CHAPTER V

THE CONSOLIDATION OF AMERICAN INDUSTRY AND FREE-TRADE

(From 1833 to 1861)

31. American tariff policy during this period; protection abandoned; gradual progress towards free-trade; brief interruption from 1842 to 1846; the tariff of 1846 renews the movement towards free-trade; this proceeds gradually; is more accentuated by the tariff of 1857 and lasts until 1861. 32. Causes of this policy; economic and industrial conditions of the United States; great industrial progress of the country; the American manufacturing industry at length consolidated. 33. Rational and historical explanation of protection. 34. The consolidation of capitalism rendered protection useless precisely when its excesses had made it intolerable; free-trade, a natural consequence of the development of the capitalist industry, would have lasted much longer in the United States but for disturbing facts that arose afterwards. 35. Effects of the American tariff policy at this time; Taussig's researches; limited influence of the tariff policy on industries; relative importance of international trade particularly in the United States . . 184-199

CHAPTER VI

THIRTY YEARS OF PROTECTION—"THE GOLDEN AGE" OF THE AMERICAN SYSTEM

(From 1861 to the present day)

36. War and protection; protection movement begun after the crisis of 1857; financial difficulties during the war cause an increase of tariff; this increase had also a protective aim; exaggerated scale reached by the tariffs. 37. Disturbances in prices and industries after the war; the protectionists take advantage of this in order to maintain and increase protection; the tariff only reduced in 1883; the reduction only fictitious. 38. The downward movement of prices increases protection; but the favourable conditions of finance demand a reduction; discussions in Congress in 1887-1888; victory of the republican protectionists; MacKinley's tariff of 1890; its character; its hostility towards all foreign importations; signs of reaction in the country against the excesses of protection. 39. The arguments now advanced by American protectionists; those of Carey now forgotten; the thesis of infant industries abandoned; important discussion on wages; protection intended to keep up American wages. 40. Protection cannot raise wages, but rather tends to lower them. 41. The high rate of American wages does not cause industry to be inferior, but it is a consequence of the great productive power of industry; Cairnes' remarks. 42. Gunton's theory; the necessity of manufactures not a novel idea, and no longer applicable to the United States;

SUMMARY OF CONTENTS

protection necessary to the advanced nations against the less advanced; criticism on this idea; it implies absolute protection; the "Chinese Wall Men." 43. The idea of absolute protection now prevailing in American tariff policy. 44. Industrial and economic condition of the United States in this period; impulse to industries during the war; crisis at the cessation of hostilities; this explains the continuation of protection for some time; but its persistence is due to deeper causes. 45. Wonderful progress of the American industries: extension of internal commerce; immense progress of certain industries; particulars of the last census; general welfare of the country. 46. The industrial depression; its character, and its spread even to the United States; explanatory theory of this serious phenomenon; the depression considered as a general crisis of the capitalist industry. 47. Industrial coalitions; the present transformations of competition; different forms of the coalitions; importance and character of the American trusts; their drawbacks and advantages; their supporters and opponents; nature and real value of the trusts. 48. Relations between the coalitions and protection noticed by several writers; coalitions considered by some as a result of protection; Dalla Volta's opinion; coalitions and protectionism are closely connected, and result from industrial depression. 49. The above considerations may afford an explanation of the American protection; industrial depression the chief cause of it; coalitions and protection a means of resistance of capitalists against depression of profits; protection as a means of lowering wages; but of less importance now than formerly. 50. The land policy in this period, and capitalism. 51. Protection as well as coalitions tend to limit production and to retard the depression of profits; Ricca Salerno's observations. 52. Other causes of the present American protection; protection as a momentary remedy for the crisis, and as a means of resistance against technical transformations. 53. Changes in international trade; crisis in capitalism leads to struggles among nations; the tendency to extend the attributions of the state. 54. Why the present protectionist reaction is not common to all countries; the causes that have prevented it in England. 55. Special causes that have favoured protection in the United States; protectionist traditions; corruption; the secession war; small importance of international trade to the United States, and growing importance of internal commerce. 56. Unimportant results gained by protection during this period; the great interests it has sacrificed   200-258

CHAPTER VII

SYNTHESIS—FREE-TRADE AND PROTECTION IN THE HISTORY OF THE UNITED STATES OF AMERICA

57. Alternate adoption of free-trade and protection in the history of the United States. 58. First period of American history; small

importance of trade; the development of manufactures impossible; prevalence of agriculture; development of international trade; necessity of free-trade; how free-trade at that time suited all classes; the demands for protection isolated and powerless. 59. The theory of free-trade and the interests of the different classes of the people; exceptions to the free-trade theory. 60. Second period of American commercial history; capitalist industry; division between capitalists and workers; divergency of their interests; protection desired by capitalists during the transformation of industry; it helped to lower the status of the worker, to raise prices, and to increase profits. Historical conditions which made protection necessary; protection though burdensome to the country finally proved advantageous to the general interests; its transitory character. 61. The interests of the agriculturists different from those of the manufacturers; reason why the latter prevailed. 62. Third period: the capitalist industry at length consolidated; the working classes already depressed enough; protection becomes useless to the capitalists; free-trade is now even advantageous to them, whilst it is necessary for agriculture and the country at large; protection and the land rent; free-trade and the labourers. 63. The last period: the struggle between the two dominant classes, agricultural and manufacturing; economic causes of the war of secession; free-trade and slavery favourable to the development of the land rent; both opposed by the capitalist manufacturers; altered conditions at the cessation of the war and the abolition of slavery; the protection to manufactures becomes comparatively useful also to agriculturists; but the increased severity of it following upon the industrial depression causes renewed antagonism between agriculturists and manufacturers; settlement by compromise uniting agricultural and manufacturing protection; importance of the agricultural protection in the United States; it paralyses the advantages to the capitalist of the manufacturing protection; struggle between profit and land rent; protection nullifies the efforts of capitalism; the land rent threats. 64. The question of international trade and the labourers; how free-trade and protection are both in their turn injurious to the labourers; uselessness of their sacrifice and of protection; the question of free-trade and protection can only be settled by such a change as will substitute, in the place of antagonism, the unity of social interests 259-281

APPENDIX

Imports into the United States from 1791 to 1893, and mean standard of the *ad valorem* duties 282-284

THIRD ESSAY

The Theory of Protectionism in the United States and the Historical Circumstances of its Development

CHAPTER I

ALEXANDER HAMILTON

1. The theory of protection in the United States; our study confined to some authors in relation to the historical surroundings in which they lived. 2. Alexander Hamilton; influence he exercised both in American politics and in the history of protection; his opinions; biographical notes. 3. Hamilton's political ideas; the Federal and Republican parties; their tendencies and their relations with the commercial policy. 4. Hamilton's financial work; arrangement of the public debt; its practical utility; Hamilton's inexact views with regard to the public credit. 5. The United States Bank; monetary arrangements; the basis of Federal finance; customs tariffs; importance of Hamilton's financial work. 6. Hamilton and the protective theory; the *Report on Manufactures*; its practical and scientific importance; contents of the *Report*; American industry as described in it. 7. The theoretical part of the *Report on Manufactures*; summary of ideas therein contained in support of protection. 8. Characteristics of Hamilton's views; he admits the advantages of free-trade, but raises the exceptions of reprisals and reciprocity; analogy with "fair trade"; importance of the political view in Hamilton's *Report*; his idea of protection is a moderate one. 9. Economic arguments adopted by Hamilton in favour of protection; these form to a great extent the basis of the protective system; necessity of the co-existence of agriculture and manufactures, and importance of the latter; necessity for a home market for the disposal of the agricultural produce of the country; heavy cost of transport which American producers have to bear; protection of infant industries. 10. Importance given by Hamilton to bounties and premiums, which he prefers to taxes as a means of protection; nature of Hamilton's protection. 11. Sumner's accusations against Hamilton; Hamilton and mercantilism; mercantilist reminiscences in Hamilton's *Report*; he is not, however, a mercantilist. 12. Connection between Hamilton and Adam Smith; criticism of physiocratic doctrines maintained by these authors; Hamilton's errors respecting the land rent; how they may be justifiable. 13. The advantages of the division of labour; importance of the means of transport; Hamilton profited by Smith's work. 14. Hamilton and List; superiority of the latter; but the elements of his system taken from Hamilton's *Report*. Hamilton and Carey; great superiority

of the former. 15. Hamilton's protective theory, and the conditions under which it developed; these conditions explain his contradictions; the political conditions of the United States justify Hamilton's mercantilist reminiscences; the formation of the capitalist class, only just commenced, justifies protectionism, whereas the general conditions of the country, adverse to protection, induce him to modify it; Hamilton the precursor of American protectionism 287-324

CHAPTER II

FREDERICK LIST

16. Frederick List an important figure in the history of protectionism. 17. List's national system; national economy; periods of the economic evolution; necessity for the development of manufactures; obstacles in their way; protection as an historical means of industrial education; during what period and under what circumstances this is necessary; theory of the productive forces. 18. Origin of List's system; condition of Germany at the beginning of the century; the multiplicity of German customs; the continental blockade and its effects upon manufactures; foreign competition after the peace of 1815; the *Zollverein*. 19. Comparison between the condition of Germany and America at this period. 20. The influence that the conditions of Germany had upon List; his work for the *Zollverein;* his doubts about the free-trade theory; as yet, however, he had no idea of protection. 21. This idea was matured in America between 1825 and 1830; influence of American surroundings upon his ideas. 22. The *Outlines of American Political Economy*, published by List in America in 1827; importance of this work: full summary of its contents. 23. Comparison with the *National System;* the fundamental ideas of it already contained in his *Outlines;* originality of these ideas. 24. Merits of List's system; reaction against the abstract ideas of the classical school; the political view; the historical method first introduced by List into the science of economics; he illustrates the historical conception of protection, and makes it the basis of his system. 25. Defects of List's system; its exaggerations, partiality, imperfections, and uncertainties; List and the capitalist theory of protection. 26. Great importance of List's system; its defects are due to the surroundings and to the novelty of the method followed by the author 325-354

CHAPTER III

HENRY C. CAREY

27. Carey and his system. 28. Summary of Carey's system; optimism prevailing throughout it; the theory of value; the theory of

SUMMARY OF CONTENTS

wages ; the theories of population and of land rent. 29. Carey's protectionist theory ; the necessity for a reciprocal development of agriculture and manufacturing; the laws of the succession of cultivations ; injury from exportation of agricultural products ; exhaustion of the land ; cost of transport ; importance of internal commerce ; necessity for favouring its growth by means of protection. 30. Criticism of Carey's system ; criticism of his theory of value and distribution of wealth. 31. Criticism of Carey's protectionist theory ; it contains elements of truth, but these are rendered absurd by his method of framing them ; the importance of agriculture and internal commerce illustrated by Carey ; his law for the succession of cultivations does not necessarily mean protection ; danger of the supremacy of one country over another ; criticism of Carey's ideas respecting exportation as impoverishing the land, and regarding costs of transport ; criticism of Carey's absolute protectionism. 32. Carey and the mercantile system ; the money ; the commercial balance ; the theory of industrial autonomy. 33. Carey's method ; its want of order ; his erroneous application of the inductive method ; its contradictions. 34. Carey and the state of affairs in America ; times in which he lived and worked ; his theories an anachronism. 35. Carey's optimism and the American situation ; his ideas regarding value, wages, population, and land rent are not sufficiently justified by the surroundings in which they were developed. 36. Carey's protection theory upheld at the very time when free-trade was necessary in the United States. 37. Carey's absolute protectionism ; its comparison with the more recent ideas on protection ; he appreciated the importance of internal commerce ; in what respect he understood the American situation. 38. General opinion upon Carey's system ; he was not equal to his fame, and his protectionist theory is much inferior to that of Hamilton and List 355-383

CHAPTER IV

SIMON N. PATTEN

39. Importance of Patten's writings ; the "Wharton School" of Philadelphia. 40. Patten's theory of consumption ; tendency of the alimentary necessities to decrease. 41. The adaptation of consumption to the condition of affairs ; possibility of supporting a more numerous population ; tendency of the excess of population to discontinue and the land rent to cease through the effect of changes in consumption. 42. Static and dynamic economy ; how Patten understood these two forms of economy. 43. Patten's protective system ; protection intended to develop the dynamic tendencies and arrest the static tendencies of the American nation ; protection apparently historical, but really permanent. 44. Patten's theory of consumption forms the basis

of his protective system; protection intended to utilise more completely the resources of the country. 45. Protection and land rent; how free-trade increases the rent of a country which exports provisions; necessity of protection to lower the rent. 46. Criticism of Patten's theories; faults of his system. 47. The distinction between static and dynamic economy is not clear, it is contradictory, and does not correspond to actual facts; starting from a premise of an historical character it leads to the conclusion of absolute protection. 48. Patten's theory of consumption has some truth, but it does not destroy the doctrines of rent and population, nor does it logically lead to protection. 49. To a certain extent Patten's protective thesis is taken from List and Carey; it is not clear enough, and is occasionally contradictory; some parts will not bear criticism, and where it is true it is not original. 50. The thesis of the influence of free-trade upon land rent in exporting countries is theoretically incontestable, but of no practical value according to the experience of the United States, where the agricultural and manufacturing protection are linked together. 51. Comparison between Patten's theory and the state of affairs in America; his theory of consumption reflects the conditions of American territory, which is sufficient to provide for all the wants of the population; the importance given to the land rent in the tariff question reflects the crisis of capitalism, and the struggle between revenue and profit. 52. The struggle between protection and free-trade is one between the two dominant classes, between profit and land rent; it can be foreseen that victory will be on the side of the landowners and land rent, either through agricultural protection or more probably through free-trade; but it will be a party victory, which will neither benefit the masses nor the country; the tariff question is only of small importance to the American people; but vastly different will be the great problem of the America of the future . . 384-411

INDEX OF THE NAMES OF AUTHORS MENTIONED . 413-414

FIRST ESSAY

THE ENGLISH COMMERCIAL POLICY IN THE NORTH AMERICAN COLONIES

B

CHAPTER I

FACTS RELATING TO THE COMMERCIAL POLICY OF ENGLAND IN THE NORTH AMERICAN COLONIES, FROM THEIR ORIGIN TO THE DECLARATION OF INDEPENDENCE (4TH JULY 1776)

1. The commercial policy which England followed with respect to her North American colonies during about a century and a half,—that is to say, from their earliest foundation to the time when, having cast off the burdensome yoke of their mother country, they declared their independence,—though it was all prompted by somewhat the same spirit and upon the same fundamental principle, was not at all uniform. It gradually shaped and developed itself into a clearer and more characteristic form by a slow process of improvement. This is deserving of minute attention, not merely from the interest afforded by the gradual development of an idea, which little by little embodies itself as a fact until it is formed into a complete system, and when at its highest perfection crumbles to ruin; but also for the reason that during the successive stages of that long evolution, there are corresponding social, economic, and industrial conditions upon which commercial policy exercises no small influence.

In this first chapter we propose, with the aid of reliable sources of information, to describe this process of development, the different stages of which do not appear to us to have been sufficiently brought to light, and briefly to survey the various measures adopted by England with regard to the commerce and industry of her North American colonies. This examination will serve as a foundation for further enquiries into the origin and consequences of colonial policy.

2. The history of the commercial policy of England towards her North American colonies may be divided into three distinct and characteristic periods.

The first period dates from the birth of the colonies to the Navigation Act, and is one of relative freedom for commerce: the second period comprises the famous Navigation Acts passed by Cromwell and Charles II., by which measures we have in the first place a system of absolute protection for the English shipping, and secondly, the monopoly of all the commerce of the colonies in favour of the mother country. The third period, from the Navigation Acts of Charles II. until the Declaration of Independence of the colonies, includes all those measures, which besides the commercial monopoly added another system of restriction and prohibition on colonial manufactures, which policy was carried out and completed in about a century.

These three periods, as will be seen even by the summary notice above, differ widely from one another; and each one is deserving of close and accurate study, for the reason that, as we said before, during the successive changes which all underwent, we have a corresponding development in the social and economic conditions of the colonies. However, when on the one hand the commercial and industrial restrictions had been applied to their greatest extent, and on the other hand the colonies had reached the highest point of economical and political attainment, then it was that the inevitable struggle began; it being no longer possible for both conditions to exist at the same time.

3. It would seem that the American colonies were predestined to become victims of a commercial monopoly. In fact, we have the first traces of colonial monopoly in England, not only before the formation of the colonies, but even before those very lands in which the first pilgrims were to dwell had been discovered. In the year 1496, when those great maritime discoveries were being effected, John Cabot, the famous Venetian navigator, applied to Henry VII. King of England, and begged protection for the discoveries he was about to undertake. The generous monarch in his license, *Pro Johanne Caboto et Filiis suis super Terra Incognita*

Investiganda,[1] granted him, instead of material and men or ships, permission to equip at his expense five vessels and to set out on his voyage, assuring him of the monopoly of the commerce, and giving him authority over all the lands he might discover, under the suzerainty of England. The king for himself claimed a fifth part of the commercial profit of the undertaking, in recompense for the protection granted to the bold navigator.

Cabot received other letters-patent in 1498 when about to start upon a second voyage, which, owing to his death, was completed by his son Sebastian, who discovered Newfoundland. Upon this occasion King Henry as well as certain merchants of London gave him pecuniary assistance; and his letters-patent were more of the nature of a scheme of colonisation than of discovery and commerce.[2]

But when Henry VII. discovered that Cabot brought home no spices, and that his attempt at colonisation was not a success, his zeal diminished, and Cabot applied to Spain.

Another instance of colonial monopoly is to be found in letters-patent granted by Henry VII. to certain merchants of Bristol who undertook a voyage in 1501, and to whom he allowed, for a period of ten years, the commercial monopoly of all the lands which they might discover.

Finally, a patent of 1502 which was granted to other navigators contains a complete plan of colonisation and monopoly. In this patent we see that Henry VII. had the intention of establishing a colony in the newly-discovered lands. He granted the discoverers and colonists an exemption from taxes for five years; moreover, the discoverers were to be entrusted with the government of the colony under the suzerainty of England; English subjects might emigrate there and carry on trade, and all commerce with those lands should, during the first forty years, be subject to a license from the king and the discoverers.[3] To Beer[4] it even seemed evident

[1] Cunningham, *The Growth of English Industry and Commerce*, vol. i. "Early and Middle Ages," Cambridge Univ. Press, 1890, p. 446. Schanz, *Englische Handelspolitik gegen Ende des Mittelalters*, Leipsig, 1881, pp. 316-318.
[2] Cunningham, work mentioned, vol. i. p. 447.
[3] Schanz, work mentioned, vol. i. p. 316.
[4] Beer, *The Commercial Policy of England toward the American Colonies*, New York, Columbia College, 1893, pp. 17, 18.

from the text of the patent that the king's intention was to limit the trade of the new lands to England alone. However, these attempts at colonisation had no results, and with them consequently vanished also the idea of a monopoly over the new lands: more than a century had to pass before these lands became permanently occupied.

/ 4. It was only during the first years of the seventeenth century that Europeans began to settle in North America; the first settlement being founded in Virginia in 1607. At first we find no trace of colonial monopoly.

James I., King of England, to favour the colonisation of America, granted in the year 1606 a large extent of land to two commercial companies; and among other concessions, he granted that during a period of seven years the companies should transport from England all that was necessary for the colonisation, free of duty; that the colonies should have full liberty to trade with other nations; and that all duties which they levied upon foreign goods, during the first twenty-one years, should go for the benefit of the colonies themselves.[1]

The first charter given to Virginia granted that all foreigners might trade with the colony, upon payment of a small duty; and this permission, as we shall see, was continued for some time.[2]

We see, therefore, that the first idea which Henry VII. had, namely, that of imposing commercial monopoly on the colonies, was disregarded from the beginning. In fact, the very first acts on the part of England towards her colonies favoured the latter economically, though they indicate the beginning of that system which must logically lead to monopoly and to industrial restrictions, by giving impulse in the colonies to the production of raw materials so as to benefit the manufactures of the mother country. Thus, for instance, James I. did much towards promoting the rearing of silk-worms in the colonies, to provide the raw silk for English manufactures; and in the year 1608 he sent out mulberry plants and silk-worms' eggs.[3]

---

[1] Robertson, *The History of America*, London, Strahan, 1803, vol. iv. p. 174.
[2] Bancroft, *History of United States*, Boston, Little Brown, 1860, vol. i.
[3] Bolles, *Industrial History of United States*, Norwich, 1881, p. 428.

In 1608 he also prohibited the cultivation of the tobacco-plant in England, encouraging it instead in the fertile soil of Virginia.[1]
But together with these interested concessions the idea soon sprang up of reaping as much advantage as possible from the colonies, and of monopolising their commerce. In exchange for the privilege of cultivating the tobacco-plant, granted to the State of Virginia, James I. levied upon the people a most exorbitant tax, and afterwards advanced certain claims to monopoly which will be remembered as the first definite attempt of its kind.

About the year 1619, the production of tobacco having largely increased, the concessionary commercial company of the colony began to export direct to Holland. This was opposed by James I., who did not wish to see England lose that trade and her customs deprived of the revenues arising from the duties.[2] A temporary compromise was arranged; but the company was dissolved in 1624 owing to fresh conflicts with the Crown. This is pointed out by Robertson[3] as the first instance of opposition between the colony and the mother country. The latter was attempting to monopolise the trade of the colonies, while the colony was claiming her right to carry her products to the best markets, on the strength of the concession of unlimited freedom of commerce granted in her charter. But the time was not yet opportune to settle this question.

Colonial monopoly was also a fond aspiration of Charles I.; but in establishing it he succeeded no better than his predecessor.

In 1628 Charles I. attempted to constitute himself sole purchaser of Virginian tobacco by first establishing London as the only market for colonial tobacco, and then reserving to himself the exclusive right of buying-in all the colonial

---

[1] Bancroft, *History of United States*, vol. i.
[2] Roscher states that the desire of monopolising the commerce of the colonies arose in the mother country, through the important trade which the Dutch, between 1630 and 1640, carried on with the Anglo-American colonies, which commerce proved the increasing welfare of the colonial market.—*Vide* Roscher and Jannasch, *Kolonien, Kolonialpolitik und Auswanderung*, Leipsig, Winter, 1885, p. 208.
[3] *History of America*, vol. iv. p. 206.

tobacco; but he did not succeed. Afterwards in 1639, in the instructions given to Berkeley, whom he named governor of Virginia, Charles I. framed the designs which were afterwards embodied in the Navigation Acts, explicitly reserving to himself for the first time the monopoly of the colonial trade. He ordered that no vessel laden with colonial merchandise should sail from the ports of Virginia for any other ports except those of England; England was to be the established emporium of all such merchandise; all traffic with the colonies in foreign ships was prohibited.

These instructions, however, dictated by Charles I. shortly before the revolution which was to end in his execution, were never applied. A protest was addressed to him by the assembly of Virginia, in which the necessity of free trade was maintained by those poor rough planters who alleged that "the freedom of commerce is the blood and the life of a republic."[1] Owing to the political state of affairs and the weakness of the English Government, which conditions did not permit of restrictions in the colonies,[2] there was free government in Virginia during the reign of Charles I., which Robertson asserts exercised a beneficial influence upon it and developed its industry and population.

The policy of the Long Parliament until 1651 was in substance one of freedom. In 1642, on account of the sympathy which the colonists of New England evinced towards the leaders of the popular faction in the English Parliament, the House of Commons exempted them from the payment of duties, either upon goods directed from England to the colonies or upon those which they sent to the mother country; the result of this was an increase in the production and the population of New England.[3] In 1646 Parliament proposed to ensure to the English shipping the whole commerce of the colonies, but with their free consent, offering in return to exempt from duties all exportations from England to the colonies. This project, however, does not appear to have been carried out at the time.[4] In 1650 those colonies which had sided with the

[1] Bancroft, *History of United States*, vol. i. p. 203.
[2] Roscher, *Kolonien*, etc., p. 208.
[3] Robertson, *History of America*, vol. iv. p. 305.
[4] Bancroft, *History of United States*, vol. i.; Anderson, *Origin of Commerce*, vol. ii.

Stuarts were forbidden commercial intercourse with foreigners, and with all those who had not a special license from Parliament or from the Council of State; but this was only a reprisal of war which lasted a very short time.[1]

Finally, we can conclude that in the first half century of their existence the English colonies of North America practically enjoyed an almost complete commercial freedom; and that the monopoly of the mother country only existed in the shape of aspirations and of partial attempts, which were without results.

5. The second period in English colonial policy commences with the Navigation Acts of Cromwell and Charles II., and it differs from the first period in well-defined and important features. In this period, however, we find in the English colonial policy two facts entirely different, and which must be kept perfectly distinct, both on account of their significance and of their scope. The Act of Cromwell and that of Charles II. often confused by writers, as if they treated of the same thing or of subjects very much alike, differ very much, and contain two distinct principles. The Act of Cromwell gave a firm basis to the protection of the English shipping and to the monopoly of navigation. The Act of Charles II. added a still more serious and important monopoly, namely, that of the colonial commerce.

The first of these monopolies forms part of an entire policy which had been more or less followed by England for 300 years, and which has now attained a brilliant completion. The second one is new in substance, because it has no other precedents than those few facts which we have just summarised. And the effects on the colonies of these two monopolies are very different, as we shall shortly see.

But let us consider a moment the subject of the protection to navigation. This idea, as we said, dates back a long time, the first practical attempts at carrying it into execution being in the reign of Richard II., when there arose the germs of those economic ideas which at a later historical period were destined to expand.

Richard, after the year 1377, inaugurated a policy of encouragement to the shipping, commerce, and agriculture of the country, which he strove to protect against foreigners by a

[1] Bancroft, *History of United States*, vol. i.

series of different measures.[1] Among others is notable the regulation of 1381 relating to shipping, and which was called the first Navigation Act. In this Act it was ruled that all merchandise imported into or exported from England should only be carried in English ships.[2] This was, however, but a temporary measure and lasted only until Easter. The state of the English shipping, which at that time formed a very small fleet, did not lend itself to such an energetic protection, and it was necessary immediately afterwards to add that, in the case where English ships were insufficient for the requirements of the commerce, the traders could avail themselves of foreign ships; and furthermore, the regulation had to be limited to exportations from England and the coasting-trade, and eventually it was decided that where masters of vessels, abusing the protection, demanded extravagant charges, the traders were empowered to engage foreign ships.

In fact, the time was not yet ripe for such protection; neither was the English shipping powerful enough for it. And in spite of the numerous petitions addressed to Richard II. and Henry IV. by captains of vessels, the attempted protection was by no means efficacious.

Another feeble attempt to protect the English shipping was made by Edward IV. in 1463, but only for three years, and it was not afterwards renewed. Henry VII. in 1485 and 1487 established a more energetic protection, ordering the exclusive use of English ships for many imports, and renewing the old regulations of Richard, by which it was permissible to employ foreign ships only when there were no available English ships in the ports. It was these measures which caused Bacon to remark that the first Tudor was really the consequent founder of a new navigation policy for England. Henry VII., however, by special licenses, frequently allowed his own protective laws to be violated.[3]

[1] Cunningham, *Growth of English Industry*, etc., vol. i. p. 338.
[2] That none of the king's liege people should from henceforth ship any merchandise, in going out or coming within the realm of England, but only in the ships of the king's liegiance, on penalty of forfeiture of vessel and cargo. (*Vide* article "Navigation Laws," by Wells, in Lalor's *Cyclopædia of Political Science*, New York, 1888.)
[3] Beer, *The Commercial Policy of England toward the American Colonies*, p. 12.

His successor, Henry VIII., also, after having for some time been bountiful in his permissions to foreign ships, initiated a more severe policy, later on confirmed and strengthened by the Act of 1540, which instituted an important advance in the policy of navigation. This Act declared that England, surrounded by the sea, was eminently adapted for the maritime transport of merchandise; that in consequence it was necessary and useful to possess a large number of ships, as in former times; that also the security of the country demanded a strong commercial navy; that, in fact, a large mercantile navy would promote national labour, giving occupation and food to a large number of persons, both sailors and mechanics, so that the country would derive benefit from it. Therefore the old navigation laws were once more enforced, and, as it had been observed that they had had the effect of raising freightage and prices of commodities, to the injury of the merchants and the consumers, limits were fixed by law upon the freightage and prices.

Schanz[1] states that the two first Tudors, Henry VII. and Henry VIII., were the true founders of the protective policy of navigation in England; that they prepared the greatness of Elizabeth and Cromwell; and that it is especially owing to their efforts that the English shipping at their time was consolidated, and that the commercial activity of England had been able to develop and expand itself so much.

According to Cunningham, however, with some exceptions respecting shipping, the Tudors not only brought England no advantages, but, instead of introducing improvements, they actually aggravated the mischief from which the country suffered through the altered conditions of commerce owing to the discovery of America.[2]

The fact remains that with Edward VI., the successor to Henry VIII., the navigation policy was partly suspended, either to increase the customs revenues,[3] or because, during his reign, the shipping had become so reduced as to be insufficient for the needs of commerce.[4] Elizabeth, also, at first, followed this policy. Afterwards, however, she renewed the system of

[1] Schanz, *Englische Handelspolitik*, etc., vol. i. p. 378.
[2] Cunningham, vol. i. "Early and Middle Ages," pp. 433, 434.
[3] *Ibid.* p. 490.   [4] Cunningham, vol. ii. "Modern Times," p. 20.

protection now traditional, reserving the coasting trade to English ships alone,[1] and even establishing a new fasting day in order to favour the fishing industry![2] Finally, with Cromwell the system of protection to shipping was established on a firm basis by a set of complete and systematic regulations, which, in spite of the times, lasted nearly two centuries.

6. Cromwell's famous Navigation Act of 1651 was not a special act of colonial policy, neither did it refer in particular to the colonies. It had two aims, the depression of the Dutch trade and the protection of the English trade and navigation. The existence of the American colonies, however, appears to have given more efficacy to Cromwell's Act than those preceding, for it was instrumental in considerably enlarging the sphere in which the stipulations of the Act were enabled to exercise their influence. England wished to become a great commercial emporium for all the nations of the world, and for that purpose to possess a large navy which would enable merchandise from all parts to find its way into her ports. Holland, then a great commercial power, which carried on nearly the whole business of transport, constituted a serious obstacle to the accomplishment of such aspirations. It was against that country that Cromwell's Act was directed, in order to strike a decisive blow at the Dutch shipping, and, at the same time, to protect that of England, the aim of the Act being that the whole of the trade between England and the rest of the world should be carried by English ships. No merchandise produced in Asia, Africa, or America was to be imported either into England, Ireland, or the plantations, unless in ships belonging to English subjects, the crew of such ships being mostly English; no products from any country in Europe were to be imported into England except in British ships, or in ships belonging to the place of production, or belonging to the parts whence those productions were usually exported; and in the English colonies, merchandise could only be imported and exported in ships which responded to the preceding conditions. These were the principal regulations of the Act;[3]

[1] Beer, *Commercial Policy of England*, etc., p. 12.
[2] Cunningham, vol. ii. "Modern Times," pp. 21, 22.
[3] *Vide* Adam Smith, *Wealth of Nations*, vol. ii. book iv.; M'Culloch, *Dictionary of Commerce*, London, 1882, and other authors. The complete text of

and these last regulations were the only ones which interfered with colonial trade, which trade, as we see, was not restricted by any monopoly, the colonies being perfectly free to buy and sell where they thought best, and only obliged to make use of their own or English ships for their trading. Even this obligation did not seriously affect the colonies, because the application of the commercial laws to the colonies was then only nominal. In fact, the schedule of reprisal of 1650 (against the Royalist colonies), forbidding certain colonies to trade with foreigners, and placing under special license their trade with England, was very soon abolished. Also, Cromwell's Act of 1651 was very feebly applied in the North American colonies;[1] traffic with Holland, though declared to be contraband, was nevertheless extensively carried on; and, a few months after Cromwell's death, the Virginians invited the Dutch and other foreign nations to trade with them. Proposals of peace and commerce were discussed without scruple by the respective colonial governments, and at length a special statute of Virginia in 1660 extended to all nations that were friendly with England the promise of free trade. Cromwell's Government had also assured independence to New England and had promoted its commerce. The American colonies remember the years of his (Cromwell's) power, says Bancroft, as the period when British sovereignty was for them free from rapacity, intolerance, and oppression. He may be called the benefactor of the English in America; for he left them to enjoy unshackled the liberal benevolence of providence, the freedom of industry, of commerce, of religion, and of government.[2]

So that, in conclusion, the first part of the period of English colonial policy, which dates from Cromwell's Act in 1651 to the Restoration in 1660, is but a continuation of the preceding period; the colonies were enjoying at this time a state of commercial liberty more or less complete. The English policy was neither oppressive nor rapacious; it allowed, so to speak, the fruit to ripen before making any attempt to gather it.

the Act can be found in Scobell's *Collection of Acts and Ordinances*, London, 1658, vol. ii. pp. 176, 177.
[1] Beer, *Commercial Policy of England*, etc., pp. 32-34.
[2] Bancroft, *History of the United States*, vol. i. p. 446; also Roscher, p. 211, states that the colonies suffered no oppression under Cromwell's Act, chiefly because Cromwell did very little towards its application.

7. It was with the restoration of Charles II. that the English colonial policy may be said to have really commenced; a policy which sacrificed completely the interests of the colonies to those of the mother country, or rather, as Adam Smith says, to the interests of the English merchants, by whom the policy was inspired.[1] It was this monarch who, following the ideas of the times in which this policy was being developed, added to the monopoly of navigation that of commerce, thus oppressing the colonies and trampling upon their rights.

The most important regulations of Charles II. relating to colonial policy are contained in the Navigation Act of 1660 (12 C. II. c. 18), which was pompously styled the "Maritime Charter" of England, and which was afterwards completed by a later Act in 1663.

It is no easy matter to pick one's way out in this confusion of regulations written in the obscure language of those times; and the number of authors who have written about them, in many cases without having understood them and sometimes confounding them with the regulations of Cromwell's Act, have rather helped to cause confusion than otherwise.

But a sufficient idea of these regulations can be obtained by going to the original sources and collecting the more important textual fragments embodied in the works of some writers, and which are more intelligible than their contradictory comments upon them.[2]

The Navigation Act of 1660 contains two different regulations, one relating to the protection and the monopoly of English shipping, the other dealing with the monopoly of

---

[1] "Of the greater part of the regulations concerning the colony trade, the merchants who carry it on, it must be observed, have been the principal advisers. We must not wonder, therefore, if, in the greater part of them, their interest has been more considered than either that of the colonies or that of the mother country. In their exclusive privilege of supplying the colonies with all the goods which they wanted from Europe, and of purchasing all such parts of their surplus produce as could not interfere with any of the trades which they themselves carried on at home, the interest of the colonies was sacrificed to the interest of those merchants."—Vide *Wealth of Nations*, vol. ii. pp. 389, 390, 6th edit., London, Strahan, 1791.

[2] See among the many authors who write about this, the works, already quoted, of Adam Smith, M'Culloch, Robertson, Bancroft, Cunningham, Wells, etc.

colonial commerce. The latter was afterwards strengthened and completed by the Act of 1663.

As regards the protection of English shipping, Charles the Second's Act merely repeats in substance the regulations of Cromwell's Act and completes them. In fact it is decreed by it (a) that no produce of any kind can be imported into or exported from England or from her colonies, or from any lands subject to the King of England, except in ships belonging to England or to her colonies; (b) that colonial produce is to be imported into England only in English or colonial ships (this stipulation is in substance the same as in the preceding clause); (c) finally (a regulation directed against foreign intermediary transport trade, especially that of Holland), that all foreign goods should be imported in vessels built in or belonging to England, and manned by English sailors, and be loaded at the place of production or at those places where the vessels are usually taken for the purpose of being loaded.

In a footnote we state, for greater precision, the text of the most important of these regulations.[1] As can be seen, up

[1] "No goods or commodities whatsoever shall be imported into, or exported out of, any lands, islands, plantations, or territories to his majesty belonging, or be in his possession, or which may hereafter belong unto or be in the possession of his majesty, his heirs and successors, in Asia, Africa, or America, in any other ship or ships, vessel or vessels whatsoever, but in such ships or vessels as do truly without fraud belong only to the people of England or Ireland, dominion of Wales, or town of Berwick-upon-Tweed, or use of the build of or belonging to any of the said lands, islands, plantations, or territories as the proprietors and right owners thereof, and whereof the master and the fourth of the mariners at least are English" (12 C. II. c. 18, s. 1).

"No goods or commodities whatsoever of the growth, production, or manufacture of Africa, Asia, or America, or of any part thereof, or which are described or laid down in the usual map or cards of those places (shall) be imported into England, Ireland, Wales, the islands of Guernsey and Jersey, or town of Berwick-upon-Tweed, or any other ship or ships, vessel or vessels whatsoever, but in such as do truly and without fraud belong only to the people of England or Ireland, dominion of Wales, or town of Berwick-upon-Tweed, or of the lands, islands, plantations, or territories in Asia, Africa, or America to his majesty belonging, as the proprietors and right owners thereof, and whereof the master and three-fourth at least of the mariners are English" (12 C. II. c. 18, s. 3).

"No goods or commodities that are of foreign growth, production, or manufacture, and which are to be brought into England, Ireland, Wales, the island of Guernsey and Jersey, or town of Berwick-upon-Tweed, in English-built shipping, or other shipping belonging to some of the aforesaid places, and navigated by English mariners as aforesaid, shall be shipped or brought from any other place or places, country or countries, but only from those of the said

to this point there was nothing new and nothing particularly oppressive to the colonies; in fact, we might almost repeat here the preceding observations made concerning Cromwell's Act.

But the novelty is found in another regulation of the Act, in which, finally putting into operation the idea expressed by Charles I. in his instructions to Berkeley, the monopoly of colonial commerce was initiated, prescribing that the products of the colonies should be brought only to England. This, however, did not apply to all products, because all of them were not required by the mother country. The products of the colonies were, in fact, of two kinds: the one either entirely unobtainable in England or only in insufficient quantity, but necessary to the mother country for her industries or for her commerce with other nations; the other, England had no demand for, either because it could be produced at home or obtained in another manner; these last named were even an annoyance to the English producers owing to the competition they caused in the home markets. The Act of Charles II. constituted the commercial monopoly of England over the products of the first class (enumerated in the Act, and which enumeration was afterwards extended by degrees), allowing only their exportation from the colonies to England or to other English plantations.[1] Among the other products (and these Adam Smith states were the most important), such as grain, wood, dried meats, fish, etc., their exportation was free, because England was not interested in them, or only interested in getting them sent as far away as possible, so much so, that eventually the importation of some of them, for instance grain growth, production, or manufacture, or from those parts where the said goods and commodities can only or are, or usually have been, first shipped for transportation, and from none other places or countries" (12 C. II. c. 18, s. 4).

These extracts from the text of the Act I have taken from Levi's *History of British Commerce*, etc., 1768-1870. London, Murray, 1872 (pp. 158-9-62).

[1] The following is the text of the regulation:—"No sugar, tobacco, cotton, wool, indigo, ginger, fustic, and other dyeing wood of the growth, production, or manufacture of any English plantations in America, Asia, or Africa, shall be shipped, carried, conveyed, or transported from any of the said English plantations to any land, island, territory, dominion, port or place whatsoever, other than to such other English plantations as do belong to his majesty, his heirs and successors, or to the kingdom of England or Ireland, or principality of Wales, or town of Berwick-upon-Tweed, there to be laid on shore."—*Vide* Levi's *History of British Commerce*, etc., p. 162.

(with the exception of rice) and salt provisions, was prohibited.[1] Perhaps, had it been possible to prohibit production altogether, Charles II., who had so resolutely undertaken the task of monopolising and despoiling the colonies, would have done it; but with regard to those products which were so plentiful in the colonies it would have been absurd. Later on we shall see England adopting this more radical system with regard to manufactories, and prohibiting the establishment of them in the colonies, so as to remove every obstacle to the importation of her own manufactures thither. And also for the same reason we shall see much later, during the reign of George III., regulations more severe than those of Charles II., intended to limit the exportation of such colonial products as were not enumerated in the Act of Navigation, to the countries of Europe situated below Cape Finisterre, which were not manufacturing countries, and from which England did not fear that ships could bring home manufactured goods.[2]

The colonial monopoly as established by the Act of 1660 was, however, not complete; with regard to certain products it confined the colonial markets to England, thus favouring the English merchants. To complete it and bestow another great advantage on the producers and merchants of England, it required that the colonial market should be reserved to the English producers and merchants. This the Act of 1663 accomplished by ordering that all European merchandise for importation into the colonies should be shipped in England. To make matters worse, this Act, as we shall see, partly did away with the advantage that the Acts of 1651 and 1661 had bestowed on the colonies by granting protection to their merchant navy together with that of England, because it laid down that all merchandise intended for importation into the colonies should be shipped on vessels built in England.[3]

With this last Act the colonial system inaugurated by

---

[1] Adam Smith, *Wealth of Nations*, 6th ed., 1791, vol. ii. p. 381.
[2] *Ibid.* p. 382.
[3] The following is the text of the principal disposition of this Act:—"No commodity of the growth, production, or manufacture of Europe shall be imported into British plantations, but such as are laden and put on board in England, Wales, or Berwick-upon-Tweed, and in English-built shipping, whereof the master and three-fourths of the crew are English."—Bolles, *Industrial History*, etc., pp. 851, 852.

Charles II. was accomplished, constituting a complete system which, revised and corrected, was destined to endure for some time.

It was framed with the idea that the colonies should only be of service to the mother country, favouring her commerce, forming a large opening for the exportation of her manufactures, and thus ensuring an important addition of trade; to this end all the interests of the colonies were to be sacrificed.

In those days the colonies, still in their infancy, only produced raw or very rough material, and, for the end in view, the colonial monopoly instituted by Charles II. was sufficient. Eventually, however, more was required; it became necessary to impose upon the colonies the maintenance of a system of production which at the same time nourished the commerce of the mother country by its exportation of raw material, and reserved to the English manufactures the entire colonial market; so that to the commercial monopoly were added restrictions respecting manufactures.[1]

8. In the third period of English colonial policy, was strengthened and completed that system which was very boldly defined by Lord Sheffield, who affirmed that "the only use of the American colonies is the monopoly of their consumption and the carriage of their produce," and by Lord Chatham, who stated that "the British colonists of North America had no right to manufacture even a nail or a horse-shoe."[2]

Let us summarise in their chronological order the principal regulations which little by little led to the putting into operation of this system in all its rigour, namely, the prohibition of carrying on the manufacturing industry which the mother country wished to reserve to herself.[3]

For some years only the Acts of 1660 and 1663 were

[1] Certain encouragements given previously to the colonial industries prove that this restrictive policy was only initiated later on in the third period. Thus, in 1662, in Virginia premiums were granted for the best productions of linen and woollen materials; in 1692 the Governor, Sir E. Andros, considerably encouraged the manufactures of the colonies. Only in 1689 did his successor, Nicholson, make the first step towards a change by recommending Parliament to prohibit the colonies from manufacturing materials.—*Vide* Bishop, *A History of American Manufactures*, etc., Philadelphia, 1868.

[2] M'Culloch, *Dictionary of Commerce*.

[3] England's system of monopoly, says Bancroft (vol. ii.), was followed inflexibly for more than a century by no less than twenty-nine Acts of Parliament.

applied, after which the new period was commenced with various regulations, which, hindering in every way the relations between the colonies, tended to limit as much as possible the productions of each colony and to extend in all of them the trade of the English merchants and producers. Manufacturing began to make its first attempts in the colonies, and the mother country, fearing her own interests, immediately attempted to crush it. With this view a regulation was framed by the English Parliament in 1672, which took away from the colonies the right of trafficking among themselves, a right which they had enjoyed until that time, and imposed heavy duties upon the importations from one colony to another.[1] Still more severe was an Act passed in 1699. Fearing the competition to English wool and materials which the colonies might be able to cause either in their own terri tories or abroad, the English Parliament laid down that from the 1st December 1699, neither wool nor woollen goods produced in any English plantation of America should be shipped in any vessel under whatsoever pretext, nor carried by horse, cart, or any other means of transport, to a destination within any of the English colonies or to any other place.[2] The object in view was that the products of the colonies should only and exclusively supply the needs of the places of their production, and the expansion of these colonies was thus confined, as it were, by an iron band.[3] A step further and they would have destroyed the first rudimentary manufactories, and altogether prohibited manufacturing.

✓ As early as 1688, the English aristocratic revolution, one of the chief features of which was the application of the mercantile system in its severest form, had renewed and further strengthened throughout the colonies all the preceding regulations, which secured to England the monopoly of the colonial commerce, and from that time the regulations became still more severe and restrictive.

The counsels of Governor Nicholson were very soon followed.

[1] Bancroft, *History of the United States*, vol. ii.   [2] *Ibid*.
[3] In 1684 a law of Virginia which encouraged the manufacture of wool was annulled by the English Parliament.—*Vide* Bolles, *Industrial History*, p. 369. .

In 1719, in fact, the system of prohibiting colonial manufacture was for the first time solemnly confirmed in England. The House of Commons declared that "the establishment of manufactories in the colonies tends to render them more independent of Great Britain," and, following upon this premise, they prohibit the establishment in the colonies of any furnace for the production of cast iron or for the manufacture of any kind of iron.[1]

Again in 1732, alarmed at the development of the commerce and industries of the colonies, which were constantly infringing the odious English restrictions, the House of Commons ordered a Commission of Inquiry "with respect to the laws made, manufactures set up, or trade carried on, detrimental to the trade, navigation, or manufactures of Great Britain."[2] Bolles gives some fragments of this inquiry, among which is to be found a most interesting description of the state of colonial industries of these times, and one can see with what jealousy England watched the growing prosperity and development of the colonial manufactures.

In 1732 the exportation from one colony to another of felt hats, the production of which was beginning to develop, was prohibited, and in 1750 a hat manufactory established in Massachusetts was declared "a nuisance," and was suppressed.[3] In that same year the establishment in the colonies of any water mill for iron works, or furnace for the manufacture of steel, was prohibited, and those existing narrowly escaped destruction. Meanwhile, iron-working having developed in England, and it being found next to impossible to stop the production and exportation of cast iron, for which the colonies, with their abundance of mineral and timber, were so well adapted, not only was the prohibition of 1719 on raw material removed, but the production of it was encouraged by exempting it from all import dues in Great Britain, in order to furnish the raw material for the English manufacturers. Encouragement was also given to the colonies to produce and export the different materials for shipbuilding and other purposes.

This policy of favouring the production of raw material in

[1] Bancroft, *History of the United States*, vol. iii.
[2] Bolles, *Industrial History*, p. 855.   [3] *Ibid.* p. 371.

the colonies by rewards and encouragement was broadly applied by the English Parliament, for it was thought that the more the colonial commerce of rough materials was extended, the greater would be the advantage that England would receive from the colonies by the importation of a larger quantity of their merchandise, and England at the same time would be making herself more independent of other nations for her supplies.[1] On the other hand, it was observed that in proportion to the broader basis given to exportation, by which means the colonists could pay for the importation of manufactured goods, so much less was the stimulus to the colonists to devote themselves to manufacturing.[2] The commercial restrictions were especially directed against the colonies of New England, either on account of the manufacturing tendencies they had already manifested, or because their main produce (grain) was the same as that of England, whilst the Southern colonies, which produced sugar, tobacco, etc. (not produced in England) were even encouraged. In effect, in 1798, 33 2, an Act of Parliament, recognising the prosperity of the sugar colonies in America as of the greatest consequence to the trade of England, imposed a duty on rum, molasses, and sugar imported from foreign colonies into any of the British plantations, so as to favour the production of sugar in the latter.[3] In 1758 the "London Society for the Encouragement of Arts, Commerce, and Manufactures" offered prizes for the production of wine, hemp, opium, olives, etc., in the American colonies, and the English Government at various times granted considerable sums towards the promotion of silk production, indigo cultivation, and other industries.[4]

9. The last years of the English domination over the North American colonies were of exceptional importance as regards colonial policy, for, by a strange coincidence which hastened matters, exactly at the time when the economic and social progress rendered the colonies less adapted and less disposed to support trade monopoly and restrictions of their in-

[1] Roscher, *Kolonien, Kolonialpolitik*, etc., pp. 217-19.
[2] Beer, *Commercial Policy of England*, pp. 93, 94.
[3] Bancroft, *History of United States*, vol. iii. For a fuller treatise of this subject see Beer, *Commercial Policy of England*, pp. 107-122.
[4] Bolles, *Industrial History*, pp. 8, 9.

dustries, the oppressive system of England became suddenly aggravated.

The regulations of the Navigation Acts had been less damaging to the colonies, because their application had only been moderately enforced, and some of them had fallen into disuse, and on account of the frequent smuggling which had been tolerated. The English custom-house had come to a compromise, and was very indulgent, and the restrictions also with regard to the manufactures were not always applied in all their severity. But this condition of affairs was radically changed by Grenville, the English Minister, in 1763 and the following years, re-enforcing in their greatest severity all the most restrictive regulations.

Bancroft[1] well depicts this man, whose scanty knowledge of the condition of the colonies, and whose obstinacy in refusing to recognise the exigencies of the times, hastened perhaps for Great Britain the loss, in any case inevitable, of her American colonies. Grenville, born too late for his ideas, and imbued with mercantile theories, beyond the range of which he could not see, had a blind reverence for the Navigation Acts and the colonial policy. His opinion was that if these were not rigorously adhered to the colonies would have no reason for existing, and he explicitly declared that exigencies of State compelled Great Britain to prevent the establishment of manufactories in America as being contrary to the general welfare.

The whole administration of that minister, which was fatal to England, though providential for the colonies, inasmuch as it gave them the last impetus towards vindicating their liberty, was directed towards the carrying out of those ideas and to the resumption in all its severity of the colonial system.

In 1763 the most strict injunctions were given to the customs officials to apply the Navigation Acts in all their rigour. The governors of the colonies were instructed that the suppression of the prohibited commerce with foreign nations was to be the object of their constant and immediate care. And in order to render these regulations more efficient it was laid down that every English warship should, when

[1] *History of the United States*, vol. v. pp. 160, 184.

necessary, watch over the merchant shipping and prevent smuggling. Not only was this an odious task to impose upon men whose calling was to defend their country and not to play the part of customs officers, but it also caused the English sailors to commit many acts of injustice, because, little versed in the complicated customs regulations, and perhaps occasionally given to plunder, they laid hands indiscriminately on legitimate or forbidden merchandise, and interfered with vessels which were acting in conformity with the navigation laws.[1]

In this manner, says Bancroft, those acts which had fallen into disuse (including all the industrial prohibitions) were once more enforced, and the customs officials and the military being interested in the contraventions, the Acts were applied with energy and excess; the colonies were, in fact, treated as a hostile country in time of war.

But that was not sufficient. In 1764 trading was prohibited between the English and Spanish colonies in America, by means of which the former supplied the latter with the manufactures from England, and received in exchange gold, silver, and live stock; also the trading between the colonies and the French West Indies was forbidden.[2] In that same year, moreover, an Act was promulgated which modified the one of 1733 in a manner disadvantageous to the colonies, with an extension of the Navigation Acts, which made England the emporium for all the Asiatic trade, and with various regulations protecting English manufactures, to the prejudice of those of the colonies.[3] The restrictions with regard to industries were applied in full force; and, in order to protect English printers, the colonists were even forbidden to print the Bible![4][5]

[1] Botta, *Storia della Guerra dell' Indipendenza degli Stati Uniti d'America;* Milano, Schiepatti, 1829, vol. i. p. 37.
[2] *Ibid.* p. 38.
[3] Bancroft, *History of United States,* vol. v. pp. 187, 188.
[4] The emigration of artisans to the colonies was also prohibited for fear of facilitating the establishment of manufactories; and, later on, when the period of mechanical inventions commenced, England prohibited the exportation of machinery to the United States.
[5] In an article in the *Edinburgh Review* (January 1891, "The Fiscal System of the United States") there is a remark curious enough to be worth reproduction here: "Mr. Andrew Carnegie, the Scottish-American champion of modern

At the same time the system of facilitating the production and exportation of provisions and raw material was continued; and Grenville attempted to gain the favour of the colonies by establishing prizes for the exportation of raw hemp, which England stood in need of, by allowing the transport of rice in all parts of America, and by considerably reducing the taxation upon the whale-fishing industry.

10. This summary of the English commercial policy towards the American colonies can now be considered as completed; the other regulations, up to the Declaration of Independence, are either provisions of a fiscal kind which gave the last impetus to the revolution, or schemes of reprisals and war, intended to punish the colonists and to overcome their resistance; properly speaking, they had no real commercial bearing or character.

It is well known how the American colonies, although recognising English sovereignty, loudly proclaimed their right not to be taxed by the English Parliament, in which they were not represented, and in which their representation would have been practically impossible and inefficacious. Grenville, nevertheless, in 1764, insisted, almost to provocation, in his proposal of taxing the colonies, and advocated the Stamp Act, which, at first postponed owing to the agitation it caused in the colonies, was afterwards approved by Parliament in 1765. In 1766 the Stamp Act was repealed, but at the same time Parliament proclaimed absolute power over the colonies, and the commercial restrictions were made more severe; in 1767, for fiscal reasons, duties were established in the American colonies upon glass, paper, dyes, and tea. All this helped to aggravate the already excited feelings of the colonists.[1]

From that time we find only several measures of war and reprisals in which the commercial restrictions are nothing but

American protection, gravely assured Mr. Gladstone, in the course of their curious controversy over the M'Kinley Bill, that manufactures had been forbidden by law under the English dominion in the colonies of North America. Where he picked up this fantastic notion does not appear, and it is probable that he was thinking when he made the assertion, not of the American colonies at all but of Ireland." This is about one of the most singular cases of polemical blindness that can be found, for it goes so far as to deny the existence of facts affirmed by the English Parliament, and admitted by all writers since Adam Smith.

[1] Bancroft, *History of the United States*, vol. v.

a lever intended to assist in bringing the rebel colonies into subjection. In 1774, in order to punish Boston, one of the chief centres of the rebellion, the English Government closed its port and transferred its customs office to another place; in 1775, the war being actually commenced, an Act of Parliament prohibited all trade with the colonies, and declared that any of their vessels captured by English ships would be kept as prizes.

But now the colonies had severed all the links that bound them to the mother country. They had freed themselves, and had put an end to that system of prohibitive legislation which, in Adam Smith's own words, was "a manifest violation of the most sacred rights of mankind."[1] They had now attained that condition of maturity when they could look after their own interests, and the unsuitable measures of Grenville and Lord North only served to hasten and to render more violent the rupture with England. On the 4th July 1776 the North American colonies declared their independence; and here finishes the English commercial policy in the colonies and that of the United States commences.

But we are still far from having completed the study of the American colonial policy in this first chapter. Up to the present we have merely sketched the historical outlines of the English legislative regulations which helped to shape it. We will now proceed to examine the factors of the English colonial policy and its relation to the historical and scientific surroundings existing at the time of its formation, and we will follow its growth through the development of the economic and social conditions of the colonies during its application to them, investigating also its effects upon them.

[1] *Wealth of Nations*, vol. ii. p. 387.

CHAPTER II

THE GENESIS OF THE ENGLISH COMMERCIAL POLICY IN THE
NORTH AMERICAN COLONIES

11. The elements from which the English colonial policy draws its origin are of two kinds, practical and scientific. The former we have already seen in the facts gathered in the foregoing chapter.

We need not repeat here, for it has already been shown, how protection to navigation was traditional in English politics even before the Acts of Cromwell and Charles II. We have also examined the attempts at colonial monopoly long ago thought of by English sovereigns but only realised at a much later date. There is still, however, to be added, the influence which the policy of other European countries, contemporaneously developing, must have exercised upon the commercial policy of England. These are the first stages of English commercial policy which, conjointly with the conditions of those times of which we will speak further on, constitute the elements of fact which gave rise to the Navigation Acts and other restrictions on the commerce and industry of the colonies.

The scientific elements we find in the economic theory which predominated at that period, and which had succeeded in exercising a great influence on the commercial policy of the States—namely, mercantilism.

The mercantile theory, at first favoured but afterwards rejected by economists, and often misjudged or but little understood, has had through modern criticism a reconstruction and a vindication which, in our opinion, constitute one of the best fruits of the application of the historical method to the study of economic questions. Roscher,[1] Held,[2] Bidermann,[3] Cunningham,[4] Cossa,[5] von-Heyking [6] and others have given to mercantilism the place which was rightly due to it in the economic history, considering it in its bearings with the conditions of the times in which it was evolved, and at the same time they have given us a clear and exact idea concerning it.

The following are the fundamental characteristics of mercantilism :[7]

First, the exaggerated importance attached to the number of population and its density; second, the exaggerated importance given to the quantity of money (confused by mercantilists with capital), by applying to public economy an idea, obvious enough in private economy, that the possession of money opens the way to all other riches,[8] an exaggeration which frequently assumes the form of a real thirst for gold; third, the exaggeration of the importance of foreign trade, which alone can procure gold and silver for a country without mines; fourth, and finally, the exaggeration of the capacity of the State, which, according to mercantilists, should regulate in its own manner and on the basis of the ideas already stated, the foreign commerce of the nation, and influence the exportation and importation of merchandise so as always to make the former predominate over the latter, with the object of preserving and increasing as much as possible the circulation of money in the State.

Amidst the various and complicated machinery of the mercantile policy, all directed towards the already-mentioned end, figured the colonial policy, which, as shown in the preced-

[1] *Geschichte der National-Oekonomie in Deutschland*, München, Oldenbourg, 1874.
[2] *Carey's Socialwissenschaft und das Mercantilsystem*, Wurzburg, Stuber, 1866.
[3] *Ueber den Mercantilismus*, Innsbruck, Wagner, 1870.
[4] *The Growth of English Industry and Commerce*, Cambridge University Press, 1890-92.
[5] *Introduzione allo studio dell' Economia Politica*, Milano, Hœpli, 1892 (English edition, by Macmillan).
[6] *Zur Geschichte der Handelsbilanz-Theorie*, Berlin, 1880.
[7] Roscher, *Geschichte*, etc., pp. 228-38.
[8] Cossa, *Introduzione*, p. 217.

ing chapter, was to have opened up for the mother country a vast market for exportation and to favour its exporting industries, causing a great importation of raw colonial produce, the price of which was artificially kept down by its being excluded from the foreign markets.

We do not intend, and it would indeed be a useless task, either to give an extensive explanation of the mercantilist theory and policy, or to repeat the criticisms which from Adam Smith downwards have been both justly and unjustly passed upon mercantilism; but we consider it useful for our purpose to dwell shortly upon those considerations, which, as we were just remarking, by confronting the theory with its historical surroundings will give us a just conception of its value.

12. Although mercantilism was founded upon an idea, partly exaggerated and partly erroneous, of money considered as the basis of the economic system, upon the error of considering as antagonistic the interests of the States, and in general upon the exaggerations noted above; although the ideal which it pictured was erroneous, and, in its last expression, was reduced to an absurdity, since it was impossible to hinder the depreciation of a superabundant currency,—nevertheless mercantilism was not only justified in its existence by the conditions of the times, but, granted those conditions, its theory was partly true. Sufficient proof of this could be found in the economic and political power which the Navigation Acts imparted to England,[1] and the active impulse given to French manufacturers by Colbert; whilst at the same time the exaggerations proved fatal, and subsequently that system became untenable, as was the case with the colonial policy which England tried to maintain with too much energy and for too long a period. There is a whole series of economic and political facts which partly justify mercantilism.

The great discoveries in the New World, which had brought to Europe an afflux of precious metals, and had hastened the transformation of exchange in kind into that of money, and the importance hence assumed by the metallic circulation, which had not then as it had afterwards so

[1] Cunningham, *Growth of English Industry*, ii. pp. 17, 112, 256, etc.

many substitutes, all go to explain the exaggerated idea which the mercantilistic school had concerning money.

The numerous colonies of recent formation, rich producers of raw materials and precious metals, and dependent upon the governments of Europe which were in want of money, excited these governments to a policy of expoliation. The great development of shipping and of foreign commerce led to an exaggerated importance being attached to the latter.

The political conditions of the various States in those times, moreover, perfectly explain the adoption both in theory and practice of this commercial system, the chief object of which was to promote the political power of the State.

The formation and the consolidation of the large States, which had become conscious of their individuality, and the permanent armies which were being raised to support them, necessitated a large quantity of men and of money, and on that account rendered the increase of the population and of money a matter of the utmost importance. The political antagonism of the various States rendered natural a commercial policy which was based upon economic antagonism, at a moment when agreement was not possible and while the States were struggling to balance their power; and politicians were able to observe the connection which existed between political and commercial power. Finally, a system which gave to the State an immense authority and a right of interference in the economic life of the people, and even placed it at the mercy of the State, was perfectly in accordance with the absolute monarchism of those times.

The thesis of mercantilism, says Roscher,[1] does not find its only excuse in the necessary imperfections of an infant science: a theory which predominated for a century in science and in practice could not be altogether erroneous. And, in fact, the pretensions of mercantilism represented an actual need of the times in which it flourished, and they were the theoretical expression of a certain stage in the evolution of economy. In the history of the economy of the peoples more importance is given, at first, to the foreign than to the home commerce, because the former supplies the products which the latter

[1] Roscher, *Geschichte*, etc., p. 233.

cannot procure, whilst the division of labour among the various provinces of a country, which will regulate in the best manner the supply of products, is usually of a later growth. So also maritime commerce becomes developed sooner than that on land.

Without a certain diffusion of the manufacturing industries economic life cannot attain maturity, neither can agriculture arrive at full development. Agriculture remains at a standstill for centuries, whilst the manufacturing industry, if stimulated at the proper moment, is capable of changes and rapid progress. We can therefore understand how, towards the close of mediæval economy, when the agricultural element predominated over town industries, it was possible by artificially directing it, to hasten the growth and maturity of economy.

In England especially (and it is of this country that we must now treat) the mercantile doctrine found a most favourable soil. The great development of maritime commerce [1] naturally brought many adherents to a theory which attached the greatest importance to foreign commerce, and the conception of a favourable commercial balance was perhaps in England more correct than anywhere else.

The idea of a favourable balance being considered as a criterion of the prosperity of a country is erroneous, because it identifies to a certain extent exportation with production and importation with consumption, considering the former as an advantage and the latter a disadvantage to the country; this, however, does not necessarily follow, because exportation could also consist of capital which would drain the country of its productive forces; also, importation could be composed of material necessary for the industries of the country, and thus be a co-efficient of production and wealth. The commercial balance, whether it be favourable or unfavourable, to use a mercantilistic expression, does not therefore necessarily indicate an enrichment or impoverishment of the country, and the balance theory is false. But if such a theory be false, it does not follow that the indication furnished by the balance must always be erroneous; it may be false, it may be imperfect, but it also may be true. And this last possibility will be the

[1] Child calls attention to this development, which was conspicuous in England between the years 1640 and 1670.

more easily verified in proportion as the commercial relations are the less intricate.

There existed a condition of affairs in England during the seventeenth century which made such a possibility quite feasible.

England at that time, as Cunningham rightly observes,[1] herself produced all that she required; her exports consisted of the surplus of the most useful goods which she produced. Her imports, on the other hand, were composed only of articles of luxury, spices, wines, silks, etc. Now, if the value of the imports exceeded that of the exports, this showed that the country was consuming a quantity of articles of mere luxury greater than the excess of useful goods which she produced: if, instead, the opposite was the case, she was consuming actually less than such excess. The commercial balance, therefore, really served as a rough criterion of the economic conditions of the country.

We must not overlook the importance which the accumulation of money had in an age in which public treasure was the chief means of maintaining power, and of ensuring the existence of the State, when the easy mechanism of a public debt was not yet ready to come to its aid. Later on, commencing from the end of the seventeenth century, we shall see how things changed, and little by little how the theory of a commercial balance underwent a great transformation.

The commercial condition of England in the seventeenth century shows us how the idea of an energetic protection of the manufactures of the country should naturally flourish. That was the actual period of the foundation of English manufactures. Up to the sixteenth century England produced but few manufactured goods, and those only for home consumption; her exports consisted of raw material, especially of wool, tin, and lead, and her imports were iron, wines, timber, furs, velvets, linen, silk, and fine woollen materials. The great manufacturing centre of Europe was Flanders; but towards the end of the sixteenth century a change took place;

---

[1] Cunningham, *Growth of English Industry*, etc., 1882 edition, p. 315. This particular edition is quoted because in the more recent one the matter is treated more broadly, and this idea, which seems to us remarkable, is not so clearly reproduced.

Antwerp having lost its position, London became the principal commercial market of Europe. With the beginning of the seventeenth century the English shipping received a great impulse; the international trade carried on directly by England largely increased, and the great commercial companies sprang into existence.[1]

Already, under Henry VII., at the end of the fifteenth century, the first symptoms of the factory system showed themselves, and had commenced that transformation which was to change England from a country exporting wool to one manufacturing it. The palmy days of guilds were ended. The manufactories had been transferred into villages; in many of the industries it is possible to trace in those times something similar to the modern factory system, by means of which the master manufacturers, tired of the restrictions of the guilds, had organised in the country small communities for industrial purposes, arranged in such a way as to bring into operation the combination and division of labour. Merchandise was not only manufactured for local use but also for sale throughout the kingdom. The whole industrial system was no longer one of small domestic industry, characteristic of the preceding centuries, but a system of centralised labour, organised on a capitalistic basis, with a large number of workmen, and under the direction of one man, namely, the manager or proprietor of the industrial village. It was from such communities as these that the villages of Manchester, Bolton, Leeds, and Halifax sprang up, and afterwards became the great manufacturing cities of our own days.[2]

All this went on increasing with time; the industrial transformation made rapid progress in the seventeenth century, and there was also great progress in the textile industries, the production of which constituted two-thirds of the English exports; also progress in the production of paper, iron, glass, etc. The development of the shipping trade was enormous, and the increase of commercial and industrial companies was

---

[1] De Gibbins, *The Industrial History of England*, London, 1890, pp. 100, 102, 132, etc.; Th. Rogers, *A History of Agriculture and Prices in England*, Oxford, 1887, vol. v. p. 129, etc.

[2] De Gibbins, "A Short Outline of the Growth of English Industry," in the *Co-operative Annual*, Manchester, 1890, pp. 283, 284.

so great that that century was called the age of commercial companies.[1]

The new industries that were developing, in face of the difficulties attending their transformation, required support, and the anxiety of ensuring to them by means of commercial polity a wide and certain outlet for their products can be easily understood. The commercial classes, owing to the rapid development of foreign trade, increased in number and power, and exercised a great influence on politics.

13. Among the English writers of the seventeenth century there is not to be found a complete agreement upon any one economic doctrine; the growth of economic research is not marked by mercantilism alone.

"The century of habeas corpus and of parliamentarism could not give rise in England to an economic literature, which, like mercantilism, was characteristic of despotism."[2] This opinion of Held is, however, rather exaggerated, for even if in that century there were in England writers who were in advance of their times, as we shall see, still that doctrine, which for a century and a half was the favourite economic scheme of English statesmen and merchants, had many followers among writers.

In the numerous publications, more or less of an empirical character, of merchants about the beginning of the seventeenth century, appear the first rough outlines of the doctrine of the commercial balance; an attempt is made to regulate the currency of precious metals either by prohibiting the exportation of them or by obliging the exporters of merchandise to import part of the price of their goods in cash (system of the "balance of bargains ").[3] Later on, after a long struggle, this crude idea, opposed by Mun, was abandoned, and, still keeping in view the object of ensuring an abundance of money, they aim to arrive at it indirectly and more reasonably by means of a commercial policy which would tend to reduce importation, and by maintaining a favourable balance, to cause gold to flow

[1] Th. Rogers, *History of Agriculture and Prices in England*, vol. v. pp. viii., ix., 102, 129, etc.
[2] Held, *Carey's Socialwissenschaft und das Merkantilsystem*, Wurzburg, Stuber, 1866, p. 26.
[3] Cossa, *Introduzione*, etc., pp. 220-224.

spontaneously into the country and augment the treasury of the sovereign.

The mercantilist theory continues to detach itself more from the idea of the increase of money as its ultimate object: commercial development asserts itself; and instead of the idea of the importation of money there is substituted that of the importance of national trade.

The fundamental idea of the balance is that the consumption of foreign products should be less than that part of the national production which is sent abroad. If they had said that the national consumption should be less than the national production, they would have been correct; but, for them, consumption meant that of foreign goods, because it took money out of the country; whereas the consumption of home goods did not do so, because the money which is employed in internal trade remains in the country and serves for other transactions. They therefore confused money with capital, and to a certain extent trade with production, looking to exchange and not to labour and capital as the means of obtaining wealth (*vide* Heyking).

The development of the North American colonies in the seventeenth century contributed to give rise in England to an economic literature and to researches into the nature of commerce and traffic. The attention of the writers of that century was especially turned to the colonies; and, according to them, the favourite means of rendering the colonies more profitable to England are the laws prohibiting the transportation of colonial products from their place of production to any other place except England; those prohibiting such products to be imported into England in a manufactured state; and those preventing the exportation from England of raw material to be manufactured in the colonies when it was to the interest of England that they should be manufactured in the kingdom.

In this respect the writer who exercised the greatest influence in England was Thomas Mun, with whom mercantilism shorn of its empirical exaggerations is raised to a political and commercial system.

Mun places in relief the great importance of foreign commerce, and he delineates the policy which ought to base itself on the excess of exports over imports, thereby propounding the augmentation of exports and the increase of the national merchant navy. This author, whose writings in England were considered as standard works, exercised great influence in his own country, and being himself a merchant he treated the subject practically and from the point of view of English interests;[1] and certainly he contributed to give an impulse to that commercial policy, which, as we have already seen, was chiefly the product of the existing conditions.

Mun's influence was not destroyed by those English writers (Child, Temple, Davenant, Locke, Petty, North) who, towards the end of the seventeenth century, rose to clearer and more precise ideas regarding wealth, production, labour, value, and commerce, and who started the theories of free trade.[2] Their theories were in advance of the times, and they did not succeed in exercising any influence on commercial politics, and their scientific value was only vindicated much later.

The first appearance of a new theory barely in its infancy could not certainly triumph over a doctrine which at the end of the seventeenth century was conspicuous in science and practice; the theory was not yet formed, neither could it have been put into practice then. The importance of these writers is certainly considerable : the doctrine of the extreme mercantilists that the national wealth depended upon the accumulation of money was shown by those writers to be false, and the importance of natural resources and of labour, the true source of wealth, was brought to light; and in these writers the exaggerated importance given to foreign commerce is modified, and more appreciation is shown to agriculture. In the practical part, the idea of a commercial balance is treated in a less absolute sense, and the systems of commercial policy adopted by the States are more or less opposed, and industrial freedom is spoken of.[3] All this, however, is but imperfectly expressed, and freedom is claimed with much reserve: in

[1] With regard to Mun, see works of Roscher, *Zur Geschichte der Englischer Volkswirthschaftslehre*, Leipsig, 1851-52 ; Cossa, *Introduzione*, etc. ; Gobbi, *La concorrenza estera e gli antichi economisti italiani* ; Held, *Carey's Socialwissenschaft* ; Twiss, *Progress of Political Economy since the Sixteenth Century*, etc.

[2] Cossa, *La teoria del libero scambio nel secolo* xvii. (in the "*Saggi di economia politica*," Milano, Hoepli, 1878).

[3] Ingram, *History of Political Economy*, Edinburgh, Black, 1888, pp. 48-54.

many instances some of these writers display an uncertainty, an eclecticism, which may be perfectly explicable and justifiable, but which at the same time also accounts for the small practical influence they obtained. Dudley North alone vigorously upholds the complete freedom of trade.[1] The others, instead, waver; Temple accepts the balance theory, and Davenant, while admitting free-trade in his own country, advocates restrictions on colonial trade. Finally, Sir Josiah Child (who is certainly one of the greatest of all these writers, and takes a broad view of the commercial balance theory, because he looks upon it only as an index of the prosperity of a country and as an effect and not a cause), approves the Navigation Act, upholds complete monopoly of the colonial trade, and admits the formation of privileged commercial companies.

"New England," says Child in his *Discourse on Trade*, " is the most prejudicial plantation to this kingdom. Of all the American plantations, His Majesty has none so apt for the building of shipping as New England, nor none comparably so qualified for the breeding of seamen, not only by reason of the natural industry of that people, but, principally, by reason of their cod and mackerel fisheries; and, in my poor opinion, there is nothing more prejudicial, and, in prospect, more dangerous to any mother kingdom than the increase of shipping in her colonies, plantations, or provinces."

These were, then, not the class of writers to arrest on its course, or even to seriously modify, a commercial policy, which, as we see, had so many claims for existing, and which was only partially opposed by them.

It is a fact fraught with singular scientific importance that, even before the mercantile theory had attained its apogee, a new theory should have already risen up prepared to overthrow it. But this importance must not be over-rated, as it appears to have been by some, and especially by Held,[2] by laying too much stress upon those premonitory symptoms, and attributing to them a character which they only partly possessed. As a matter of fact, mercantilism pervaded the political as well as the commercial theories existing in England in the seventeenth century, and we can attribute to

[1] Cossa, "*Saggi*," pp. 59-64.
[2] Held, *Carey's Socialwissenschaft*, pp. 25-28.

it the Navigation Acts, also the restrictions imposed on commerce and upon the colonial industries, of which we are treating.

14. Since we are studying mercantilism and the English commercial policy in its relation to economic literature, it may be permissible for us to dwell somewhat longer on this subject before passing on to study from facts the effects of such a policy on the colonies, and to examine the view taken of it by the two great authorities on economic science, Adam Smith and Ricardo.

We can hardly expect to find in the two founders of the classic school a complete criticism of the English commercial policy of the seventeenth and eighteenth centuries. Adam Smith certainly gives the final blow to the theory of the balance of trade, which had been tottering since the end of the seventeenth century, at the same time collecting and organising in a rational and scientific system the many criticisms concerning it which had already appeared; he, however, strenuously defends the Navigation Act. He criticises the English colonial system, showing by a series of arguments that it was equally injurious to the colonies and to the mother country, and he especially attacks the prohibitive system with regard to the colonial manufactures. But his work displays a certain want of harmony, if it does not actually lapse into contradiction, when, comparing the colonial policy of England with that of other European countries, he praises it and maintains that in many points it was not damaging, and that it was sometimes even advantageous to the colonies.

Ricardo, confining himself to the strictly theoretical aspect of the question, confutes the thesis of Adam Smith that the colonial monopoly was injurious to the mother country, and points out the advantages which accrued from it.

The argument is so important that an analysis, if even somewhat lengthy, of the subjects treated by those great writers will not be out of place.[1]

---

[1] Adam Smith, *An Inquiry into the Nature and Causes of the Wealth of Nations*, book iv. (For my references I have made use of the 6th English edition, London, Strahan, 1791.)

David Ricardo, *Principles of Political Economy and Taxation* (chap. xxv. "On Colonial Trade" under "Works." London, Murray, 1852, pp. 204-9).

In the fourth book of Adam Smith's great work, that which we may call the partially practical defence of English commercial policy precedes the theoretic criticism; we will follow in the same order.

The Navigation Act is approved by the great Scotchman only as one of the exceptions which he makes to the criticism of the mercantilistic system of encouraging home industry by means of oppressing foreign industry; and this exception partakes of a political character. Before wealth there is the struggle for existence; and when a certain industry is indispensable to the defence of a country, it must be sustained even when the means adopted for that purpose are not economically correct. This is Smith's thesis—

"There seem, however, to be two cases in which it will generally be advantageous to lay some burden upon foreign, for the encouragement of domestic industry. The first is, when some particular sort of industry is necessary for the defence of the country. The defence of Great Britain, for example, depends very much upon the number of its sailors and shipping. The Act of Navigation, therefore, very properly endeavours to give the sailors and shipping of Great Britain the monopoly of the trade of their own country, in some cases by absolute prohibitions, and in others by heavy burdens upon the shipping of foreign countries."[1]

"The Act of Navigation is not favourable to foreign commerce, or to the growth of that opulence which can arise from it. . . . As defence, however, is of much more importance than opulence, the Act of Navigation is, perhaps, the wisest of all the commercial regulations of England."[2]

We observe incidentally that this all-important reason of defence, being more important than wealth, consisted in the essentially commercial struggle between England and Holland; the political and economic elements were perfectly fused together, and the political defence had necessarily to be based upon the economic increment, and upon the development of English shipping and commerce; the shipping and commerce

[1] Adam Smith's *Wealth of Nations*, vol. ii. p. 192.
[2] *Ibid.* pp. 194, 195. Child calls the Navigation Acts "the Magna Charta of the English shipping"; and Anderson, "the palladium of the maritime power of England."

being the principal resources of England. Adam Smith's opinion, therefore, that the Navigation Act had only a political justification, does not seem to us to be correct, inasmuch as the political and economic justifications were inseparable.

Passing on to the English colonies of North America, their prosperity, according to Adam Smith, is due, conjointly with the abundance of new land, to their political institutions. The colonial laws compelled the proprietors to cultivate and improve their lands under pain of being deprived of them, and they facilitated in various ways the division of property. The English policy with regard to her American colonies has been more favourable than that of any other European state towards its colonies. The English colonists have never had to contribute towards the defence of the mother country, but have on the contrary always been protected by the latter entirely at her own expense. According to Smith, among all the different systems of colonial monopoly adopted by various countries, the English system was certainly the most favourable to the colonies, because, instead of granting the monopoly of the colonial trade to one privileged company, or confining that trade to one single port of the mother country or to her own ships, as other nations have done, England has left colonial trade free to all her subjects and to all her ports, so that the competition between the English merchants prevented them from realising exorbitant profits, and safeguarded the colonies.

" Under so *liberal a policy* (note well this expression) the colonies are enabled both to sell their own produce and to buy the goods of Europe at a reasonable price. But since the dissolution of the Plymouth Company, when our colonies were but in their infancy, this has always been the policy of England." [1]

It may be added that with regard to the export of colonial produce the English monopoly was limited to the articles enumerated in the Navigation Acts, while the others, and among them the chief products of the colonies, such as grain, timber, salted meats, fish, etc., were left free; and among the articles enumerated pig-iron, for instance, was exempted on entering England from the heavy duties to which that of

[1] *Wealth of Nations*, vol. ii. p. 378.

other countries was subjected; so that in one sense these duties contributed rather to the encouragement of the American foundries than to their detriment. These advantages, however, as Adam Smith admits, accidentally arise from measures framed to protect the interests of England.

Where Smith gives vent to a fierce protest against the English colonial policy is with regard to the prohibition of manufactures in the colonies, due, as he says, to the unjust influence exercised by the English merchants and manufacturers upon the legislators of their country.[1]

"While Great Britain encourages in America the manufacturers of pig and bar iron, by exempting them from duties to which the like commodities are subject when imported from any other country, she imposes an absolute prohibition upon the erection of steel furnaces and slit-mills in any of her American plantations. She will not suffer her colonists to work in those more refined manufactures even for their own consumption; but insists upon their purchasing of her merchants and manufacturers all goods of this kind which they have occasion for. She prohibits the exportation from one province to another by water, and even the carriage by land upon horseback or in a cart, of hats, of wools and woollen goods, of the produce of America; a regulation which effectually prevents the establishment of any manufacture of such commodities for distant sale, and confines the industry of her colonists in this way to such coarse and household manufactures as a private family commonly makes for its own use, or for that of some of its neighbours in the same province."[2]

And he continues sharply stigmatizing such a system:

"To prohibit a great people, however, from making all that they can of every part of their own produce, or from employing their stock and industry in the way that they judge most advantageous to themselves, is a manifest violation of the most sacred rights of mankind."[3]

Smith, however, adds that these prohibitions, although unjust, had not up to that time (that is, up to 1773, when he wrote the chapter to which we refer, as can be gathered by the context) been very injurious to the colonies, because land was

[1] *Wealth of Nations*, vol. ii. p. 385.
[2] *Ibid.* pp. 386, 387.   [3] *Ibid.* p. 387.

so cheap and consequently work so dear, that the finer materials would have cost more if made there than if imported from England; so that also without the prohibitions their own interests would have suggested to them the inutility of establishing such industries.

In conclusion, the English commercial policy towards the American colonies is spoken of by Adam Smith as 'iniquitous' with respect to the manufacturing prohibitions, and as partly relatively liberal, and partly absolutely liberal with respect to the commercial monopoly—and he writes about it just when the revolution had already begun. This must be borne in mind, because we shall have to compare it with the conditions of the colonies during the whole time in which it was developing, and when in full vigour.

Strangely enough Smith, shortly after, having in spite of criticisms repeatedly called this a "liberal policy," says that it was inspired by the English merchants more eager for their own interests than for those of the colonies or of the mother country. "In their (the merchants') exclusive privilege of supplying the colonies with all the goods which they wanted from Europe, and of purchasing all such parts of their surplus produce as could not interfere with any of the trades which they themselves carried on at home, the interest of the colonies was sacrificed to the interest of those merchants."[1]

After all this, passing to the consideration of the colonial policy from a more scientific and theoretic point of view, Adam Smith (who reappears as the demolisher of mercantilism) criticises it at length, in all its aspects and without omissions, and he sums up his criticisms in this manner.[2] Colonial monopoly, like other expedients of the mercantile system, depresses the industry of all other countries, but principally that of the colonies, without in the least increasing, in fact diminishing, the industry of the country for whose advantage it is established.

Monopoly prevents the capital of that country, whatever the extent of that capital may be at a specified time, from supporting such an amount of productive work as it otherwise might, and it prevents the industrious inhabitants from obtaining such a good income as they would otherwise obtain. And

[1] *Wealth of Nations*, vol. ii. p. 390.   [2] *Ibid.* pp. 434-37.

as capital can only be increased through the increase of income, monopoly, by diminishing that income, retards the formation of capital.

By increasing the rate of mercantile profit, monopoly discourages the improvement of the land and maintains a high rate of interest on the market. Monopoly, indeed, increases the merchants' earnings; but in order to benefit a small class of the inhabitants of a country, it injures all the others, and also all those of other countries.

The colonial monopoly injured England, says Adam Smith, because it diverted English capital from other necessary uses and from other trades, and caused it to largely return to the colonial trade; it also rendered precarious the condition of English trade which, through the rebellion of the colonies, was seriously compromised.[1]

15. Ricardo[2] criticises this thesis of Adam Smith regarding colonial monopoly being injurious to England.

The fact of having the monopoly of the colonial market for the sale of their products, brought no benefit to the English producers and merchants in regard to their being able to dispose of their products in the colonies at a higher price than in England or elsewhere, remarks Ricardo; that would only have been possible for a company possessing the whole colonial monopoly, whilst in the case of the English sellers, their competition on the colonial market would maintain the price of their goods at its proper level.

It may be well to mention here that a somewhat similar remark is also made by Adam Smith; but whilst the theory is true, the reasoning of Ricardo clashes with a fact, of which he does not treat, and which requires an explanation.

---

[1] Cunningham, speaking of Smith's criticism on mercantilism, mentions that Smith did not sufficiently understand the standpoint of the English mercantilists, who did not devote themselves so much to increasing the wealth of their country as to increasing the political power, and to establish the political supremacy over other countries. Thus the criticism on the colonial system, formed upon an economic principle, does not hold good, because English mercantilists did not think of augmenting the wealth of the country by the restrictions to the colonial trade, but only endeavoured to augment the political power; and the succeeding events, Cunningham says, proved them to be right.—*Vide* Cunningham, *Growth of English Industry*, vol. ii. pp. 434, 435.

[2] Works, *Principles of Political Economy*, pp. 204-209.

The fact is that in reality prices were frequently higher in the colonies than in the mother country; and this fact of a specific raising of the value of products sold abroad is verified also at present in all countries governed by a protective system, as the English enquiry into industrial depression shows by numerous examples. For this to happen it is not necessary for the exporters to enjoy any monopoly (this monopoly, however, could sometimes exist in the colonies if English exporters were few and agreed among themselves). In fact, in order that protected producers might be able to sell abroad at a higher value than at home, it would be sufficient for the excess of the foreign value upon the cost to be exactly balanced by an equal inferiority of the national value below the cost; since, granting that, these producers only obtain on the whole the reimbursement of their outlay, or in other words they receive nothing which competition could deprive them of.

But colonial monopoly, says Ricardo, benefited the mother country in a different manner, by ensuring for her products a market which might have been taken away from her by others; by being able to produce and sell to the colonies, at the normal price of home production, goods which were elsewhere produced at a less price; which goods, if trade with the colonies had been open to all, would have been carried to the colonies by other countries, and would have shut out English importation.

As regards the colonies their loss was not in being compelled to buy English goods at a higher price than in England, but in being obliged to buy from England those products which they would have been able to obtain elsewhere at a lower price.

"It is evident," concludes Ricardo, "that the trade with a colony may be so regulated, that it shall at the same time be less beneficial to the colony, and more beneficial to the mother country, than a perfectly free trade." [1]

16. To these views of Ricardo may be added others of an historical character; and as we are not entering fully into the question (for our researches refer especially to the effects of the English commercial policy upon the colonies, and not

[1] *Principles of Political Economy*, etc., p. 207.

upon the mother country), we only just give them a passing glance.

We have seen what were the industrial conditions of England when the colonial monopoly was founded: the manufactures were developed and the capitalist system of industries was initiated. The difficulties were indeed considerable that the English manufacturers and traders had to overcome in order to firmly constitute that which was then only an attempt not yet realised—the industrial and commercial supremacy of England; still, there undoubtedly existed in the country a conspicuous natural disposition for industries; meanwhile England at that time, with its colonial possessions, could avail itself of a territory extremely varied and vast, so that her system of commercial restrictions could not certainly be called a system of economic isolation.

In these conditions, as will be seen in another essay treating of the young industries, protection was able to benefit the industrial and commercial development of the country; and colonial monopoly, as Ricardo shrewdly observes, secured exclusively to the manufactured goods of the mother country a vast market, and placed them beyond the influence of foreign competition; this monopoly, I maintain, constituted a form of vigorous protection; a protection analogous, observes Roscher, to that advantage admitted by Adam Smith, which a country can obtain by such commercial treaties as assure it the preference over other countries in a foreign market.[1]

Roscher notes how difficult it is to sustain the Smith theory as to the different remunerations upon various branches of commerce, and the inferiority of colonial commerce compared with others, keeping in view the tendency, illustrated by Ricardo, of the rate of profit to level itself in all the different employments of capital, according to the delay of returns, or according to the risk incurred by such capital.[2] This, however, concerns the advantage to the separate capitalists, and as regards that, the tendency to levelling cannot be theoretically doubted.

But as regards the general interest of the country, it

[1] Roscher, *Kolonien, Kolonialpolitik*, etc., p. 236.
[2] *Ibid.* p. 232.

seems to us to have been benefited—not the interest of only a few merchants and manufacturers—by a system which in an epoch of industrial and commercial transformation helped to place the economic life of the country in that groove for which it had most pronounced natural aptitudes, and established close relations of trade between a country comparatively densely populated and productive of manufactured goods, and a country thinly populated and productive of raw materials. The system might have been temporarily injurious, favouring perhaps employments which at the time were but slightly profitable: but this could only have been a passing evil to be afterwards compensated by future benefits. As a proof that the colonial restrictions were of no real advantage to England, the fact is generally brought forward that, at the separation of the North American colonies from the mother country, instead of English manufactures and trade being severely damaged, there followed a greater progressive development in the commercial relations between England and the United States, and also in the English industries. But it seems to us that, if this constitutes the condemnation of the colonial system at the time of its abolition, it does not equally condemn it at the time of its initiation by England; in the same way as illustrating the advantages obtained later on by England through free trade, does not imply an absolute condemnation of the systems previously adopted.

Everything has its proper time, its beginning and its end; and England, the great maritime and industrial power at the end of the past century, no longer needed those means, which since the time of Charles II. had facilitated the gradual formation of her power, now established and triumphant, and had no necessity to be supported in her latter transformations, because she was certain of her primacy in the world.

17. But as it is not necessary to dwell more at length upon a question which would be perhaps out of place here, we now close this long digression. Neither is it the time to examine critically certain statements of Adam Smith concerning our subject; because, according to the method which we should keep in view, namely, that the examination of facts should precede conclusions, for the present we confine ourselves to passing a few general remarks upon the opinions of

the great economist. As we have already said, the question of the English colonial policy is not very harmoniously treated by Adam Smith, and his criticism, frequently so powerful, is occasionally to be found struggling against a certain defensory tendency, which places the author almost in contradiction with himself. Consequently Smith's treatment on the whole is rather undecided, and leaves the reader uncertain and only partly persuaded. But in our opinion this uncertainty and this apparent contradiction were not only absolutely inevitable at the time when the great economist wrote, but were even from a certain point of view creditable.

Adam Smith dealt the last vigorous blows to the mercantilist doctrine, which both in theory and practice was then faulty on all sides; and from the impulse of his genius sprang a new science which the coming times would explain. It was certainly not the moment for mercantilism to find completely favourable criticism and that historical justification which was only possible a century later. Besides, precisely at the time when the American colonies, tired of English oppression, were throwing off the yoke, an entirely impartial judgment on the English colonial policy must have been very difficult even for such a well-balanced mind as that of Adam Smith; especially as the elements of fact, indispensable for judging the effects of the monopoly and industrial restrictions on the colonies, must have been uncertain, difficult to procure, and often falsified.

Finally, we must not neglect to observe that Adam Smith judged the English colonial system as it existed in his time, at the beginning of the American revolution: a complicated system, the result of numerous regulations, following each other little by little, as we have seen, during a long period, and the judgment of which must have been very different according to the consideration of them as then existing, or as they had been separately dictated in their turn.

Uncertainty was therefore inevitable; but to our thinking (and here lies Smith's credit), that uncertainty is not only to be attributed to those difficulties which we have noted, and to that contrast which must have arisen in Smith's mind, between the sentiments of the loyal citizen of the mother country struggling against the rebellious colonies, and the scientific plans of the founder of economic liberalism; but also perhaps to that historical sentiment, which often shows itself in his great work, making him completely approve the Navigation Act, and which must have caused him to perceive, although confusedly, in the colonial policy, both the condemnation of the present and the justification of the past.

CHAPTER III

THE EFFECTS OF THE ENGLISH COMMERCIAL POLICY UPON THE NORTH AMERICAN COLONIES

18. First of all let us endeavour to clearly picture the economic and social conditions of the American colonies before the Navigation Acts. The date of their foundation in itself tells us a good deal: the first permanent European settlement in North America was that of Jamestown (Virginia), founded in 1607; the colonisation of New England commenced in 1620 with the colony of Plymouth, founded by the pilgrim-fathers; the next was that of New Hampshire, founded in 1623; Massachusetts in 1629; Connecticut in 1633; Rhode Island in 1636; Maine in 1639. The colony of New York, founded by the Dutch in 1613, only came into the power of the English in 1664.

The first settlement founded in New Jersey dates from 1624; Delaware dates from 1627, etc.

In short, the real colonisation commenced within the first thirty years of the century, and the Navigation Acts, coming at about the middle of the century, fell upon the colonies in their earliest stage of existence.[1]

[1] The causes which in the beginning of the seventeenth century gave an impulse in England to colonisation were complex: an increase in the population had been manifesting itself during the reign of Elizabeth; the agricultural transformation substituting for the old triennial cultivation, that of pasturage and cattle rearing, had produced a profound and general crisis among the agricultural classes, who were without work and without food; the establishment of peace during the reign of James I., following after a long period of warfare, induced many adventurers to seek an occupation in other parts, and finally political struggles, persecutions, and religious strife. The colonisation was therefore brought about by economic, political, and religious causes; and whilst the Spanish colonies were founded for the purpose of the discovery of

We know what was the life of the pilgrims and puritans who emigrated to New England; they were not rich colonists arriving with the necessary stores and capital for colonisation; they were for the most part not even supplied with necessaries, and they had to struggle for a long time against hunger and want, against the severity of the climate, and with the difficulties of a virgin soil and unexplored lands. In other colonies, of a different origin, the conditions of the early times must have been less trying, owing to the help afforded by companies and proprietors who had promoted and organised their foundation.[1]

Historians represent the life of the early American colonists, especially those of New England, as one of poverty, hardship, and misery. But the energy of the colonists, combined with the abundance of the new and free lands open to all, soon changed the condition of affairs, and there followed a period of comparative prosperity based upon labour.

Numerous are the evidences of the economic welfare of the American colonies in the middle of the seventeenth century. The colony of Virginia was very prosperous in 1648;

precious metals, the English colonies were founded in order to obtain new products, to open new markets, and to relieve over population. "America was all the more attractive because, whilst offering, from a political and religious point of view, to independent men every liberty, at the same time, from an economic point of view, it offered them every facility for enriching themselves" (*Vide* Roscher, *Kolonien*, etc., p. 188 ; and Leroy Beaulieu, *De la colonisation chez les peuples modernes*, Paris, Guillaumin, 1874, pp. 94-8, 117).

[1] The original colonies in North America were divided into three classes: Crown colonies, proprietary colonies, and charter colonies. The first were founded by emigrants, and established entirely by their own resources ; so in reality were those of New England, for also the colony of Massachusetts, originally founded by a company, was afterwards left to its own resources. The proprietary colonies were founded by wealthy Englishmen who had obtained from the Crown absolute power over the territories occupied by them. And finally, the charter companies were those founded by privileged commercial companies, by which they were governed.

Whilst, therefore, the independent members of the Crown colonies were left to their own resources, the other colonies were assisted by the companies and proprietors interested in them. Virginia was in this manner supported by the company which founded it ; and in the case of Pennsylvania, William Penn, the founder, spent so much money on the colony that he finished by being imprisoned for debt ; and Lord Baltimore spent about £40,000 in works connected with the colony of Maryland, founded by him.

abundance of lands, free markets for products, and practically all the prerogatives of a free State. The colonists there, says Bancroft,[1] enjoyed all that prosperity which a virgin soil, equality of laws, and general uniformity of conditions could produce: their number increased, their houses were full of children, and their ports were full of ships and immigrants. The colonies of New England were also very thriving; signs of prosperity were evident from about 1640, and they soon established shipbuilding and commenced exporting skins, timber, fish, and grain.

We are speaking of the general welfare and prosperity, not of wealth, because it was, evidently, only a comparative prosperity. To give an example, in 1678 (thirty years later), New York contained only 343 houses, a population of 3430 inhabitants, and its trading employed ten or fifteen ships.[2] A thousand pounds would then have been a fortune, and a person with half that sum was a rich man.[3]

The industry carried on in the colonies during these very early periods was primitive indeed, as we can well understand. It consisted almost exclusively of agriculture and mining, and both worked in the very roughest manner.

Bolles describes at some length the agricultural life of the colonists: they lived alone, far apart, and scattered over their farms, unprovided with the most necessary instruments; the agricultural rotations were unknown to them, and they made no use of manures. For a century and a half the colonists remained in a stationary condition, and their instruments, few and imperfect, were never improved.[4] The production, and consequently the exportation, consisted mostly of grain, timber, tobacco, etc. Some attempts were made to extract and work iron, in which the whole country was very rich. The first establishment was started at Lynn in 1634 for the casting of pig-iron; and others followed in the succeeding years, but they were all small and most primitive.

There were numerous saw mills and flour mills driven by

[1] Bancroft, *History of the United States*, vol. i.
[2] Bishop, *History of American Manufactures*, vol. i. pp. 60, 61.
[3] Bancroft, *History of the United States*, vol. i. p. 407.
[4] Bolles, *Industrial History of United States*, p. 14.

water power; the first turning to account one of the principal productions of the country, the timber from the forest clearings, the other supplying the most important necessary of life. The abundance of timber and tar, together with the long extension of sea-coast which the colonists inhabited, gave rise to the industry of shipbuilding, which industry rapidly increased, and in which the colonists soon excelled. We also find some indications of attempts to produce glass, earthenware, hides, and woven materials. The colonists in general being so isolated could not confine themselves exclusively to agriculture; every one, to supply his own wants, was obliged to devote himself also to the industries connected with it, and the local industries carried on in a small way by artisans provided them with the rest. The wants of the colonist families, accustomed to a simple, rough, and isolated life, were very few; house, food, and often instruments and clothes were all prepared by the same planters, who were at the same time blacksmiths, carpenters, weavers, etc.;[1] and only for a very small part of the household wants was it necessary to fall back on products manufactured out of the country.

The most marked characteristics of the economy of the English colonies, during the first half century of their existence, were the fertile and unlimited lands, open to all, the prevalence of agriculture, and the isolation of the farmers.[2] Connected with these characteristics, both as to cause and effect, were, in our opinion, the welfare of the colonies, the equality of conditions, the scarcity of industries, the primitive state of life and social institutions, also the small importance of internal and international trade.[3]

" Before the close of the first half century of their history,"

[1] Goss, *History of Tariff Administration in the United States*, New York, 1891, p. 10.
[2] In Virginia, between 1652 and 1660, the inhabitants, says Bancroft, were all agriculturists, scattered, unassociated, averse to trading or to assembling together in a town; there was very little commercial industry, and no important accumulations of commercial wealth.
[3] In the midst of such social prosperity, writes Loria, extracting from a letter dated 1688, there was a tendency among the colonists to isolation. In such a vast extent of land each immigrant was stimulated to cultivate more ground than he could manage. The plantations extended themselves into large tracts of country, and farms of one to three thousand acres were common. Consequently each colonist was separated from his neighbour by great distances which were

states Bishop, "the older colonies were rich and prosperous to a degree scarcely exceeded during the time they continued as dependencies of Great Britain."[1] "Labour was valuable; land was cheap; competence promptly followed industry. There was no need of a scramble; abundance gushed from the earth for all. . . . It (Virginia) was the best poor man's country in the world."[2]

In the community of New York, composed essentially of agriculturists, there prevailed a great equality of conditions; there were few merchants, few servants, and very few slaves.[3]

Notwithstanding that the population began to increase, labour was scarce, and this constituted the principal obstacle to the existence of manufactures. This fact we will study better later on with the help of Benjamin Franklin's observations. Meanwhile we may mention here that the welfare, the equality of conditions, the absence of accumulated wealth, the prevalence of agriculture, the difficulty of finding workers, the want of manufacturing industries, were all the consequences of the existence of free land.[4] The isolation of the agriculturists, necessary in order to cultivate the best and easiest lands, and to occupy them in large tracts, caused, so to speak, the social life to be very limited; frugality was general; trading rare, and carried on in a most primitive manner; barter and exchange by means of shells (wampum), originally used by the colonists with the Indians, had become the common system of trading among the colonists themselves; and shells as monetary currency were only suppressed about 1650, when by their superabundance they had become valueless. Also, beaver skins in the north, tobacco and rice in the south, were used as money, and even the taxes were paid in kind. Coined money, which was very scarce, came afterwards through the trade with the West Indies and with the immigrants from Europe; it

impossible to traverse for want of roads. Hence the scantily populated country, the solitary life, the unfrequent and unimportant trade.—Vide *Analisi della proprietà capitalista*, Torino, 1889, vol. ii. p. 23.

[1] Bishop, *History of American Manufactures*, vol. i. p. 324.
[2] Bancroft, *History of the United States*, vol. i. p. 234.
[3] *Ibid.* vol. ii. p. 407.
[4] *Vide* Loria's theory, which we only note in passing at present, but of which more will be said later on.

was mostly used for the payment of the importations from England.[1]

Commerce was generally very scarce; and, considering all these conditions, the mode of life and the few wants of the colonists, it was natural that the importance of international trade should be limited.

19. We will now pass on to examine what were the effects and the importance of the Navigation Acts on the colonies at the time when they were introduced. In order to arrive at a conclusion we must bear in mind two other elements besides the social and economic condition of the colonies: the opinions of historians and other writers, with the facts testifying the injuries caused; and the complaints raised in the colonies through those famous Acts which we have analysed in the first chapter.

Cromwell's Act might have damaged the colonies by limiting their freedom of trade, and by placing obstacles in the way of their foreign commerce, but, as we have seen in the first chapter, besides being very feebly applied, the damage it might have caused was certainly paralysed by the advantage that it actually brought to the colonies; for by restricting the trade solely to English or colonial ships, at the same time that it protected the English shipping, it gave an impulse to the shipping of the colonies, thus greatly benefiting them.

It might be supposed that, if the Act of Cromwell was harmless to the colonies, that of Charles II., expressly directed towards restricting their commerce and favouring the commercial and industrial interests of England, must have been very injurious to them; and, that being obliged to purchase in England all the goods they required, and to sell there most of their own products, it must, in short, have arrested their economic development, or diverted to other channels the prosperity resulting from their labour and their free land.

This is the reasoning of the greater number of writers, and we will give an example from the most positive and the most reliable among them, the great American historian. England, says Bancroft, adopted from the Spanish a system of monopoly through which the merchants of the mother country enriched themselves by selling to the colonists goods much above their real value, and obtaining their products, of which

[1] Bolles, "American Finance" in Lalor's *Cyclopædia*.

they were the only buyers, at rather less than their value; and by this system, fatal to the colonies, the colonists lost that which was gained by the merchants (not by the people generally) of England. The Act of Charles II., continues Bancroft, constituted an unjust oppression, which could only be maintained by force, and which was itself sowing the seeds of the future insurrection of the colonies; it contained the pledge of the final independence of America.[1]

An example of the damage caused to the colonies by the Act of Charles II. is pointed out by Bancroft in the state of affairs in Virginia; their tobacco trade suffered considerably, and their market was restricted, whilst the prices of goods imported increased, to the serious detriment of the population, which was entirely agricultural and had not, like New England, an aptitude for industry.

We are far from denying the enormous injustice of that colonial policy which began with the Act of Charles II., but we hold that the injury which, at least in the commencement, it must have caused to the colonies, was less than appears at first sight.

We have found mention of very little actual damage caused to the colonies by the Act, and it can be easily understood how injurious it might have been to Virginia, because that colony imported everything from England;[2] whilst tobacco, the only product it exported, and by the sale of which the colonists provided themselves with everything, was included among the enumerated goods which were to be exported exclusively to England.[3] But the other colonies were differently situated. For a country, in which everything, as it were, spoke of freedom, political freedom, religious freedom, which had attracted many of the emigrants; free lands accessible to every one; equality of conditions in a general modest welfare;

---

[1] Bancroft, *History of the United States*, vol. ii. p. 46.
[2] "... plenty encouraged indolence; no domestic manufactures were established; everything was imported from England." This is what Bancroft states with regard to Virginia.—*Vide* vol. i. p. 335.
[3] This was not altogether a disadvantage, for as Beer observes, with regard to tobacco, the colonies had practically the monopoly of the English market, for not only was Spanish tobacco dearer, but it was surcharged in England with duties three times higher.— Vide *Commercial Policy of England*, etc., New York, 1893, p. 49.

for a country which for thirty years or more had enjoyed almost complete freedom of maritime trade,—the Act of Charles II. might have been a terrible blow and might have raised, not only general discontent, but actual revolt.

We are not now concerned with the investigation of the causes which perhaps made a successful reaction of the colonies impossible in the beginning of their career ; but, as regards the dissatisfaction and the complaints raised by the Act of Charles II. in the first years of its application, it appears on the whole that they were less than might be supposed. Great resentment was displayed by Virginia,[1] which attempted to revolt, and by Maryland,[2] both tobacco-producing colonies. Sir William Berkeley, Governor of Virginia, in 1671 summed up the complaints of that colony as follows :—" Mighty and destructive have been the obstructions to our trade and navigation by that severe Act of Parliament which excludes us from having any commerce with any nation of Europe but in our own ships ; we cannot add to our plantations any commodity that grows out of it, as olive trees, or cotton, or vines. Besides this, we cannot procure any skilful men for our hopeful commodity of silk, and it is not lawful for us to carry pipe-stems or a bushel of corn to any place in Europe out of the King's dominions."[3] These complaints might also to some extent have been made by the other colonies, but we do not find many traces of them ; and Robertson, speaking only in a general way, says that against the Navigation Acts protests were immediately raised in the colonies, which were unheeded (perhaps the author alludes to the petition to Charles II. in 1661 from Virginia, to be allowed free-trade : *vide* Bancroft, vol. ii.), and that the English Government tried hard to enforce the law, whilst the colonies were trying, and with some success, to elude it by means of smuggling.[4] That this allusion of Robertson is to Virginia alone is confirmed by the following words of Bishop :—" These laws were very little regarded by the colonies, with the exception of Virginia, where they excited remonstrances and almost

[1] *Vide* Bancroft, vol. i. p. 335.   [2] *Ibid.* p. 326.
[3] Well's article on " Navigation Laws " in Lalor's *Cyclopadia.*
[4] *The History of America*, London, Strahan, 1803, vol. iv. Roscher (*Kolonien, Kolonialpolitik*, etc., p. 211) accepts Robertson's assertions without comment.

rebellion, and were not, until a later period, enforced upon them."[1]

This opinion seems to be very important, for it is accepted also by Bolles, who brings it into his *Industrial History* without mentioning his authority.[2] The oppressive and unjust acts of Charles II. were at the time of their promulgation "little regarded" by the colonies. And this must be true, at least to a great extent, because it is supported by later facts and opinions, of which we shall speak further on, among others, in the explicit declarations made by the colonies a century later, in which they admitted England's right to "regulate the colonial trade."

But why were such Acts so little heeded from the beginning, especially when, through their novelty, they were likely to be more difficult to bear? Evidently because the injuries they caused to the colonies were very few and hardly felt under the conditions in which the colonies then found themselves.

Let us call to mind the observation of Adam Smith mentioned in the second chapter, to the effect that the principal products of the colonies, exclusive of Virginia, were timber, grain, fish, etc., which were not enumerated in the Acts, and were free from restrictions.

This fact somewhat explains the indifference of the greater part of the colonies, whose exportations were little interfered with by the new laws. Let us add also that the colonies of the north were just those in which there was a certain industrial aptitude, and in which there was developing a home manufacturing industry which supplied the wants of the agriculturists, and which was not then, as it was afterwards, hampered and crushed by the English laws, so that the rise in price of the products of importation, consequent upon the monopoly established by Charles II., could not affect them very seriously. We have already seen in the preceding paragraph how the primitive economic and social condition of the colonies reduced the importance of international commerce, so that any law restricting such commerce must have been easily tolerated. Goss[3] points out that, "though we hear

[1] *History of American Manufactures*, vol. i. p. 88.
[2] Bolles, *Industrial History*, etc., p. 852.
[3] *History of Tariff Administration*, p. 10.

much of a flourishing illicit traffic, we find that the colonial marine was engaged mainly in the fisheries, and that general commerce was small in amount, and confined to a few articles." Finally, those injurious effects which the Navigation Acts might have caused, the colonies succeeded to some extent in neutralising in two ways—by smuggling [1] (even though limited for the reasons already noted, to our thinking most appropriately, by Goss) and by the home manufacturing of goods.

It was therefore precisely that monopoly, by means of which the mother country sought to bind the colonial trade, to the advantage of her own merchants, which compelled the work and the capital of the colonists to be dedicated to the neglected field of domestic manufacture. From the time when the English colonial monopoly commenced, says Bishop, we find an increased attention of the colonies to home manufacturing.[2]

This result was also largely contributed to by those regulations which, in order to favour the English proprietors, prohibited the importation into England from the colonies of grain, preserved meats, etc.; in fact, the principal products of the New England colonies. These colonies, when they did not assist themselves by smuggling, must have found very little advantage in exporting their products to other countries, from which, unless they intended to infringe the English laws, they had to send back their ships empty or send them to England for a cargo. This condition of affairs must naturally have caused those colonies to neglect the production and commerce of those products, and must have stimulated them to organise manufactures for the supply of their own needs.[3]

In conclusion, the navigation laws, at the time when they were introduced into the colonies, were certainly not a benefit

---

[1] Smuggling was more carried on in the Northern States than in the Southern; the former, in fact, producing few commodities which could find sale in England, were obliged to communicate with other countries, and were thus tempted, and to a certain extent forced, to buy there some products; whilst the latter, producers of tobacco, rice, etc., found their natural market in England. —Vide Beer, *The Commercial Policy of England toward the American Colonies*, p. 134.

[2] Bishop, *History of American Manufactures*, vol. i. p. 324.

[3] Beer, *Commercial Policy of England*, etc., pp. 74, 75, 136-38.

to them, neither were they very injurious, since the conditions in which the colonies then were caused them to be but little affected by the action of the colonial policy which was then being formed.

And that this is the case is proved ultimately also by the prosperity of the colonies a few years later.

Bancroft, after having severely criticised the policy of Charles II., describes in glowing terms the general welfare of New England about the year 1670.

Trade was considerably increasing. In Boston roadstead were to be seen Spanish, Italian, French, and Dutch vessels; the ships of Massachusetts went to the farthest regions; the country enjoyed a general prosperity; the towns increased; begging and thieving were almost unknown; and, on the whole, the people were enjoying a real independence.[1]

20. The last period of the English commercial policy in the American colonies is marked, as we have already seen, by an increased severity of application. It commences about the end of the seventeenth century by enforcing more vigorously the Navigation Acts, which at the beginning had only been lightly applied; afterwards came the restrictions on the internal colonial trade and upon the exportation of colonial manufactures. During the first half of the eighteenth century the prohibitive system towards the colonial manufactures was broadly applied; and finally, shortly afterwards, in the years preceding the revolution, the whole colonial policy became fatally oppressive. There is therefore to be observed a continual increase in the severity of this policy all through the period from the end of the seventeenth century until the revolution. What can be the reasons?

The reasons, to our thinking, are complex. Above all we must bear in mind the commercial theory then dominant; the system of mercantilism was certainly undergoing a change, and was gradually losing its primitiveness; the importance given to money was not the same as formerly; and the significance given to the balance of trade was also changed. This, however, did not bring any material change in the commercial policy. At the end of the seventeenth century the development of Joint-Stock Companies and of credit had placed the State in

[1] Bancroft, *History of the United States*, vol. ii.

the position of finding other means besides the public treasure to ensure her power; the accumulation of money, therefore, was no longer the direct aim of the commercial policy; there was instead a tendency towards encouraging the development of industry and the trade of the country. The favourable balance of trade was held to be a certain indication of the prosperity of the country's industry, consequently all the efforts of the English policy were directed to maintain it.

With this character the doctrine of the balance of trade continued to dominate with nearly all writers and in all the legislation of the first half of the eighteenth century. The State was still endeavouring to promote the welfare of England without regard to its dependencies and in antagonism with other nations; it still maintained a systematic interference with commerce and industry; but it was entering upon a new phase of the mercantile system. All this was done not so much with the view of directly increasing the power of England by means of the balance of accumulated wealth, as with the view of obtaining material advantages not only for merchants but for the nation at large. It was only after the time of Adam Smith that this policy was really discontinued.[1]

Therefore, although the mercantilist theory was somewhat perfected, it nevertheless continued to inspire the English commercial and colonial policy.

But the strengthening of this policy, and especially the system of prohibiting colonial manufactures during the period on which we are engaged, is linked with other facts which help to confirm our reasoning.

We have previously observed how the English commercial monopoly had directed colonial capital to be dedicated to manufacturing. This impetus was certainly not very strong, as we shall shortly see when speaking of the conditions of American industries; but that such an effect, although to a small extent could, and in fact should happen, appears quite natural; and if it remained limited, it was because the

[1] Cunningham, *Growth of English Industry*, etc., 1882 edition, p. 367. This edition is quoted because this important item does not appear to be in the more recent edition of 1892, vol. ii.

economic and social conditions of the colonies did not yet allow the development of manufactures.

As matters stood it seems that the prohibitions on colonial manufactures, only just beginning, helped, towards the end of the eighteenth century, to complete and improve the English commercial policy, thus joining the commercial monopoly to the industrial monopoly and paralysing in the former that tendency, which we might call self-destructive, by which the higher price of imported manufactures gave stimulus to home productions and lessened the importations; and the commercial monopoly naturally resulted in the destruction of that trade which it was striving to render so productive to the mother country.

It would, however, be a mistake to give to this fact a greater importance than that of a secondary co-efficient in the strengthening of the colonial policy. The principal factor of such strengthening was the condition of English industry in the eighteenth century.

21. English industry was at that time far from being in the same primitive state as that of the colonies; it had a history of centuries, and for centuries the English Government (long before the institution of colonial monopoly) studied to increase and strengthen it by a whole system of laws, commencing from 1337 with the prohibition of Edward III. forbidding the exportation of wool and the use of materials which were not of home manufacture, up to the strange decree of Charles II. ordering that all corpses should be buried wrapped in woollen cloth.

We have already seen[1] how the English manufactures were developing during the sixteenth and seventeenth centuries, and how in England the rudiments of capitalism were beginning to shape themselves.

This movement, in the eighteenth century, became rapidly more pronounced, and the system of capitalism and use of machinery became extended.

As early as the commencement of the eighteenth century the mania for speculation, and the formation of innumerable companies for every kind of undertaking, showed signs of the abundance of English capital and the wealth of the country,

[1] *Vide* pp. 31, 32.

resulting from the development of industries and commerce and the improvement of agriculture.

And if, up till the latter part of that century, there were no large factories, there were, however, all through the century signs of an approach of the modern capitalist methods of production upon a large scale ; the custom of employing a large number of persons under one roof, or at least under the superintendence and management of an employer, became more general. At Nottingham there were fifty manufactories which had about 1200 looms at work.[1]

But the great industrial transformation, already showing itself during the preceding years, received an immense stimulus in the second half of the eighteenth century by that series of inventions which produced a complete revolution, firstly in the cotton industry, and afterwards in all the weaving industries.

In 1767 Hargreaves invented the famous spinning-jenny, which performed the work of thirty spinners ; Arkwright improved it in 1768 by his spinning frame, driven by water power ; and finally Crompton in 1775 united the two machines in his mule-jenny. Cartwright, a poor clergyman of Kent, in 1787, with his power-loom, did for weaving what the former had done for spinning.

Immediately there sprang up in Lancashire and other counties numerous manufactories employing workmen from every part of England ; the factory system at once entered upon its triumphant career, and soon took the place of the smaller industries and the domestic productions of cotton spinning, so general in England until then.[2]

The new machinery was soon used for wool and flax, producing in those industries a similar transformation.

Important improvements were likewise introduced in the production and working of iron ; new systems for ventilation of furnaces, the adoption of the process of puddling and lamination of iron, etc. ; the manufacture of pottery also became wonderfully improved. All the industries received an immense impulse, and most of them became entirely transformed by the powerful invention of Watt, who, in 1769,

[1] De Gibbins, *The Industrial History of England*, pp. 146, 147.
[2] Sismondi, *Studi intorno all' Economia Politica*, Capolago, 1840.

obtained the patent for his steam machine, which was applied to manufacturing in 1785.[1]

This short period of twenty years between 1763-1783, which Levi calls the period of the foundation of the English industries (we might more correctly say " of the great English industry "), was also fruitful in chemical discoveries; it was the age of Cavendish, Priestly, and Lavoisier; great changes also took place about this time in the means of transport, and the roads, which until then had been few and bad, were greatly improved.

A few figures will help to show the industrial progress during the eighteenth century.

The English cotton manufactures exported in 1697 represented only a value of £5915; in 1741 they amounted to £20,709; in 1751 they were £45,986; in 1764, £200,354; in 1765, £248,348; in 1780 they reached £355,060; and in 1785 they were £864,710.[2] From this date the yearly progress continued to advance by rapid strides through the marvellous power of machinery.

Levi depicts in glowing colours the economic transformation which had occurred in England. Industry and commerce gradually underwent a marvellous change through the expansion of the principal manufacturing and commercial towns throughout the country. Liverpool reaped enormous advantages through the extension of the Lancashire manufactories, the rapid increase of population and wealth of the American colonies, the new English acquisitions in Canada, and through the extended cultivations in the West Indies. Birmingham felt the whole advantage of the opening of the Birmingham, Staffordshire, and Worcestershire Canals, which brought to that town all the supplies of coal and materials for manufacturing and building at much lower rates of transport than formerly. Manchester was surrounded by a group of active and prosperous manufacturing towns. Bristol, for a long time without competition, carried on .a considerable foreign trade and enjoyed all the advantages arising from the confluence of several rivers; Glasgow at

[1] *Vide* works mentioned of Levi, M'Culloch, De Gibbins, etc.
[2] M'Culloch, *Dictionary of Commerce*, under the heading "Cotton Manufactures."

the same time greatly extended its relations with the West Indies.[1]

Montefiore, referring to a somewhat later period, namely, the end of last century, describes the condition of industries. "The division of labour, and invention of machinery applied to our manufactures, enables this country to bring a variety of different articles to great perfection and at a low price. The labour of more than a million persons is done by fire-engines, which reduce the price of raw materials as well as of the manufactured article."[2]

The period in which the "factory system," or, as the Germans call it, the capitalist industrial system, was established in England, can be fixed at the last quarter of the eighteenth century. But a new institution does not arise all at once and as a whole; it must necessarily be the product of an evolution, gradual in proportion to the importance of the fact of which it treats; and the great inventions of the latter part of the century, about which we have spoken, could not do otherwise than hasten the economic evolution which had already begun, and of which they themselves were actually an effect.[3]

From all the facts which we have collected it seems clear that the capitalist system was in the course of formation during the whole of the eighteenth century, and that the industries were in a state of transformation during that period.[4]

Returning at last to our subject, this fact perfectly explains the strengthening of the English colonial policy. Under the impulse of an increasing population, and in consequence of dearness of commodities, the English manufactures underwent a gradual process of development and a necessary transformation;[5] and the State, which had been so constantly influenced by traditions of economic interference, and had protected the public industries for centuries, considered that a greater protection was opportune. Besides, such action was at that time

[1] Levi, *History of British Commerce*, etc., p. 21.
[2] *Commercial Dictionary*, London, 1803.
[3] Loria in his *Analisi* clearly demonstrates how the great industrial transformation which occurred towards the end of the last century was nothing more than an effect of the conditions of the population and of the land.
[4] Loria, *Analisi*, vol. ii. pp. 219-20, also dates the industrial transformation in England from the beginning of the eighteenth century.
[5] *Ibid.* p. 220.

fully justified by the difficulties against which manufacturers had to struggle in order to proceed gradually from a small to an extensive industry; it was a transformation not only of capital but also of labour, the beginning of which must have been very difficult.

In the same way Colbert, towards the end of the seventeenth century, " having resorted to protection of industry as the only method by which the dearness of commodities and the increase of population could be counteracted," carried out his industrial policy, introduced powerful machinery, and " in a short time France underwent an industrial metamorphosis which built up on a large scale the wealth, power, and splendour of great factories upon the ruins of small manufactories."[1] The English Parliament, at the beginning of the eighteenth century and afterwards, protected the national manufactures which were undergoing a process of transformation, and made its policy towards the American colonies still more oppressive.

First there were obstacles thrown in the way of the interior commerce of the colonies, and afterwards all manufactures were forbidden, with the purpose of preventing the colonists from improving their own industry and supplying their own requirements, in order to prevent the closing of that great and privileged colonial market which English monopoly secured to English producers, whilst, by allowing the colonies to produce only raw materials, the manufactures of the mother country were strengthened.

This policy, however iniquitous and oppressive, attained for a while its object, and was tolerated by the colonists, although it wounded their feelings of independence much more than a mere commercial monopoly; but this toleration lasted, as we shall see presently, only as long as the system was in point of fact of little inconvenience to the colonies, and consequently of but small advantage to England.

22. That which shows a really continual increase, studying the economic and social conditions of the colonies at the present time, is the population. In 1688, the twelve old colonies, Massachusetts (including Maine), New Hampshire, Rhode Island, Connecticut, New York, New Jersey, Pennsyl-

[1] Loria, *Analisi*, vol. ii. p. 220.

vania, Delaware, Maryland, Virginia, and the two Carolinas (including Georgia), numbered altogether not more than 200,000 inhabitants; in 1754 the thirteen existing colonies had a population of about 1,165,000 whites, 260,000 negroes; and in 1774 about 2,100,000 whites and 600,000 negroes.

At the end of the first period of sixty-six years (1688-1754) the population had increased sevenfold, which is equivalent to a duplication about every ten years; in the second period of twenty years (1754-1774) it doubled itself only once.[1]

These figures show an increase of the American population greater than that admitted by Malthus in his famous essay, and thought by him to be the greatest possible. Malthus reckoned that, in 1643, the population of New England alone was 21,000, and that in 1760 it was 1,000,000; and he inferred that as an average the population there doubled itself in twenty-five years; he also held that, on the whole, in the Northern States, from the first American settlement until 1800, the period of doubling was shorter still—a little more than twenty years—whilst in the interior colonies the population increased more rapidly, and doubled itself in fifteen years.[2]

It is not possible to say which of these data is the truest, because during the colonial period there was not the help of those splendid statistics which were afterwards collected every tenth year in the United States.

If the figures of Bancroft are sufficiently exact, they show that the population during the colonial expansion met with some obstacles which hindered its full development, a fact which is anything but surprising.

At any rate, it is proved that, in the period we are speaking of, the population underwent a continued and rapid increase. But, rapid as it was, it could not be excessive, because there was plenty of free land accessible to all, as we shall see further on.

Some other data point to rather a slow tendency towards concentration in the towns. New York, which we have seen with 3430 inhabitants in 1678, had 6000 in 1699; 22,750 in 1774; 33,131 in 1790; 60,000 in 1800.[3]

[1] Bancroft, work mentioned.
[2] *An Essay on the Principle of Population*, pp. 3 and 287.
[3] M'Culloch, *Commercial Dictionary*.

In the eighteenth century the international trade of the American colonies made considerable progress; the figures concerning imports and exports mentioned by several authors are certainly not very precise and uniform, but they are sufficient to give us an idea of the development of the commercial activity.

According to Franklin the imports from England consisted of only £640,114 in 1744; in 1746 they rose to £754,945; in 1748 to £830,268; in 1754 to £1,246,615; in 1756 to £1,428,720; in 1758 to £1,832,948.[1] From 1766 to 1775 they were on an average £2,000,000 per year.[2] According to another author, Eyma,[3] their annual average from 1756 to 1771 was £2,500,000, and from 1771 to 1773, £3,000,000; whilst during the latter years of this period the exports from the colonies to England amounted to £4,000,000.

These data, although somewhat discordant and comprising periods rather different, do not perhaps really contradict each other.

We know also from another source that the English colonies of the American continent had a considerable trade before they shook off the yoke: New England and the neighbouring colonies exported furs, hides, flour, corn, salt-meat, fish, etc.; Pennsylvania—corn, pulse, meat, cheese, tallow, hides; the colony of New York—corn, flour, timber, fish-oil; Virginia and Maryland—corn, pulse, and especially tobacco; the Carolinas and Georgia—rice, tobacco, cotton, indigo.[4]

Thus the time when international trade had little importance for the colonies was over; in the eighteenth century, and especially in its second half, the importance of the colonies increased, and their activity in exporting raw material and importing manufactured articles became more remarkable. The colonies, therefore, in consequence of this progress, began to have more numerous and more refined wants; but their manufactures not increasing in the same proportion, as we shall see, the importation of foreign manufactured produce was destined to become greater; and the restrictions imposed upon

[1] *Works*, etc., 1806. [2] Levi, work mentioned.
[3] *Les trente-quatre étoiles de l'Union Américaine*, Paris, Levy, 1861; also Leroy Beaulieu, *De la colonisation*, etc., p. 137.
[4] *Encyclopédie méthodique*, Padova, 1784.

the colonial trade by England were consequently destined to become heavier.

With regard to manufactures, we find mention of some industries having moderately developed and having risen above their primitive condition of domestic products; for instance, the manufacture of felt hats increased so much that the English Parliament thought it advisable to forbid the exportation of such articles; the boot manufacturing industry also was so extensive that in 1731 it almost completely supplied the requirements of the country. Paper manufacturing had reached a certain development; the first paper mill was established near Philadelphia in 1693; and in 1769 there were about forty mills in the States of Pennsylvania, New Jersey, and Delaware.[1]

Lastly, a branch of industry which, as will be shown hereafter by an important document, seemed to be destined to acquire a firm footing in New England, was iron smelting and manufacturing, but the prohibitions of the English Government tended to its suppression.

23. However, the circumstances just mentioned must not lead to the belief that there was a serious progress in the manufacturing arts, and still less an industrial transformation; the manufactures were still not only scarce, but had, till the end of the colonial period, the character of household industries. This is confirmed by information derived from various sources concerning the period comprised between the beginning of the eighteenth century and the revolution.

At the beginning of the eighteenth century, says Bishop,[2] linen, cotton, and woollen fabrics were very coarse, and made by the peasantry with the help only of rough tools, and for the use of their own families.

We get important evidence in the following extracts from the Report of the Enquiry on American Industry ordered by the House of Commons in 1731, and quoted by Bolles. There was evidently at that time a certain amount of vitality in some of the productions, especially in the manufacture of iron, and in hat-making, but weaving was still altogether a household occupation.

[1] Bolles, work mentioned.
[2] Bishop, work mentioned, vol. i. p. 338.

"The Governor of Massachusetts Bay informed us, that in some parts of this province the inhabitants worked up their wool and flax into an ordinary coarse cloth for their own use, but did not export any; that the greatest part of the woollen and the linen clothing worn in this province was imported from Great Britain, and sometimes from Ireland, but, considering the excessive price of labour in New England, the merchants could afford what was imported cheaper than what was made in that country; that there were also a few hat-makers in the maritime towns, and that the greater part of the leather used in that country was manufactured among themselves; that there had been for many years some iron-works in that province, which had afforded the people iron for some of their necessary occasions, but that the iron imported from Great Britain was esteemed much the best, and used wholly by the shipping, and that the works of that province were not able to supply one-twentieth part of what was necessary to the use of the country. They had no manufactures in the province of New York that deserved mentioning (their trade consisting chiefly of furs, whalebone, oil, pitch, tar, and provisions); no manufactures in New Jersey that deserved mentioning, their trade being chiefly in provisions shipped from New York and Pennsylvania. The chief trade of Pennsylvania lay in the exportation of provisions and lumber; their clothing and utensils for their houses being all imported from Great Britain. By further advices from New Hampshire, the woollen manufacture appears to have decreased; the common lands on which the sheep used to feed being now appropriated, and the people almost wholly clothed with woollens from Great Britain. The manufacture of flax into linen, some coarser, some finer, daily increased by the great resort of people from Ireland thither, who are well skilled in that business; and the chief trade of this province consisted, as for many years past, in the exportation of naval stores, lumber, and fish. By later accounts from Massachusetts Bay, in New England, the Assembly have voted a bounty of thirty shillings for every piece of duck or canvas made in the province. Some other manufactures are carried on there, as brown hollands for women's wear, which lessen the importation of calicoes and some other sorts of East-India goods. They also make some small quantity of cloth made of linen and cotton for ordinary shirting and sheeting. By a paper mill set up three years ago they make to a value of £200 yearly. There are also several forges for making bar-iron, and some furnaces for cast-iron or hollow-ware, and one slitting mill, and a manufactory for nails. The governor writes concerning the woollen manufacture, that the country people, who used formerly to make most of their clothing out of their own wool, do not now make a third part of what they wear, but are mostly clothed with British manufactures. The same governor, Belcher, by some of his letters of an older date, in answer to our annual queries, writes that there are some few copper-mines in this province, but so far from water-carriage, and the land is so poor, that it is not worth the digging. The Surveyor-General of His Majesty's Woods writes that they have in New England six furnaces and nineteen forges for making iron; and that in this province many ships are built for the French and the Spaniards in return for rum, molasses, wines, and silks, which they truck there by connivance. Great quantities of hats are made in New England, of which the Company of Hatters in London have likewise lately complained to us that great quantities of those hats are exported to Spain, Portugal, and our West-India islands. They also make all sorts of iron-work for shipping."[1]

A lapse of thirty years did not bring any change in the textile industry of the colonies. From 1732 to 1763, Bishop states that there was not much progress in this industry. The population of the interior became more numerous, and they somewhat improved in their domestic manufactures, which amounted to a considerable value; but their importation of English goods continued to increase, together with the wealth and luxuries of the people.[2]

The high price of the imported textile fabrics caused by the monopoly, compelled the colonists to make great use of skins as clothes, and at the same time was a stimulus to the domestic industry of weaving, which, however, could only be carried out almost secretly within the walls of private houses and with primitive implements. "The women learned to weave and spin; and a large quantity of woollen, hemp, and linen cloth and other goods, was made in the privacy of the

[1] Bolles, work mentioned, pp. 855, 856.   [2] Bishop, vol. i. p. 344.

household throughout the whole country. Nearly every family wove a part or the whole of its own clothing and blankets; and many which had skill in the art had many pieces over and above their own wants to sell to the merchant. The law could not reach their private factories. . . . Every village and country had its fuller and dyer, and this individual was the only one in the industry who carried on his business publicly and for a number of customers." [1]

It would not be possible to describe with more precision (and we only quote a few lines) the circumstances of a production so entirely domestic, which only in a few instances modestly endeavoured to assume the extent of a local industry.

A few years after, in 1767, a report of Governor Moore confirmed the fact that the woollen manufacture continued to be entirely domestic, and that almost every house had its looms.[2]

Only in 1770 was there the first sign of the industrial transformation, which had still some time to wait before developing. Soon after the hostilities with England, which, as we shall see, imparted a great stimulus to the national manufactures, a spinning-mill with some mechanical contrivance was set up at Cambridge, Massachusetts.[3]

But this transformation was to proceed very slowly: until 1789, says Bishop, the American industrial activity consisted only of isolated manual work.[4]

In the colonies of the north the industrial production was scanty and scarcely progressive; whilst as to those of the south there was none at all; things were in the same condition as one hundred years previously.[5] In the two Carolinas the activity was exclusively agricultural, and was favoured and encouraged by England. The colonists cultivated their lands by slaves, and they lived frugally; but the soil being free and fertile, there was a general welfare, and in three or four years the colonists were able to double their capital. In Virginia also agriculture was the only source of production; there was not any town of importance, the colonists living

---

[1] Bolles, work mentioned, pp. 370-372. (This description refers to the middle of the eighteenth century.)   [2] Bishop, vol. i. p. 371.
[3] *Ibid.* p. 376.   [4] *Ibid.* vol. ii. p. 14.
[5] Beer, work mentioned, pp. 70, 71.

scattered and isolated on their lands.[1] What sort of agriculture there was we hear from Loria, who, in the description he gives of it, designates its features as permanent throughout the colonial period, implying thereby that it did not progress. "The general system of cultivation in America in this period was that nomadic and extensive agriculture which, after having exhausted an extent of land, kept passing on to cultivate fresh lands. In point of technical agricultural knowledge the colonies were not inferior to the mother country; and Jefferson in his notes on the state of Virginia, p. 163, says that the stationary condition of agriculture did not depend upon want of knowledge, but upon the large amount of land which could be freely exhausted, adding that in Europe they exhausted the soil because there was plenty of labour, while in America they exhausted labour because there was plenty of soil. The report of the Massachusetts Board of Agriculture, 1876, speaking of this industry during the earliest period of the American colonisation, says that the cultivation of the land was very simple and primitive—primitive because skill would have been superfluous. There was no lack of advice for improving the cultivation and rendering it more productive, but the colonists answered plausibly that the ground was so fruitful that it was not worth while troubling about a more careful production or employing a larger capital."

And these conditions of agriculture, says Loria, were the cause of the other industries not progressing. "The scattered industry was incompatible with progress, because in the colonies, the large extent of uncultivated land attracting every worker caused the industrial manufactures to remain quite a domestic concern. It was women who in the America of the seventeenth century spun and weaved, as in the early ages of Europe; produce was rarely brought to market, and manufactures were of the greatest simplicity."[2]

24. The works of Benjamin Franklin are for us a very rich source of authentic information respecting the economic conditions of the colonies in the period immediately preceding their independence, and they are of very great importance, because not only do they help us to an exact idea of those

[1] Bancroft, vol. iv.
[2] *Analisi della proprietà capitalista*, vol. ii. pp. 29, 30.

conditions, but also because they help to elucidate a certain change in the frame of mind of the colonists at that time; and these circumstances will be easily elicited by our consulting Franklin's works, successively according to their dates, which comprise a period of about twenty-five years.

The first of his works we have is *Observations concerning the Increase of Mankind*, which was written in Pennsylvania in 1751; in it are considered the conditions of the colonies in the first half of the eighteenth century, and it explains why England should not be alarmed at the increase of American manufactures. Land is so abundant and cheap in the colonies, says Franklin, that an active man, with a practical knowledge of husbandry, can in a short time make sufficient money to buy some land and settle on it with his family.

"So vast is the territory of North America, that it will require many ages to settle it fully; and till it is fully settled, labour will never be cheap here, where no man continues long a labourer for others, but gets a plantation of his own; no man continues long a journeyman to a trade, but goes among those new settlers, and sets up for himself. Hence labour is no cheaper now, in Pennsylvania, than it was thirty years ago, though so many thousand labouring people have been imported from Germany and Ireland. The danger, therefore, of these colonies interfering with their mother country in trades that depend on labour, manufactures, etc., is too remote to require the attention of Great Britain." [1]

Further on, in speaking of the slaves, after having said that their work in the colonies was of little effect and dearer than that of the free workmen of Great Britain, he points out that at any rate slavery was necessary, "because slaves may be kept as long as a man pleases, or has occasion for their labour, while hired men are continually leaving their master (often in the midst of his business) and setting up for themselves." [2] In short, Franklin in 1751 describes the situation as a whole population attracted to agriculture by the abundance and fertility of the land, with the consequence that hired work was impossible, and manufactured articles were produced for private use, or at the most as a small local industry, and even

[1] Franklin, *Works*, etc., 1806, vol. ii. p. 385.   [2] *Ibid.* p. 386.

that was very limited, because the cultivation of the land was more profitable. Franklin implicitly gave to England the advice to do away with her restrictions because they were derived from the fear of an imaginary danger.

The great scarcity of hired work, and the facilities open to workmen to abandon their employment and become farmers and landowners are confirmed later on by Sir H. Moore, Governor of the Colony of New York, who, in 1767, answering a question of the British Government concerning the condition of manufactures in his province, mentioned the tendency of the workmen to prefer the fields to the workshops, as a fact which was to be considered as a counteraction against the incipient manufactories. Even servants brought from Europe for different purposes left their employments as soon as their engagements expired, and obtained a small plot of land. The pleasure of thinking that they were landowners, says Moore, caused them to endure every privation for years preferably to the comforts they had enjoyed in their former employments; and this observation shows that the rate of wages must have been very high—a fact which can be reckoned as another hindrance to the foundation of industrial establishments in the colonies. Governor Moore added that the owner of a glass manufactory, which had been established in his province a few years previously, but had since failed, told him that the cause of his ruin was the desertion of his workmen, whom he had brought into the country at great expense. And other employers had suffered the same fate.[1]

25. But let us go back to Franklin. The second of his

---

[1] Bishop, vol. i. pp. 236, 237. To understand the words of Governor Moore, it is necessary to know what was meant by the "indented servants" to which he alludes. They were free men shipped from Europe to America at the expense of a master, under the obligation of working for him for a certain time, during which they were entirely under his authority. This system, says Loria, was started by the masters and capitalists with the idea of creating wages and profits in a country where they had been impossible, owing to the ease with which land could be obtained; but it did not succeed, because, as Loria observes and proves with facts confirmed by Moore, the servants, on putting foot on the American shores, broke their contracts, abandoned their masters, and spread themselves over the free lands. (*Vide* Loria, *Analisi della proprietà capitalista*, vol. ii. pp. 174, 175.) Respecting the impossibility of hired work in the American colonies, *vide* Loria, work mentioned, especially pages 17, 18, 151, 153, 175.

works to be examined by us concerns the interest of Great
Britain in her colonies and the acquisition of Canada and
Guadaloupe.[1] It was written in 1760. In it we find
described a condition of affairs somewhat similar to what we
have seen above; but what is specially important is that
Franklin, with a keen intelligence of economic phenomena,
points out how such a condition might change, and indicates
the means of preventing it; he did not hold that the manufacturing industries were necessary to the colonies, whose
welfare was derived from agriculture, and it was in the
stability of agricultural economy that he foresaw the means of
conciliating the interests both of the colonies and the mother
country. The work in question belongs to a time when there
was not yet much friction between the colonies and England;
the Navigation Acts were feebly applied, and Grenville had
not yet begun that system of severity and coercion which was
to incite the colonies to resistance more on political than
economic grounds. Franklin considers the interests of the
colonists and those of England as identical, but in his work he
started more particularly from the English point of view. He
argued against those who thought that the territory of the
colonies should be as limited as possible, and that their expansion should be forbidden and Canada left to the French, and
he maintained that the coalition of the colonies against the
mother country was impossible, and that their territorial
expansion was useful and necessary in order to keep them
busied only with agriculture, because in such case they
remained open to the English importations. He held that if
the colonial territory was to be kept within narrow limits
manufacturing would undoubtedly develop, because the population would become more dense, and in this respect he observed,
long before Malthus, that the duplication happened every
twenty-five years. He therefore advocated the occupation of
Canada, which, in fact, was given up by France in the Treaty
of Paris, 1763.

The American colonies, said Franklin, speaking of the
time in which he wrote, have so little aptitude for establishing manufactories that they are even losing the few which

[1] "The interest of Great Britain considered, with regard to her colonies,
and the acquisitions of Canada and Guadaloupe." *Works*, etc., vol. iii. p. 89.

are accidentally profitable. The armourers, cutlers, pewterers, as well as the hatters, who came to the colonies, gradually ceased to make the articles of their trades, and imported them from England, whence they got them cheaper and of better quality. They still kept their shops, but more as sellers than makers. And even the hat-manufacturing industry which had developed in New England through the facility with which beaver skins could be procured, gradually collapsed as the beavers became scarce, and not only the exportation of hats came to an end, but they could hardly produce sufficient for themselves, and many were imported from England at a cheaper price.

The continual expansion of the colonies towards Canada and the other unoccupied territories, says Franklin, will for centuries limit the colonies to agriculture, notwithstanding the increase of population; the present colonies will be unable to supply manufactured articles for their own requirements, and still less for the needs of others, and thus the trade of England will go on increasing for centuries, and will supply the colonies till they are as thickly populated as the mother country.

"They who understand the economy and principles of manufactures," says Franklin, "know that it is impossible to establish them in places not populous: and even in those that are populous hardly possible to establish them to the prejudices of the places already in possession of them."[1] But if the colonies had not large territories around them where they could expand, and were compelled to remain within the same limits, the value of the land would rise tenfold in a few years, and, the population increasing, the price of labour would become cheaper, and then manufactures would spring up in the colonies to compete with the mother country and become independent of her. "Manufactures are founded in poverty: it is the multitude of poor without land in a country, and who must work for others at low wages or starve, that enables undertakers to carry on a manufacture, and afford it cheap enough to prevent the importation of the same kind from abroad, and to bear the expense of its own exportation. But no man who can have a piece of land of his own, sufficient by

[1] Franklin, *Works*, etc., 1806, vol. iii. p. 121.

his labour to subsist his family in plenty, is poor enough to be a manufacturer and work for a master. Hence, while there is land enough in America for our people, there can never be manufactures to any amount or value."[1]

But suppose that the population becomes numerous in the colonies, then any restriction, any coercion put upon its industry will be in vain. "Unprejudiced men well know that all the penal and prohibitory laws that ever were thought on will not be sufficient to prevent manufactures in a country whose inhabitants surpass the number that can subsist by the husbandry of it."[2]

It is not opportune for us now to examine critically Franklin's argument about the possibility and utility of a new country busying itself with agriculture only—an argument which was contested later on by the protectionists, and above all by Alexander Hamilton,[3] who in this matter endorsed the opinion of Adam Smith.[4] Nor can we enter into an analysis of the deep reasoning which led Franklin to the belief that the cessation of free land would be the first cause of social inequality;[5] nor of the reasoning which led to the wish of preventing such result even at the cost of keeping the colonies in a state of inferior social-economic conditions, and which caused him to foresee the inevitable growth of an extensive manufacturing activity under the sway of capital, for such indeed is the only means of employing workers for whom there is no more free land to take possession of, and whose needs force them to accept scanty wages. What actually requires our attention is simply the fact that Franklin in this second essay describes the economic conditions of the colonies as stationary, and yet he considers a change, the premonitory symptoms of which must have been then manifest, as approaching; and, indeed, whilst in his writings ten years before he declared that the danger of a colonial competition against England was too remote, that free land was plentiful and

[1] Franklin, *Works*, etc., 1806, vol. iii. pp. 107, 108.   [2] *Ibid.* p. 107.
[3] *Vide* his *Report on Manufactures*, which we will discuss later on.
[4] *Wealth of Nations*, book iv. chap. i. pp. 161-165.
[5] There was and is still land materially free in the United States, but the difficulty of workers with little or no capital settling on it must be taken into consideration—a difficulty ever increasing.

accessible to all, and that the rate of wages notwithstanding immigration was the same as in the preceding thirty years, in the essay of which we are speaking he describes the same conditions, but adds that if the colonial territory were not expanded, these conditions would soon be altered, the wages would become lower, and the existence of manufacturing establishments would be an inevitable and irremediable event. Franklin made a mistake with regard to the remedy he suggested, because the annexation of Canada did not prevent the development of the American manufactures soon after; but he foresaw that the economic transformation of the country was near; and we have already mentioned some of its latent causes.

However, the indications of the coming change must have been very slight, as can be inferred from the facts stated previously, and from Franklin's essay itself, because it does not contain any complaint against the industrial restrictions then extant, nor allusion to any injury done by them to the colonies.

We find such complaints later on; but although the work under our consideration points out how useless restrictions would be if the manufacturing activity were really to develop, yet it does not contain any protest against the prohibitory laws of England, which makes us believe that such restraint caused but little harm and resentment, because manufacturing as an industry scarcely existed.

26. There is a letter from Franklin to Governor Shirley without date; but it was published in 1766, and was probably written a little before.

The subject and tone of this letter are different; the interests of the colonies and those of the mother country are no longer described as identical; but from the colonial point of view the right of England to impose taxes is contested, and there is an enumeration of the injuries they had sustained, and from which England had derived advantage.

"(1) The taxes paid in Britain by the landholder or artificer must enter into and increase the price of the produce of the land and manufactures made of it; and a great part of this is paid by consumers in the colonies, who thereby pay a considerable part of the British taxes. (2) We are restrained in our trade with foreign nations; and where we could be supplied with any manufacture cheaper from them, but must buy the same dearer from Britain, the difference of price is a clear tax to Britain. (3) We are obliged to carry a great part of our produce directly to Britain; and where the duties laid upon it lessen its price to the planter, or it sells for less than it would in foreign markets, the difference is a tax paid to Britain. (4) Some manufactures we could make, but are forbidden, and must take them of British merchants; the whole price is a tax paid to Britain. (5) By our greatly increasing the demand and consumption of British manufactures, their price is considerably raised of late years; the advantage is clear profit to Britain, and enables its people better to pay great taxes; and much of it being paid by us, is clear tax to Britain. (6) In short, as we are not suffered to regulate our trade, and restrain the importation and consumption of British superfluities (as Britain can the consumption of foreign superfluities), our whole wealth centres finally amongst the merchants and inhabitants of Britain."[1]

After this enumeration, which in its plain language is a vigorous invective against the colonial policy, Franklin adds (and this is at first rather surprising) that the colonists did not complain of these kind of secondary taxes, though they had no share in laying or disposing of them, but they refused to pay the new heavy taxes which Parliament imposed upon them.[2] This apparent contradiction can be easily explained and further elucidated by official documents. For the present we shall only point out that the words *we do not complain* were certainly said by Franklin with reluctance, as can be clearly inferred from the next letter to the same person, in which the writer, regretting that the colonists were treated differently from the other English subjects, asks: "Would it be right to deprive such inhabitants of the common privileges enjoyed by the other Englishmen, the right of vending their produce in the same ports, or of making their own shoes,

[1] Franklin, *Works*, etc., vol. iii. pp. 35, 36.
[2] *Ibid.* p. 36. In the same year, 1766, Franklin repeated, during his examination before the House of Commons, that the colonies did not contest the right of the English Parliament to regulate their commerce.

because a merchant or a shoemaker living in the old land might fancy it more to his advantage to trade or to make shoes for them?"[1]

27. Events followed one another rapidly: the revolution took place; the tone of Franklin's language changed altogether; there were no half measures. Strong complaints of the colonists were expressed in a letter published in London in 1766. This letter bears a significant title, "Causes of American discontent before 1768," and a still more significant motto, "The waves never rise but when the winds blow."[2] It speaks mostly of the discontent at the English claims to impose taxes on the colonists without their consent, but there are also expressions of resentment against the commercial policy.

The English monopoly, said the colonists, makes the imported goods ten, twenty, and even fifty per cent dearer. English fancy goods brought into the colonies become fashionable and annihilate the local trade; the interests of any company, however small, of British merchants or manufacturers, are preferred to those of the king's subjects in the colonies.

"Iron is to be found everywhere in America, and beaver are the natural produce of that country; hats, and nails, and steel are wanted there as well as here. It is of no importance to the common welfare of the empire whether a subject of the king gets his living by making hats on this or on that side of the water. Yet the hatters of England have prevailed to obtain an Act in their own favour, restraining that manufacture in America, in order to oblige the Americans to send their beaver to England to be manufactured, and purchase back the hats, loaded with the charges of a double transportation. In the same manner have a few nail-makers, and still a smaller body of steel-makers (perhaps there is not half a dozen of these in England), prevailed totally to forbid by an Act of Parliament the erection of slitting-mills or steel furnaces in America, that the Americans may be obliged to take all their nails for their buildings, and steel for their tools, from these artificers under the same disadvantages."[3]

[1] Franklin, *Works*, etc., vol. iii. p. 39.   [2] *Ibid.* p. 225.
[3] *Ibid.* pp. 233, 234. Author writing in England, and the "we" refers to the English.

These are explicit complaints without reserve. Later on, when the revolution of the colonies was in its acutest stage and discussion became useless, Franklin uttered words full of a biting irony against England. In 1773 he wrote that very strange pamphlet in which he imagines an edict of the King of Prussia proclaiming his right over England, and prescribing a complete system of commercial measures to her detriment, forbidding her to carry on industries which competed with those of Prussia, compelling all ships going or coming from England to pass through the port of Konigsberg, etc. Such measures, says in conclusion the King of Prussia in this witty edict, must seem reasonable to England, because they are copied from those which she has imposed on Ireland and America.

And the irony of this calm old American becomes truly cutting when, in another writing of the same date, he, foreseeing the final success of the colonies, lays down the ways which a government must follow in order to lose its colonies, stating precisely those of the English colonial policy!

28. The analysis of these writings of Franklin has facilitated our task with regard to the last point we have to consider in this chapter, namely, the opinion of the colonists concerning the English commercial policy from the beginning of the eighteenth century to the revolution, and the complaints and opposition which that policy caused in the colonies.

We shall also mention here a series of successive facts, recommending the reader to remember also those stated towards the end of the first chapter, after which the conclusions and general apprisement of the English commercial policy in the colonies will be easily arrived at.

In the early part of the eighteenth century we find no evidence of complaint in the colonies. Although Bancroft mentions so many facts showing the discontent which broke out later, neither he nor any other of the authors that we have consulted make any references to earlier discontent. This can be perfectly well accounted for if we take into consideration the economic conditions already stated, the rather mild application of the Navigation Acts, and later the smuggling, which increased proportionally with the commercial activity, and was till 1763 almost tolerated by the English authorities.[1]

Nine-tenths of the American merchants, says Wells, were smugglers; one quarter of all the signers of the Declaration of Independence were bred to commerce, to the command of ships, and to contraband trade; among them were Hancock, Trumbull, Hamilton.[2]

The prohibitive measures against the colonial manufactures began almost with the century; and although the colonies were already then showing some industrial activity, as we have seen especially in the report of 1732, there is no evidence of dissatisfaction caused by such measures till 1750, when the manufacture of iron was prohibited by the Government; and Bishop says that this abrupt measure, which caused the immediate closing of several establishments, was considered as an infringement of the natural rights of the colonies.[3]

Although this branch of industry was then comprised within narrow limits, the oppressive interference of the Government must have caused a deep sense of injury, not only in those who suffered a material loss, but also amongst the whole population, whose self-esteem was wounded. According to Leroy Beaulieu,[4] intelligent observers who travelled in America about 1750 were strongly impressed by the symptoms of a general and persistent irritation, which only awaited an occasion to show itself.

And it was precisely at that time that two very different men—Peter Kalm, a Swedish traveller, who visited New York in 1748, and Turgot in France in 1750—both predicted that the secession of the colonies was near.

But Leroy Beaulieu in the work mentioned gives too much importance to the resentment of the colonies, which, according to our opinion, was at that time more of a desultory than persistent character. After 1750 and until 1761, we find no complaining, and the right of England to regulate the

[1] Bancroft, vol. v. p. 158.
[2] See the article on the American Merchant Marine, in Lalor's *Cyclopædia*.
[3] Bishop, vol. i. p. 491.
[4] *De la colonisation*, etc., p. 125. Roscher also, *Kolonien*, etc., pp. 220, 221, speaks of the resentment against England which Peter Kalm found in New York in 1748, and of his prediction that within thirty or fifty years the American colonies would become independent.

commerce of her colonies was not seriously questioned even after. "The people of the colonies had previously exercised a somewhat indefinite power to make their own laws. . . . It was conceded that, in all matters of what may be denominated imperial concern, the common legislature of the realm must legislate for all the dominions of the Crown, and that under this head fell the commerce of the colonies with the mother country and with other nations and colonies."[1] This right was not seriously contested by the colonies, and they did not even complain of its application. Davis says that there were few complaints until the English Parliament under George III. attempted to impose taxes on the colonies.[2]

In 1761 the colonists began to complain. In Boston they protested against the restrictions to commerce (Bancroft); and when in 1763 the commercial monopoly and the industrial prohibitions were again fully enforced by Grenville, the Minister of State, they encountered resistance.[3] The means of resistance adopted, before resorting to arms, was the abstention from English goods; it was an idea which pervaded the whole revolution and constituted an economic form of patriotism.

The combination began in Boston, 1764; the citizens solemnly agreed not to use any article of English origin, and not to eat lambs so as to promote the local manufacture of wool. Throughout the colonies in 1765, formal resolutions were made not to have any more commercial intercourse with England, and not to purchase English products; the New York merchants decided not to give further orders in England, to cancel those already given, and to accept no merchandise

[1] Thomas M. Cooley, *General Principles of Constitutional Law in the United States of America*, Boston, 1880, p. 4.
[2] Thorold Rogers says: "So inveterate and wide-spread was the delusion, however, as to the benefits of a sole market, that it does not appear that the colonist resented an arrangement under which he got all the losses and the British manufacturer and merchant all the gains of this regulated monopoly, for he was blinded to the true meaning of the relation by differential duty put on goods like his, but produced on colonial soil."—Vide *Economic Interpretation of History*, London, 1888, p. 328.
[3] There cannot be any doubt that, not to speak of taxation, the very display of excessive rigour was one of the main causes of the American Revolution, by aggravating an almost universal discontent.—Leroy Beaulieu, *De la colonisation*, etc., p. 136.

CHAP. III *ENGLAND'S POLICY IN AMERICAN COLONIES* 83

till the Stamp Act was repealed. In 1767 further resolutions were passed to prevent the importation and use of a great number of English manufactured goods; in 1769 the resistance in this way became more general and intense. In 1770 the protective combination of the colonists seemed to collapse, notwithstanding Franklin's exhortations, because it had not been carried out everywhere with the same zeal; but it was resumed with increased vigour in 1774 through the initiative of Boston, the port of which town was closed by the English; the Continental Congress embodied the resolutions of the citizens in a decree whereby, from 1st December 1774, no English merchandise was to be imported, and, by another decree in August 1775, no American produce was to be exported to England or to the English possessions.[1]

This method of warfare had certainly a great economic and commercial importance, because the stoppage of the English imports gave a stimulus to the American manufactures; but its character and purpose should not be misunderstood, for it would be erroneous to think that the resolution to oppose importations was only a retaliation and a resistance against the commercial monopoly of England. No one will deny that there was discontent against this monopoly and against the manufacturing prohibitions at the commencement of the revolution; we can trace it in the publications of that period.

The colonists said that to impose taxes on the imported goods after having forbidden manufactures in the colonies was an enormity, and it is an historical fact that when they protested against that taxation they looked on it more as a political and fiscal act than a commercial one. We are, said Dickinson, the famous agriculturist of Pennsylvania, in the condition of a besieged town surrounded by the enemy on all sides but one, and if this last one is also closed we must surrender. In 1765 the validity of the Navigation Act was openly contested in New York, where the merchants claimed the same freedom of trade as in England.[2] But in those days incidents of that character were not frequent, and they were not the direct cause of the resolutions agreed upon by the colonists to oppose the English importations. These means were

[1] Bancroft, Botta, works mentioned. [2] Bancroft, vol. v. p. 360.

adopted to compel Parliament to repeal the Stamp Act and some similar measures of a political character which offended the Americans in what they believed to be their right, not to be taxed by England without their consent; the opposition to the English goods was essentially a protest against the English political authority, which the colonies, already ripe for freedom, could endure no longer.

To be sure the hostile feeling against the commercial policy of England, and the material damage caused by it, made these ways of resistance popular and effective, but they were not the principal cause of the contest; and this is shown by the deliberations of the people as well as by those of the legislative assemblies. It has been seen that in 1765 the merchants of New York resolved not to receive any imports until the Stamp Act was repealed, and in a similar frame of mind the Assembly of Virginia, by Washington's advice, decreed in 1769 that no English goods should be imported until the taxes imposed by the Parliament were repealed. In 1774 the complete suspension of commercial intercourse with Great Britain was accepted by South Carolina for reasons exclusively political, and as a support to the sister colonies, though, being an exporter of agricultural produce and an importer of English manufactures, her interests were thereby considerably damaged; the Continental Congress enacted that, from the 1st September 1775, all exports to England were to be stopped if the claims of the colonies were not admitted.[1]

But there is a still more significant fact, that whilst the public discontent was on the increase, we find explicit declarations, whereby the right of the mother country to regulate the commerce of the colonies was admitted. Botta in his valuable history draws attention to these almost contradictory feelings of the colonists which we have observed in Franklin himself; and in the same part of his book, where he shows the injury inflicted on the colonies by the commercial monopoly, and states their complaints, he makes also the remark that the colonists did not consider themselves either offended or oppressed.[2]

[1] Bancroft, work mentioned.
[2] *Storia della guerra*, etc., vol. i. p. 18.

In September 1774, the Continental Congress, assembled at Philadelphia, decided, on the motion of John Adams, to accept the Navigation Act, and to admit the right of the British Parliament to regulate the commerce of the colonies, provided that no taxes either internal or external were imposed without their consent. In the petition sent by the Congress to the King the same year, there is indication of the acquiescence of the colonies to the commercial and industrial restrictions.[1] And lastly, in 1775, when the war had practically begun, the following conciliatory proposal, which, however, had no effect, was made by the Colonial Congress: England to abolish the monopoly, granting to the colonies the same commercial rights as those obtained by Scotland when united to England; free commerce with other nations to be allowed; the colonists to pay to England £100,000 a year for a hundred years, and if England were unwilling to give up the Navigation Act, the abolition of which, says the document, *was never our intention*, the suggestion was made of arriving at an understanding on the basis of the recognition by the colonies of the right of England to maintain that Act for one hundred years.[2]

29. And now we can briefly sum up the results of our researches, which, we must confess, have led us to conclusions somewhat different from those which we imagined when we undertook the task of investigating this branch of economic history.

Before Cromwell there is no instance of restriction of the colonial commerce, which till then enjoyed perfect freedom. Cromwell's Act put some limits to the trading of the colonies, by forbidding the traffic which was carried on there by foreign ships, but whilst he thereby protected the shipping and trade

[1] Bancroft, work mentioned.
[2] Even Alexander Hamilton admitted, in one of his writings in 1774, the right of England to regulate the commerce of the colonies.—*Vide* Sumner, *Alexander Hamilton*, New York, Dodd, 1890, pp. 5 and 21.

"The colonial system, as it was administered before 1763, contributed but slightly in bringing about the revolution of 1776. As Ramsay has said (*The History of the American Revolution*, i. 40), if no other grievances had been superadded to what existed in 1763, they would have been soon forgotten, for their pressure was neither great nor universal. It was only when the fundamental basis of the Acts changed from one of commercial monopoly to one of revenue that the Acts became of vital political importance."—*Vide* Beer, work mentioned, pp. 157, 158.

of the mother country, those of the colonies were also protected and increased.

The commercial monopoly began with Charles II., but it worked much less oppressively than is generally thought. In the first place, although it placed the commerce of the colonies under considerable restraint, yet it gave some stimulus to their shipping by forbidding the trade with foreigners; at the same time it enacted that English ships were to carry only goods destined for the colonies (Act of 1663), so that the export trade was effected only by the English and colonial ships. Secondly, the provisions of the Acts concerning shipping were mildly applied till 1688, and even later on in the eighteenth century they were little by little relaxed, whilst industrial restrictions were strictly enforced.

On the other hand, even if the Navigation Acts had been applied with more vigour than they really were, the consequences would not have been very different; the economic activity of the colonies was so little developed and in so primitive a state, the production so localised, social life so rare, that the exchanges were few, and for a long time the importance of the international commerce of the colonies was very small. Lastly, as regards exports we have seen that the Navigation Acts restrained those exports, which, for the great majority of the colonists, had less importance; and left the others free or nearly so, whilst household manufacturing partly supplied the wants which could not be satisfied by obstructed importations. In short, for a considerable time the Navigation Acts could not injure the colonies on account of the manner in which they were applied, and more especially on account of the economic condition of the colonies.

The system of industrial restrictions must not be estimated differently. Properly speaking it was begun before the end of the seventeenth century, because the prohibition of the internal exchange of manufactured articles was in reality a hindrance to industry; and this system was in course of time gradually confirmed and strengthened. But shortly after the middle of the eighteenth century the colonial manufactures were almost exclusively of a household character; the hindrance to their progress arose much more from the conditions of the country than from the English restraint, and if the latter was the cause of the greater or less injury to some traders, the economic activity of the country on the whole must have suffered but little damage.[1]

After the middle of the last century there was some change in the commercial and industrial conditions of the colonies: the foreign trade was becoming more important and the industries were passing through the early stages of transformation. This change was yet of so little importance that it could scarcely have any influence on the efficacy of the colonial policy as applied up to that time; but most imprudently just then this policy was enforced with a greater rigour than ever.[2]

We shall support our argument by a remarkable passage, quoted from the work of a well-known Italian economist,

[1] On this point it might even be affirmed that the English policy, which consisted in giving to the colonies a stimulus towards the production of raw material and repressing the manufacturing industry, did nothing else than place the colonial activity on its proper footing, causing thereby the same effects which would have probably followed from a policy of free trade!

[2] Let us mention some opinions from the admirable work of Merivale: *Lectures on Colonisation and Colonies*. London: Longmans, Green, and Co., 1861.

"The trade of the North American colonies," says he, "was not, perhaps, much affected in the long run by the Navigation Acts. The prohibition to manufactures for themselves was a prohibition to do that which, on a large scale, nature itself had forbidden them to do, by calling them to the more profitable occupation of agriculture. The restriction of the use of English manufactures could not, except in a few articles, subject them to much extra expense" (p. 97).

The monopolising of the trade of the colonies by compelling them to send all their produce to the mother country, although a principle of the old colonial system, was so difficult to execute that it was never seriously applied; so that this attempt made by England on the North American colonies in the first period of the Navigation Acts was soon abandoned as useless (p. 188).

The part insisted upon was to compel the colonists to use solely the goods of the mother country.

As to the prohibition of the colonial manufactures, a strict order not to make articles which were of common use was impossible, and with regard to a more extensive production, the very conditions of the colonies, the abundance of land, and the rate of wages, prevented it; therefore such prohibition was little more than nominal.

But there were some industries, the prohibition of which was really very injurious to the colonies, as, for instance, when the production was of an extensive character and could easily be worked on the spot, such as sugar refining (p. 220).

Beer endorses Merivale's opinions and says that the prohibition of manufactures had somewhat beneficial consequences, because their diffusion in young countries would only be a *pis-aller* (Vide *The Commercial Policy*, etc., p. 135).

who with a superior intelligence and deep historical perception grasped by intuition that truth which we have reached only by a slow and minute study; and we are glad that our book may be considered as an explanation of only one page of the *Analisi della proprietà capitalista*, which exercises so much influence on economic ideas.

In this work Loria says: " This necessity, which forced the colonists to import the commonest goods from the mother country, was a powerful cause of their political dependence; and when, in 1750, England forbade the iron trade to the colonies, an industry which, according to Lord Chatham, they had no right to exercise, and when a weaving business set up in Massachusetts was declared *a nuisance* and suppressed, the colonies could not defy the authority of the English Government, because their industry was so poor that they could make neither instruments nor arms, and they were dependent on Great Britain for all products except those of agriculture; but these very prohibitions which England imposed on the trade of the colonies revealed that the latter had no means of carrying out extensive manufactures, and indeed the prohibitions were opportune and possible only because nature itself prevented the colonists from manufacturing. This observation concerns a particular case of a general economic principle, that a measure is effective only when it agrees with the circumstances of the times. And that is why the colonies shook off the yoke as soon as there was a cessation of the territorial conditions which disqualified them from manufacturing." [1]

Our conclusions, although we draw from the same historical facts as Loria, differ from his in some points.

We do not deny that the difficulty of making arms and ammunition may have delayed the revolution (as to ships, their construction was flourishing in the colonies); but from the facts of the case, and from what Loria himself implicitly says later on, it seems quite clear that if the colonies did not revolt sooner, it was because they had no economic reason for doing so, and that, leaving out political considerations, the commercial and industrial system of England was not, at least for a long time, so oppressive to them as to cause a revolution.

[1] Loria, *Analisi della proprietà capitalista*, vol. ii. p. 31.

We accept with some reserve the opinion expressed in the latter part of the above passage where Loria seems to believe that the American revolution may have been caused by a change in the economic position of the colonies. This idea which, indeed, is endorsed by most authors,[1] our investigations show not to be quite consistent with truth, for it seems to us that the economic and industrial policy of England was only a secondary cause of the revolution. This cause acted more forcibly towards the end, when the restraint became suddenly harsher; but the economic condition of the country was not such as to make the effects of that policy seriously felt, nor in reality did the colonists show themselves excessively intolerant of it, since they acknowledged to the last the right of England to regulate their commerce. We cannot inquire here into the political causes which led to the American revolution—we could not do so properly in a few words; but we believe that if the colonial system, suddenly aggravated, partly led to it, the determining cause was the national conscience of a new people having already the character-

[1] Among whom Lecky (*History of England in the Eighteenth Century*, London, 1883, vol. iii. p. 302). "It is undoubtedly true that the commercial policy of England had established a real opposition of interest between the mother country and her colonies; and, if the policy which was the proximate cause of the American revolution was chiefly due to the King and to the landed gentry, the ultimate cause may be mainly traced to the great influence which the commercial classes possessed in British legislation. The expulsion of the French from Canada made it possible for the Americans to dispense with English protection. The commercial restrictions alone made it their interest to do so. If the *Wealth of Nations* had been published a century earlier, and if its principles had passed into legislation, it is quite possible that the separation of England and her colonies might have been indefinitely adjourned. A false theory of commerce, then universally accepted, had involved both the mother country and her colonies in a web of restrictions which greatly retarded their development."

To his opinion, however, may be opposed that of other writers, who interpret the facts in a manner similar to our explanations; and in addition to those we have occasionally mentioned, we may add the authoritative words of Professor Seeley: "It is the custom to describe the old colonies as sacrificed to the mother country. We must be careful not to admit that statement without qualification. It is supposed, for instance, that the revolt of our own American colonies was provoked by the selfish treatment of the mother country, which shocked their trade without rendering them any benefit in return for these restraints. But that is far from being true. Between England and the American colonies there was a real interchange of services. England gave defence in return for trade privileges. In the middle of the last century, at the time

istics of a separate nation, and feeling its strength and right to freedom.

The industrial and commercial conditions of the colonies were very little altered during the last years of the English rule, and they remained unaltered even during the first years of independence; it was the aggravation of the colonial policy which, co-operating with the political causes, gave the final impulse to the revolution.

Our opinions and the observations made upon the assertions of Loria do not detract from the truism laid down by that author, namely, that the British prohibition to manufacturing in the colonies (and we might also add the commercial monopoly) was at that time *historically reasonable and practicable*. Such was certainly the case with respect to the commercial policy in the colonies for a considerable time, but it was no longer so when finally it became aggravated. These conclusions, so different from those generally admitted, prove once more the efficiency of that mode of study which recognises in economic phenomena a changeable and historical character. The colonial policy, so much opposed, can yet be justified, not only by the condition of the mother country during a certain historical period, but also by the condition of the colonies at a certain stage, during which, if monopoly was not actually a benefit, it could not certainly disturb very much the colonial economy. This justification, however, must be considered as concerning only a certain period, beyond which the monopoly having become irrational and impracticable, was naturally doomed.

when the American quarrel began, it was perhaps rather the colonies than the mother country that had fallen into arrear."—Vide *Expansion of England*, Leipsig, Tauchnitz, 1884, p. 75.

In the pages following, Prof. Seeley admits that the interference of England in the colonial commerce was unjust, because it subjected the colonists to the interests of the traders of the mother country, and he considered the colonies as lands to be exhausted (p. 79). And lastly, elsewhere the same author gives an opinion which may almost seem contradictory. "It was not then simply because they were colonies that our colonies rebelled. It was because they were colonies under the old commercial system, and at a moment when that system itself was administered in an unusually narrow-minded and pedantic way" (p. 165). But in reality there is no contradiction, because the author ascribes the American revolution not to the colonial system in general, but to its last and ill-advised exaggerations, which hurried on the events just when that system began to be intolerable to the colonists.

Every phase of economic evolution has that commercial policy which is suitable to it; and we shall see the confirmation of this statement in the following pages, where we shall inquire into the causes which determined the commercial policy of the United States.

SECOND ESSAY

THE CAUSES OF THE COMMERCIAL POLICY OF THE
UNITED STATES

CHAPTER I

FROM THE DECLARATION OF INDEPENDENCE TO THE
ESTABLISHMENT OF THE CONSTITUTION

1. The period between 1776, when the North American colonies declared their independence, and 1789, when, in accordance with the constitution of 1787, the first congress was called together, was a period of suspense for the American commercial policy, because the English rule having ceased, and with it the colonial commercial policy, no other national system was put in its place. The commercial disorder of those days was more the consequence of unavoidable circumstances than of faulty administration.

It will be as well to give beforehand a few brief historical data, in order to co-ordinate the political with the economic facts, as they are so closely connected with each other.

The war between the colonies and the mother country, which commenced in 1775, lasted several years. The great struggle was decided by the famous victory of Yorktown, 19th October 1781; but hostilities were continued for about two years later, during which there was desultory fighting, several American towns remaining in the hands of the English until the treaty of peace signed in Paris, 3rd September 1783, when England recognised the independence of the United States.

The *Continental Congress* of the American colonies, which met for the first time at Philadelphia in 1774, and which was the first organisation of an American national character that the revolted colonies set up in opposition to the mother country, maintained the form of revolutionary government until 1781.

In that year the *articles of confederation*, agreed to by the Congress of 1777, were enforced. The revolutionary government was followed by a somewhat less irregular one, which lasted till the constitution of the United States was established.

The first form of regular government was an unhappy one. The new states were suspiciously vigilant against one another, meanly selfish, and they would not give up any part of their own independence in favour of the Federal Government, which had therefore no authority, and its finances depended entirely upon their caprice.

According to Sterne,[1] the Government was allowed to contract debts, but the means of settling them were refused; it could raise troops and gather fleets, but there were no means of paying them, unless the states granted the money; it could sign treaties with foreign powers, but could not compel any of the states to observe them. In short, it was a Government which could proclaim the law, but could not punish the infringement of it.

Of course such a state of affairs affected above all the public treasury, and the Confederation, which had already so many difficulties to contend with, had also, through the ill-will and want of cohesion of the states and citizens, to struggle against the difficulties of a disastrous financial condition, whilst the states even refused the means for the payment of the public debt. The general disorder was such that Washington was justified in saying that the Confederation was like a shadow without a body, and that the Congress was a sham.

2. The states did not give up to this *mock assembly* the right of regulating the commerce, which right, after the cessation of the English domination, belonged to them individually, and thus the Congress, though having theoretically the right of stipulating treaties and arranging the commercial relations with foreign nations, was practically powerless to dictate strict rules to the separate states of the Confederation in matters concerning inland or foreign commerce; besides, Congress was also debarred from decreeing any tax whatever without the consent of the states, which repeatedly refused to authorise a tax of five per cent on importations for an exclusively fiscal purpose.

[1] Simon Sterne, *Constitutional History of the United States.*

Hence the strange aspect and confusion of the commercial policy of the United States in the first period of their existence; for we find treaties and proclamations of free-trade emanating from a Congress having no real power with regard to commercial policy. On the other hand we find, in a union of States desiring a collective national existence, each State acting in matters of commercial policy exclusively in its own interest, so that the measures adopted by one State neutralised those of another.

This was a condition of affairs which, as we shall soon see, gave later on the greatest stimulus to the formation of the constitution, and compelled the refractory States to yield to the National Congress that right of regulating commerce which, if held by themselves, was only a source of internal struggles, ineffective efforts, mutual enfeeblement, impossibility of protection for the general interest of the whole country, and also the very negation of the national existence.

3. Our investigation of the American commercial policy of this period must be divided into two parts—first, the lapse of time from the beginning of the war in 1775 to the Treaty of Paris, 1783; and, secondly, the few years which followed until the meeting of the first Congress of the United States in 1789. This division is necessary, because the conditions of the foreign commerce of the United States in these two periods were very different.

The commerce between England and the American colonies, already deeply shaken through the resolutions passed by the colonists forbidding the importations from the mother country, ceased completely at the beginning of the war, because the English Government in its turn rejected the importations from the colonies. And even the American trade with other countries, which formerly, on account of the English colonial policy, was carried on by smuggling, must have been almost completely paralysed by the war.[1] Botta says that although during the war the American trade with

[1] Speaking of the year 1775, Bancroft (vol. viii. p. 57) says that there was no commerce, therefore no hope of revenue from duties on imports, and (p. 250) that the foreign trade was completely suspended in 1776. Eyma states (vol. ii. p. 60) that of course during the revolution the commerce of the United States not only with Great Britain, but also with the rest of the world, was completely suspended.

England ceased, it went on freely with other countries, especially with French and Spanish ports, which not only were open to American ships, but supplied ammunition to the colonists;[1] but the importation of foreign goods in the United States, especially manufactured ones, had probably very little importance during the war, and that we infer both from the historical evidence produced and the consideration of the consequences which, according to many authors, the war had on the American industries.

And, indeed, if it cannot be said that the American manufactures underwent in this period a considerable modification in their conditions, they nevertheless received some stimulus from the war. According to Mason, the revolution, by stopping the commerce with other countries, compelled the colonists to supply their own wants from their internal resources; the interruption of intercourse acting as a prohibitive tariff increased the local manufacturing activity, so that, although manufacturing was still a household occupation, or nearly so, and carried on with rough instruments, all articles of first necessity were abundantly produced, especially in those States which had skilled workmen and the necessary materials.[2] Moreover, the historians of the American manufactures, Bishop[3] and Bolles,[4] state that the revolution greatly promoted the manufacture of iron, because the importation being stopped there was the necessity of turning the raw material to account and making the articles required for the war on the spot, and that at the end of the revolution this industry attained a considerable development, which would have increased rapidly if after the peace it had not been stifled by the invasion of foreign manufactured goods.

The foreign commerce then being almost stopped, whatever policy was followed by each of the States and the Congress itself during the war was practically of little importance; but from our point of view it is important, because it shows

---

[1] *Storia della guerra*, etc., vol. ii. p. 336; the same author, also speaking of the year 1778 (vol. iii. p. 386), states that the commercial intercourse of the Americans with England, and to a great extent with other nations, was stopped.

[2] *A Short Tariff History of the United States*, Part i., 1783-9, Chicago, 1884, p. 18.

[3] Bishop, vol. i. p. 630.   [4] Bolles, p. 198.

the tendency and the requirements of the country at that time.

As we have said, the policy of each State was different from that of the Continental Congress. Let us examine each of them separately.

4. It is strange, and almost unnoticed by writers,[1] that whilst the colonies were under the sway of the English policy, and acknowledged till the end the right of Great Britain to regulate their commerce, on the other hand they carried on now and then a sort of commercial policy of their own, supporting their own industries, putting taxes on the imports and exports, and competing with each other by means of protective measures. They did not admit the right of England to burden them with taxes, and they reserved the duties for themselves; England sometimes objected to their measures when she thought them adverse to her interests, but at other times she did not interfere.

The ideas of monopoly and industrial protection were the leading ones of the time, and in the shape of mercantilism they inspired the English commercial policy, which was also imitated by the colonies in their turn; and they carried it out as far as they could under the suspicious and vigilant eye of their rulers—a point on which it will be necessary to give a few details.

As we have seen, England had practically encouraged the production of raw material in the colonies, and the colonists took advantage of this to turn it to the profit of their own manufactures. Virginia in 1662 and Maryland in 1681 forbade the exportation of raw hides; Massachusetts, besides prohibiting the exportation, punished those who killed animals without preserving the skins for tanning; and the manufacture of leather was regulated by special laws.[2] In 1651 the Assembly of Massachusetts prohibited the exportation of wool, and the slaughtering of lambs was only allowed when they were intended for family consumption; in 1656, in consideration of the scarcity of textile material and foreign im-

---

[1] We must except Hill, who deals extensively with this subject; see *The First Stages of the Tariff Policy of the United States*, American Economic Association, Baltimore, 1893.

[2] Bolles, *Industrial History*, etc., p. 445 and following.

ports, the Legislature ordered that those persons who could be taken from less important occupations, whether men, women, or children, should devote themselves to spinning, and that the *select men* of every town should select from each family one or more spinners according to circumstances, and bind them to supply a certain amount of yarn for thirty weeks.[1] The Governments of the colonies often granted pecuniary loans, concessions of lands, and other favours to those who set up industrial establishments. In 1752 the Government of Massachusetts granted to a firm the exclusive right of making glass for the whole province;[2] the Legislature of Maryland also encouraged a similar manufacture by a considerable loan.[3] In 1643 the Government of Massachusetts granted to a company, formed with the object of smelting and manufacturing iron, exemption from taxes and the exclusive privilege of producing iron for twenty-one years, provided that within two years enough was made to supply the wants of the colony.[4] In 1772 Massachusetts and Rhode Island gave prizes for the making of sailcloth.[5] In other instances the Governments set up some industries themselves. England did not always tolerate all these decrees; in fact they were not unfrequently cancelled.[6] Other measures encouraged agriculture; in 1652 Massachusetts prohibited the importation of corn, flour, and meat; Virginia prohibited tobacco, and other colonies the importation of cattle.[7]

It will not be out of place to mention also some facts about the duties. Although the mother country regulated the commerce of the colonies, occasionally some of them took upon themselves to impose customs duties which were generally of a fiscal character; but frequently protection was also the object. Of this latter description were those decreed in 1673 by the Government of Massachusetts on the importation of malt to promote the local production of it, and in 1704 Pennsylvania taxed the importation of hops for the same purpose.[8] In this year also the same Legislature put a tax upon the tonnage of all the ships which did not belong entirely to the inhabitants

---

[1] Bishop, *History*, etc., vol. i. p. 311.   [2] *Ibid.* p. 235.
[3] *Ibid.* p. 243.   [4] *Ibid.* p. 472.   [5] *Ibid.* p. 334.
[6] *Ibid.* p. 321.   [7] Hill, *The First Stages*, etc., pp. 14, 15.
[8] Bishop, vol. i. pp. 249 and 260.

of the colony in order to promote their shipping, an example which was followed by New York in 1709, and Massachusetts in 1718; and, as this last Act contained also a tax on imported English goods, the governor sent a sharp reprimand to the Assembly.[1]

But the idea of protection had taken hold of the colonies from their beginning in the shape of a rivalry against one another, as we shall see again later on, whereby the colonies, forgetting that solidarity of interests which should have bound them together against the common ruler, quarrelled with one another respecting their commercial interests.

In 1694 the Legislature of the colony of New Jersey, with the purpose of increasing commerce and shipbuilding in Perth-Amboy, a rival port to New York, prohibited the exportation of timber for the construction of ships, excepting those intended for the high sea. In 1714 duties and other hindrances were thrown in the way of the exportation of some goods intended for the adjacent colonies, and this system was continued with considerable energy until the revolution.[2]

5. Now, if this spirit of monopoly, privilege, and protection, which was characteristic of the time, existed in the colonies during the English supremacy, and in spite of the colonial system, it could not be expected to suddenly disappear at the beginning of the revolution; it was even natural that on the fall of the English dominion, and with it the colonial policy, the independent States, on becoming entitled to regulate their own trade, should profit by their newly-acquired right according to their particular capabilities. And they did make some use of it after the war, though next to none before the war, the reason being not because, as some authors think, the principles of the commercial system of England were discredited, which cannot be the case, since, as we have seen, the colonies themselves imitated it whenever possible, but rather, as we shall show presently, because traditional feelings were overruled by actual necessities.

But tradition and urgency agreed on one point, namely, the encouragement, by subsidies and prizes, of the national manufactures, especially of iron and woollen, which were required for the war, at the beginning of which such assistance

[1] Bishop, vol. i. p. 54. [2] Bolles, p. 851.

was general in the colonies, either by each separate State or through the Congress, which made frequent appeals to the whole country for the supply of the things urgently required during the war, and which could only very rarely be obtained from abroad,[1] owing to the importations being stopped.

6. We have already said that the commercial policy of the Congress had little effect during the war, because trading with foreign countries was completely suspended, and also because, neither during the war nor after it, did the States acknowledge the right of the Congress to regulate their commerce; but the attitude assumed by the latter is none the less remarkable. Even before the Declaration of Independence, in April 1776, Congress forbade the slave trade, and proclaimed free-trade with the whole world except the countries belonging to England. "In this manner," says the great historian of the United States,[2] "the colonial system was swept away for ever from the continent, and the flag of every nation invited to its harbours. The vote abolished the British customhouses, and instituted none in their stead. Absolute free-trade took the place of hoary restrictions; the products of the world could be imported from any place in any friendly bottom, and the products of American industry in like manner exported, without a tax." However, the observations we have previously made show that, as a matter of fact, this *absolute free-trade*, spoken of by Bancroft, must be taken with considerable reserve; but the declaration of the Congress is remarkable in itself, and requires an explanation, considering that the traditions of the country were quite mercantilist.

Later on, in 1778, the representatives of Congress—Franklin, Deane, Lee, and Gerard—concluded with France a treaty of alliance and commerce, declaring on that occasion that the advantages of commerce were founded on reciprocal utility and on the sound principles of free-trade. This free-trade which inspired the first acts of the American commercial policy was perhaps partly an expression of the tendency of the leaders of the revolution, who with few exceptions were, theoretically at least, in favour of free-trade, but it was more particularly the outcome of the political and economic conditions of the country, which urgently required it.

[1] Bishop, vol. i. pp. 381, 382, 390, 391, 615, 616, etc.   [2] Bancroft, vol. viii. p. 323.

Free-trade was, more than anything else, a retaliation and a blow struck at England, inasmuch as all foreign goods, except those from England, were accepted. In the treaty with France it took the shape of a reciprocal arrangement, whereby France, desiring new markets for her goods, offered in return to help the new republic with money and fighting men. The free-trade proclaimed by the Congress was another way of inviting into the United States the goods of which they had most urgent need, and of supplying the army in a moment when the importation of English manufactures was stopped, and the local ones were still in their infancy ; and that is why the Congress not only encouraged manufactures, but even set up some at its own expense. In 1776 the Congress directed several provincial assemblies to do all in their power to promote the cultivation of hemp, flax, cotton, and the production of wool ; to establish in each colony societies for the improvement of agriculture, arts, manufactures, and commerce ; to study the best means of introducing the manufacture of sailcloth and steel.[1] When the colonies began the revolution, says Bolles,[2] they were very poorly provided with the necessary materials for war. They could scarcely make any weapons; they had no skill, no machinery, and no capital. The complete cessation of imports from England made it necessary for them to stimulate their own iron industry, and private enterprise not being adequate for the task, the Congress established iron manufactures in several places suitable to the object in view.

But obviously all this was not enough. The national manufactures could not be created suddenly and produce at once all that war required. The necessities of war were most urgent, and their immediate satisfaction had to prevail over every other idea, and over all traditions, and no single State would have thought of throwing obstacles in the way of attaining such an object ; hence the proclamation of free-trade, with the view of attracting to the Federal ports arms, ammunition, and cloth for the revolutionary army.

Besides, as we shall see later on, free-trade was the system which on the whole was for some time the most suitable for

[1] Mason, *A Short Tariff History*, etc., p. 16.
[2] *Industrial History*, p. 198.

the emancipated colonies, whose industrial conditions could certainly not be suddenly changed by the new political events. The industrial transformation took place slowly in the course of years. The colonists only raised agricultural produce and raw material; they were still incapable of undertaking manufactures on a large scale, because easily cultivated land was free and plentiful. The articles they made were almost exclusively the scanty outcome of domestic industry, so that a protective commercial policy would have been for the new States premature and inefficient; and, in such circumstances, it was even inconceivable and still less practicable. Moreover, as industrial restraint had not injured the colonists, free-trade was to their advantage, because thereby they could purchase cheaply in foreign ports what they had not at home, and also because it opened easy channels through which they could dispose of the abundant produce of their free lands. Free-trade was the natural policy of the United States in the first stage of their evolution.

7. As we have incidentally stated, the War of Independence, by stopping the foreign importation and creating a greater demand for certain articles, promoted the increase of the national manufactures, and was unconsciously a sort of protective system. "The long War of Independence," says Carlo Cattaneo,[1] "considerably accelerated the formation in America of a large commercial and industrial class. The importation of British goods and the exportation of indigenous produce was suddenly stopped; there was an immediate want of arms and ammunition, and still more of tackle, sailcloth, and ironwork for ships. It was not easy to get them in foreign ports owing to the vigilance of the enemy's ships. It was necessary for the colonists to rely on their own hands and on what the country could naturally supply. This was not very difficult to men who had a short time before left the busy shores of England, and were not new to practical engineering. Funds were collected, workshops organised; workmen came from all parts. The whole nation was rejoicing."

[1] "Notizie sulla questione delle tariffe daziarie negli Stati Uniti d'America," published in the *Annali di Statistica*, Milan, March 1833. Cattaneo, *Opere edite ed inedite, raccolte da Agostino Bertani*, vol. v. p. 86, Firenze, Lemonnier, 1888.

But the stimulus which the war gave to the American manufactures must not be exaggerated. The production increased indeed, but as to industrial transformation there were nothing more than slight indications, as had already appeared before. There was not yet sufficient skill in the country, not sufficient capital, not the machinery which in those days was being invented in England, and the exportation of which the English Government strictly forbade; besides, a great transformation could not be expected in the seven years of agitation and warfare.

The manufacture of wool did not change its domestic character immediately after the war; spinning and weaving were also still household occupations. It was only in 1790 that the first modest factory with new appliances was set up; whilst the invention of the "cotton-gin" by Whitney, which gave such stimulus to cotton manufacture, took place in 1792.[1]

Some machinery slowly found its way into the country. A few manufacturing companies were formed some years before the constitution, and the manufacture of iron improved. The revolution especially excited the activity of those industries which supplied articles requisite for the war, but the household industries still continued and increased.[2]

On the conclusion of peace, in 1783, the activity which had been imparted to the national industry came to an end. There being no longer the urgent requirements caused by the war, and the trade with foreign nations being resumed, it is quite conceivable that the national industry was unfavourably affected by these circumstances, the more so that it was yet in its infancy. American authors depict with dark colours the effects caused by the arrival of quantities of goods, especially English, into the United States ports soon after the peace, owing to the free-trade policy adopted by the Congress, or, to speak more exactly, owing to the inability of the Congress to impose protective duties. But their sources of information are somewhat suspicious, because those authors were almost all protectionists; therefore we refer to others. For instance M'Culloch,[3] in order to show the uselessness of the English

[1] Bolles, work mentioned.   [2] Bishop, p. 395, etc.
[3] *A Statistical Account of the British Empire*, London, Knight, 1837.

colonial policy, tells us that after the peace Great Britain continued to have the same ascendency in the American market as before, because the United States were pre-eminently agricultural, and no other country but Great Britain could supply them so cheaply with the greater part of the manufactured goods they required; whilst on the other hand the attempt of the Americans to expand their manufactures by means of protection did not succeed. And Levi,[1] adopting the same views, tells us that the British trade, far from losing ground, on the contrary increased after the war; and, coming to figures, he gives us for the period 1766-1775 an average of £2,000,000 a year for the English exportations to the American colonies, and £3,000,000 as the annual average for the period 1784-1792.

The fact remains that foreign merchandise invaded the American market from all parts of the world, especially from England. The long interruption of commerce with America must have caused a glut of merchandise in the English markets, and the English producers and merchants must have been anxious to recover the rich American market they had lost; therefore the strange assertion that English goods were cheaper in the American ports than in London or Liverpool need not seem very surprising.[2] Certainly the American manufactures could not sustain such a competition, the less so because after the end of the war the great demand for certain produce, especially manufactured iron, ceased; and also because the currency was involved in difficulties through the enormous issue of paper money made by the Congress, to whom the States gave no other means of providing for its financial wants.[3] The development of the national manufactures, says Matthew Carey,[4] was arrested: the weaver, the bootmaker, the hatter, the saddler became bankrupts; their establishments were closed, their workmen reduced to beggary.

8. Such being the state of the country, it is easily conceivable how the idea of protecting the national industries could gain ground, particularly amongst the manufacturing

---

[1] *History*, etc., p. 57.   [2] Bishop, vol. i. p. 395.
[3] Bolles, "American Finance," in the *Cyclopædia* of Lalor.
[4] Matthew Carey, in the *New Olive Branch*, quoted by Mason, p. 23; see also Hildreth, *History of the United States*, vol. iii. pp. 466, 467.

and merchant classes which suffered most; an idea for which there were already precedents, not only in the acts of the colonial governments, as we shall see, but also in the mercantilist traditions still extant and not easily effaceable.[1] The cry for protection therefore became louder, and the States which individually preserved the right of regulating their own commerce, and had already imposed duties to defray the expenses of the war, adopted protective measures. Connecticut, for instance, within the years 1784-1788, imposed duties on imported goods partly for a fiscal and partly for a protectionist purpose. New Hampshire in 1786 did the same, declaring still more explicitly the protectionist character of its duties;[2] and so on in Pennsylvania, Rhode Island, Massachusetts, there were duties with a double purpose, which sometimes reached as much as 25 per cent *ad valorem*. The idea of protecting agriculture and industry went even to the extent of completely prohibiting, as did in 1786 Massachusetts, the importation of such goods as were produced within the State in sufficient quantity for the public consumption.[3]

9. But it is obvious that the measures of commercial policy which were undertaken by the separate States could have no efficacy. They were not uniform; each State acted on its own account, and was inspired solely by its own interests, which often differed from those of other States. The measures taken in one State were paralysed by those of another, or clashed with them, so that instead of forming an obstacle to foreign importation, they hindered the development of the interior commerce of the whole nation. We have seen that in the years following the peace the importations increased enormously, and this is a proof that the individual efforts of the States were of no avail. They even manifested some antagonistic tendencies which threatened to destroy the faint image of national unity then existing.[4]

The eastern States claimed a Navigation Act; those of the south claimed slavery and free importations. The central

---

[1] We see clear signs of mercantilism in a pamphlet of that time quoted by Mason (p. 28) and in other documents.
[2] Hill, pp. 43, 44.   [3] *Ibid.* pp. 46, 55.
[4] O. L. Elliott, *The Tariff Controversy in the United States*, 1789-1833, Palo Alto (California), 1892, p. 20.

States objected to both, and whilst this contest was going on, Congress was completely inert, because it had no authority in the matter. The authorisation to impose a duty of 5 per cent on importations for a fiscal purpose was denied to the Congress, and the treaties which Congress had concluded with Holland, Sweden, and Prussia concerning commercial stipulations were allowed to exist without objection on the part of the States not because the latter had relinquished the idea of their own sovereignty, but simply, says Johnston,[1] because there was almost no commercial intercourse between those countries and the United States.

Such a position could not last; it injured too seriously the great economic and political interests of the country. These interests required a uniformity of commercial policy, solid bonds of unity, and removal of the antagonism which jeopardised its existence.[2]

The necessity of committing the commercial policy to the Federal Congress was urged by another motive both political and economic. After the loss of the American colonies, the English Parliament endeavoured to retain the economic ascendency of England over them by means of expedients taken from her traditional policy. An Act of 1783 allowed the importation of American raw material into England upon payment of normal duties, provided they were imported by English subjects and in English ships; and the English statesmen, considering the industrial power of England, the possibility of her merchants selling on credit, the kind of goods required by the United States, and the fitness of England to supply them, thought it best not to make any treaty with the United States, because as a mere sequence of circumstances, England would attain the utmost benefit without making any concessions. The English hoped that the United States would have continued to supply raw material and would become the great

---

[1] *Vide* "Jay's Treaty" in Lalor's *Cyclopædia*.
[2] "The mutual jealousies among the States even went so far as to lead to a war of tariffs among themselves, with retaliatory and discriminating duties. It was principally this unseemly state of affairs, together with the unsuccessful attempt to give Congress the power to impose a 5 per cent import duty, that led to the formation of the new Federal Constitution, which went into effect in 1789, and under which the United States now lives."—*Vide* Smith and Seligman, *The Commercial Policy of the United States*, p. 5.

market of the English merchants, and by prohibiting the exportation of machinery and by other measures of similar character, they shaped their commercial policy so as to convert their hope into a reality, and to regain the advantages which they had lost by the secession of the colonies.

But the national feelings of the Americans and the consciousness of their financial interests, which required a free development of all the productive forces of the country without exterior hindrances, demanded that those English plans should be effectually opposed, so as to ensure commercial independence to the American people. It was necessary that the American nation should protect herself energetically against the attempts of the English economic policy; such a defence could only be undertaken by the Federal Congress, and not by the single States.[1]

The example of the United States can be adduced as a proof of the theory, so well illustrated by Loria, of the influence of economic phenomena upon the constitution of the state; a doctrine which seems to us incontrovertible.[2]

It cannot be doubted that the formation of the constitution of the United States, that monument which after a century is still venerated by the Americans, was brought about by economic causes. We certainly do not intend to say that these causes were the only ones or even the most essential; that would be paradoxical. But it seems evident that the last energetic stimulus which induced the States to give up part of their sovereignty and to approve the constitution, arose from injuries which their discordant and selfish commercial policy had caused. And this is not only confirmed by a long series of authors whose evidence it would be tedious to repeat,[3] but it is shown also by historical facts, because the first proposal for a new constitution was made in 1786, at Annapolis, ·in the assembly called together by Virginia to investigate the means of arriving at a uniform commercial system for all the

---

[1] Adams, *Taxation in the United States, 1789-1816*, Baltimore, John Hopkins University, 1884, pp. 15-16.

[2] Vide *Les bases économiques de la constitution sociale*, Paris, Alcan, 1893.

[3] We mention some names at random: Bancroft, Lodge, Bishop, Sumner, Mason, Thompson. Bancroft says that the necessity of regulating the commerce was the immediate cause of improving the constitution.—*History of the Formation of the Constitution*, vol. i. p. 146.

States; and the constitution drawn up by the Federal Assembly of Philadelphia in 1787, granted to the Federal Congress the power of regulating the inland and foreign commerce of the States, a power which till then the States possessed individually.

The American protectionists go further; they assert that the constitution was adopted in order to have a single and effective system of protection for the national manufactures.

But this is a risky assertion indeed, because if it is true that when the constitution was drawn up there were numerous demands for protection for the manufactures, on the other hand we must observe that if such demands were so prevalent as to determine the formation of the Federal Constitution, they would have prevailed also in the first Congress of the United States, which met two years later, in 1789, and would have imparted a serious protectionist character to the first Act concerning the commercial policy of the country, passed in the same year; but it was not so, as we shall soon see.

It seems evident that the constitution empowered the Congress to make laws concerning the commerce, and that this grant of authority implied the right of imposing protective duties, therefore the objection of some American free-traders that the protectionist tariffs were unconstitutional is not tenable: but it appears to us none the less clear that the essential object was to establish a single system of commercial policy in accordance with the requirements of the nation.

We shall now investigate those requirements, and the character assumed by the commercial policy of the United States in the first period of their existence under the new constitution.

CHAPTER II

THE TARIFF OF 1789

THEORETICAL PROCLAMATION OF PROTECTION IN THE UNITED STATES AND ITS PRACTICAL IMPOSSIBILITY

10. The economic history of the United States in the first century of their existence is very interesting, and opens a fertile field of inquiry into social facts. During this century the United States preserved and developed the political structure which the great founders of the national unity created by the constitution of 1789. When the great American people became free they occupied little more than the eastern coast of the continent, divided into a few States, and although there had been constant progress during the colonial period, the colonists at the time of the revolution were still in an almost patriarchal condition of life. They spread rapidly over immense territories mostly unexplored, comprising all climates, capable of yielding every produce, and suitable for every kind of economic development. They managed by their activity and their exceptional aptitude to turn these natural advantages to account, and so rapidly indeed that the progress achieved in every ten years seems the work of a century, influencing even the old nations, and becoming a leading factor in the future of the human race.

The natural wealth of the American continent spread. happiness and comfort among the rapidly increasing population. The extent of the territory, its variety and distance from Europe, gave to the economic and political growth of the United States a decided character of individuality and independence, which continued to increase together with the development of the American nation, though without preventing the increase of their intellectual and economic relations with other nations, and exercising at the same time a great influence upon their economy. The doctrine of Monroe, America for the Americans, as generally understood, did not only apply to the political, but also to the economic relations. It meant giving the fullest development to its great resources, and making it also economically independent of other nations—a complete world by itself, as it were. Such an ideal may be disputable and even absurd, but surely it is undeniably a vast and powerful one, because we find it deeply rooted and popular in the United States during the whole century; it is one of the chief factors of their commercial policy, and the argument most frequently brought forward in favour of protection.

In the history of the United States the economist observes the free development of economic agencies, and the phenomena which naturally arise in the dealings of man with land. The commercial policy of that country is a matter of most interesting research, it is parallel to its economic movement, and seems to be a direct consequence of it. The circumstances and nature of the economic and social evolution of the United States are peculiar, therefore they cannot lead to conclusions applicable to other nations, but they will be none the less useful to the economic science.

We do not intend to relate the history of the commercial policy of the United States, that may be found in other works, although it has seldom been written with that impartiality and freedom from prejudice which are indispensable conditions of every scientific research; nor do we intend to make a special investigation of the practical consequences of protection in that country. We must mention them occasionally, but a scientific determination of this matter is so difficult and unsafe, the complication of facts so enormous, the isolation of them so unmanageable, the clear distinction between cause and effect so perplexing, that we have not the courage to undertake the task; we propose to ascertain the causes which have produced the evolution of the economic policy of the United States, and particularly those of the so-called American system — that is, the protection of industry by means of duties imposed on importations. The subject is interesting enough; it has been partly treated by others, but it is not yet exhausted, and if we have the disadvantage of dealing with it at a distance, and only by the aid of books, on the other hand we are thereby enabled to speak without prejudiced ideas; and we hope that viewing the facts from far we shall be as an observer who, watching from a high point the expanse around, does not see such minute details as people moving to and fro in the streets, or the many varieties of grasses in the fields, but takes in at a glance the general aspect of the country and its salient features.

11. In the history of the commercial policy of the United States we find three different elements which have exerted great influence. The fundamental element always present is the productive condition of the country; it is the basis on which the structure of its commercial policy is laid; the latter may in its turn occasionally exert an influence, but for the most part it is only an effect of this condition. The two other elements to be considered are war and the exigencies of Federal finance. Three wars, the War of Independence, the War of 1812, and lastly the War of Secession, variously influenced the industrial and commercial life of the country, and at their conclusion the commercial policy underwent great changes, as we shall see later on; but we believe that such changes would not have happened, or at least would not have lasted so long if they had not been supported by the industrial conditions of the country.

The War of Independence was the one, as we have partly seen, which exerted the least influence, because although the national industry was then extended, the country was not yet ready for a greater industrial expansion; therefore there was absence of the very conditions which required the application of protectionism; but in 1812 when the country, after a long period of national existence, was thoroughly prepared for the expansion of industry, the war gave it a great stimulus, and when peace was restored, capitalism, which was in course of formation, caused the adoption of the American system of protection.

Lastly, the Secession War was the original cause of the abolition of free-trade and resumption of protectionism. At first the customs duties were increased for merely fiscal purposes, but afterwards protection was continued with increased severity for many reasons which we cannot now investigate.

A third element, and a troublesome one for the tariff system, was the condition of the Federal treasury. The whole history of the United States is an example of the unpardonable error whereby the tariff has been made both the main financial source of income of the Government, and a means for protecting the national industry. The reluctance of the States to allow Congress to impose general taxes, and the imperfect financial ideas which considered the customs duties as a lighter burden for the people, were the source whence this error was derived and kept alive; a social error, because it led to the heavy taxation of many articles of first necessity, and also a financial error because it rendered the condition of the Federal treasury fluctuating and unsafe, and exposed it to the evil of a sudden interruption of revenue when, as in case of war or commercial crisis, the wants of the state required it most; but these sides of the question, which we merely point out, do not concern us. The idea was especially faulty and inconsistent from the point of view of the commercial policy itself, because it subjected the latter to the vicissitudes of the Federal finances; and indeed in the history of the *American system* we see several times a sudden rise or exaggeration of duties to supply the needs of the state, with the consequence that the protectionist policy has been accidentally or unwillingly initiated or intensified; and for this reason we have also seen several times that phenomenon, strange and unusual in Europe, namely, the surplus revenue causing a reduction of tariffs and bringing about a remarkable change in the commercial policy of the country.

This influence of the financial policy upon the economic policy is to be met at every step in the history of the United States; occasionally it has been useful, but generally the reverse, for it was one of the principal causes which contributed to the establishment of protectionism, especially after the War of Secession.

Besides these main factors of the tariff policy of the United States, there have been others more or less important at different times, namely, political events which exercised an influence upon industry and commerce; the antagonism of interests between the north and the south which has been a source of struggles and compromises; questions of internal policy; the vicissitudes of parties; financial crises.

All these and other causes influenced in their turn the commercial policy of the United States, but on the whole they were rather concomitant causes contributing to but not determining the events; and some authors by exaggerating their importance have well nigh lost sight of the general and most important lines of the history of the subject we are investigating.

12. Before entering into a minute analysis of the facts, it will be convenient to make some brief historical statements, which will be completely justified and explained later on.

The history of the commercial policy of the United States from the formation of the constitution to our days can be divided into four great periods. The first, about a quarter of a century, from 1789 to 1815, is the period when the protectionist policy was being prepared, but had not yet been applied. For about twenty years until 1807, the American manufacturing industry was still in its infancy; the industrial conditions requiring protection were wanting. Protectionism was frequently invoked and began to be popular; it even prevailed in some tariffs, but was not paramount. At the same time the manufacturing industries gradually and slowly increased; the capitalist stage of industry commenced, and soon afterwards the point was reached when capital, to establish its own sway, compelled the Government to set up protection. This event was first delayed in the United States by the Napoleonic wars, which for many years made the commerce of the neutral nations very profitable, thus causing the American capital, which was neither extensive nor venturesome, to be employed in international trade, instead of in the national industries, which were in great want of transformation and improvement. But after 1807 and until 1815, first the cessation of the neutral commerce, and then the war with England, which completely stopped the American trade, also the great decrease of importations, and the urgent need of articles for the war, placed at the disposal of manufacturers the capital which till then had been invested in commercial pursuits, and gave great impulse to the industrial activity of the country; and thus industry received a spontaneous and undesired protection, the result not of the tariff policy but of fortuitous events. The transformation of industry, which had proceeded slowly, suddenly expanded, and the sway of capital became the most prominent feature of the economic aspect of the country. We must here observe that the historical events aforesaid must have exerted an influence on the industrial activity inferior to that which is apparent at first sight, because the Napoleonic and English wars had neutralising consequences, so that we may say that if manufacturing had not been at first hindered and afterwards protected, it would have arrived at the capitalist stage either during this period or a little later.

The formation and the consolidation of the capitalist system of industry eventually caused in 1816 the establishment of the *American system* of protection, which had been advocated but not carried out till then, a system which continued to develop until 1832, and comprises the second great period of the commercial policy of the United States. At the end of this really distinct period of the history of American protectionism, the manufacturing industries were, on the whole, firmly established; their infancy and household character were altogether at an end, and capital assumed the leading part in the industrial activity of the country. The protectionist policy which had already become almost superfluous, and the severity of which was in some respects injurious to the country, and especially to some of the States, began to decrease through the famous *Compromise Act;* there was also a third and long period during which the country, with the exception of a short interruption from 1842 to 1846, passed gradually from protectionism to free-trade, which was indeed consistent with the general prosperity of the manufacturing industry. This movement lasted about thirty years, and was abruptly interrupted by a political event, the Secession War, when the import duties were repeatedly raised for fiscal purposes in order to supply the enormous wants of the Federal treasury in that fratricidal struggle.

Hence a vigorous protectionist reaction; following upon which there were several modifications of the tariffs, the last and most serious of all being that of 1890, when, through the instrumentality of the famous MacKinley Bill, the American system, which seemed to have been forgotten, was resumed more energetically and more severely than ever.

We do not wish to express opinions and conclusions which might seem premature, but we can confidently assert forthwith that this revival of protectionism in the United States and its counterpart in Europe, are in both cases an effect of the crisis which capitalism is undergoing; a crisis which seems to point out the necessity for a social and financial transformation, whose main features are not yet clearly apparent. Perhaps the capitalist system, as actually existing, is close upon its end, and capital does its utmost to defend itself; it leans upon protectionism, and tries in Europe as well as in America to revive its strength by those newly-devised huge coalitions called *Trusts*.

13. But resuming our argument, let us come to the first Acts of the Congress of the United States concerning the commercial policy of the Government.

As soon as the two branches of the American Legislature were organised in 1789, one of the first laws voted was that of 4th July, which settled the duties on importations. They were partly *ad valorem* and partly specific, and ranged from 5 to 10 per cent of the value. To mention only the most important items, iron was to pay $7\frac{1}{2}$ per cent; linen, woollen, and cotton fabrics, 5 per cent; glassware, 10 per cent. Some raw materials, such as cotton, wool, hides, were exempt from duties, and all other goods not mentioned in the tariff were to pay 5 per cent. The goods imported on ships built or owned by Americans were allowed a deduction of 10 per cent.[1] As an average it is reckoned that the duties on importation were $8\frac{1}{2}$ per cent *ad valorem*.[2]

Another Act of the same year decreed some differential duties on the tonnage of the ships which entered the American ports, namely, 6 cents per ton upon American-built and American-owned ships, while foreign-built and foreign-owned vessels were charged 30 cents, and upon vessels both built

---

[1] Vide *The Existing Tariff, etc.—Comparative Tables of Present and Past Tariffs*, Treasury Department, Washington, Gov. pr. aff. 1888.

[2] *Vide* Sumner, Ford, and others.

and owned by foreign subjects an entry fee of 50 cents per ton was imposed.[1]

We must stop a while to consider these Acts which mark the origin of the American commercial policy, because the epoch when they were made was a decisive one; and it is important to acquire a clear notion of the character which such policy assumed at its origin: not an easy task, because authors differ very much.

They generally take into little consideration the second of the aforesaid Acts concerning the tonnage, with the exception perhaps of the protectionist authors who wish to extol the good results of protectionism applied to the American shipping by assertions which are very disputable, as we shall see. Wells[2] says that the Act was the result of a compromise which took place at the time of the formation of the constitution, between the States of New England, which were greatly interested in shipping, and those of the South, which upheld slavery; by this compromise there was inserted in the constitution the power of regulating the commerce and carrying on the slave-trade until 1808; and, as soon as Congress met, New England claimed the execution of the provisions which concerned her, namely, the differential duties on tonnage, which gave such decided preference to American shipping.

We have already seen in the preceding chapter the motives which caused the constitution to allow Congress the right of regulating the commerce, a right which of course included the power of decreeing protective tariffs. It seems clear to us that the maritime interests which were paramount in New England succeeded in obtaining that protection which manufactures could not yet obtain. There cannot be any doubt that the object of the differential duties on tonnage was the promotion of the American shipping; but we shall see later on what effect they had.

Most of the authors deal with the duties on importations imposed by the Act of 1789, and show a discordance of opinions truly wonderful. To have an exact idea of the importance and character of this Act, we must examine two questions.

Was the tariff enacted with a view to protection, and did it

[1] Adams, *Taxation in the United States*, Baltimore, 1884, p. 40.
[2] "Navigation Laws," in Lalor's *Cyclopædia*.

supply a widespread want in the country? Did it have any protective effect upon the American manufactures? The authors who have treated these questions may be divided into two categories contradicting each other. Some say that the tariff of 1789 had a protective purpose, and that it initiated the *American system;* others, on the contrary, say that it was established for merely financial and political reasons, and that as a matter of fact the *American system* was introduced much later.

We must inquire into the grounds of this dispute, which has the greatest importance for our subject.

14. The protectionist thesis is upheld by many arguments by Bishop, Bolles, Mason, Thompson, and others. Above all, they assert that the constitution was accepted with great enthusiasm by the agricultural, industrial, and manufacturing classes as a palladium for the future industrial interests of the nation, and that the protection of American industry was one of the chief advantages which the people expected from the new Government.[1]

According to these authors, there are many facts proving that there was at that time a strong public sentiment in favour of protection of the national industry. At Hartford, Halifax, and other places associations of ladies were formed with the object of reducing domestic expenses and encouraging the national manufactures; at Richmond there was an association for promoting the national commerce and manufactures; another in Boston for preventing the use of foreign produce, especially fancy goods, and encouraging the national manufactures; another with similar objects in Pennsylvania which supported its claim by the consideration that there was plenty of raw material and natural produce in the United States, and that their distance from Europe made it necessary for them to have their own manufactures. Similar ideas were expressed in meetings and in publications[2] all over the country, and as soon as the Congress was called together such declarations took the shape of petitions requesting the representatives of the nation to adopt a protective policy.

[1] Bishop, work mentioned, vol. ii. p. 14, and Mason, p. 70.
[2] Thompson, *The History of the Protective Tariff Laws*, Chicago, Peale, 1888, pp. 32-37; Mason, work mentioned, etc.

The merchants and manufacturers of Boston, New York, Philadelphia, Charleston, and New Jersey invoked protection; those of Charleston especially for shipbuilding. Seven hundred mechanics and workmen of Baltimore petitioned Congress for protection, deploring the decadence of arts and manufactures after the revolution. They said that the Government, which was the first legitimate one they had had, should make the nation as independent in fact as in name, by encouraging and protecting the home manufactures, and by taxing those foreign goods which could be produced in America, so as to give a decided preference to Americans.[1]

According to the protectionists, all the great American statesmen of that time were inclined to grant protection to the manufactures. One of these was Hamilton, the author of the famous *Report on Manufactures* who, as we shall see, explained the basis of the protectionist system by a series of arguments, which were later on reproduced and renovated, but rarely surpassed. Jefferson was a protectionist who hated the development of the foreign trade, and who had his own plan of industrial organisation, which he would have brought into practice even by compulsion. He wished to secure for the United States what he called the balance of employment, and in 1809 he was delighted that the embargo, though destructive for the American international commerce, had called the attention of his compatriots to the necessity of establishing useful manufactures, and had hastened the balance of the various branches of economic activity, and reduced the foreign trade to the mere exchange of what was superfluous to the United States for such goods as were wanted by the Americans, but which they could not themselves produce.[2]

Madison was a protectionist who, in the discussion of the tariff of 1789, declared himself friendly to free-trade, and expressed a wish that commerce would be freed from the hindrance of tariffs and preferences, but, at the same time, proclaimed the necessity of protection, and said that the single States had entrusted to Congress their right of regulating commerce with the expectation that Congress would feel

---

[1] Bishop, vol. ii. p. 15; and also among others, Tucker, *History of the United States*, vol. i. p. 348.
[2] Jefferson, *Works*, vol. viii. p. 163.

bound to protect it;[1] and later on, when Madison became president of the United States, he invited the Congress to adopt a protectionist policy.

Lastly, Washington, the most perfect and well-balanced genius of his time, was a protectionist, as his messages to Congress show: in the first Congress he recommended that the new and useful inventions from abroad should be encouraged; in the second he advised the encouragement of navigation in order to make the commerce and agriculture of the United States less dependent on foreign ships; and in the last he explicitly pointed out that Congress had already several times, and not without success, directed their attention to the encouragement of manufactures, adding that "the object was of too much consequence not to ensure a continuation of their efforts in every way which shall appear eligible."[2]

But the strongest argument in favour of the assumption that the tariff of 1789 had a protective purpose, may be drawn from the preamble and discussion of the Act itself. According to the supporters of this opinion, the discussion shows that protection to the infant manufactures was considered originally as an essential part of the whole legislation. The minute discussion which followed upon the tariff, and the antagonism of interests which was manifested, showed the protectionist intentions of the representatives of the country. The members for Massachusetts claimed a duty on rum in favour of the producers they represented, but were opposed to a duty on molasses; those of Pennsylvania wanted a duty on iron and steel, which was objected to by the Southern States; and the same antagonism was to be seen in the other States.[3]

Fitzsimmon, the chief author of the tariff, moved an amendment to somewhat increase the duties, proclaiming at

---

[1] Thompson, work mentioned, p. 66.
[2] *Ibid.* pp. 43, 70. Levi, in his *History of British Commerce*, says that Washington recommended the extension of the American manufactures, but that he did not request protective duties; however, the sense of Washington's words which we have given above seems to justify Thompson's argument.
[3] *Vide* Worthington C. Ford, "Tariffs of the United States," in Lalor's *Cyclopædia*; *vide* also in W. Hill's work, already mentioned, an extensive summary of the discussion on the tariff, and the arguments in favour of the various industries.

the same time his intention of supporting thereby and protecting the "infant industries" of the country; his amendment was approved with only a few dissentients; and others in favour of the tobacco and glass manufactures were also approved. The little opposition, says Thompson, had not a free-trade character, but proceeded from adversaries of the Federal Government, who wished to weaken it by opposing the tariff.[1]

Finally, as a decisive argument, the authentic preamble of the Act is adduced, where it is said that in order to support the Government to discharge the debts of the United States, and to encourage and protect the manufactures, it was necessary to impose duties on goods, wares, and merchandises imported.[2]

Hence the assumption that the tariff of 1789 was a satisfaction given to the claims of the protectionists, and was the beginning of the protectionist policy of the United States; a conclusion indeed not very safe, because the difference between words (even the words of an act) and facts is sometimes considerable.[3]

15. The protectionist theory of the origin and character of the tariff of 1789 is opposed by the political and financial theory brought forward with considerable vigour especially by three American economists, Ely,[4] Taussig,[5] and above all Henry Carter Adams in his splendid monograph, several times quoted by us, on taxation in the United States from 1789 to 1816.[6] According to the opinion of these economists the thesis of the protectionists is superficial, and we might also add biassed, because it is to their interest to show that protectionism has always been almost connatural with the political life of the United States from their origin. The motives which determined the tariff of 1789 should not be attributed to the desire of protecting manufactures, but rather to the

[1] Work mentioned, pp. 58-62, and Bishop, ii. 17.
[2] Bolles, *Financial History*, etc., 1789-1860, p. 75.
[3] See Bishop, Bolles, Thompson, etc., in the works already mentioned. It is strange that Levi, Cattaneo, and Sumner accept this thesis, and admit that the protective policy commenced in the United States in 1789.
[4] *Problems of To-day*, New York, Crowell, 1888.
[5] *The Tariff History of the United States*, New York, Putnam, 1888.
[6] *Taxation in the United States*, etc., Baltimore, 1884; *vide* also Smith and Seligman; *The Commercial Policy of the United States*, Leipsig, 1892.

financial needs of the Government and the political feelings of the time.

As soon as the Federal Government came into existence, the first problem that arose was how to supply the treasury; and not wishing to adopt direct taxation or indirect internal taxes, because these measures were disliked by the people and the States, and it was advisable not to provoke them at the very moment when they were submitting themselves to central authority, the Government had no other resource than to take the customs duties as the basis of its finances. The tariff of 1789 had the special object of procuring an income and of re-establishing the public credit: this, says Adams, was its real object, not that of establishing the manufacture of beer bottles or encouraging the growth of hemp. "He who does not recognise this is not in mental harmony with the period, and so fails to grasp the true meaning of these first debates."[1]

There is further the consideration that the demand for protection for the manufactures, the opposition to the importation and consumption of foreign goods, and the concessions to protectionism were essentially of a political character. The first Congress of the United States was to defend the country against the attempts of the English commercial policy, which, as already stated in the preceding chapter, had given the impulse to the adoption of the constitution; the commercial restrictions were demanded with the idea of reaction and defence against the English policy; the aversion against foreign produce, manifested in so many ways in the country, was a display of nationalism which the Congress was inclined to support. The first tariff was a confirmation of the central authority, and was to serve also another political purpose, namely, to strengthen by a common tariff the union of the States, which was not yet firmly established, and to stimulate the commercial intercourse between State and State.[2] Specific duties were imposed on some articles because it was necessary to secure their supply in case of war.[3] The seemingly protective preamble was only an ostensible display, a colour put on to win the votes of those who wanted protection.[4] And with regard to the petitions

[1] Adams, work mentioned, p. 62.
[2] Ely, p. 42.
[3] Taussig, p. 15.
[4] Adams, p. 30.

to Congress, they show that the petitioners wished for protection; but they were interested manufacturers, therefore such petitions do not prove that the desire for protection was very prevalent.[1] Even Hamilton's famous *Report on Manufactures* has a more political than economic foundation, says Adams; Hamilton's object in advocating protection was the same as he had in framing the scheme for a national bank, and other measures of his, namely, to secure executive centralisation and to build up a sentiment of nationality, an object which was paramount with the whole federalist party.[2]

In short, according to the thesis assumed by Adams, the idea of protection in the United States was not at first an industrial conception distinctly expressed in clear, definite terms, but rather the adjunct of a comprehensive and decidedly aggressive political programme; protectionism as a purposely framed system, independent from politics, appeared much later in the history of the United States. Besides, such a system could not emerge suddenly, it could not clearly assume the shape of a policy in 1789, because manufactures were then rare in the country, and the field within which protection could be employed was a very limited one.[3]

We concur with this way of interpreting facts, and these arguments persuade us much more than those of the protectionists. These considerations also explain the apparently contradictory attitude of the great men of the time. Madison, Adams, Jefferson, were on the whole averse to commercial restrictions; they were so on account of their studies and inclinations, and because they saw how predominant the agricultural and commercial interests were then in their

[1] Adams, p. 33.
[2] Work mentioned, p. 31. We may add that in this report there was another political object vigorously expressed, that of retaliation against the restrictive and prohibitive measures of other States.
[3] *Vide* also Smith and Seligman, *The Commercial Policy*, etc. "A careful review of the debates in Congress, of the discussions by the public, and of the provisions of the Act itself (of 1789), shows clearly that the paramount consideration was that of revenue. The chief need of the times was an adequate provision for the Government expenses; and the manufacturing interests were so utterly insignificant, that the main stress was laid on the revenue feature. . . . The same is practically true of all the tariff Acts until the close of the war of 1812 with England " (p. 6).

country, how little the importance of manufactures, and how small the possibility of their expansion;[1] and if practically they accepted measures of commercial restriction, and even proposed some themselves, they did so mostly for political reasons, as a retaliation against England, with which country they did not see a way of establishing a system of commercial reciprocity.[2]

Indeed all exaggerations must be avoided; we must own that they had not an absolute faith in the freedom of trade, and their belief in it must have been lessened still more later on. Madison accepted free-trade only on condition of reciprocity, and it cannot be denied that the concessions made to protectionism were not only inspired by political motives, but also because protection was desired in some quarters. On the whole the mercantilist traditions were still alive amongst the masses; and as a matter of fact there were some branches of industry which, though they had received great impulse during the war, were afterwards weakened by the excessive importations which followed the conclusion of peace, and Congress wished to help such industries by the imposition of certain duties, as it appears from the discussion which took place on the matter. Undoubtedly there was a certain amount of opinion favourable to protectionism in the country as well as in Congress. But in our opinion the truth lies entirely in that saying of Adams that the idea of protectionism was mixed up with politics, and that the latter prevailed over the former with the consequence that many petitions in favour of protection had a political and not an economic aim. And even Bolles says that there was a wish to protect manufactures by means of duties not only for their own sake, but also because revenge was sweet, even if obtained at considerable cost;[3] and Thompson, an exaggerated protectionist, admits repeatedly that the main motive of the petitions for industrial protection was the desire of becoming completely independent of England.

[1] As a matter of fact the predominance of the agricultural and commercial interests counteracted protectionism. According to Elliott (work mentioned, p. 72) the commercial interests although they were not adverse to manufactures, prevented the enactment of tariffs which might cause a diminution of the foreign trade. [2] Hill, pp. 86-90, and Elliott, pp. 38-52.
[3] *Financial History*, 1789-1860, p. 79.

Now, if we look at the figures of the tariff of 1789, it seems quite clear that in its general lines it was not a protective one : duties of an average of $8\frac{1}{2}$ per cent, often scarcely 5, and only in a few cases reaching 10 per cent, could not be protective ; there were a few very moderate specified duties of a distinctly protective character, but nothing more.

We are then quite justified in saying that if the first tariff is to be described as a protective one, it is so only nominally ; the protective intention must be feeble, because the measure was brought forth more for a political than for an economic purpose ; the tariff was and remained for a long time, as we shall see, exclusively fiscal, and this is proved by the fact that the duties, even modified as they were in course of time, remained still under the limit which experience shows can be reached in order to get a good fiscal result; whilst on the other hand, since 1792, there were interior taxes on some manufactures which destroyed any possible advantage obtainable by means of the tariff. But here this objection might be made: granting that protectionism was put forward mainly for a political purpose, namely, as a reaction against England, but at the same time there was some economic reason for it, the two motives coalescing should have given not only a nominal but also a really protective character to the tariff. We can meet the objection by saying that this was not the case, because the need of protection from an economic point of view was a weak one, whilst on the other hand the political motive was not sufficiently urgent. Neither could the losses suffered by some manufacturers subsequently to the conclusion of peace compel the Government to give effect to a protective policy, nor could the political motive be carried to such an extent as to become injurious to the economic condition of the country. And probably it is for this reason that even Hamilton, as we shall see, whilst theoretically he advocated the protective system, practically he suggested a very moderate application of it. In short, the protective policy was not distinctly adopted in 1789, nor for many years after, because on the whole the industrial condition of the country did not require it, and would not have allowed it; and before proceeding any further we must see closely what this condition was, because, as we have said, the commercial policy of a country is a consequence of it.

16. For the description of the American industry in 1789, and about that period, we have plenty of information among the many notices which are contained in the famous *Report* of Alexander Hamilton,[1] and these have been completed by the recent researches of Bishop, Adams, Taussig, and especially Wright.[2]

The industrial condition of the United States had undergone but little change from what it was before the Declaration of Independence, the great industrial progress already begun in England twenty years before had not yet spread itself on the other side of the Atlantic; there were some new industries recently developed after the war, and a few machines, but they were very rare; in other respects there was no change.

Agriculture was still the prevailing industry. In 1789 Franklin reckoned that the wealth and population employed in commercial and industrial undertakings represented only one-eighth of that employed in agriculture, and according to Tench Coxe nine-tenths of the whole population were engaged in agriculture.

Adams divides the products to which agricultural labour was applied into three classes: (*a*) vegetable food-products (wheat, corn, rice, potatoes, etc.); (*b*) products of animal life (beef, mutton, pork, hides, wool, butter, lard, etc.); (*c*) other productions of the soil (tobacco, cotton, indigo, hemp, timber). The first were obtained chiefly in Pennsylvania and the southern part of New York; the second in the other parts of New York and in New England; tobacco in Virginia and Maryland; the other southern States in addition to tobacco produced rice, indigo, and cotton. It was in these latter States that agriculture mostly prevailed. The northern States, on the contrary, were more especially dedicated to commerce, which ranked next to agriculture, and which through political reasons, as we shall see, soon expanded greatly. Last in order of importance came the manufactures,

---

[1] *Report of the Secretary of the Treasury on the Subject of Manufactures*, made the 5th December 1791, Philadelphia, Skerret, 1824.

[2] *Comparative Wages, Prices and Cost of Living*, Boston, Wright and Potter, 1889.

which were still very few and restricted to articles of easy production for local use; and for these the central States showed a special tendency, though of course limited.[1]

According to what we read in Hamilton's *Report*, few manufactures had attained during his time a noticeable development. The rich deposits of iron-ore which existed in the country were worked with profit, although only charcoal was used for smelting; forges were much more numerous than one might have believed; nails were made in quantities by water-power machinery; agricultural and other sharp-edged instruments and firearms were also made; and also steel was produced: the art of casting metals was, however, in its infancy. Copper was as abundant as iron; its manufacture and that of brass were both extensively carried on, for such materials could be easily and cheaply worked. The dressing of skins, especially tanning, was of some importance either as a special branch of industry or as a household occupation. The extension and progress of distilleries and breweries were remarkable, the latter supplying almost all the requirements of the country. There were plenty of saw-mills, flour-mills, and brick-kilns; the manufacture of paper, one of the first industries introduced into the colonies, was a thriving business; there was also a good number of printing-presses and several glass-works. The cotton manufacture was still in its infancy, but Hamilton looked on it with confidence, because the raw material grew in the country, and because this industry, requiring the use of machinery, suited the United States, where "a defect of hands constitutes the greatest obstacles to success."[2] It was Hamilton who announced the formation of a great company with a capital of half a million dollars for the manufacture and printing of cotton goods.[3] This company (certainly one of the first of such undertakings formed in the country), and the introduction of the whole series of Arkwright's improved machinery, adopted for the first time in 1790 by Samuel Slater at Pawtucket, Rhode Island, began in the United States the era of cotton manufacturing, which was to develop so greatly later on.[4]

But, whilst this industry was in its infancy, wool manu-

[1] Vide *Taxation in the United States*, etc., pp. 11, 12.
[2] Vide *Report* p. 115.   [3] *Ibid.* p. 115.   [4] Bishop, vol. ii. p. 26.

facturing did not show any tendency to change and to abandon the domestic stage; with the exception of hat-making and fulling, it was carried out exclusively by the family circle, whence the few industrial experiments that had been attempted failed to remove it.

Shipbuilding, however, was a remarkable exception to this pitiable condition of industry, for ships were better and more cheaply made in the United States than in Europe; so much so that previous to the war one-third of the tonnage under the British flag was of American construction.[1]

But the American manufactures on the whole showed little signs of improvement, and made hardly any efforts to rise above the level of a local production enough to satisfy the immediate wants of the agriculturists. There were several causes for such a state of affairs; for instance, the scarcity of hands, especially skilled hands, high wages, the want of machinery, the dearth of capital, and the heavy competition from abroad. The attempts towards progress were very few and far between, and generally speaking the movement towards capitalism, of which we see the first signs in the following years, had not yet begun.

Wright describes with a masterly hand this condition of affairs, and we cannot refrain from briefly summarising his remarks.[2]

The factory system had not yet displaced the domestic or individual system of labour. In the process of production there was no division of labour. Apprenticeship was the method in vogue, and apprentices had to learn an entire business, not only a single branch as now; a shoemaker, for instance, had to learn the whole process from tanning a hide to finishing a shoe; thus there was a great waste of productive force and time, to the loss of both producer and consumer. This system caused a closer intercourse between masters and workmen than in our days. Industries were not carried out by corporations. Few and rough were the tools used; there was neither the ability nor the means to construct machinery; the inventors of those days were often obliged to invent the very tools with which they carried out their ideas. In the

[1] Bancroft, *History of the Constitution*, etc., vol. i. p. 63.
[2] *Comparative Wages*, etc., pp. 6-12.

United States steam was applied to industry only in 1800; in short, nearly all industrial work was done by hand. To this backward state of industry in general was to be added a wretched lack of means of transportation and communication. The roads were very poor; canals, which later on had such splendid development till the introduction of railways, were also in a primitive state of construction; the experiments of navigation by steam began only in 1807. The postal service was insufficient and very costly; letters were often sent by private carriers. The business centres were comparatively isolated; traders and merchants were informed with difficulty of the state of distant markets, and all this must have contributed to give to industry a strictly local character.

17. These conditions, which also represent the whole colonial life, did not admit a protective policy; free-trade was the only economic system which could satisfy the interests of the country. Protection is grounded on capitalism. When in a new country the production begins to be under the power of capital, and manufacturing begins to assume large dimensions with wage work as a basis, capital has to contend against great difficulties — that is, mainly against the low price of manufactures caused by foreign competition, and the high rate of wages brought about by the presence of free land, which the labourer will prefer to wages. The advent of capitalism divides the producers into two classes, capitalists and workers; the former have interests different from the latter, and can only firmly establish their undertakings by raising the prices of manufactures and lowering wages. This purpose is fitly served by protectionism, which by obstructing importation raises prices, whereby the circumstances of independent workers are made more difficult, the possibility of choosing their employment is restricted, and the cultivation of free land is rendered more difficult, more costly, and more in need of capital.

When, on the contrary, the capitalist stage of industry has not yet begun, as long as the production is brought about by independent workers, there can be no capitalist motive for protectionism, and there is then only one class of producers, which unites the interests of both capital and labour, and can turn to account all the advantages of free-trade.

This theory includes Loria's observations on the influence of free land, and is cleverly expounded by Ricca Salerno in his most original work.[1] We cannot admit all the explanations given by this author, as will be seen elsewhere, but we accept such of them as are consistent with the statements made above. The idea that protectionism is a consequence of capitalism seems to us altogether a happy one, and will be confirmed by the facts we are about to mention, especially if elucidated by some observations.

Let us point out that the independent workers spoken of above, such as they were in the colonial period and after the meeting of the first Congress, did not form, generally speaking, a special manufacturing class; they were either husbandmen or those who supplied the wants of husbandmen; they carried on domestic manufactures to supply their own requirements. Their manufactures were coarse and were principally those which it would not have been convenient to order from abroad, and in which no foreign makers would have attempted to compete; they were not capable of producing any other goods. It was to their common interest that their agricultural produce should be largely exported; there was no fear of it rising in price because land was abundant. It was to their common interest to allow the importation of such commodities as could not be produced in the country, and the price of which it was naturally not to their interest to have raised; the low price diminishing the cost of consumption was advantageous to all, and especially to the cultivators of free land, because it rendered less capital necessary.

For the colonial period industrial restrictions were almost harmless, because manufactures could not expand; and for the same reason the natural policy of the United States in the first years of their existence was free-trade, the more so that the wants of the country increased, whilst the manufacturing activity did not proportionately develop.

It was only later on when the conditions were changed, when the factory system began, when there was wage work, machinery, large undertakings—developments which were hindered during the first years of independence, as we have

[1] "Protezionismo e libero scambio nei paesi vecchi e nuovi," *Giornale degli Economisti*, Roma, April-May 1891.

seen—that protectionism could benefit a class, the capitalists, by raising the price of commodities and lowering the wages. Moreover, the adoption of protectionism, in spite of its evils, was justifiable not only on account of the state of affairs, but also because it actually benefited the country by giving firmness to the great capitalist industry, the advent of which was a necessity of the economic and social evolution.

The capitalist nature of protectionism was clearly shown in Congress during the discussion of the first tariff by Fisher Ames, when he said that it was necessary to protect the young American industries, because otherwise the working people would abandon them for the rich free lands.[1] This assertion, which recalls to mind the observations previously expressed by Moore and Franklin on the peculiar obstacles to manufacturing in the colonies, shows clearly the influence which free land exerted against capitalism and wage work, and why protectionism was advocated, in order to destroy such influence.

The time, however, was not ripe; and these were merely the first attempts of the factory system. Although manufacturing had received a stimulus from the war, it was not yet transformed, and a commercial policy in favour of capitalism, while manufacturing was still in its infancy, would have been inopportune.

The request for protection made to the first Congress, the reasons urged in its favour, and the aversion shown to importations can for the most part be explained, as we have seen, by political motives, and also by the capitalist tendencies which were gradually coming to the front. On the other hand, the general conditions of the country described by us show that neither the capitalist interest nor the political motives could prevail so far as to enforce a protectionist policy which would have utterly ruined the country; and they explain also how some little concessions to protectionism, and an ideal declaration to this effect, took place to calm down those interests and motives; and thus we can further account for the strange attitude of some great statesmen of the time, Jefferson and Madison for instance, who were at first favourable to the freedom of trade and afterwards yielded gradually to protectionism, till at last they accepted it even on principle.

[1] Sumner, p. 22.

Their gradual changes were compromises between their economic ideas and the surrounding circumstances and opinions; and thus we can also account for the attitude taken up by Hamilton, who was the prophet of American capitalism and protectionism.

CHAPTER III

THE AMERICAN TARIFFS FROM 1789 to 1807—FARTHER
IMPRACTICABILITY OF PROTECTION

18. From 1789 to 1808 there were twelve Acts concerning the tariffs, which underwent several modifications. To put matters clearly before the reader, we have made a synopsis of those items which were considered most important at the time.[1]

Date.	Iron.	Cotton Goods.	Woollens.	Linens.	Glass Wares.	Unenumerated Articles.
1789	7½	5	5	5	10	5
1790-1791	...	7½	...	...	12½	...
1792	10	...	7½	7½	15	7½
1794-1795	15	12½	10	12½	20	10
1797-1800	...	15	12½	...	...	12½
1804-1808	17½	17½	15	15	22½	15

As can be seen from this table, the duties were successively increased till they were nearly tripled in about twenty years; but this increase does not indicate, as might at first sight be imagined, the gradual development of the protective policy.

The main and almost exclusive cause for the successive augmentations of the customs duties was the needs of the treasury, as is testified by almost all the authors, whom it is needless to mention.

We have already said that the customs were almost the only source of the Federal revenue; the increasing expense of the United States could be supported by no other means. It is easily imaginable that the wants of the Government grew much more rapidly than the revenue derived from the custom-house, and we need not go into the detailed financial history of Bolles and others

[1] We take these figures from the work *The Existing Tariff*, etc., already mentioned; they show the duty per cent *ad valorem*.

to be convinced of it. The extraordinary demands were met by loans, and the readjustment of the public debt was one of the great feats of Hamilton ; but the public debt also required a share of the ordinary public income, hence the inevitable increase of the tariff for a merely financial purpose ; and we see this increase proceeding cautiously, and remaining for a long time below that limit beyond which a tariff, through its oppressiveness diminishing importation, loses its financial efficacy.

This limit was, perhaps, exceeded only in 1812, when, in order to provide for the requirements of the war declared by the United States against England, the taxes were doubled ; but this measure did not have the desired effect, for the revenue from the customs diminished instead of increasing, and from about thirteen million dollars it decreased to less than eight millions, as may be seen by the following table.

Receipts of the United States (in dollars).
1789-1816.[1]

Dates.	Customs.	Interior Taxes.	Direct Taxes.	Public Lands.	Income from various Sources.	Total of Ordinary Revenue.
1789-91	4,399,473	...	...	...	10,478	4,409,951
1792	3,443,071	208,943	...	...	9,919	3,661,933
1793	4,255,306	337,706	...	...	21,411	4,614,423
1794	4,801,065	274,090	...	...	53,278	5,128,433
1795	5,588,461	337,755	...	...	28,318	5,954,534
1796	6,567,988	475,290	...	4,836	1,169,416	8,217,530
1797	7,549,650	575,491	...	83,541	399,139	8,607,821
1798	7,106,062	644,358	...	11,963	58,193	7,820,576
1799	6,610,449	779,136	...	...	86,188	7,475,773
1800	9,080,933	809,397	734,224	444	152,712	10,777,710
1801	10,750,779	1,048,033	534,343	167,726	345,649	12,846,530
1802	12,438,236	621,899	206,566	188,628	1,500,506	14,955,835
1803	10,479,418	215,180	71,879	165,676	131,945	11,064,098
1804	11,098,565	50,941	50,199	487,527	139,076	11,826,307
1805	12,936,487	21,747	21,883	540,194	40,382	13,560,693
1806	14,667,698	20,101	55,764	765,246	51,122	15,559,931
1807	15,845,522	13,051	34,733	466,163	38,550	16,398,019
1808	16,363,550	8,190	19,159	647,939	21,823	17,060,662
1809	7,257,507	4,034	7,517	442,252	62,163	7,773,473
1810	8,583,309	7,431	12,449	696,549	84,477	9,384,214
1811	13,224,623	2,296	7,667	1,040,238	59,211	14,422,634
1812	8,958,778	4,903	859	710,428	126,165	9,801,133
1813	13,224,623	4,755	3,806	835,655	271,571	14,340,410
1814	5,998,772	1,662,985	2,219,497	1,135,971	164,400	11,181,625
1815	7,282,942	4,678,059	2,162,673	1,287,959	285,283	15,696,917
1816	36,306,875	5,124,708	4,253,635	1,717,985	273,782	47,676,986

[1] From Spofford's *American Almanack*, New York, 1888.

A writer wittily commenting on this fact says, that in the arithmetic of taxation two and two instead of making four, often make only one; but in this case the observation is more witty than true, because the decrease of income was then caused mainly by the war, which immensely diminished the importations, so that from seventy-seven million dollars in 1812, they sank to twenty-two millions in 1813, and to thirteen millions in 1814.

It cannot be denied that the protectionist ideas were slowly making headway in the country, although at that time they did not exert a serious influence on the determination of the customs policy; but at any rate the fact is evident, as will be more clearly seen later on, that the imposition of duties for a merely fiscal purpose led unconsciously and even unwillingly to the establishment of protection; and this was another of the injurious consequences derived from drawing the Federal revenue almost exclusively from the customs, because, leaving out the question whether protective duties are useful or not, it is quite certain that they can only be applied with satisfactory results when they are in harmony with the industrial conditions of the country, and not when they are imposed almost at random, to serve quite different purposes.

Bolles, whilst admitting that the burdens of which we have been speaking were imposed with the object of supplying the Government with funds, and paying the interest on the public debt, adds that the idea of protecting industry contributed to the adoption of such a course, and that if in those years questions concerning protection had little importance in the Congress, it was because the principle of protecting the national manufactures against foreign importation was largely accepted, both by the people and the Congress, much more than is the case in our days.[1] This, however, is obviously a great exaggeration, because, if it were true, the tariff would have been much higher, as happened later on when protectionism was carried out in earnest.

19. A most important feature in the history of American protectionism was the famous *Report on Manufactures*, presented on the 5th December 1791 by Alexander Hamilton,

[1] *Financial History*, etc., 1789-1860, p. 78.

Secretary of the Treasury, to the House of Representatives, which had entrusted him with the formation of a scheme for the encouragement and protection of the national manufactures. The scientific part, however, of this famous document (as will be analysed by us in another essay) was, in our opinion, more important than the practical part. The theory of protectionism contained in it is truly remarkable, but it seems to us that the vigour with which Hamilton advocated its application in the United States was not consistent with the very mild nature of the practical proposals which he presented to Congress, and which were only to a small extent approved. Hamilton's *Report* has been the foundation and authority upon which afterwards were laid the arguments of all the American protectionists; however, one of the most remarkable things in it, which proves further that it had more scientific and historical importance than influence in the commercial policy of his country, is that the author conceived protection in quite a different manner to that which was later on adopted in the United States; for whilst the American protectionists demanded protection almost exclusively in the shape of duties upon the importation of foreign goods, as was applied when the *American system* was carried out, Hamilton, although he accepted such duties as proper means to the end, and even recommended them to Congress, still attached much greater importance to bounties and premiums to be granted directly to the various branches of industry, and insisted on the adoption of them either exclusively or conjointly with the customs duties.

We repeat, Hamilton's proposals to Congress for protecting the manufacturing industries were very mild when compared with the protectionist exaggerations of more recent times. What he wanted were moderate duties, exemption for raw material, bounties and premiums, as we will endeavour to show at greater length elsewhere. Let us sum up the main lines of his scheme, adding also the tariff of 1789 and its re-adjustment after his report in 1792:—

Items.	Tariff of 1789-90. Duty per cent ad valorem.	Hamilton's Proposals in 1791. Duty per cent ad valorem.	Tariff of 1792. Duty per cent ad valorem.
Iron manufactures	7½	10	10
Firearms	5	15	10
Steel manufactures	5	7½	10
Copper manufactures	7½	10, and exemption for the raw material.	10
Leather manufactures	5	15	7½
Linens and manufactured hemp	5	10-12½ bounty and premiums.	7½
Woollens	5	On carpets, 7½; premiums for the production and importation of wool.	7½
Cotton manufactures	7½	Extension of the duty of 7½ to every manufactured article. Bounty to the production of raw and manufactured cotton. Exemption for raw cotton.	7½
Silk manufactures	7½	Premiums. Exemption for the raw material.	10
Glass wares	12½	12½ bounty to the production.	15
Coal	2 cents per bushel	Bounty and premiums.	4½ cents per bushel

As it may be observed in this table, the taxation on foreign goods proposed by Hamilton was not very high, and in many cases, especially for textile fabrics, protection was to be brought about only in the shape of bounties. We shall not enter into the question concerning the originality of this idea, which Hamilton may have borrowed from Colbert or from the English policy, nor can we discuss here the economic value of the plan of protecting infant industries by means of bounties, but we must acknowledge that Hamilton's proposals possessed at the time the advantage of being remarkably opportune. The adoption of a system of bounties instead of duties, as the basis of American protectionism, would have really been a fortunate thing for the United States, inasmuch as it would from the outset have prevented that deplorable fusion of protective and fiscal taxation upon which Federal finance was exclusively based, and which was always the origin of the most grave inconveniences, and one of the principal causes of the instability and excesses of the tariff.

It must, moreover, be noticed that the state bounties and premiums suggested by Hamilton were then the only means whereby the protection of incipient manufactures could be carried out without serious injury to the country.

When Alexander Hamilton recommended state subsidies, he was anxious about the increase in the price of commodities, and about the scarcity which might have been caused by heavy protective taxation. State subsidies and premiums would have been what Gide happily terms *protection without protective duties*.[1] If then Hamilton was in advance of his time when he formulated a protective system not yet suited to the wants of the country, he nevertheless practically supplied those wants by proposing subsidies and low duties.

But only a small part of Hamilton's proposals—some mild customs duties—were accepted by Congress; the premiums and bounties were rejected. Sumner reckons that the average of duties *ad valorem* in 1789 was $8\frac{1}{2}$ per cent; the average for 1790-91, with a modified tariff, was 11 per cent; and that of 1792, when the tariff was again altered after Hamilton's *Report*, was $13\frac{1}{2}$ per cent. So that, according to these statements, Congress in 1792 increased the duties by only $2\frac{1}{2}$ per cent, as may be seen also by the tax on unspecified items, the average of which was from 5 to $7\frac{1}{2}$ per cent; it must be noted also that every one is agreed that the tariff of 1792 was adopted chiefly for financial purposes. We can then, without fear of exaggeration, conclude that Hamilton's protectionist proposals were almost entirely rejected by Congress.[2]

Neither need this surprise us if we recall to mind the observations of the preceding chapter, which tend to demonstrate that protection was premature at that time; whilst, on the other hand, the principle of bounties, although better and wiser, could not be well received by Congress, because, instead of procuring the desired increase of income for the Government, it would have led to greater expenditure, and

---

[1] "La protection sans droits protecteurs," *Revue d'Économie Politique*, Paris, September-October 1891.

[2] Bishop (vol. ii. p. 44) says that the duties of 1792 were imposed also with a protective view, but he admits that they were increased for exclusively financial reasons.

also because it did not satisfy the widely-spread political feeling of a desire to openly injure British commerce and industry.

20. Between the years 1792 and 1808 the tariff was several times increased, as before mentioned, for exclusively fiscal purposes. There were several petitions in favour of protection, which were not always ignored by Congress, and they tend to show that the protective system did not suddenly spring into existence, but that it required a long preparation.

Bishop has recorded the petitions for protection presented to Congress in 1793 by the rope-makers, printers, etc.,[1] and others in the following year by coal merchants, glass-blowers, iron manufacturers, hat makers, etc., such petitions being sometimes opposed to one another.[2] In 1802 the citizens of New Jersey requested an increase of duties on raw iron and nails.[3] In 1803 protective duties were demanded by the Franklin Association and many traders for various branches of industry, and the Committee of Commerce and Manufactures of the House of Representatives acknowledged the justice of their demands, declaring at the same time that it was opportune to grant protection either by exemption of taxes on raw material or by taxation on foreign imports to such of the national industries as could supply goods in quantities adequate to the public wants; they even advised the Treasury Secretary to draw up a new plan of special duties, but in such a manner as not to alter the income derived from the customs.[4] In 1804, in answer to fresh petitions from traders and manufacturers, Congress unanimously increased by about $2\frac{1}{2}$ per cent the duties on importation, added some special ones, and imposed 80 cents per ton on all foreign ships entering the ports of the United States; the surplus revenue accruing from such increase of taxation was to form a fund to fight the pirates;[5] it is clear enough that this increase was not for a fiscal purpose. This observation and the further progress of the protective idea are confirmed by a message of President Jefferson, who in 1806, when treating of the surplus of the Federal revenue, said that it should not be assigned as a reason for abolishing the duties in favour of the American industries, that American patriotism

[1] Bishop, vol. ii. p. 47.   [2] *Ibid.* p. 54.   [3] *Ibid.* p. 92.
[4] *Ibid.* p. 98.   [5] *Ibid.* p. 104.

ought to uphold it, and that the surplus should be applied to purposes of public utility.[1]

21. The political conditions of the time and the industrial conditions of the United States explain their commercial policy during this period. The factory system, which, as we have seen, struggled against obstacles in its attempts to take a firm hold of the country, was also delayed in its development by the political events which diverted the economic activity of the American citizens from manufacturing and turned it towards international commerce. The wars which afflicted Europe at the end of last century and the beginning of this were the cause of this diversion. The proclamation of the neutrality of the United States made by Washington in 1793, and the fact that they were then the only important nation in the world acknowledged as neutral, caused them to be for fourteen years the carriers of the trade between the European colonies and Europe. Goods from the European colonies were carried to the American ports, whence, protected by the neutral flag of the United States, they were sent to Europe. This condition of affairs lasted until 1807, and gave great stimulus to American shipping; but at length the commercial war between France and England became so obstinate that even the neutral trade was destroyed.

At the end of 1793 the tonnage of the United States exceeded that of every other nation except England; their foreign trade ranked in point of value next to that of England, and, proportionally to the population, the United States were the first commercial nation of the world. From 1789 to 1807 the increase of the tonnage of the United States was truly wonderful; from 127,329 tons it reached 848,306, an amount which after 1807, the conditions of the international commerce being changed, considerably diminished, and it did not again reach that amount until after 1837, when it was surpassed.

The exportations from the United States were also enormously developed during this period, as may be clearly seen in the table following. Only part of these exportations consisted of merchandise of the country, mostly agricultural produce, the price of which having increased in consequence

[1] Bishop, vol. ii. p. 115.

of the war caused also an increased production; as for the rest, more than a half consisted of foreign colonial produce, which, as has been said, was brought to the United States, whence it was shipped to Europe. In order to find in the commercial statistics of the United States an amount of exportation of a value superior to that of 1807 we must go on to the year 1835.

These conditions exerted a great influence in the economy of the United States. The capital possessed by the country was not very great, and all, or nearly all, the disposable part of it was invested in international commerce, shipbuilding, and in agricultural pursuits, which were encouraged by increased prices. The industrial activity must have experienced a severe crisis; manufacturing was naturally at a standstill. When the capital of a country is scarce it cannot effectively stimulate several branches of economic activity at the same time. The very conditions which were favourable to agriculture and commerce were necessarily unfavourable to manufactures, which, therefore, made little or no progress.[1]

[1] For all this information see the works already mentioned of Bishop, Adams, Ely, Levi, etc.

CAUSES OF THE COMMERCIAL POLICY

Date.	Political and Diplomatic Events.	Total Exportation from the United States.	Exportation of National Merchandise.	Exportation of Foreign Merchandise.	Importations.
1791	....	19,012,000	..		29,200,000
1792	....	20,753,000	..		31,500,000
1793	Treaty of the allied powers	26,109,000	..		31,100,000
1794	Jay Treaty negotiated with England	33,026,000	..		34,600,000
1795	....	47,989,000	..		69,756,000
1796	....	67,064,000	..		81,436,000
1797	French cruisers allowed to capture American vessels for any cause recognised as lawful ground of capture by British Treaty	56,850,000	..		75,379,000
1798	Order in Council granting "special indulgence" to American shipping. French Treaty declared void by United States, and merchantmen allowed to arm	61,527,000			68,551,000
1799	....	78,527,000	35,000,000	43,665,000	79,069,000
1800	....	70,971,000	35,000,000	35,971,000	91,252,000
1801	....	94,115,000	40,000,000	54,115,000	111,363,000
1802	Treaty of Amiens, followed by reinforcement of the colonial policy by Great Britain	72,483,000	40,000,000	32,482,000	76,333,000
1803	European hostilities renewed, followed by relaxation of colonial policy. Orders in Council not to molest trade with French colonies	55,800,000	42,205,000	13,594,000	64,666,000
1804	....	77,699,000	41,467,000	36,231,000	85,000,000
1805	....	95,566,000	42,387,000	53,179,090	120,600,000
1806	Berlin Decrees issued. American vessels trading in British goods threatened	101,536,000	41,253,000	60,283,000	129,410,000
1807	(a) Jay Treaty expires. (b) Monroe Treaty rejected. (c) British Orders in Council issued, requiring license to trade with Europe. (d) Interpretation of Berlin Decree making it effective against America. (e) Milan Decree issued, denationalising ships submitting to British orders. (f) Congress lays embargo on all American shipping	108,343,000	48,699,000	59,643,000	138,500,000
1808	British orders repealed as applied to Spain	22,430,000	9,433,000	12,997,000	56,990,000
1809	Embargo repealed by Congress, June 28	52,203,000	31,405,000	20,797,000	56,400,000
1810	....	66,757,000	42,336,000	24,391,000	85,400,000
1811	....	61,316,000	45,294,000	16,022,000	53,400,000
1812	War declared with Great Britain by American Congress, June 18	38,527,000	30,032,000	8,495,000	77,030,000
1813	....	27,855,000	25,008,000	2,467,000	22,005,000
1814	....	6,927,000	6,728,000	145,000	12,965,000
1815	End of the war with England	52,377,000	45,974,403	6,583,000	113,041,000
1816	....	81,920,542	54,831,896	17,138,556	147,103,000

N.B.—The amounts are in dollars. This table is partly taken from Adam's *Taxation in the United States*, pp. 72, 73.

With regard to the American manufactures, then, we can say that their position was the same as that of 1789, which was described by us as a characteristic one, and free-trade continued to be natural and necessary to the country, the more so as the international commerce was developing. A protective policy at any rate was still impossible, and we have seen that it was not enacted at that time. If the Government of the United States had unwisely attempted it then, it could not have helped the progress of industry, because it would have been difficult and even injurious to divert the American capital from the investments to which it was irresistibly attracted by the conditions then extant; and moreover it was so scarce that it could not have served the double purpose of both commerce and industry.

A protective policy could not have been enforced then, nor for some time afterwards. It would have been too inconsistent with the predominant interest of the agricultural and commercial classes, the former being adverse to measures which could cause a diminution in the exportation of the agricultural produce, and the latter suspiciously vigilant against any hindrance to the greater development of international intercourse.

On the other hand it must be acknowledged that manufacturing was not completely inert; its progress was hindered but not destroyed, and the capitalist phase was undergoing the process of evolution. In this period there were two great events: Whitney's invention in 1793, which was to give an immense stimulus to the production and manufacture of cotton; and Robert Fulton's application of steam to navigation, for which he obtained a patent in New York State in 1803. The patents for new inventions taken out in those years in the United States are comparatively numerous.

Bishop not only mentions the introduction of many mechanical contrivances, the successful establishment of new manufactures, and a considerable industrial activity in many places (of which Philadelphia was one), but he records also the formation of some Joint-Stock Companies with a comparatively large capital. For instance, in 1800 there was a company formed for the manufacture of iron with a capital of 330,000 dollars; another in 1805 for the same purpose with 450,000 dollars. These facts, which indicate the first struggles of capitalism, become afterwards so frequent that it is not possible to record them individually, therefore comprehensive statistics must be used. During these struggles the factories surrounded by unfavourable conditions and striving against numerous difficulties appealed for assistance; hence the petitions to Congress for protection; and although the commercial policy of the United States had not yet been altered, these were favourably received, and sometimes they even obtained slight satisfaction.[1]

[1] How faulty is often the protectionist's logic! Thompson, for instance (*History*, etc., pp. 84, 85), ascribes the great progress of the foreign trade of the United States after 1791 to the enactment of the protective tariffs. But which ones were they? Perhaps he alludes to the tax on tonnage imposed in 1789 to promote the American shipping. But we have seen that the great commercial activity was promoted mainly by political events extraneous to the commercial policy. List (*Das Nationale System*, etc., Eheberg's edition, Stuttgart, 1883, p. 93) ascribes the flourishing state of the American manufactures, agriculture and commerce, spoken of by Washington in his Message of 1791, to the duties, though small, which were imposed in 1789; whilst indeed the tariff of 1789 could have no other effect than the readjustment and unification of the commercial policy; and besides the industrial conditions of the United States in 1791 were essentially the same as those of 1789.

CHAPTER IV

THE FOUNDATION OF THE FACTORY SYSTEM AND THE
PROTECTIVE POLICY

(FROM 1807 TO 1832)

22. The classic period of American protectionism which, as we shall see, corresponds with that of the foundation and consolidation of the capitalist industry in the United States, comprises the lapse of time from 1816 to 1832. The nine preceding years, however, from 1807 to 1816, are closely connected with this period, and not only had a great influence over the successive advancement of the protective policy, but, also during this period, political causes spontaneously brought about similar results which were afterwards produced by economic measures. It seems therefore convenient to include in one period the twenty-five years, from 1807 to 1832, which have such a great importance in the history of American protection.

It is necessary at the beginning to mention some historical occurrences. The state of things so favourable to the development of the foreign commerce of the United States, which we described in the preceding pages, ceased towards 1807, and to this succeeded a period in which that commerce was almost completely interrupted.

Already in the preceding years the American commerce had more than once suffered injury and loss through the English policy; but towards the latter part of 1806, the war between England and France becoming more bitter, and changing into a commercial struggle, both countries tried to put an end to the neutral commerce which aided the belligerents, and to constrain the United States to abandon their neutrality, which had been so profitable to them, and to declare for one or other of the combatants. It would be outside our province to narrate the vicissitudes of this commercial war; we will keep only to the most prominent facts that may be of interest.

Towards the end of 1806 (in order to paralyse the resources of the enemy, to impede their commerce and to prevent their obtaining supplies), England declared all the coast, ports, and rivers of Europe from Brest to the Elbe to be blockaded; Napoleon, then in the apogee of his power, responded haughtily by the Decree of Berlin of the 12th November, proclaiming the blockade of the British Isles, and dictating a series of measures against British commerce and shipping. The English Government, not to be behindhand, prohibited by the Order in Council of January 1807 all commerce with the French ports, and ordered the captains of English ships of war, or privateers, to intimate to any neutral vessel they might meet, bound to any port of France or of its allies, to suspend their voyage under pain of being captured. Napoleon, in reprisal, ordered the confiscation of all the English merchandise and colonial produce found in the Hanseatic cities: England by another order of the 11th November 1807 declared a state of blockade against all the French ports, those of their allies, and of all the countries from which the English flag was excluded (that is, of all Europe except Sweden); and ordered that all ships bound to such ports should be subjected to English examination and to the payment of taxes. Napoleon immediately replied by the famous Decree of Milan of the 17th December 1807, declaring that any ships of whatever nation which submitted to the English orders should be considered as denationalised and thus a rightful prize, and at the same time he placed the British Isles in a state of blockade, and ordered that all ships coming from England or her colonies or bound to England should be captured.

It is not necessary here to inquire into how far this struggle was effective and how far hypothetical (especially on the part of Napoleon who had no navy), nor to examine the results, except as far as concerns the United States. The position of the United States, as a neutral nation, became insupportable: their rights were trampled on, their ships captured, their commerce to a great extent was suspended and greatly damaged. In this condition of affairs President Jefferson judged that it would be better to prohibit foreign commerce, in order to induce France and England (by suspending such American exportations to those countries as were necessary for their munitions of war) to revoke the measures adopted against neutral commerce. And on the 22nd of December 1807 was promulgated the "embargo," which prohibited American ships from leaving the ports of their country, and ordered all foreign ships to sail at once, whether empty or with the cargo they had on board at the moment of the proclamation of the embargo.

This act was another blow to international commerce, already sufficiently compromised and damaged by preceding measures; the exports and imports of the United States diminished considerably, and would have been still more reduced had it not been for smuggling, which continued to flourish. The embargo did not produce the wished-for result; on the contrary, as may be imagined, it greatly injured American interests: it was nevertheless maintained until 1809, when there was substituted the "non-intercourse law," which prohibited every commercial relation with England and France, and closed the American ports to the ships and the merchandise of those countries. That this commercial struggle should end in war was inevitable; and the war with England broke out in 1812 and lasted till the end of 1815. This, as far as concerns commerce, only made matters worse, producing the almost complete cessation of the international trade of the United States, which only regained vigour after the peace of 1815.[1] All these changes are clearly shown in the statistics of the imports and exports of the United States from 1807 to 1814, as set out in the table printed in the preceding chapter.

To complete our sketch, we must add that in 1812, at the commencement of hostilities, in order to provide for the necessities of war, the Congress adopted financial measures by which the import duties on the principal products were raised to 30 and 35 per cent.

[1] For these facts see Levi, work mentioned, and other writers; also Johnston, "Embargo in United States History," in Lalor's *Cyclopædia*.

23. The changes which almost completely destroyed the commerce of the United States from 1807 to 1815 exercised a corresponding but very different influence on the manufactures. The great diminution of foreign imports caused naturally a considerable rise in the prices of manufactures in the American markets, and this rise and the necessity of manufactures for the use of the country gave a greater encouragement and impulse to the colonial manufactures than any protective tariff could have done. The war with England, with the death-blow it dealt to the already ruined commerce, and with the increase of interior demand that it caused, made prices rise higher, and exercised that influence which otherwise the tariff of 1812 would have done; that, however, had no protective efficacy, for the imports of 1813 and 1814 were greatly reduced by the war, and for the same reason could not have the financial result expected.

But to proceed: we have already said that no protective measure could have given to the American manufactures a development which was not commensurable with the quantity of disposable capital. Now, the American capital, which had formerly been invested in foreign commerce, was hastily withdrawn, and that investment abandoned now that it had become not only almost profitless but also very risky; and attracted by the favourable prospects opened suddenly to home manufactures, it flowed into these and gave them new strength and caused them to increase.

"Just in proportion," says Bolles, "as the embargo laws and other kindred measures were effective in destroying American shipping, did American manufactures strike deep root, and rankly grow."[1] The numerous records we have concerning American manufactures during these years prove that there took place a rapid transformation, through which they passed from an almost completely domestic state to the factory system. Naturally such a transformation could not be produced in one or in a few years, but necessarily needed a longer period; however, it is certain that whilst the great development of commerce retarded it, the new condition hastened it all the more.

Noteworthy above all at this time is the report of Gallatin,

[1] *Financial History*, etc., 1789-1860, p. 285.

the Treasury Secretary, on the state of American manufactures in 1810, which, if historically and theoretically unequal to that of Hamilton, is none the less important as regards the description of the state of manufactures. Let us, for instance, compare with Gallatin's description the poor picture which, as we have seen, Hamilton drew of the manufactures, scarcely mentioning ten that had obtained any development, and pointing out the primitive and domestic state of the majority of them; the progress in twenty years appears remarkable; the greater part of it being quite recent and due to late events.

Gallatin[1] divided American manufactures into three groups. (a) Products which satisfied the consumption of the United States, inasmuch as their export exceeded their import; (b) articles the production of which was established, and which provided for the consumption of the country; (c) articles the production of which had received a stimulus, though not enough to fully satisfy all requirements.

To the first group belong all goods in which wood was the chief material, hides and analagous manufactures, soap and tallow-candles, oil and spermaceti candles, linseed oil, refined sugar, common earthenware, snuff, chocolate, hair-powder, and mustard. In the second group were comprised the production and manufacture of iron, cotton, wool, and flax goods, hats, paper, printing-types, books, playing-cards, alcoholic and fermented liquors, manufacture of hemp, gunpowder, window-glass, jewellery, and watches; leaden goods, straw hats, and wax candles. Finally, to the last group belong dyes, drugs, salt, manufactures of copper and brass goods, printed fabrics, pottery, glass, etc.

We have reproduced this enumeration (declared by Gallatin to be incomplete) as showing more clearly the development that manufactures had reached.

Gallatin gives afterwards particular notices on each of these industries, and on the capital employed in them, etc.; but we cannot enter into these details. He calculated that the bulk of the annual produce of American manufactures exceeded the value of 120,000,000 dollars, an important sum comparatively

[1] *Vide* the full description which Bishop gives of this report, vol. ii. pp. 146-159.

speaking for those times; and elsewhere we notice that in 1811 the United States exported home-manufactures to a value of 3,039,000 dollars. The progress in the cotton manufacture is especially remarkable; this manufacture was unsuccessfully attempted from 1787 to 1808, but in the following years it developed rapidly; in 1803 there were only four cotton mills in the United States; in 1808 there were fifteen in New England, with 8000 spindles; in 1809, sixty-two mills with 31,000 spindles, and another twenty-five mills were in course of erection;[1] in 1810 there were two hundred and twenty-six mills;[2] in 1815 the number of spindles employed in the mills was 500,000.[3] And whilst in 1800 only 500 cotton bales were worked in the United States, in 1810 the American manufactures worked 10,000, and in 1815, 90,000.[4] In two years only (1807-1809) the spinning and carding of cotton was quadrupled. Gallatin calculates that in 1809 the value of all the cotton manufactures, flax and wool, produced in the country, amounted to more than 40,000,000 dollars. Only a small proportion of this was obtained from the above-mentioned factories; the greater part was a domestic production; and even this production had received a great stimulus. Weaving was still exclusively done by hand; the "power-loom" being introduced for the first time at Lowell in 1814.[5]

Gallatin afterwards speaks of the difficulties which American manufactures encountered in their development, and his words are truly remarkable. In his opinion the result obtained up till then was most favourable, since we must take notice of the *natural causes that impeded the introduction and progress of the manufactures in the country;* the most important of these were the *abundance of land,* in comparison with the population, the high price of labour, the want of sufficient capital, *the attractions which agriculture presented,* and the difficulty of suddenly changing the economic bent of the country, which in the past years had been entirely devoted to commerce. No one can doubt the im-

[1] Gallatin's "Report," in Bishop, vol. ii. p. 148.
[2] Wright, *Comparative Wages,* etc., p. 15.
[3] Taussig, work mentioned, p. 28.
[4] Bolles, work mentioned, p. 288.   [5] Wright, p. 17.

portance of these observations; the conditions of the country were not yet such as to spontaneously develop manufactures; accidental causes had given an impulse to them by paralysing what was antagonistic to them; at the cessation of these exceptional causes, after the peace with England, protection, as we shall see, was bound to spring up vigorously as a reaction of the capitalist interests against the free land of the country, and against all the conditions which tended to impede the capitalist industry.

But in 1810 things had not reached this point. Several of the difficulties which Gallatin speaks of were, as he himself says, lessened by the cheapness of materials, the introduction of machines, which were rapidly spreading, the afflux of capital transferred from commerce to the manufactures, etc.; and the only serious obstacle to American manufacture at that time was the superiority of the capital of the first manufacturing country in Europe (England), which superiority allowed her merchants to sell at long credit and to content themselves with small profits, occasionally also sustaining losses.

The American capital was less courageous and enterprising, and it timidly turned to manufacturing, owing to the uncertainty of the political conditions, and, as Bolles says, through Congress manifesting no disposition to protect industrial establishments;[1] but notwithstanding this uncertainty the formation of capitalism proceeded rapidly. The numerous incorporated societies formed in these years are indubitable signs of this. The principle of corporate action, by which small capitals dispersed in many hands can be united, and under the direction of a few be profitably employed in industrial operations, says Wright, commenced to be utilised. Between 1806 and 1814 fifty companies were organised and incorporated in Massachusetts to carry on textile manufactures; in the last of these years alone thirty corporations

[1] Bolles, work mentioned, page 287. Curious as is this observation, it is nevertheless true. It is strange that Bolles, speaking of 1812, complains somewhat of the little inclination of Congress to protect the industries, whilst the "embargo" first and the war afterwards protected them considerably. But it is true that Congress had not yet formed any design of protection. It was resolved later on in 1816, when the "capitalist motive" was stronger and more insistent.

were authorised for the manufacture of cotton, wool, glass, wire, etc. Salaries and profits rose.[1] And some of these companies had considerable capital; one, for instance, may be mentioned with a capital of 800,000 dollars, established in 1812.[2] New machines and inventions were adopted in great number in the factories; the patents granted for new inventions, which from 1790 to 1811 had presented an average of 77, in 1812 reached 237. The progress of manufactures, wrote Niles towards the end of 1812, is astonishing; "the world has no parallel for the population of the United States, nor can it furnish any for the increase of our fabrications." And Cobbett, watching that progress from the other side of the Atlantic, exclaimed: We have before us the germs of a great event, nothing less than the complete and absolute independence of America from English manufactures.[3]

24. But the peace of 1815 threatened to destroy the new manufactures of the United States, just as the preceding war had ruined international commerce. To the peace immediately succeeded a veritable inundation of merchandises that poured into the American ports; the imports, which in 1814 were reduced to nearly twelve million dollars, suddenly rose to one hundred and thirteen millions in 1815, and to one hundred and forty-seven millions in 1816. The English manufacturers, to whose merchandise, after years of commercial war, an ample market was finally opened, rushed as if to the attack of a fortress; and it was indeed the weak and badly-defended fortress of American manufactures which they wished to conquer, even at the sacrifice of selling under cost-price. The enormous importations immediately lowered prices, which had previously been so high in consequence of the suspension of commerce, and the American manufactures felt the effects severely; many manufacturers were compelled to close their works, others, who had decided to make a stand, soon afterwards became bankrupt; the young American industries which had grown rapidly under favourable conditions were now in the greatest straits; and American capital,

[1] *Comparative Wages*, etc., p. 15.
[2] Bishop, work mentioned, vol. ii. p. 183.
[3] Bolles, work mentioned, pp. 287, 288.

which was abundantly supplied to them, was in danger of being lost. To aggravate this sad condition of affairs there was, with regard to the manufacture of cotton, the fact that the increased foreign demand for raw cotton had raised the price of it, thus making the cost of the raw material dearer.

Hence arose a great clamour for protection from those who had suffered loss. President Madison made himself their mouthpiece at Congress, and in his Message of December 1815 said that the rule of leaving industry entirely to individual initiative ought to have some exceptions, that there were special circumstances under which a country might be deprived of industries already established and adapted to it; that circumstances had given impulse to American manufactures which were now developed, and constituted such a body of interests as to require immediate protection. And to the protection of the Congress Madison especially recommended those manufactures which produced commodities necessary to the public defence, or which supplied the wants of the citizens, and those which used raw materials mainly produced by the national agriculture.[1]

The situation was so grave that Sumner, an author certainly above suspicion, and who belongs to the most extreme section of free-traders, is obliged to admit that "the return of peace, if it reopened trade and let things return to their normal condition, would be a calamity."[2]

In this state of affairs, which demanded energetic measures for the safety of the country, and to prevent the ruin of the capitalists, the "American system" was initiated. The discussion which was waged in 1816 in Congress and throughout the country on the protection of American manufactures was not a theoretical controversy, it was a practical and very serious problem that had to be solved. Protection had been at first demanded, without any practical result, from a political and patriotic point of view, to combine economic and political independence, and to thoroughly emancipate the country from England. It was now demanded to prevent the ruin of industry, and to preserve the young American in-

[1] Bishop, work mentioned, vol. ii. pp. 214, 215.
[2] Vide *Lectures on History of Protection in United States*, p. 36.

dustries of too recent a growth to be able to struggle with success against the competition of the first manufacturing nation in the world. Another argument was adopted by Dallas, the Treasury Secretary, to support the protective tariff: the necessity of creating by the development of manufactures an interior market for the agricultural produce of the country, emancipating it from the fluctuations of foreign markets and from the policy of foreign Governments. Thus, after a long discussion, the protective tariff of 1816 was approved, and its chief aim was the protection of the textile manufactures, to be brought about by imposing on goods of that class a duty of 25 per cent, and applying to other productions, principally for fiscal reasons, duties of an average of 20 per cent. This was not sufficient to satisfy the demands of the protectionists, who claimed an energetic protection, and who would have wished that the state of affairs anterior to the peace should be reproduced, which no tariff would have been able to obtain. What may have contributed to make the position appear only trifling was the fact that the duties were really lower than those which, for exclusively financial purposes, were adopted in 1812 at a time when no tax whatever would have been of any use, because the importations had been reduced almost to nothing.

But in reality the tariff of 1816 was protective, although not in an exaggerated degree. The duties, except in 1812, had never been so high; they were intended to check the impetuous current of imports, and they did in fact slacken it with respect to the cotton and wool manufactures, at the same time reaching a limit altogether prohibitive to the commoner kinds of cotton goods, the American production of which was sufficient by itself to supply the wants of the country.[1] Moreover, the tariff was for the first time doubly protective in reality and in intention. In fact, after 1789, when it had been proposed to protect American manufactures by a tariff, which we have seen was in reality only a fiscal one, the subsequent Acts of Congress had not given any more signs of protective intentions, or perhaps only feeble and incidental ones. The increase of duties had always been made with a fiscal motive, and if they had exercised any protective

[1] Bolles, *Financial History*, etc., pp. 364, 365.

influence it had been indirectly and unintentionally. And the still more recent events, embargo, prohibition of commerce, and wars, had not any protective end in view; protection, however energetic, had been so far the result of circumstances and not of any premeditated design.

However, in 1816 the protective system was explicitly initiated, although not yet fully framed. The tariff of 1816 was considered rather as a provisional one to remedy the very serious situation; an organised system of protection was not yet desired, and the duties of 1816 were only to last until 1819.[1]

25. The tariff of 1816 was, however, very soon increased. The imports which were for a while checked and which decreased in 1817 to nearly ninty-nine million dollars, rose in 1818 to one hundred and twenty-one millions, and prices of manufactures, whether for this reason or through the increase of interior competition, remained low. The peace declared in Europe after a long period of war gave a great development to European manufactures. The returning home of hundreds of thousands of soldiers lowered the price of labour and also lowered the prices of European manufactures, against which competition the American industries could not contend. Many of the manufactures were in a critical condition; only that of cotton gave undoubted signs of prosperity. The manufacturers began to say that the tariff of 1816 had been a delusion, and that as the proposition of supporting home manufactures in this time of struggle and crisis had been solemnly proclaimed, and as they had already commenced to protect them, they ought to render that protection efficient by strengthening the insufficient tariff of 1816.[2]

Numerous were the associations which were formed to promote American manufactures and to spread the doctrine of protection; numerous also were the demands for protection, with which President Monroe associated himself in his first Message.[3]

And these demands soon obtained a hearing. In 1817 a sort of Navigation Act was approved, which limited importa-

---
[1] *Vide* Taussig, work mentioned, p. 18.
[2] Bolles, work mentioned, pp. 272-275.
[3] Bishop, work mentioned, vol. ii. pp. 237, 238.

tions to the produce brought by ships from the place of their production, and reserved the coasting trade solely to American ships. In 1818 some modifications of the tariff were approved in the direction of protection, especially in favour of the iron industry. The duties then corresponded to an average of nearly 35 per cent *ad valorem*.

In the meantime, however, the country was in a state of great depression. The crisis had spread even to agriculture. The English corn-laws and the improved European harvests caused a diminution in the exportation of American agricultural produce; the prices of provisions, of cotton, and other raw products of the United States were greatly reduced. The manufactures continued in a bad condition. "Manufacturers," says Bishop, "were forced to abandon extensive and flourishing establishments, reared as if by magic in the last few years, and with their operatives and multitudes of handicraft workmen entered into competition with the cultivators of the soil, and swelled the products of agricultural labour, for which there was no longer a market." [1]

If, however, demands for protection were started by the central States, where the manufactures were more widely spread, and also by some of the agricultural States, which saw in the development of the manufacturing industries a means of enlarging the sale of their raw produce, the States of New England, on the contrary, where commercial and maritime interests prevailed, were from the first averse to these measures. Afterwards the position was entirely changed, and towards 1820 the protective policy found its warmest partisans in New England, where the cotton and wool manufactures had received a great impulse, and its most energetic adversaries in the Southern States. These last opposed the high duties for several reasons: because slavery rendered the development of manufactures impossible; and as it was necessary for them to import goods, protection increased their prices, and indirectly lowered the prices of their agricultural produce, rendering their exportation more difficult because it impeded foreigners obtaining them in exchange for their manufactures; and finally, because they feared that England, as a reprisal against the heavy duties on her manufactures, might in her turn

[1] Bishop, vol. ii. p. 250.

impose duties, or prohibit the importation of cotton, the principal produce of the Southern States.

Whether on account of this contest, or because the general condition of the country was really gradually improving, and some industries, especially the cotton manufactures, were working well, for some years the demands for protection, although always supported by President Monroe, did not obtain a hearing in the Congress, which repeatedly postponed proposals to revise the tariff in a protective sense. But the increase, so long invoked, was at last granted by the tariff of 1824.

It is strange how, in order to sustain the two opposite opinions, the conditions of the country were described in exactly contradictory ways. Clay, energetically supporting the bill, described the depressed condition of every branch of national industry, attributing it to the tariff policy of the country, and recommending the adoption of "a genuine American system of encouraging national industry"; whilst Webster maintained instead that the country was in a state of extraordinary prosperity, and that the diminution of prices and of profits, and some pecuniary embarrassments were derived from other causes.[1]

The tariff of 1824 brought duties from an average of 35 per cent to nearly 40½ per cent, and had for its principal end the encouragement of the production and manufacture of wool, iron, hemp, lead, and glass. The duties on the manufacture of cotton, already sufficiently protected, were increased very little; but in its protective zeal the tariff increased the duties on several merchandises, such as silk, cutlery, etc., for the production of which the country was not in the slightest degree prepared.

The "American system" was like Dante's wild beast

"Che dopo il pasto ha più fame che pria,"[2]

for the tariff of 1824 did not long satisfy the protectionists. In order to conciliate the demands of the producers and manufacturers of wool it had at the same time raised the duties on

[1] Bishop, vol. ii. p. 292.
[2] "Which after its meal is more hungry than ever."

raw wool and on manufactured goods, thus really affording to these latter a very slight protection. In other industries, however, the vigorous protection had given a stimulus to production, and thus created a lively interior competition which caused a fall in prices. Political disputes were added, which affected the protective question in different manners; but after a long and lively discussion, notwithstanding the energetic opposition of the Southern States, the protectionists triumphed with the tariff of 1828—"the abomination of 1828," as its adversaries called it, which raised duties, bringing them to 50 per cent and still higher.

Then only were the American protectionists satisfied, and there are -some who, like Carey, affirm that the protective system was only then for the first time really adopted in the United States. In reality, the tariff of 1828 marked the culminating point of the first period of protection for American industries, and a reaction was imminent. From the South there arose a growing and threatening clamour of protests and revolt against the system which, it was claimed, only served the interests of one part of the country; on the other hand the Federal revenue was in excess, and showed the necessity of reducing the tariff so as to reduce the revenue, since it was not constitutional to call upon the country to make greater sacrifices than what was necessary for financial requirements. But the protectionists of the North only desired those duties to be reduced which had not a protective aim, whilst the free-traders of the South tried to strike the protective system at its root.

The contest became sharper; the free-trade movement was accentuated. A free-trade convention, in which delegates from fifteen States took part, met at Philadelphia in 1831, and protested against the existing tariff, declaring it " unnecessary, unequal, unjust, oppressive, and as manifestly violating the spirit of the constitution."

President Jackson declared the revision of the tariff requisite, as it pressed too heavily on some articles of necessary consumption, protected some interests too minutely and only locally, and attempted to acclimatise in the country certain manufactures for which it was not yet ready. His voice, however, was not listened to. In the meantime the struggle was threatening to compromise the unity of the country. In South Carolina the agitation against the tariff turned into open revolt, and Congress, moved at last by the perils encountered and by the necessity of terminating the dispute, approved the tariff of 1832, which, still maintaining its protective character, considerably diminished the duties; and afterwards, as this concession was not sufficient to calm the agitation, Congress also approved Clay's compromise Act of 1833, which established a gradual reduction of duties, to take place every two years until 1842, when they would have been reduced to a maximum of 20 per cent.

With this Act, so famous in the history of the American tariff, ended the first period of protectionism; and if the "American system" was not wholly abandoned, as the protectionists claim, it tended to slowly prepare the country for the transit from an energetic protection to a comparative free-trade.

26. The facts which we have collected, and which refer to the period 1816 to 1832, have need of some fuller explanation. The great impulse given to the manufactures by the political events which destroyed commerce from 1808 to 1815, effectively hastened the industrial transformation; and when, at the declaration of peace, this stimulus failed, a serious crisis followed which necessarily demanded energetic measures for the economic salvation of the country. There can be no doubt about the stagnation from which the manufactures suffered during the period 1815-1820, and this explains the adoption of the protective system of 1816. But we must not give to these facts an importance greater than they really possessed. As the events of 1808-1815 hastened the industrial transformation, so the peace and the revival of commerce, with their inevitable injuries to manufactures, hastened the adoption of the protective policy. But both these facts would equally have happened; and, on the other hand, the crisis in the manufactures, if it explains the first tariff in 1816, and perhaps its increase in 1818 (for at that time it would certainly have been possible to establish a higher tariff, which would still have been inferior to the prohibitions and the embargo), it does not explain the protective movement and the successive increases of the tariff in 1824 and 1828.

The whole of the protective movement of this period is, however, made clear to us, as usual, by the analysis of the industrial conditions of the country. The period from 1815 to 1830 in the United States is qualified by Wright as "a period of industrial transition"; this commenced with the introduction of the factory system, and finished when that system was completely established in the great textile industry, and slowly but surely it proceeded to transform the other industries. The machines, essential to the present system of manufacturing, became now an important factor in the industrial problem. The transition was gradual; the greatest progress was made in Massachusetts, in the cotton manufacture, and the new system adopted in this industry spread eventually to the other branches.[1] This period, in fact, was for the United States the period of formation of capitalist industry; the rudiments of it in the preceding years had only been a preparation, hastened by the events of 1808-1815; and now the long-prepared transformation was rapidly completed.

One of the circumstances that greatly aided the cotton manufacture in the critical times of 1815, says Bishop, was the introduction of the power loom;[2] other industries were also stimulated by the continually spreading adoption of the new machines. From 1817 steam was generally used in the cotton mills and in breweries; in 1823 the first railway concession was granted in Pennsylvania, and in 1827 the first railway commenced to work.[3] The patents for new inventions which, as we have seen, averaged 77 per year during the period 1790-1811, gave an annual average of 192 from 1812 to 1817, and in 1830 reached the figure of 544.[4] The development of the capitalist enterprises under the form of companies of capitalists, incorporated or not, for the exercise of industries, was especially considerable, and their importance was an indubitable sign of the solid foundation of capitalism. From 1820 to 1824 in Massachusetts alone the formation of industrial companies with a capital of 6,840,000 dollars was authorised, and this only with regard to incorporated companies.[5] There existed in the State of New York in 1823

[1] *Comparative Wages*, etc., p. 14.   [2] Bishop, vol. ii. p. 213.
[3] Wright, *Comparative Wages*, etc., pp. 16, 17.
[4] Bishop, *passim*.   [5] Wright, p. 17.

206 incorporated manufacturing companies whose capital amounted to 20,350,500 dollars, and there were besides hundreds of companies not incorporated.[1] In 1824 the capital authorised to the incorporated manufacturing companies in eleven States of the Union amounted to over 70,000,000 dollars; at Lowell one manufacture of cotton raised its capital in 1825 to 1,200,000 dollars. In this year the consumption of cotton in American manufactures was nearly 100,000 bales; the number of spindles was 800,000. A third of the cotton manufactures in New England (centre of the cotton industry) and all the newer manufactures had their machinery made after the best English models, and some were improved. The bulk of capital employed in the manufactures of the United States in 1826 was calculated to be 156,500,000 dollars.[2] In 1829, 235 industrial incorporated companies existed in Massachusetts for the production of cottons, wools, iron, glass, copper, linen, etc. The cotton manufacture was the most prosperous, but in many places those of wool, boots, etc., were also prosperous. At Lowell seven cotton mills employed 1200 women. The introduction of machinery gave a great stimulus to most industries; the new system of production exercised an immense and continual influence in the increase of the productive capacity of the workers, and in the diminution of prices of products.[3]

The condition of the two largest manufactures, cotton and wool, towards 1832, is most important. The statistics regarding the manufacture of cotton in twelve States in 1831 gave the following data:—Amount of capital embarked in the factories, 44,914,984 dollars; number of spindles at work, 1,246,503; number of workmen employed, 67,607. American looms, according to Bishop, had almost superseded English ones; and from 1824 cotton manufacturers no longer demanded protection, because they had no need for it.[4] And so, too, the woollen industry had largely developed during the preceding years,[5] and in 1828 it was established on a firm basis; machinery was extensively used, the factories provided with adequate capital, the cost of operations, to believe business

[1] Bishop, vol. ii. p. 283.   [2] *Vide* Bishop, vol. ii. pp. 294, 299, 309, 312.
[3] *Vide* Wright, work mentioned, p. 17.
[4] *Vide* Bishop, vol. ii. pp. 357, 361, etc.   [5] *Vide* Taussig, p. 41.

men, not greater than it was in England, and if Americans had been able to obtain raw materials at the price they cost in England, they would have been able to sell their manufactures at an equally low rate.

In 1832 President Jackson's Message confirmed the exceedingly prosperous condition of agriculture and national manufactures; and even more boldly than he, the Secretary of the Treasury declared that protection could only be transitory and would not exceed a certain limit, with a view solely to guard the general welfare of the country and not special interests. They had now gained, he said, their proposed ends of stimulating American industry, making themselves independent of foreign supplies, counterbalancing the greater abundance of capital and the inferior rate of wages in foreign countries, safeguarding the investments of money in manufactures, and ensuring means for common defence in time of war.

"From the year 1789" (says Carlo Cattaneo, in the admirable work which we have more than once quoted) "a course of forty-three years had marvellously multiplied the wealth of the republic, and had made American industry an object of admiration to the most distant and the most hostile nations; and the plentiful supply of necessaries, together with the increased population, the skilfulness of the artisans, the diffusion of knowledge even among the poorest classes, the lightening of burdens on raw materials and commodities of first necessity, *had by this time removed all inequalities to which native industry had been subject, and consequently, the necessity for protection against foreign competition, which had previously been asserted.* To continue such a favour would be to acknowledge a perpetual obligation to support certain trades, which with the progress of time would go on increasing in force and exigency."[1]

The industrial condition of the United States thus makes perfectly clear to us the reasons for the protective policy adopted between 1816 and 1832, when capitalism was being consolidated. And we are able to associate ourselves, in conclusion, with two observations which we find in Professor Taussig's excellent work, which we have so often quoted. The rising up of a considerable commercial class (in 1808-1816)

[1] *Vide* Cattaneo, *Opere*, .v. p. 105.

whose success largely depended upon the maintenance of protection, brought about with energy in those years by political circumstances, formed the basis of a strong movement in favour of a more decisive limitation of foreign competition,[1] and so protection was introduced. But the first protective movement ended with the year 1832: in the ten years that followed, the strong popular feeling for protection died away, and this is to be explained, says Taussig, by the fact that the cause which had produced this feeling had ceased to exist,—the desire to facilitate the transformation of agricultural into manufacturing industries was no longer expressed, because manufactures had already been adequately developed.[2]

27. The fundamental idea on which the demands of the protectionists and the American protective policy of the 1816-1832 period are based, is that of a temporary protection to enable the new national manufactures to hold their own against the competition of old countries, whose industrial enterprises are well supplied with capital and skilled workmen. When this had been accomplished, the native industries would no longer require artificial aid, they would be self-supporting, and the scheme of protection, having answered its purpose, might be thrown aside.

This is in substance the theory of the protection to "young" industries, which, though especially maintained at this period, is expounded by the principal protectionist writers, and accepted even by other writers. We will stop for a moment and briefly examine the theory in order to confront it with the capitalistic interpretation which we have put upon protection.

We first find attention drawn to the idea of protection for the young industries in Alexander Hamilton's *Report* among the other arguments advanced by him in favour of that policy. It is always hard, says he, to make a start, when we endeavour to rival long-established industries; force of habit and fear of failure render all innovations difficult. The spontaneous birth of new industrial undertakings is not effected without painful labour: sometimes the birth is premature, at other times it is delayed too long. It is necessary

[1] *Vide* work mentioned, p. 17.   [2] *Vide* work mentioned, p. 107.

therefore for the Government to foster the confidence of capitalists and to encourage them in new enterprises.[1]

This theory is, in substance, the basis of the system of Frederick List who, assigning an historical character to protection, claims it as a means of educating the industries of a country during their transition from an agricultural to a manufacturing phase, and to guarantee against loss those who devote their capital, their talents, and their energy, to the foundation of new industries.

John Stuart Mill (to pass to a different order of thinkers) has given, with many reservations, and setting forth with admirable clearness the essential conditions, his adhesion to the theory of the protection of young industries in a famous chapter of his *Principles*, which protectionists have carried in triumph as if it were a standard captured in war. In this portion of his work, after having refuted at considerable length the protective arguments, and exposed the doctrine of free-trade, he states that "the *only case* in which on mere principles of political economy, protecting duties can be defensible is when they are imposed temporarily (especially in a young and rising nation), in hopes of naturalising a foreign industry, in itself perfectly suitable to the circumstances of the country. The superiority of one country over another in a branch of production often arises only from having begun it sooner. There may be no inherent advantage on one part, or disadvantage on the other, but only a present superiority of acquired skill and experience. . . . But it cannot be expected that individuals should, at their own risk, or rather to their certain loss, introduce a new manufacture, and bear the burthen of carrying it on until the producers have been educated up to the level of those with whom the processes are traditional." (It is notable that these last words are almost the identical ones used by Hamilton as well by List). "A protecting duty, continued for a reasonable time, will sometimes be the least inconvenient mode in which the nation can tax itself for the support of such an experiment. But the protection should be confined to cases in which there is good ground of assurance that the industry which it fosters will after a time be able to dispense with it; nor should the domestic producers ever be

[1] *Report on Manufactures*, edition quoted, pp. 42-45.

allowed to expect that it will be continued to them beyond the time necessary for a fair trial of what they are capable of accomplishing. . . . The expenses of production being always greatest at first, it may happen that the home production, though really the most advantageous, may not become so until after a certain duration of pecuniary loss, which it is not to be expected that private speculators should incur in order that their successors may be benefited by their ruin. I have therefore conceded that in a new country, a temporary protecting duty may sometimes be economically defensible; on condition, however, that it be strictly limited in point of time, and provision be made that during the latter part of its existence it be on a gradually decreasing scale."[1]

It will be seen that this theory, so clearly set forth by John Stuart Mill, does not invalidate the theoretical principle of free-trade and the doctrine of comparative cost, which forms the basis of it, the value of which we will point out in its proper place; but it merely constitutes an exception of an historical character, allowing, during a given historical period in the economy of a people, the operation of the law of comparative cost to be temporarily suspended, and substituting for the free action of competition, which is based on the immediate speculative interests of private individuals, a provident collective action, which, keeping in view the future interests of the country, and considering, as it were, the welfare of the child that is to develop into a man, carefully wraps in swaddling clothes the infant, which, if left to itself, would not wax strong in that free condition suitable only for adults.

Nevertheless not even this exception, expounded with so much prudence and so many reservations by John Stuart Mill, has been accepted by a large number of extreme free-traders, who are unwilling to admit a very simple truth, namely, that it is quite impossible that protection, widespread as it is both in theory and practice, should be merely the offspring of diseased imagination and economic error, and have no possible justification; that it should not, in fact, have in it a scintilla of truth! Certainly the difficulty of distinguishing between trades deserving and those undeserving

---

[1] *Principles of Political Economy*, people's edition, London, Longmans, 1891, pp. 556, 557.

support may be admitted, and likewise the yet greater difficulty of throwing off protection, when once it has taken root in a country, and even the efficacy of state aid as an energetic impulse to industrial development may be doubted; but it is beyond the bounds of criticism and borders on the ridiculous to assert, with Amasa Walker, that the existence of a healthy industry must be vigorous from the very beginning; that capital adapts itself easily to experiments and to the initial outlays of such enterprises, that every good and sound industry springs adult and fully armed as another Minerva from the head of Jove.[1]

Quite recently Mr. Francis A. Walker, in an admirable article directed against protection, but replete with robust historical sense,[2] has made honourable amends for the sins of his father . . . Let us not digress, however, but get back to our subject.

At the beginning of the century, and about the period under discussion, there existed in the United States those very conditions which, according to Mill, would justify protection, which was invoked as a prop to new industries. The country was tending to emerge from a purely agricultural state, and factories were everywhere springing up; there was yet wanting, however, that supply of machinery with which England was so richly furnished; nevertheless that industrial transformation which had occurred in England between 1760 and 1780, here, too, was on the eve of accomplishment. The new native industries were undoubtedly in a position of inferiority to those abroad, and with regard to many of them it was indeed merely a question of temporary and accidental inferiority, as, for instance, in the cotton manufactures, which were abundantly supplied with raw material and intelligent artisans, but which lacked machinery and experience, etc.

But the simple theory of the protection of young industries will not alone explain the protective tendency of the period in question; the capitalistic interpretation of protectionism completes, and at the same time makes the movement more clear.

[1] *Vide* A. Walker, *The Science of Wealth*.
[2] "Protection and Protectionists," in *The Quarterly Journal of Economics*, April 1890.

American free-traders make an acute observation on this point. Professor Sumner says that the tariff of 1816 actually carried into effect the proposals made by Dallas, the Secretary of the Treasury, who divided the articles subject to duty into three classes, according as the native supply of them equalled the demand, only partly satisfied it, or failed altogether to meet the requirements; and he proposed graduated duties on all three categories, the heaviest on the first. But, says Professor Sumner, the incongruity of such an idea is manifest. If the object was to foster infant industries, the heaviest duties should evidently have been laid upon articles producible in the country, but which were not in fact produced at all, or only in insufficient quantities; but instead of that, prohibitive import duties were levied on those classes of goods, an adequate supply of which was forthcoming from native sources, whilst merely a revenue tax was laid on articles made at home in limited quantities; and all this in contradiction to the theory maintained.[1] And Professor Ely also says that notwithstanding the fact that protection was claimed for the so-called "infant industries," the real "infant industries" never got any protection at all, and in the tumultuous clamour of special private interests only the powerful succeeded in obtaining Government aid.[2]

The observation is indeed just and acute; all the more so if we reflect that it was precisely Mill's intention to justify protection only in the early stages of a new industry, to encourage "experiments"—nothing more. But the capitalistic interpretation completes and elucidates, as we have said, the theory of "protection to infant industries."

28. By "protection to infant industries" must be understood encouragement to manufactures during their transition from the domestic to the capitalistic phase, and during the consolidation of the latter. We have already shown, in its proper place, how, during the first-named phase, protection would be not merely useless, but even hurtful to the producers and to the entire country. Nor yet at the very outset of capitalistic enterprises is a decided protective policy possible: some encouragement, some assistance, such as that given to particular industries even from colonial times, might indeed

[1] *Vide* work mentioned, p. 37.   [2] Vide *Problems of To-day*, p. 55.

be granted; but broader protection is not possible at this stage. For protection to be established, there must exist a class of capitalists already sufficiently powerful to have made their influence felt, and to induce the country to incur an immediate evil in order to guard their own interests, and perhaps in this way also those of the nation at large. For there can be no doubt that if at the time of its inauguration protection does prove advantageous to the capitalistic manufacturers of a new country in their competition with old-established and flourishing industries (owing to higher prices and lower cost of labour), it is none the less a burden to the country, both on account of the increased cost of living, and as a result of the—at all events temporarily—less productive direction given to manufactures. In order, therefore, to dispose a country to such a sacrifice—even if it may prove advantageous for the future—capitalism must already have acquired a certain weight. That is why we see protection rising up in the United States when the transition-state of their industries had already begun and was hurried on by accidental circumstance; protection, which had long been invoked, only became a reality at the time when capitalistic enterprises were about to complete their transformation, to fully develop and consolidate themselves.

Whether protective duties really bring about the desired results, or whether they do so to a greater or less extent, is another question by no means easy to answer, and that can only be approached by examining each individual case when all the facts are before us; but that we have in this theory the explanation of the first period of American protectionism appears to us evident.

Nor, indeed, can it be said that a coalition of particular interests has weighed, to the detriment of the country, on its general interests. For the establishment of full-grown industries must ensure new sources of wealth; and, even if we look upon protection merely as necessary in certain circumstances for the foundation of capitalistic industries in a new country, it may be observed that this is an inevitable historical phase, that is necessary for the progress of the country, which would in any case have to pass through it at one time or another; so that it is best to make its advent easy. Protection in new countries, when it is directed to the encouragement of such industries as are impeded by artificial difficulties only, occasioned by their development *pari passu* with rivals in old-established countries, may, in certain circumstances, be for a certain length of time not merely necessary and beneficial to a particular class—the capitalists, but it may also be justified by the exigencies of social progress. Be it noted, however, that we say justified, as an historical fact: not that the fact in itself, its *raison d'être*, and its effects are ideally just; indeed, but too often do we find historical necessity and justice in disaccord with one another, and history presents many necessary facts and economic phases that were or are the negation of all social justice. The true reason, therefore, of the rise of protectionism in a new country is to be found in the formation of a class of industrial capitalists, who, as soon as it is in their power to do so, devise means for safeguarding their own interests. The theory of protection to infant industries, allowing such means during a given period in the economic development of a nation, admits that, at such a moment, the measures adopted may satisfy not only the actual needs of the capitalists, but also the future requirements of the country generally. But, this once accepted, in no way obscures the purely class-interest origin of the protective movement.

A defence of the consolidation of capitalistic industry in a new country, which finds itself in rivalry with others better educated to the trades and generally ahead of it, may be demanded for various reasons, some of which have already been put forward.

In the old countries the disappearance of free land determining the value as a function of the rate of profit, and the law of decreasing returns occasioning the diminution of the rate of profit, and the preponderance of the employment of technical capital in production, bring about a sensible lowering of prices in a vast class of commodities that assure to the old nations a decisive triumph in international commerce. Hence there is nothing surprising, says Professor Loria, in the British commercial monopoly, nor in the free-trade theories which have prevailed in England during the last centuries, in opposition to the protective principles ruling in

Germany, America, and generally in countries where the degree of the limitation of soil-production is not so far advanced.[1]

It is necessary, consequently, that in new countries prices should be raised if it is desired that industry should accomplish its capitalistic transformation. But it will be handicapped not only by the low prices of foreign manufactures, but also and chiefly by the high standard of wages resulting from free land: and protection is for this very reason invoked to ensure in these conditions a profit for the capitalists, and thus sustain the industries which depend on them.[2]

As has already been pointed out elsewhere, protective duties, by raising the price of manufactures, increase the difficulties of independent workmen, shackle their free occupations, render harder the cultivation of the unappropriated land, and hence reduce salaries and wages, give rise to the capitalistic profit, and consolidate capitalism.[3]

[1] Vide *Analisi della proprietà capitalista*, vol. i. pp. 128, 129.
[2] See Loria, *Analisi*, vol. ii. p. 190.
[3] See Ricca Salerno, "Protezionismo e libero scambio nei paesi vecchi e nuovi," in the *Giornale degli Economisti*, April and May 1891, Rome. Professor Loria and Professor Ricca Salerno hold, on this point, different views. According to the latter, protection serves to prevent the rise of wages, or even to occasion a reduction, and hence tends to the accumulation of money in the hands of capitalists. Loria, on the contrary, maintains that protection effectually limits both production and the increment of accumulation, which causes the rise of wages; and in this way aids indirectly in keeping up profits. For our part, we hardly dare to express an opinion in so grave an argument when conflicting views are set forth with such acumen and so much learning by our two distinguished authorities. If, however, we might venture a remark upon the subject, it would be that in both views there appears to us to be some truth, but not the whole of the truth. We should modify Ricca's statement by observing that during the first period of capitalism protection does not raise profits, but rather paves the way for them under the new industrial *régime* that is in course of evolution, and hence favours the development and the consolidation of capitalism. And in this economic phase, protection may bring about this result, either by raising prices, or else by lowering at the same time the condition of workmen, excluding them from the free land and consequently forcing them to labour for hire, or else by reducing wages. Loria's theory, on the other hand, seems to have some truth, inasmuch as it serves to explain (contrary indeed to the same author's ideas) another fact. In the later development of capitalism, when it is worried and undone by the immoderate competition of investments, protection, by means of the fetters which it imposes, the aid it renders to monopolies, and the limitation of production, may prop up the capitalist interests and prevent the fall of profits. And this may perhaps throw some light on the actual revival of protection both in Europe and in America. But, as we have pointed out, this interpretation is at variance with

In this interpretation of the first period of American protectionism we find a confirmation in the argument maintained by Carey in his work, *The Past, the Present, and the Future*.[1] In it the author repeatedly deplores the fact that the American people effect settlements in the far West to cultivate lands distant from markets and by no means fertile, rather than turn to account, by disforesting, draining, and tilling them, the far richer soil in the northern valleys of the State of New York, and many other fertile spots comparatively close at hand in the old States. Instead of the cultivation in those poor and distant regions of grain for exportation, he would like to see husbandry applied to the lands which were nearer and more fertile, although requiring the expenditure of greater labour and capital, so that cattle, dairy produce, and timber, might be obtained from them for domestic consumption; a state of things which would be possible only when the development of industrial manufactures had created a home market for such products.

If you ask the planter, says Carey, why he does not disforest the rich soil which is close to the poor ground he is now cultivating, his answer will be that he has offered 20 dollars an acre to any one who will fell the trees, but in vain; no one cares for the work; no one wants timber; his neighbours have gone far away to settle in sterile regions. If now we inquire into the true significance of Carey's words, we find that, as a matter of fact, he deplores that labourers should settle down on free distant lands requiring but the rudest agriculture and little capital; he deplores the fewness of wage-earners and the high standard of wages; he would like to see the rich, less remote districts put under cultivation (although they need for disencumbering and draining the soil

Loria's own statement (which, all the same, is not very accurately borne out by facts) that with the decreasing productiveness of the soil, free-trade becomes more and more general, since the profit, which has now become automatic, no longer need ensure its own continuance by an artificial limitation of production. On this point, however, we propose to dwell at greater length at its proper place (vide *Analisi*, vol. i. 605, 606; and the last pages of Ricca's article which we have quoted).

[1] *Vide* the second edition, London, Trübner, 1856. The first edition appeared in 1848, when the author's conversion from free-trade to protective principles was not yet quite complete; and this work bears witness to the opposite tendencies which were at work in him.

the expenditure of a large amount of capital), in order to create an agricultural and industrial wage-earning class. Carey, therefore, really invokes a reaction against the influence of free land in favour of capitalism, since the cultivation of lands which are more fertile, but at the same time more difficult, and which require considerable capital and the establishment of manufactures, brings about the necessity for the capitalist and the wage-earner—a necessity which does not exist when an easily tilled soil is cultivated by independent labourers. Hence it is the institution of capitalism in agriculture and manufactures that Carey expects from protectionism. And this is even more clearly set forth in other parts of this author's work. In fact, when drawing a picture further on of the happy state of things when, the richer lands having been cultivated and factories built close to them, producers and consumers shall find themselves near one another, he says : new and better ground would be occupied, the remuneration of labour would rise, and the land would be divided into smaller allotments, and in course of time the planter would become the landlord of well-to-do tenants cultivating the soil on their own account, and the slaves would become free men and their owners rich and prosperous. From all of which it is evident that his ideal was the substitution, in the southern States, of relations between wealthy proprietors and hired workmen, in place of those between masters and slaves.

Hence we conclude (and many other passages might be quoted in support of our argument) that Carey's conception of protection is in fact a capitalistic one ; and that he desires it with a view to the establishment of capitalistic industries, and to react against the influence of free land, which tends to disperse labourers and to make the existence of a class of hired workmen difficult or impossible.

Now such a thesis and such ideas might have passed muster in a writer of the colonial period or first ten years of the century, but they appear altogether out of place in Carey's mouth. We have seen how difficult it was, during the preceding period to find hired workmen, and how the factory system was not possible; since then (1808 to 1832) it had effectively risen and consolidated itself ; yet even in these years difficulties were encountered of the kind to which we have alluded above, since we saw that, in 1819, Bishop noted that in consequence of the crisis manufacturers and workmen were abandoning the factories in great numbers in order to take up agriculture. But at the end of this epoch, and all the more so at the time when Carey was writing, the state of affairs had altered. In several States, and in the New England States particularly, the industrial transformation was complete, and capitalistic industries had been established on a sound basis; and this is admitted by the last-named writer, who adds that the machinery in the American factories was even better than that in England. The largely increased population, and the ever-growing difficulty of cultivating the soil without adequate capital, brought to the factories a large contingent of hired labourers. On the other hand, the southern States ranged themselves against protection: their economy, founded on slavery, was not adapted to an industrial development, whilst protective duties, by enhancing the price of the provisions consumed by the slaves, adversely affected their owners.[1] Thus the interests of the agricultural capitalists and those of the manufacturing capitalists were in opposition.

Carey wished to see the industrial transformation effected in all the States, and the consumer placed everywhere by the side of the producer; and protection would have served to abolish slavery. But, putting on one side the possibility of giving an identical industrial constitution to the most diverse regions, and some of them particularly well adapted to agriculture, protection, of which the most advanced States were now in no need, would in the other States necessarily replace the slavery of the blacks by the servitude (for hired services are often no better than servitude) of white men.[2]

---

[1] *Vide* Ricca Salerno, article quoted.
[2] All this will perhaps explain why, in Hamilton's time and also later, the proposals to encourage manufactures by means of premiums, bounties, or exemption from taxes were not accepted. It has been seen how much importance Hamilton gave to the system of bounties. And Prof. Ely (*Problems of To-day*, pp. 56, 57) also observes how advantageously an exemption from taxes might have been substituted for import-duties. But neither of these systems of encouragement would have been able to influence capitalistic industries in the recondite way we have demonstrated; and which was indeed perhaps unconsciously what the capitalists wanted.

But that of which only a glimpse had been caught by Carey (whose writings, as we shall note, were an anachronism) was clearly seen by Edward Gibbon Wakefield, the theorist of systematic colonisation, who intended to build capitalism on the artificial basis of the wages system in the new countries.

And Wakefield's observations serve to explain the acquiescence of the agricultural States in the *régime* of protection, as vigorously applied from 1816 to 1832, to give impulse principally to the industrial interests.

The protective policy, observed Wakefield in 1834, produces a great advantage in the United States, namely, the concentration of the population. Without the manufactures maintained by protection, the population would not be so concentrated in towns, and it would be a scattered agricultural population without association of labour: it would have no rational and productive agriculture effected by the application of capital and hired labour, but a dispersed agriculture, divided into small farms far from each other, and but slightly productive, such as we see in the American States where there is no slavery.

Slavery in the southern States is, like the tariff in the northern States, an expedient for neutralising the dispersion of the population. The protective tariff is useful to the American people, and they will maintain it until the price of the land has considerably risen through the increase of the population in the course of a century, or perhaps sooner, if the legislature augments the price of the concessions of free land.

If the price of the new land were such that free labour was always obtainable for the combination in agriculture (*i.e.* hired labour), then, with a better produce obtained from capital and labour, with increased profit and higher wages, the Americans would be able to produce corn at a lower price than at present, and they would be able to relinquish protection.[1]

29. But Wakefield had not seen everything. Although he penetrated deeply into the relations between protection, land policy, and slavery—all instruments of the capitalist domination—and demanded laws to augment the price of the concession of free land, he did not perceive that that which he asked for had happened a long time ago, and not only that

[1] Wakefield, *England and America*, New York, Harper, 1834, pp. 227-231.

the price of land had been augmented, but labourers were completely excluded from the land sold in enormous tracts to speculators only.

The land policy of the United States is in perfect accordance indeed with their commercial policy. The stress laid by Gallatin on the natural difficulties which the development of manufactures encountered owing to the abundance of land available for cultivation and on the attractions of agriculture (see *supra*, p. 151), and Carey's disapproval of the diffusion of the population over the far West, find a counterpart in the obstacles that for so long a while were placed by American land legislation in the way of the colonisation of the United States by independent labourers. Even during the confederation public lands had only been sold in a few vast concessions, in such a manner as to favour large speculative enterprises, and to discourage individual colonists. This was recognised by Congress in 1789, without, however, any remedy being approved; as it was feared that by offering the public lands on too favourable terms, emigration to the distant regions would be too freely stimulated, and the eastern States would be deserted: that is to say it was feared to open more widely the way of independence to the scant labourers, whose reluctance to work for wages constituted the chief difficulty in the development of manufactures. Alexander Hamilton, the prophet of American protection and capitalism, in 1790, maintaining the expediency of satisfying the requirements of three classes of purchasers—capitalists who would buy lands for the purpose of re-selling them, associations of persons who wished to colonise them, and single individuals or families desirous of emigrating to the West—proposed that the public lands should be sold in allotments of any extent, at the price of thirty cents per acre, credit being allowed to purchasers of ten square miles at least. This suggestion was not approved at that time; but a little later on, in 1796, it was decided that the lands should be sold by auction in lots of not less than *nine square miles*, and (no doubt for financial reasons, as the enormous size of the lots would in any case bar out the labourers), at the price of not less than two dollars per acre, and then leave was given to defer payment for long periods so as to favour speculation all the more.

Thus, at an epoch when it was not yet possible, as we have seen, to initiate a protective policy which would only have made for the interests of too small a class of capitalists, a land policy was nevertheless introduced, which favoured all the interests of the capitalists, whether manufacturers—by excluding labourers from the soil, and compelling them to work for wages—or agriculturists, by leaving the field open to speculative undertaking on a large scale exclusively.

Labourers were absolutely prevented from acquiring public lands; whilst hundreds of thousands of acres in separate lots became the property of capitalists or corporations, who either kept them for themselves, constituting enormous estates, or else re-sold them with great profits, to the colonists. Thus, with the full approval of Congress, says Sering, the public lands were handed over to the speculators.

Later on, when industrial capitalism, in its onward course at the beginning of the present century, had made its influence felt, and had obtained protective tariffs, the exclusion of labourers from the soil, which tallied so well with the interests of capitalists, was none the less maintained; for the laws of 1796 were substantially unrepealed. In vain did the labourers appeal to Congress in 1814, declaring that thousands of poor and industrious citizens were in want of land and were unable to acquire it, and demanding that it should be sold to them in allotments of 160 acres at the price of $12\frac{1}{2}$ cents per acre. The land was denied to them, whilst the great sales, made on credit to speculators, were continued!

It was not till 1830, and that at a time when capitalism had securely established itself upon the foundations of the wage system, that the first reform was effected; and then only as a provisional measure. It was made permanent in 1842, and granted the right of pre-emption for a tract of ground not exceeding 160 acres to colonists who had squatted far away upon waste lands, and had cultivated them in spite of the laws and repeated decrees of Congress: so great was the earth-hunger in them!

But after all the concession was insignificant; it did not throw open new regions to immigrants, but merely regulated the condition of those who had illegally occupied the land which it had been intended to reserve only for speculators.

Soon after 1830, when industrial capitalism was quite consolidated, the excesses of protectionism, assailed by the agricultural interests, were at length restrained, and finally, as we shall see, a *régime* of relative free-trade followed. But the reforms of the land-laws, which all the capitalistic interests agreed in demanding, had to be waited for, for a long time yet—till, in fact, the Homestead Law of 1862.

For when industrial capitalism no longer needed support either from tariffs or from land laws, the interests of the landed capitalists placed them in opposition to every kind of reform; and especially was this the case with regard to the free-traders and slave-owners of the south, who strove to maintain the land-monopoly which was indispensable for securing the immense extension of the possessions required by their system of despoiling culture.[1]

30. Finally, as the last investigation regarding the period under discussion, it may be asked what influence the duties exacted between 1816 and 1832 had on the protected manufactures. This is indeed an investigation which we propose to leave aside, or only to touch on incidentally, as we are content in this work to examine specially the causes which led to the adoption of the protective system and the relations between this system and the condition of the national manufactures. And the investigation in question would be, moreover, one of exceeding difficulty in consequence of the great complexity of the phenomenon, the effects of which it is next to impossible to isolate with any certainty from other facts produced by different causes; and to us the difficulties would be multiplied by the distance of time and space.

Be it noted, however, that the greater number of writers participate in one of the conflicting theories, and either attribute all the industrial progress to protection, and all the crises and troubles to its not having been adopted or having been abandoned, or else *vice versa.* To give an example, List says that up to the year 1837 the manufactures of the United States had largely developed, *in spite of the reductions effected in the* 1828 *tariff;* whilst, on the other hand, Sumner

---

[1] *Vide* Max Sering, *Die landwirthschaftliche Konkurrenz Nordamerikas in Gegenwart und Zukunft,* Leipzig, Dunker und Humblot, 1887, pp. 111-115; and Loria's *Analisi,* vol. ii. pp. 251-252.

maintains that from the war with Great Britain up to 1837 America enjoyed great prosperity, *in spite of protection;* and that the injuries which it did were not felt by the people, since the protective policy rather prevented a state of greater well-being than actually created indigence, the prosperity of the country being so great that all that protection could do was to diminish but not arrest it! And any number of such examples might be adduced.

On this point Professor Taussig's remarkable work, which is ably written in a calm and objective spirit, deserves frequent quotation; the results of his researches, however, are not altogether encouraging, since the conclusions which he draws are few and far between, and by no means positive. For all that, it may not be inopportune to briefly recapitulate them.

He investigates the effects of the tariff, from 1816 to 1832, upon the three principal manufactures—cotton, wool, and iron—which during that period were supposed to be strongly protected by import duties.[1]

The difficulties which, at the beginning of the century, were experienced by the cotton manufacturers, were, says Taussig, to a large extent artificial; but the development of this industry would in any case have been very slow—in the then condition of commerce and of the country generally— had it not been for those particular circumstances which affected it so favourably from 1808 to 1815. When peace was signed in 1815, the cotton industry was fully developed and provided with new machinery. The tariff of 1816, which put a duty of 25 per cent upon cotton goods, with a minimum by which woollens worth less than 25 cents a yard were taxed as though valued at 25 cents, was of little effect at first, because the value of the greater part of these goods was above the limit; but from 1819, the price of cotton goods having constantly fallen, the minimum duty proportionately rose, and in a few years it was felt to be positively prohibitive as far as the importation of the coarser kinds of stuffs was concerned—and the products of the American looms were chiefly of this nature. According to Taussig, the period of "youth" during which protection would have been

[1] Vide *The Tariff History,* etc., "Protection to Young Industries," chaps. iii., iv., v., vi.

useful and even necessary. for the American cotton manufactures was from 1808 to 1815: and it was precisely at this epoch, without there being any need for protective duties, that fortunately a strong system of protection was in force. Henceforth,.protection would no longer have been strictly necessary: and it was certainly far inferior to that which the events of the preceding years had furnished; but it was none the less useful to the cotton industry in the critical condition in which it was placed for a few years. The tariff of 1816, says our author, may be considered—so far as the manufacture of cotton is concerned—as a judicious application of the principle of protection to infant industries. But about the year 1824 the cotton industry had taken firm root in the United States, and stood in no need of further encouragement; so that all the later tariffs were useless, and, so far as they produced any effect, hurtful. The woollen manufactures experienced pretty much the same vicissitudes as the cotton trade; the really effectual protection was that given by the events of 1808-1815; they breathed the spirit of vitality into an industry which had hitherto existed merely as a domestic production. The years that followed 1815 were for the woollen, as well as for the cotton manufacture, a period of difficulty; the tariffs of 1815 and of 1824 protected it, but far more moderately than they did the cotton manufacture, either because no minimum was applied, or because it being at the same time desired to encourage the production of wool, duties were placed on the raw material, the importation of which was necessary for the manufacturers; so that the efficacy of the duties on manufactured articles was partly paralysed by those on raw material. Anyhow these duties fostered the growth of the woollen industries; although even on this point the writer somewhat hesitatingly adds that possibly there was no need for them, as the industries in question were already adult. But in 1828 the manufacture of wool had quite passed out of the period of youth, machinery was largely employed, and the undertakings well supplied with capital; in fact, this industry was well able to take care of itself, and the increased protection of 1828 was by no means justified.

Finally, regarding the production of iron, Taussig shows that the strong and continuous protection, which varied from

40 to 100 per cent ad valorem, from 1816 to 1832, did not enable this industry to consolidate itself. so as to be in a condition to overcome foreign competition by producing goods as cheap, if not cheaper; but it contributed to make such a transformation unnecessary, rather than to favour it. It cannot be said that the obstacles to the progress of this industry were principally due to protective duties, since its inferiority compared to foreign rivals was chiefly owing to its not being able to make use of coke in the foundries on account of the distance of the bituminous coal-fields from the manufacturing centres, and the difficulty of transport. But the fact remains that, whilst in other industrial countries, and especially in England, a complete revolution had for some time been effected in this trade, the United States continued to use charcoal in their foundries; and the new technical processes which transformed that production were not adopted till the years 1830-1840, when the import duties had reached their lowest point. So that it may, at all events, be asserted that the influence of protection was not felt in this industry.

The final conclusion to which Taussig arrives regarding the effects of protection during the 1816-1832 period, is that, although all the circumstances were then supposed to be favourable to protection of "infant industries"—for the country was young and but little developed, in a phase of transition from a purely agricultural condition to one of greater industrial complexity, combined with important technical changes which always render the establishment of new industries more difficult—yet, in spite of all this, little or nothing was gained by the protection which the United States enforced during this period. And the reason of this was because the great aptitude of the American people for mechanical pursuits on the one hand, and on the other the excessive protection afforded by the commercial restrictions during the exceptional period from 1808 to 1815, gave such an impulse to manufactures that they stood in need of no further protection, nor did they reap any advantages from it. Finally, as regards the production of raw iron and other similar industries, protection failed in its object, as their development was not effected till a much later epoch.

We do not wish, however, to attribute a greater weight to

Taussig's opinions than he does himself. There is no more difficult or complex analysis than that of the effects of protective duties; and we must not lay too much stress on the results which they seem to furnish; and that is the very reason why we have restricted our investigation to that of the causes of protection. And further on, Taussig, after a long and minute study, based closely upon facts and free from all theoretical preconception, ends with the following frank but melancholy confession:

"It is very doubtful whether, with the defective information at our disposal, we can learn much as to the effect on the prosperity of the country of the whole series of Tariff Acts. Probably we can reach conclusions of any value only on certain limited topics, such as the effects of protection to young industries during this time; as to the general effect of the protective measures, we must rely on deduction from general principles."[1]

And, in truth, these conclusions are discouraging, so much so as to raise doubts in the minds of all who have not, as we have, a firm and entire belief in the efficacy of the inductive method applied to the study of economic questions. But where shall we find other studies of the effects of these tariffs, written objectively and with the same strict impartiality and freedom from all scholastic prejudice, that are the distinguishing traits of Taussig's invaluable book? We certainly do not pretend to know all that has been written on the subject, but we feel sure that there are not many works of such value.

To be so quickly disconcerted, however, and to say, as Taussig does, that for general results one must trust entirely to deductions, is indeed to show small confidence in the method adopted, and too great impatience to arrive at conclusions. And here a happy simile of H. C. Adams occurs to us. Replying to some one, who was quoting instances of the incapacity and corruption which so often mark American administrations, as an argument against state interference, Adams observed that American free-traders had treated the state as the old physicians used to treat their patients, prescribing copious blood-letting as a cure for every infirmity: what wonder, therefore, if the organism of the state has been

[1] *Vide* work mentioned, p. 108.

enfeebled?[1] Thus, in political economy, an exaggerated use is made of the deductive method; the inductive method being seldom and wrongly applied, and nearly always with prejudice, and in confirmation of the results of theoretical investigations. And then it is complained that the outcome is barren!

We certainly do not maintain that the inductive method will completely solve every question, nor yet the one under discussion: we merely remark that it would not be wise to reject it only on account of the difficulties it presents, and to trust entirely to deductions; which, taken alone, in the great question of international exchanges, point to the conclusion of absolute free-trade and a thorough condemnation of protection. Now the contrast between this theoretical, though vigorously logical, conclusion, and the reality of things, which is so strongly permeated by protectionism, is too glaring; and, as Ricca Salerno has well observed, it is not reasonable to believe that a system which has lasted so long a time, and which is constantly being revived in different places and periods, should be altogether founded on error; but we must rather infer that, in the historical development of society, there are causes which determine its existence.[2]

[1] See H. C. Adams, *Relation of the State to Industrial Action*, p. 65, Baltimore, Am. Ec. Ass. 1887.
[2] Vide *Protez. e lib. scambio*, etc., art. quoted.

CHAPTER V

THE CONSOLIDATION OF AMERICAN INDUSTRY AND FREE-TRADE

(FROM 1833 TO 1861)

31. The history of the American tariff policy during this period may be summed up in a few words. Whether Clay's " Compromise Act," brought about by the state of affairs to which we have alluded in the preceding chapter, was in reality a transaction between free-traders and protectionists, and between the conflicting tendencies and interests of the different States, as is generally supposed to be the case, or whether it was merely, as Sumner maintains,[1] the result of a political makeshift in which neither public nor private interests had any consideration, it undoubtedly effected a gradual lowering of the protective tariff, which continued uninterruptedly for ten years, until, finally, in 1842, it brought the duties down to a comparatively moderate level. And even if it cannot be said, with Bishop,[2] that this Act practically abandoned the system of favouring native industries, it was none the less a fact that, besides the immediate reduction of many duties, it was decreed that all of them should be progressively lowered in such a way that in 1842 not one of them should exceed 20 per cent *ad valorem;* which, coupled with the yet more significant fact that the provisions of the " Compromise Act " were effectively applied during the whole decennial period, clearly indicate that the American tariff policy had taken a new direction; that there was a tendency to substitute little by little—so as not to cause too violent a shock to various interests—measures of relative free-trade, for

[1] *Vide* Sumner, work mentioned, p. 51.   [2] *Vide* Bishop, vol. ii. p. 375.

the so-called "American system"; and that the country adapted itself with good grace to the new policy which was being gradually applied.

In 1842 this free-trade movement was abruptly interrupted, and the tariff enforced that year, by lessening the number of commodities exempt from duty, and raising the duties to an average of 33 per cent, restored the "American system." It is essential, however, to note that although protection was at that time advocated by the manufacturers of the north, it was not popular among the people at large, to whom the principle did not seem so attractive as from 1824-1832;[1] and this is borne out by the fact that this return to protection was of very short duration—lasting during one legislature only—and immediately afterwards, in 1846, the movement initiated by the "Compromise Act" redoubled in vigour, notably in 1857, and continued till the outbreak of the Civil War.

Taussig[2] disputes the statement that the 1846 tariff was effectually an application of free-trade, and after a careful analysis arrives at the conclusion that it was merely moderate protection; but the fact remains that, on the whole, its duties amounted on an average to about 24 per cent ad valorem,[3] a level not much above that of the minimum reached in 1842; and that to find in the American tariffs duties below this limit—except in the last named year—it would be necessary to go back to the years before 1816, that is to say, to a period anterior to capitalism and the "American system."

Not without significance, on the other hand, is the way in which the tariff of 1846 was considered by those who brought it forward; it having been introduced by the then president and secretary of the Treasury as a measure that substituted simple fiscal taxation for the protective duties; which was equivalent to saying that the idea of abandoning protection was then popular, if presidents and ministers would only run the risk of proclaiming it openly.[4] Sumner, too,[5] admits that the period from 1846 to 1860 was one of relative

---

[1] Taussig, p. 113.   [2] Ibid. p. 114.   [3] Bishop, p. 431.
[4] Ibid. passage quoted, and also W. C. Ford, "Tariff of the United States," in Lalor's Cyclopædia.
[5] Work mentioned, p. 55.

free-trade, that the tariff of 1846 was a low one, that its protective scope was limited, and that it was called "a revenue tariff with incidental protection." It remained in force, without giving rise to much opposition, up to 1856, when, on account of the superabundance of the revenue, it was proposed, with a financial view especially, to reduce the duties still further, and this was carried out in 1857, in spite of some protests and the indifference of the public, who took little or no interest in the matter; whilst the manufacturers of the east seemed more inclined to favour the free importation of raw materials than to claim increased duties upon manufactured articles. "It is worthy of notice that this Act (of 1857) was attended with very little public discussion, and that the manufacturing interests raised no objection. The country had, in short, become accustomed to the era of comparatively low duties, and the matter seemed to have disappeared from the political arena."[1]

The tariff of 1857, which effectually paved the way for free-trade, and that even Cairnes describes without circumlocution as a free-trade measure,[2] lasted till 1861; the country was satisfied with it, and agitation for protection had almost ceased,[3] when overshadowed by other issues and especially by the slavery struggle, that terrible hurricane, the Civil War, bursting upon the country, convulsed its economic and financial life and completely changed for a long time the basis of the tariff question.

To sum up, the "American system," spontaneously evolved between 1807 and 1816, and since then successively strengthened by high tariffs, from 1816 to 1832, had since the year 1833 been practically abandoned, and thus, on the whole, it enjoyed but a brief existence, corresponding to the period of the foundation of the American factory system. And the

[1] Vide R. Mayo Smith and E. R. A. Seligman, "The Commercial Policy of the United States of America, 1860-1890," in the volume, Die Handelspolitik, etc., published by the Verein für Social Politik, Leipzig, 1892, p. 10; and Bishop, volume quoted, p. 432.

[2] This most important fact is also stated by Wells, who says that from 1850 to 1860 the question of protection or free-trade was altogether left aside, and excited no interest whatever in the country. Vide Cobden Club Essays, 2nd series, 1871-1872. Taussig, too, states that the reduction of 1857 had been approved of by many business men.

[3] Taussig, work quoted.

epoch of nearly thirty years, from 1833 to 1860, if it may not be called an era of free-trade, marks at all events the fall of a policy of decided protection, and the adoption of a system of gradual preparation, which was only momentarily interrupted, for a *régime* of complete commercial freedom.

And this will become clear—in the absence of more accurate data regarding the average *ad valorem* duties (which are always most difficult to extract from tariff-returns having duties of various kinds, chiefly specific)—by dividing, for each separate year, the total of the imports on which duties have been levied, by the figure of the corresponding annual revenue of the custom-house.

In fact, according to these data (as we have deduced them from the Statistical Abstract of the United States), whilst the average of the tariff in the eleven years from 1821 to 1831 had been 38·68 per cent *ad valorem* on all duty-paying goods, in the following eleven years (1832-1842) it had descended to 31·43 per cent; and, leaving out of consideration the four years 1843-1846, during which, as we have said, there was a short protective reaction, the reduction in duties seems to have progressed uninterruptedly in the following years till 1861; the average duty during these fifteen years having been 24·27 per cent, with a minimum of 18·84 per cent in 1861.

32. It is now time to inquire into the causes of the great change introduced into the American tariff policy during the thirty years under consideration. Following the system adopted in our researches, we shall prepare the way by examining the economic and industrial conditions of the country during this period. In spite of the fact that during these years the United States passed through two grave crises —and the one of 1837 and the following years was of no ordinary severity—on the whole the period under consideration may be looked upon as one of prosperity. The great industries, the foundations of which had been so laboriously laid in the preceding period, were now extending their operations by leaps and bounds; and the ever-increasing spread of machinery, the adaptation of natural products to the wants of man, the multiplication of new inventions for turning all these products to account, these were the chief characteristics

of the new industrial era, characteristics which have set a stamp upon the industry of the present day.[1]

One proof of this great fact, among the many that might be quoted, is the gradual increase in the number of industrial patents granted. These, as we have already seen, averaged 77 per annum from 1790 to 1811, and 192 from 1812 to 1817; from 1840 to 1850 the annual average had risen to 646; from 1850 to 1860, to 2225; and to quote a few figures more particularly, there were 435 patents issued in 1837, 473 in 1840, 602 in 1850, and 4819 in 1860.[2]

Even at the beginning of this period signs were not wanting, not merely of a great industrial development, but of a certain national economic independence: the country gave indications of being almost self-sufficing. In 1834 the total value of all commodities manufactured annually in the United States was calculated at 325 millions of dollars; whilst that of foreign produce consumed in the country—tea, wines, coffee, and spices, which the United States do not produce, being deducted—amounted to less than 50 millions of dollars.[3] In 1836 it was reckoned that the capital employed in the United States in the production of cotton was 800 million dollars, and that engaged in its manufacture 80 million dollars. There were about 1,750,000 spindles at work, and in each factory recently established the average number of spindles was from 5000 to 6000, and the capital sunk in each undertaking varied from 140,000 to 200,000 dollars.[4]

This development of the cotton manufacture was no doubt far inferior to that of England, where twice as much capital was employed, and where steam machinery was much more largely utilised; but, considering the different circumstances, the development of the industry in America is a very notable fact.

But in order justly to appreciate the state of affairs, the opinions of contemporaries are even more important than statistics. Bishop, an ardent protectionist, opens the chapter of his work which deals with the period from 1840 to 1850, saying: "We are now approaching a period when the

[1] Wright, *Comparative Wages*, etc., p. 23. [2] *Vide* Bishop, *passim*.
[3] *Ibid*. vol. ii. 383. [4] *Ibid*. vol. ii. pp. 398-401.

manufacturing industry of the country, established upon a solid and permanent foundation, had attained such wonderful expansion that it is no longer possible to trace its progress in detailed statements or isolated facts. In spite of temporary checks and adverse litigation, the Anglo-Saxon widened the circle of his enterprises, until the sound of his hammers rung throughout the whole extent of the populated portion of the republic." [1]

And farther on—still speaking of 1840, that is of a time when duties were exceedingly low, and were hardly in fact protective—the author adds that although the English competition with its increased production and consequently reduced prices was no doubt severely felt by American industry, which was handicapped by high salaries and interest, nevertheless, in spite of the fact that many manufacturers were crushed by it, the prompt adoption of all the new industrial methods had placed American manufacturers in a position to cope with it.[2] The advance made by trade generally was most remarkable: there were many new industries that had by this time obtained a firm hold on the favour of the public; machinery was employed more and more; and the notable development of means of transport came to the assistance of many, enabling them to avail themselves largely of the vast mineral resources of the land.[3] Many were the inventions made during these ten years, among them two of the greatest of the century—the sewing-machine and the electric telegraph.

No less startling appears the progress and prosperity of the country if we pass on to the following decennial period, 1850-1860. Statistics of American manufactures in 1850 (we are still quoting Bishop) reveal the astonishing fact that the capital employed in the national industries exceeded 550 million dollars, and that the annual product was valued at 1019 millions. Ten years later on the produce of American manufactures had increased by 86 per cent, having in 1860 reached the figure of 1900 million dollars.[4] At the last-named epoch, the industrial development of the United States had assumed colossal proportions; it was fed by innumerable manufactures, fostered by countless inventions

[1] Bishop, vol. ii. p. 419.   [2] *Ibid.* p. 423.
[3] *Ibid.* pp. 425-427.   [4] *Ibid.* pp. 452-457.

and machines of all kinds, and the historian of the American manufactures attributes this extraordinary development to the great natural resources of the land for raising the necessaries of life and raw materials; to the abundance of hydraulic forces; to the easy communications in the interior of the country; to the large growth of capital, although this was less rapid than in other countries; to the immigration from abroad; and above all to the amount of liberty enjoyed by labour and capital in the American republic.

And it is well—if it be only for the sake of confirming it—to compare with this hymn of praise of American industrial progress sung by Bishop, the statements made by free-traders; they likewise dwell upon the well-being and prosperity of the United States from 1850 to 1860, and attribute it to the effect of the low tariff. Wells tells us that during those ten years, and especially during the last three of them, the progress in every branch of industry and commerce was greater than in any similar period of subsequent date; that the wealth of the nation increased 126 per cent; that comfort was general, and pauperism almost unknown.[1] And Sumner, too, declares that the years 1846 to 1860 were, in the United States, years of great and solid prosperity, that all industries made continuous and genuine progress, without however, sudden and exorbitant profits; that the shipping rapidly increased; that the production of cotton augmented; everything being stimulated by the great discoveries of gold in California, which gave a wonderful impulse to the national prosperity; so that industrially and economically, the period from the Mexican War to the Civil War was for the country a golden age.[2] We have said that during these years there were two crises: and especially serious was the one in 1837, chiefly caused by the abuse of credit, and its effects were felt for several years; there being a general depression of trade which lasted till 1842. The crisis of 1857 was of shorter duration. It, too, was occasioned by over-speculation and by bank operations; but all evil effects had disappeared within a twelvemonth.

33. And now the explanation of the American tariff

[1] Vide *Cobden Club Essays.*
[2] *History of Protection in the U.S.*, p. 55.

policy during this period does not appear to us to be difficult. To make it all the more clear, however, a few remarks may not be out of place. In studying this question, we repeat, it has not been our design to accurately weigh the effects of protective policy; we are chiefly concerned in indicating its determining causes, and in searching in the various historical periods for that rationality which surely must be found in it, since the permanence and immense importance which have accrued to the protective system absolutely forbid us to set it down as a wholly unreasonable or delusive institution.

It is essential, however, to note the distinction between the determining causes, the *raison d'être*, and the effects which may result from the system: for it may be perfectly rational and easily understood, and yet by no means bring about the state of things which had been hoped for; or the results may merely benefit the few persons or classes who have known how to subordinate the general welfare to their own interests. We think it necessary to state this in order to make it clear that, in treating of protection, it is by no means our intention either to attack or defend it, or even justify its existence. Had this been the object of our investigation, it would have been necessary to collect other materials. All we desire to do is to explain the causes, the due appreciation of which is necessary for further researches. But to return to our argument.

With regard to the justification of protection, it seems to us best, with a view to making ourselves perfectly intelligible, to make a few distinctions.

We do not contest the position assumed by free-traders on the ground of abstract theory; protection is undoubtedly an obstacle to production, it directs the commercial activity of a country into less productive channels, and hence necessarily occasions a diminution in its general wealth.

But, before all, we must discriminate between the general welfare of the country and the particular interests of individual capitalists, and the capitalist class as a whole.

If the general welfare of the country be considered, then the principle of free-trade is unassailable, and the exception that we made in favour of protecting young industries and aiding the establishment of capitalistic industries is, as a matter of fact, hardly an exception to the rule, since, as we have pointed out, it is only a question of a providential act which can be done by the collective wisdom of the nation, sacrificing the general interests of the time being for those of the future.

But if the particular interests of the capitalist manufacturers be considered, then the matter may assume a different aspect, and the exceptions become more frequent. It may be observed, it is true, that it is also to the interest of the capitalists to embark their money and energy in undertakings which, in the actual circumstances of the country, will prove the most productive; and that it is difficult to understand what interest they can have in embarking on less remunerative enterprises which need the support — always uncertain in duration and in its effects — of the state. And it may also be asked, what are the beneficial effects of protection where it is indiscriminately granted to all?

But this abstract reasoning, though essentially sound, loses much of its force when carried into the domain of practical affairs. Indeed, absolutely universal protection is an impossibility, hence it is needless to consider a situation in which all would benefit equally. Protection as a matter of fact is an advantage to some, and a disadvantage to others, and represents the triumph of those who succeed in making their interests prevail. On the other hand, we must not look upon capitalists as the possessors of money which they are free to employ as they please, and to whom it is a matter of indifference how they utilise their capital and their energy as long as the undertakings prove remunerative; nor, in considering enterprises already set on foot, ought we to assume the absolute mobility of the business and the capital invested in it; for such a mobility does not in reality exist, especially in the great industries of the present day. If we could make this assumption, of course, there would be no flaw in the argument. But we should be starting on false premises.

It has already been shown that, more particularly at the starting point of enterprises where much capital is embarked, protection may have a temporary justification. And for this very reason, even if the premises were admissible, too rigorous conclusions could not be drawn from them.

Let us now endeavour to picture the industrial condition of a country in its full development. In its normal condition protection would find in it no *raison d'être*: all industries—if in themselves endowed with vitality—will live spontaneously. But circumstances change: a temporary crisis, due to technical or economic causes, overtakes one or more industries, rendering it impossible to meet foreign competition. It may be said that the system cannot be altered on this account; that one must adapt oneself to the new conditions and give one's capital to the most productive employment actually open to it.

But these are mere words: a great mechanical trade will not be able to transform itself into a great agricultural enterprise. Whatever the general interest of the country may be, the interest of individuals will certainly be to uphold their own business and to prevent a transformation or liquidation, which would, in the greater number of cases, prove a failure.

And here it appears reasonable enough that capitalists should invoke the aid of protection, which gives them the hope of holding their own by means of a rise in prices and a reduction of wages. This protection may, in point of fact, bring about results more or less advantageous or disadvantageous; and even if of advantage to a few, it may be hurtful to the country at large; for I cannot admit that, if applied simply as a temporary expedient, it could be absolutely disadvantageous for ever. Its effects will depend upon a series of circumstances, which it is not possible to examine here, due to its mode of application and to the state of the country; but the capitalist's appeal for protection—in the case we have assumed—will appear perfectly reasonable; whilst reasonableness would vanish if the condition of the country at large or of the particular industries were prosperous.

Now, what amount of attention will such a petition for protection command? The appeal will be more or less general and more or less urgent in proportion as it reflects a general condition and a want felt by the industries; the attention paid to it will be in proportion to the influence exercised by the capitalist class over the political powers, and hence in accordance with the extent to which this want manifests itself in the country. And not only this; but the system of protec-

O

tion adopted (whether it prove on the whole beneficial to the country or otherwise) will last more or less long in exact proportion to the reality and permanence of the conditions set forth as its *raison d'être*. Finally, the system will continue as long as the damage which it does to the country, either by its mere existence or owing to its excesses, does not raise up against it a coalition of opposing interests, strong enough to do away with it.

All this may appear obscure and vague; nevertheless, we think it will become clear when we apply it to the history of the period under consideration, and even clearer when we come, later on, to more recent dates.

34. The protective policy had been enthusiastically adopted in the United States from 1816 to 1832; and we saw how it was (at least, partly) justified by the industrial condition of the country. But, towards the close of that period, it had exceeded its bounds in such a way as to conflict too strongly with opposing interests, which coalesced to undermine it. Whilst, however, this coalition was acting energetically, going so far, indeed, as to threaten national unity, the causes which had brought the protective system into force, and had made its adoption popular, gradually ceased to exist. We have seen how in the 1833-1860 period the protectionist policy lost its popularity in the United States, and the reason was that it was no longer necessary for the capitalists, and even less so for the country at large.

The industries depending on capital were now consolidated and in course of full development: they no longer needed support; if they had required any, it would have been absolutely contrary to the interests of the country, since it would have bolstered up artificial undertakings. The population was increasing rapidly: in twenty years, from 1830 to 1850, it almost doubled, rising from twelve to twenty-three million inhabitants; and in the following ten years it increased by a third, reaching thirty-one millions. The land in the Eastern States was entirely occupied, and it was only to be had in the far West, where, owing particularly to the comparative difficulties of transport at that period, a considerable outlay of capital was requisite;[1] and the workmen, being unable to occupy the

[1] List quotes the fact to show the inopportunity of giving an undue impulse

land on their own account, were more easily driven to work for wages; which was very advantageous to the factory system, then in want of hands. For even if they were attracted by the unoccupied land, the laws then in force (which, as we pointed out, were not radically modified till after 1860) effectually barred their projects.

The manufacturers were therefore in a prosperous condition and able to do without protection at the very moment when its excesses had brought about a reaction against it. The capitalist industries were then passing through a phase of normal and prosperous development; and it is just to such an historical phase that the theory of free-trade is applicable; it is the policy adapted to the normal conditions of growth of the factory system.

And it may be observed, incidentally, that the complete adoption of free-trade principles in England dates from the very moment when the consolidation of the factory system had been fully effected.

And as, by these criteria, we can explain the gradual displacement of protectionism by a free-trade policy in the United States during the period in question (a process naturally slow, for otherwise it would have adversely affected both private interests and that of the country at large); so, at the same time, it explains the brief return to protection in the years 1842-1846. It was brought about by an abnormal state of affairs, during the existence of which, through the change in the political, economic, and financial conditions of the country, the manufacturers were able to bring home with greater force their requests, which were perhaps partly justified.[1] But, occasioned by temporary causes, this return quickly passed away with the removal of these causes; since the economic and industrial state of the country, when once it had relapsed into its normal condition, rejected a protective policy.

And if fresh disturbing factors had not supervened to revolutionise American economy, and if, when these factors had passed away, capitalism had remained in a phase of solid

to agriculture in the United States, and the necessity of encouraging manufactures by means of protection.
[1] Smith and Seligman, p. 9.

and increasing prosperity, the United States would probably have become, little by little, the classical land of economic liberty, and would have possessed together with that perfect freedom of exchange which exists within its extensive frontiers, an international freedom of commerce. But first of all the Civil War, and subsequently the depression and industrial crisis, changed the entire aspect of affairs, and cut short at the very moment of its triumph the career of American free-trade.

35. Finally, a few remarks may be made on the effects of the American tariff at this period. We do not gather much from authors on this point, and they are as usual contradictory.

The protectionists, beginning with Carey and coming down to the very latest writers—Bolles, for example—attribute the crisis which reached its highest point in 1837 to the reduction of duties effected by the Compromise Act; the prosperity of 1842 to the protective tariff which was enforced that year; and the panic in 1857 to the undue lowering of the duties. The free-traders, on the other hand (see Walker, Wells, Cognetti,[1] Sumner, etc.), extolling, as we have already seen, the prosperity of the period from 1846 to 1860, refer it entirely to the gradual abandonment of the protective system.

Among so many discordant voices and in the midst of such complex phenomena, it is difficult to see one's way clearly; nevertheless, to the student who examines the question objectively and without prejudices certain facts are patent.

It may be admitted that the imports, which during the years 1834-1837 had increased out of all proportion, were a disturbing element in the national industries, or that they were one of the co-efficients of the crisis: it is admitted by Wright, an impartial observer.[2] But it cannot be stated with certainty that this increase was caused by the reduction of duties; since (as Taussig opportunely observes) the reductions made in those years were very slight, the important reductions not having been effected till after 1840. Nor can it be denied that the crisis in those years was chiefly brought about by

---

[1] *Vide* his most interesting essay upon the circulation of wealth in the United States, preceding Walker's translation (*Bibl. dell' Econ.* Serie 3ª, vol. i.)
[2] Vide *Comparative Wages*, etc., p. 192.

other factors: such as over-speculation, unlimited credit, an excessive circulation, a bad harvest, etc.¹

That it was the protective tariff of 1842 that put an end to the crisis, and caused the prosperity of the following years, as the protectionists maintain, and as Wright himself insinuates,² to a certain extent, appears to us a rash conclusion, for it is evident that a crisis occasioned by transitory causes such as those in question, could not be of long duration, and that in a vigorous country like the United States, prosperity would necessarily return of its own accord. Taussig,³ however, admits that protection in the years 1842-1846 may have contributed to the re-awakening of commercial activity: and it is, indeed, easy to understand how it may have temporarily lightened the difficulties of the most oppressed branches of industry; an advantage enjoyed afterwards, if not by the country, at all events by individual capitalists.

The same author proceeds to show the effects produced on certain industries by those duties, which even in this period of gradually lowering tariffs might be considered as protective.

We are unable to enter into details, since we have not at hand sufficient data to discuss Taussig's most minute analysis; and we must refer the reader to his excellent work. Some of the author's conclusions, however, appear to us to confirm what we have stated in the preceding paragraphs. On the whole, he notes the limited influence of the duties upon industries which no longer required protection, and which did not cease to develop even when the duties were little by little withdrawn. He affirms, on the other hand, the influence which the high duties on iron, that lasted in various shapes from 1831 to 1841, exercised upon the iron trade. These duties had a protective effect, impeding, or rendering importation very rare, and raising the price of iron, and thus keeping in existence antiquated furnaces which would otherwise have disappeared. But in so doing they did infinite harm to the country, since they fettered the progress of iron industry in the United States, and maintained at a high price

¹ *Vide* Taussig, Wright, *supra*.
² Wright, *Comparative Wages*, etc., p. 192.   ³ Taussig, p. 119, 120.

a commodity which is one of the most potent factors in our civilisation.

The resolute protection from 1842 to 1846 made these effects all the more marked; and it was only after 1846, under a milder *régime*, that the iron trade, stimulated by foreign competition, began to develop rapidly. Protection, consequently, was hurtful to the country; it injured manufactures which now no longer required artificial support; but it was of temporary advantage to those capitalists whose money was sunk in the older processes of production which they hesitated to abandon, since every transformation is costly.

And now we pass on to a brief statement of the free-trade thesis which attributes the prosperity of the period, specially from 1846 to 1860, to the relative freedom of exchange. That the giving up of the "American system" resulted in good to the country appears to us undeniable; since, as we have seen, protection had absolutely no longer any *raison d'être*, and had become injurious, and free-trade was naturally bound to stimulate progress on the part of native industries now quite able to hold their own with those abroad.

The comparative freedom of trade would necessarily be a co-efficient in industrial progress; but the opinion that the general well-being — the golden age which the United States enjoyed from 1846 to 1860—was due to it alone, or even principally, seems to us altogether one-sided and beyond the mark.

The United States were passing through a happy epoch in which all industries, having consolidated themselves, were being developed to their utmost capacity, and they availed themselves of the boundless natural resources of the land. The growth of the American economy was merely the effect of natural causes, and the general welfare and vitality of trade were to a certain extent also due to other reasons, such as the discovery of gold in California; so that, on the whole, without under-estimating the benefits necessarily following the removal of impediments to international trade, we are led to consider this relative liberty rather as an effect than as the cause of the general well-being and industrial prosperity, which no longer required uncertain and artificial support; an effect which none the less became in its turn a cause and an effective co-efficient of progress.

Nor ought we, all the same, to exaggerate the importance of international commerce, as it is exaggerated, with the most misleading results, both by free-traders and by protectionists. It is observed by Taussig that the alterations in duties during this period produced far less effect upon industry than is generally supposed; the development of manufactures proceeded uniformly, and seems to have been but slightly stimulated by the heavy duties in 1842, and but little shaken by the more moderate ones from 1846 to 1857. Generally speaking, the extent to which the mechanical industries were created and kept alive by means of the protective system, has been much over-estimated by the advocates of the latter; indeed, both the character and the growth of these industries were far less influenced by the tariffs than might have been logically expected.[1] And the same may be said of the exaggerated influence attributed to free-trade. Foreign trade is one of the elements of the economic life of a country, but it is by no means the most important one; internal commerce is a far weightier element. This was insisted upon by Adam Smith, who, rebuking merchants for considering inland trade merely as an auxiliary to foreign trade, spoke of it as " the most important of all, the trade in which an equal capital affords the greatest revenue, and creates the greatest employment to the people of the country." [2]

Nor must we lose sight of the fact that we are dealing with the United States; a vast country increasing rapidly in population, and all of whose inhabitants naturally looked to the interior of the land—an immense virgin region—rather than to foreign prospects. It was above all things the development of native resources that would fix the attention of·the American people: and this explains, on the one hand, the spring of action, the *leit-motiv* of Carey's protectionist writings, and, on the other, as protection was now unnecessary, the comparative indifference with which, as we have already seen, Americans viewed the tariff question during the whole of this period.

[1] Vide *Tariff Hist.* p. 154.
[2] *Wealth of Nations*, book iv. ch. i. p. 147, edition of 1791.

CHAPTER VI

THIRTY YEARS OF PROTECTION—"THE GOLDEN AGE OF
THE AMERICAN SYSTEM"

(FROM 1861 TO THE PRESENT DAY)

36. With the year 1861 was inaugurated in the history of the American tariff policy a new and singular evolution which has left indelible traces: the free-trade movement, which had been slowly expanding during the preceding period, and to which the country seemed readily to adapt itself, was suddenly arrested. And the United States were plunged at the same moment into all the horrors of a civil war and into the excesses of a protectionist policy that even now, after a course of thirty years, shows no sign of abatement, and seems to have broken the tradition, made good by the whole history of the country, that the same tariff policy could only last for a few years at a stretch.

The historical facts of this epoch are so close at hand and so well known that there is no need to recall them: familiar, too, are the vicissitudes of the American tariff policy during the last thirty years; whilst, on the other hand, the importance of this singular period has, in our opinion, been inadequately appreciated and but little light thrown upon its true significance. We shall therefore pass rapidly over the historical events, in order to dwell at greater length upon those facts which seem to us greatly to elucidate the nature and characteristics of modern protection.

Ever since the crisis in 1857 there had been growing in the eastern States, and particularly in Pennsylvania, a feeling in favour of protection, which in the 1860-1861 session had led to the approval of the Morrill tariff, that, under cover of substituting specific for many *ad valorem* duties, as a matter of fact somewhat increased the burden on industrial products, notably on iron and woollens. But this protective tendency would in all probability have enjoyed but limited and ephemeral success had it not been singularly aided by events. The Morrill tariff had just been passed, when the turmoil broke out; it had hardly been applied before Fort Sumter fell.

The tariff question in the United States is, says Ellena, intimately bound up with that of the Federal budget;[1] and this fact, which we have more than once observed, is to be met with anew at this moment, and during the following years. The truth is that it was financial necessity that dictated these excessive duties, which would never, in other circumstances, have been tolerated by the country.

The needs of the Federal finances during that titanic struggle gave rise to one of the most curious and complex financial experiments that have ever been made, and one that put the great economical vigour of the country to the severest test. In a very short space of time an enormous public debt was created, and simultaneously heroic steps were taken for its extinction; a forced currency was resorted to, and a rapid depreciation of paper money ensued; after having fallen into desuetude for half a century, internal taxes were revived, and the result was a system of imposts which for its universality and singularities has had no parallel in history, nor is it ever likely to be imitated in the future.[2] Government had been seized with a rage for taxation in view of the financial exigencies; and, by laws passed from 1862 to 1864, a complicated and curious system of taxation was introduced that weighed heavily on every kind of manufacture, assessing in more ways than one production as well as sale, and confiscating from 8 to 20 per cent of the value of commodities.[3] Naturally at a time when all was done to

[1] Vide *Relazione della commissione d' inchiesta per la revisione della tariffa doganale. Parte industriale*, Roma, Botta, 1886.
[2] *Vide* Wells, "The Recent Financial, Industrial, and Commercial Experiences of the U.S.," *Cobden Club Essays*.
[3] For further particulars regarding the imposts levied in the United States during this period see Wells' work, and especially W. C. Ford, "Internal

increase the revenue, recourse was had to means for augmenting the returns of that which was its most important source, namely, the customs duties, and in fact, they were successively raised during the war, and specially in the years 1862 and 1864. The higher duties were, moreover, justified by the necessity of compensating national manufacturers for the enormous increase in internal taxation, and enabling them to compete with foreign rivalry in the unfavourable circumstances in which they then found themselves.[1]

Nevertheless, it is certain that the protectionists then in power availed themselves of this state of affairs, and that, under the pretexts mentioned above, they raised the tariff exorbitantly, the average duties in 1862 amounting to 37·20 per cent, and in 1864 to 47·06 per cent. Every increase of import duties demanded by native producers was granted; the general welfare was entirely lost sight of, and laws were made to favour special interests; and on the foundations laid by the war and by political corruption was erected the edifice of absolute protection, fostered by the sentiment of national exclusiveness and isolation.[2]

37. At the conclusion of the war the extraordinary requirements which had given rise to the tremendous taxation of which we have spoken naturally ceased: the national debt was regulated, the internal duties were little by little abolished, and the financial organisation tended to reassume its normal aspect. Hence, the exorbitant customs tariff, which necessarily weighed heavily on the country, should likewise have been reduced; but the interests which had grown up around it were by no means inconsiderable; the moment was a critical one, and the protectionists seized the opportunity of the general perturbation in prices and of the cessation of the demand for goods on the part of the state, in consequence of the termination of the war, to oppose every reduction, and not only this, but to increase protection by abolishing those duties which had no protective character and raising the others, so as to deprive the tariff of all fiscal attributes.

Revenue of United States," in Lalor's *Cyclopædia;* also Bolles, *Financial History*, 1861-1885, etc.

[1] Wells himself admits this.
[2] Taussig, pp. 166, 167; and Smith and Seligman, p. 14.

Bolles[1] says, indeed, that up to 1872 requests for a reduction of the tariff were few; and that the agitation was confined to professors of political economy and journalists who had nothing better to do. But this sally, directed perhaps against Wells, who in those very years (1868-1870) published, as Commissioner of Revenue, his famous reports demanding a diminished tariff, is more malicious than true, especially when it is borne in mind that these reports—as Bolles himself admits—made a great impression on public opinion, and that, in 1872 a reduction of 10 per cent was approved of, not only on account of the excess of imports, but also on account of the agitation (resulting from agricultural depression), which was raised against the tariff in the west.

This, however, was only an apparent concession, since it dealt almost exclusively with unprotected commodities, and, moreover, a general and equal reduction effected in such a manner could be of little use, and laid itself open to being suddenly revoked at one time or another. In fact, after the crisis of 1873, when the Federal revenue decreased in proportion to the diminished imports, the occasion was immediately seized, in 1875, to annul the reduction made in 1872, and the war tariff, which had been merely aggravated by the various modifications introduced into it, was restored. And this state of things lasted almost ten years longer, till 1883, notwithstanding the attempts made during each session of Congress to lower the duties.

But, especially in the closing years of this period, the demands for a reduction of the tariff became more and more pressing, and encouraged by the ever-increasing surplus yielded by the Federal revenue, they gathered strength daily. A commission, appointed by Congress in 1882, bore witness to the fact that the more enlightened public opinion of the country and the voice also of those who in former times had claimed absolute protection for national industry, desired a reduction of the tariff; and it pointed out that such a reduction would be not merely a just concession to the national sentiment and an act of justice to consumers, but would be likewise substantially beneficial to trade interests generally. Hence the commission proposed to modify the existing tariff

[1] *Vide* work mentioned, p. 452.

in such a way as to render it protective only in those cases in which the conditions of labour and of American capital placed the manufacturers of the United States in a position of inferiority to their foreign competitors, and to prevent the undue influence of high duties giving an immoderate and fatal impulse to production and speculation.[1]

However, the tariff of 1883, which was voted in consequence of these proposals, brought a very slight amount of relief; in substance it was the same tariff as before, and it was certainly not calculated to satisfy the demands of the western States that claimed a substantial and not a merely fictitious lowering of duties. The tariff of 1883 was the work of protectionists, and it was designed to meet the opinion that was growing in the popular mind against excessive duties.[2] The reductions affected those products especially in which American industry no longer dreaded foreign competition, such as the commoner sorts of cottons and wools; and, on the other hand, heavier duties were laid on fine goods that were of greater importance as an article of import.[3]

So that, the mean reduction in the tariff, according to Nimmo (the director of Federal statistics), came to barely 5 per cent; and the duties remained at about 38 per cent.

38. But during the following years, no changes being made in the tariff, the gradually lowering prices, by aggravating protection in a system of specific duties, caused a progressive rise in the percentage duty on imports, calculated *ad valorem*, which in 1884 was estimated at 41·61 per cent on total imports, in 1885 at 45 per cent, in 1886 at 45·55 per cent, in 1887 at 47·10 per cent. This average was, however, the result of a great variety of duties extending from 5 to 200 per cent.

In the meanwhile, the necessity to meet that singular phenomenon — the continuous surplus revenue — occasioned a fresh revision of the tariff. On the other hand, the discontent which it aroused, particularly among agriculturists, went on augmenting. During the year 1885 the movement in favour of reduction gained strength by the democratic victory. A scheme was discussed at considerable

[1] Bolles, p. 477.
[2] Taussig, p. 254; and Smith and Seligman, p. 22.   [3] Taussig, p. 236.

length which aimed at the lowering of the duties, and the exemption of raw materials, including wool. But the protectionists insisted on the general depression of trade, and in spite of the lamentations of the western farmers, who complained of having to pay too dearly for their agricultural implements, clothes, and furniture, the bill was rejected.

In 1887 President Cleveland sent to Congress the famous Message, in which he advocated reduction of duties and the abolition of those on raw materials.

In the 1887-1888 session the question was warmly discussed in Congress, and the divergent opinions were clearly defined; the democratic party, in favour of the moderate diminution of protection proposed by Mills and approved of by the House, maintained that the duties were excessive and weighed most heavily on the poor classes, and that, besides, a great part of the manufactures consumed in the United States could be produced there as cheaply as in England, and therefore without any need for protection. Hence they suggested a modification of the tariff on the following basis: the transformation of many specific into *ad valorem* duties, the exemption of many products, especially raw materials and wool, and the lowering of many other duties. It may be observed that the protection of wool was the corner-stone of the American system, since it purchased the assent of a large number of agriculturists to the industrial protection.[1] To Mills' Bill the Senate, where the republican party prevailed, opposed Allison's Bill, which claimed the resolute maintenance of protection, and at the same time advised the reduction of the duties on unprotected commodities, or even their total exemption, in order to effect a diminution in the revenue —in this way reducing the tariff to a mere instrument of protection.

The elections of 1888 were decided on a tariff platform, and the victory of the republicans ensured the triumph of protective principles, which culminated in 1890 in the famous MacKinley Bill. But this measure has been so amply

[1] The duty on raw wool, says Taussig (*vide* "La tariffa Mackinley," in the *Giornale degli Economisti*, Rome, January 1891), is the price that American manufacturers pay to the farmers for the continuation of the protective system.

discussed by the press of the whole world, that we may be excused for not going into many details, and confining our attention to its spirit.

The MacKinley Bill has considerably raised the duties, especially upon the textile and finer manufactures, to which the American industries are less adapted, and which are imported in great bulk: the duty on woollen manufactures has been raised on an average from 67 to 91 per cent *ad valorem*, and in some cases, on the finer products, to 150 per cent; that on raw and manufactured metals has gone up from 40 to 80 per cent.[1]

Some raw materials essential for manufactures have been exempted from duty; and as a sop to the farmers of the north and west, high duties have been laid on agricultural produce (Canadian competition especially being aimed at), tobacco and raw wool, the duty on which has been further raised from 34 to 40 per cent—this latter being a heavy fee paid, as we have seen, by the manufacturers for the maintenance of protection, and which leads consequently to exorbitant duties on manufactures.

But putting aside the forms of the tariff, the predominating characteristic of the famous MacKinley "Bills" is a spirit of absolute aversion to foreign importations and to international trade, an aversion which in the so-called "Administrative Bill" showed itself in the form of an infinite number of complicated and extremely vexatious regulations, no doubt partly designed to prevent fraud, but which none the less betray the evident intention of discouraging to the utmost extent all foreign imports.

"Considering these laws, not in their abstract economic bearing, but in their context and apparent intentions, which are revealed by countless particulars," said an American newspaper, quoted by Moireau, "it would almost seem that the chief and better part of the assembly of the richest country in the world was inspired exclusively with the strange idea that the importation of foreign commodities was an immoral traffic, and that the merchants who effect it are criminals, or little less."

[1] *Vide* Moireau, "Les Bills MacKinley," in the *Revue des deux Mondes*, 1st July 1891; and Taussig, article quoted.

And this strange idea of destroying or crippling international commerce was even quite frankly stated in Congress; for, an opponent of the tariff having said that he did not understand on what principle its supporters voted the expenses for the maintenance of lighthouses, Senator Hiscock abruptly replied that were it not for the coasting-trade he would willingly see every beacon extinguished on the shores of the United States.[1]

But we are not arguing at the present moment; we are only stating facts, and strange facts they are forsooth!

It may be well to point out, in conclusion, that a month after the MacKinley Act had been in force, the republican protectionist party met with a rebuff at the general election for the House of Representatives; it was occasioned by various political causes, but perhaps to a large extent also by the extravagant tariff policy, which had immediately brought about a great rise in the price of articles of first necessity and general use, without raising in the very least degree—which was indeed quite natural—the wages of workmen, as the protectionists had led them to expect. A reaction against the excesses of protectionism set in among the agricultural and labouring classes, the farmers probably thinking that the protection granted to some of their produce was too dearly paid for, considering that they had necessarily to bear the expenses of the industrial protection, with an increase in the cost of manufactures, and above all, with a fall in the price of agricultural produce, the exportation of which had been made more difficult. And the "National Farmers' Alliance" among the many, and at times Utopian demands which it made—such as, for example, a large increase of the paper currency and state credit—affirmed the necessity of the reform of the customs tariff.

On the other hand, the "Knights of Labour," who had on their rolls an immense army of workmen, united with the agriculturists in demanding a lowering of the duties which weighed especially heavy on labour; and there arose a loud cry from the fields and the workshops, protesting not only against the tariff, but against the banks, against the railway

[1] Vide *Edinburgh Review*, January 1891, "The Fiscal System of the United States."

companies, against trusts, against monopolies, in a word, against the prevailing capitalism.[1]

These are the facts, reduced to their simplest expression, but none the less strange and surprising. For, although for almost twenty years the whirlwind of protectionism had raged with greater or less violence in nearly all civilised countries, yet there had been no parallel to a continuity of thirty years, with constant aggravations of protective policy, and with an ultimate explosion of such magnitude, leading the disheartened economist to ask if the great scientific and practical struggles for economic liberty were to culminate not merely in a general protectionist reaction, but in the proclamation of a system of economic isolation and of the theory of absolute protection in the vastest, richest, and most progressive state of modern times.

The phenomenon is indeed most grave; and hitherto it has remained involved in considerable obscurity. In fact, if we find endless polemical discussions regarding the results of protection or the greater or less opportunity of maintaining it,

[1] These lines were written in May 1892, and our remarks dealt with the question up to that date. Subsequent events have somewhat altered the situation, without however changing it completely. The victory of the democratic party in the elections of the House of Representatives was confirmed and strengthened by the election of President Cleveland which followed in 1892. The election was made upon the basis of the tariff question; the reaction of the country against the excesses of protectionism, and the deep, popular aversion to the great corporations, monopolies and trusts, and in general to the great capitalistic interests favoured by protection, became more active, and greatly helped to ensure the triumph of the democrats, who demanded the revision of the tariff. In February 1894 a new tariff was voted in the House of Representatives to diminish the excesses of the MacKinley Act. This tariff, however, met with considerable opposition in the Senate, which greatly reduced the amendments.

The new law, as it came into force on the 27th August 1894, presents two noteworthy characteristics; a slight diminution of several duties, and the abolition of the duties on raw wool. There has been a slight reduction in the duties on textile materials, coal and iron ore, on pig iron, and on iron and steel goods; a greater reduction in the duties on earthen and china ware. The political influence of the sugar trust succeeded in maintaining and manipulating to its own advantage the duties on raw and refined sugar.

These changes, however, on the whole do not substantially modify the American protective system (according to Taussig, from whose recent important article we draw these data—*vide* "The New United States Tariff" in the *Economic Journal*, London, December 1894); they only cause a general and slight diminution.

The most important modification has been the abolition of the duties on raw

rare, on the other hand, is it to hear the question asked—the all-important question both in theory and in practice—what is the *wherefore*, the *raison d'être* of this strange fact, the persistence of protectionism in the United States of to-day ? And the explanations vouchsafed are almost always superficial when, indeed, they are not downright childish—like the one most commonly met with, that protection is simply a gigantic blunder, and that Americans are yet blind to the error of their ways!

It is the answer to this question that we propose to seek, by carefully studying in their every aspect these last thirty years of the economic life of the United States, adopting the same system that we have hitherto followed for the preceding periods.

39. Before, however, entering into a direct research, it may be well to examine the arguments for protection, as set forth during this period by its American partisans in support of their theory, and the general characteristics which the system has assumed in the United States. We do not propose to investigate now the most recent protective theories in this country: that will be the object of another essay, in which we will deal

wool. The duties on wool and on woollen materials, as we have already seen, were for a long time the backbone of the American tariff; the duties on raw wool formed the most efficacious protection conceded to the agriculturists in recompense for the protection accorded to the manufacturing industries. Now it is evident that such a change may exercise a great influence on the future; it is difficult to foretell the future, but it does not seem out of place to observe that, the compromise between manufacturers and agriculturists thus broken, the latter will not acquiesce and will demand either an increase of the agricultural duties, or more probably the gradual abolition of the protective duties on the manufactures. Now, considering on one hand that a vigorous agricultural protection neutralises the advantages that protection to manufactures can offer to capitalists, and that in reality the American agriculturists are not in want of this protection, but they have demanded it up to the present time more as a recompense for the industrial protection than for any other reason; so that it seems very slightly probable that they should demand it in preference to the reductions of all the tariffs; and on the other hand, considering the deep aversion that protectionism, as an attempt at strengthening the capitalistic interest and monopolies, begins to awaken in the people of the United States, one could, without pretending to prophesy, be led to believe that the movement towards reduction of duties, slightly perceptible in the last act, may be the beginning of greater and more general reductions. (It is, however, impossible to predict anything, as is proved by the recent defeat of the Democratic party, which has taken place during the revision of the proof-sheets of this very note.)

P

with the opinions of some of the principal American writers, and endeavour to reconcile them with the circumstances of the times in which they moved. At present we merely purpose a brief glance at the arguments most frequently brought forward, especially nowadays, and that are the most generally received, our aim being to see if we cannot discover in them some solid reason, either apparent or real, that may justify the actual state of things.

Let us then briefly refer to Carey, the principal advocate of contemporary American protectionism, pending a more detailed examination of his theories elsewhere. It is a singular fact that this writer, who enjoyed so much fame and popularity in the United States, is now slighted, even by protectionists, who, coming to him for their arguments, frequently forget to quote him (see, for instance, Gunton and Mason); whilst his theories, even if they had any influence at the beginning of the present period, seem now, in our judgment at all events, to carry no weight at all.

This curious fact may, we think, be explained by pointing out that Carey's theory (as we shall see in the last of these essays) referring, as it did, to a state of affairs which had already undergone great changes even when his chief work, *Principles of Social Science*, appeared (1858), cannot nowadays be looked upon as otherwise than an anachronism.

And, as Carey's arguments have lost their force, the motive of sustaining the infant industries of a country is no longer urged in favour of protection; for, indeed, such a motive would appear grotesque when it is remembered that, in a century of life, these "infants" had had ample time to become adults.

The more popular method of accounting for the actual American protectionism is to quote the standard of wages in the United States, which is very much higher than in Europe, and to maintain that protection is necessary, either for assuring to the working people due remuneration, or else for safeguarding American industries which, on account of a high civilisation, and therefore of high salaries, have a dearer cost of production than is the case with the European manufactures, which would for that reason be able to undersell them. And thus, removing the question from the low grounds of economic interests to the loftier ones of patriotism, it is concluded that industrial protection is necessary to prevent the high status of civilisation in America being brought down to the low level of that in Europe.

This system of defending protection, which artfully endeavours to prop up the interests of the capitalists by means of patriotic sentiment and by the labouring classes, deserves a thorough analysis.

40. Let us clearly understand the questions at issue; the first may be formulated as follows:—Can protection exercise and does it exercise raising influence on wages? And the second—Does the higher standard of wages constitute for American manufactures (or rather for some of them—for protection is not demanded for them all) an element of inferiority of such a nature as to justify state support? Let us begin with the first question.[1] Protection, it may be observed, cannot favour the workmen and raise the price of labour which they have handed over to the capitalist; because whoever has anything to sell can be benefited in two ways—by the restriction of the quantity of the commodity offered for sale and consequent rise in its price, or by the multiplication and cheapening of the things which he wants and which he will buy with the proceeds of what he has sold. Now protective duties have no influence on the supply of labour; to limit it, it would be necessary to bar not the importation of goods, but the immigration of labourers. Instead of lowering the price of articles of consumption protection raises it, hence, if it has any effect on wages, it must be to depress them, to the great detriment of the working classes. And if a solution were sought, by representing the increased demand for labour that is provoked by the impulse given to the various industries, it could be shown that such an increased demand is more apparent than real, being a mere transition from one form of production to another; for industry is in all cases limited by capital, which protection does not augment.

But that is not enough; it may be stated that protection does not merely lower wages by increasing the workmen's cost of living (which is the effect of protecting manufactures, and,

[1] *Vide* among other works, George, *Protection and Free Trade*, chapter xix.; and Ely, *Problems of To-day*, pp. 70, 72, etc.

all the more, agricultural produce), but that it does so in other ways also. Wells says that protection, by raising the cost of production, renders exportation difficult; and that the producer who, on account of the flooding of the home markets by over-production, wishes to export his goods, will do all in his power to lessen his expenses, and as he cannot diminish the cost of raw materials, which has been raised by protection, he will endeavour to effect a saving on labour, and hence will do his best to lower wages.[1] This reasoning fails to convince us for two reasons; first, because it starts with the assumption of heavy duties on raw materials, which might be removed; and secondly, because it is evident that every employer does his utmost to reduce the cost of labour to the lowest possible degree, but the doing so effectually does not depend upon himself, but upon the condition of the labour-market.

Let us rather turn to a line of reasoning previously suggested and more than once referred to by us, and observe how protection tends to sustain the interests of capitalists, to aggravate, by the rise in prices, the condition of workmen, to render money-saving on their part more difficult, and to increase the number of wage-earners and consequently lessen their remuneration.

The subject will be touched upon again by us when we come, before long, to consider the actual economic conditions of the United States; but the general tendency to which we have alluded has, we think, been made sufficiently clear by what we have already stated; and it is in complete antithesis to protectionist pretensions.

"By a strange inconsistency," says Ricca Salerno, in the excellent work which we have so often quoted,[2] "the terms of the question are inverted, and it is asserted by some that protective duties are necessary to defend rich American labour against the depressing assaults of its poor European rival. But it is evident that the labour in question is none other than that which is at the service of capital; and the defence which it is proposed to set up consists in beating down the claims of the labourers. . . ."

41. The other leading argument of American protectionists

[1] Vide *Practical Economics*, New York, Putnam, 1887, p 111.
[2] Vide *Giorn. degli Econ.* April-May 1891.

of to-day is based, as we have seen, upon the supposed position of inferiority to their European rivals in which the native industries would be placed on account of the higher standard of wages. Here, too, answers are numerous, and it must be admitted exhaustive, although not all of equal value. It is pointed out that if American labour costs dearer, it is, on the other hand, more productive,[1] and is rendered more effectual by a more intelligent application of machinery. Wages are higher in the United States in the non-protected than in the protected industries, which would seem to indicate that the cause of inferiority, if there is any, is not due to the wages. For if that were the case, the southern States, where a lower standard of remuneration prevails, ought to have an industrial advantage over the northern States, which is absurd. Moreover, considering the relatively small proportion in the total cost of production that in many large industries can be assigned to wages, and, on the other hand, the expenses to transport which burden all products imported from abroad, it is maintained that American producers would be able to hold their own, even if they paid higher wages.[2] Finally, many

[1] We may here note a few reservations which Professor F. Walker (in an article most moderate in tone and full of common sense, "Protection and Protectionists," in *The Quarterly Journal of Economics*, April 1890) makes to the theory that high wages do not raise the cost of production, because their effect is to proportionately augment the efficiency of the work done. Walker says that that is true generally, but not always; it is not true in regard to industries in which there enters but little intelligence and skilled labour. In the latter cases it may well be that American industries, or some of them, might, owing to the high wages paid, find themselves at a decided disadvantage, having indeed a cost of production greater than that of other countries. It would then be for statesmen to consider whether the capital and labour applied to such relatively unsatisfactory, though state-aided, industries should continue to be protected at the charge of the nation. "Now, whilst I am so much a free-trader," says Walker, "that I can with difficulty conceive a situation in which I should give a vote, as an individual or a representative, in favour of initiating a protective system—and certainly I should not have done so in this country, holding the opinions I now do, in 1789, 1816, 1824, 1828, 1842, and still less in the 1863-1867 period—*nevertheless, I am so much a protectionist* that I should act in an essentially conservative spirit when dealing with the mass of labour and capital which had been once fully engaged in any branch of industry. And I should be moved to this, not by the interests of this accumulation of capital and labour, but by those of the general welfare."

[2] Wells (*Practical Economics*, p. 97) asserts that of the total value of the finished article, labour represents: in the manufactures of wool 16 per cent,

say that, as a matter of fact, the actual progress of American industry is such that in many of its branches it can enter into competition with foreign manufactures, even successfully, without any need of protection.[1]

But these are all observations of facts requiring a minute statistical analysis, which would be out of place here, all the more so as further on we shall speak at considerable length of the actual state of the manufactures in the United States.

The protectionist argument can also be refuted in more general terms from a theoretical standpoint, and such a refutation is to hand from the pen of a distinguished English economist, Cairnes.

His remarks on the subject, in his classical *Leading Principles*, apply to the year 1874, and yet they seem to have been written at the present moment, for, during the course of twenty years, the American protectionists have not apparently learned anything very new; they go on repeating the same arguments, without so much as thinking of replying to those of the English economist. The argument of the higher standard of American wages, adopted since the war, proves too much, says Cairnes. Wages in the United States are high in all industries, and not merely in those requiring protection; and if high wages was a proof of high cost of production, and this occasioned the necessity of protection, then the farmers of Illinois and the cotton-planters of the south would require it quite as much as the spinners of New England or the Pennsylvania founders. The highly remunerative character of American industry, both in wages and profits, is a consequence of its productive power. Capitalists

---

of iron and steel 21 per cent, of cotton 22 per cent, in the iron mines 41 per cent. Now, calculating that the transport of foreign goods from their place of origin to the United States, including insurance, commission, etc., cost 5 per ent of their value (and if the goods are conveyed by land the expense is greatly increased), it may be concluded that American producers would be able to pay their workmen—even if they had no protective tariffs—an average wage 25 per cent higher than that received by the artisans of competing nations.

[1] *Vide* Wells, p. 85; Schoenhof, *The Industrial Situation and the Question of Wages*, New York, Putnam, 1885. Mills, a member of the House of Representatives, in his report in 1888 in favour of the reduction of the tariff, confirms Senator Sherman's opinion that nine-tenths of the manufactures actually consumed in the United States could be made there as cheaply as in England, without any need for protection.

and operatives are highly remunerated in America, because their industry produces much. Now a richly fruitful industry implies a reward which is great when compared with the sacrifice endured; it means the low cost of the thing produced.

High profits and wages in the United States, instead of indicating a high cost, on the contrary indicate a cheap cost of production. Such is the state of American industry for a large class of products. The weakness in certain manufactures is due to the fact that these industries are not so constituted as to be able to give profits and wages up to the usual standard in the United States, which is higher than that in Europe, taking the average of its various countries. It is not that the United States are incapable of obtaining such produce, but that they cannot turn it out in such favourable circumstances as the other products. And this explains the inability of American producers to compete with European "pauper labour." They cannot do it and at the same time be compensated for their work on the American scale.[1]

Cairnes' reasoning is so close and logical that it is easy to understand American protectionists having left it altogether aside, for what answer could they make to arguments which cut away the ground from beneath their most important and recent contentions? And, as a matter of fact, we, who have conscientiously performed the by no means amusing task of perusing a large number of the volumes and pamphlets which advocate, frequently in mere childish fashion, protection in the United States, have hardly ever alighted upon any allusion to Cairnes' criticisms, or, if they are dealt with, the replies are quite inadequate. One of the latter, supplied by Hoyt,[2] naïvely points out that in the agricultural industries and in the production of many other articles of consumption, worth about 6700 million dollars out of the 10,000 million, at which the annual produce consumed in the United States is valued, the country has certain natural advantages which more than balance the high rate of wages; whilst it enjoys no

[1] Vide Cairnes, Some Leading Principles of Political Economy, London, 1874.
[2] Vide Protection versus Free Trade, New York, Appleton, 1888, p. 290 et seq.

such advantages in other industries, and so for these latter, the high wages aggravating the cost of production, protection is necessary. But this is exactly what Cairnes says, namely, that the weakness of certain industries is not occasioned by the rate of wages, but depends upon other innate causes; it is a relative weakness which makes them less productive than others; but this does not lead logically to the conclusion that it is necessary or opportune to protect them.

42. On the question of wages, with which we are now occupied, a singular opinion is held by Gunton, an American economist, who enjoys a certain reputation in his own country. In a recent work[1] he unfolds the theory of international trade from a somewhat novel standpoint, and his views are so paradoxical that we cannot refrain from touching upon them—only, however, in so far as they bear directly upon the matter at issue.

According to Gunton, the development of manufactures is an indispensable condition of social progress, since they alone among industries tend to concentrate and socialise the people—agricultural pursuits having the opposite effect. And to encourage manufactures, it is necessary to assure for them a market, which cannot indeed be created by the state, but which the state can maintain by protecting to a certain extent national products; and this market should be at home, which is far preferable to outlets abroad. Protection is most advantageous to all, because it promotes the concentration and differentiation of industry, creates more complex social relations, stimulates the growth of new desires and a higher phase of existence. The higher the standard of life of the workmen, the higher will be their wages. Thus the protection of national industries, by raising the social standard of the country, betters the condition of all the workpeople.[2]

Up to this point we discover nothing new in this explanation of the advantages of protection, for it all comes to the idea of the necessity of manufactures for social progress, and for a complex social life, which is Carey's fundamental idea, although Gunton carefully abstains from quoting him, and which, to go somewhat farther back, is also Alexander Hamilton's opinion—

[1] Vide *Principles of Social Economics*, New York, Putnam, 1891.
[2] *Vide* work mentioned, pp. 223, 225, 228, 533.

a view, in fact, which within certain bounds[1] is contested by no one, but which does not necessarily lead to protection; and which cannot finally be looked upon as anything but an anachronism in the United States of to-day—a country which has attained a great complexity of life and civilisation, where the manufacturing industries are established on broad foundations, and do not, for the most part, need protection; a country, in short, which might be disturbed, but not convulsed, by a change—especially if a gradual one—of its tariff's policy.

But Gunton's singularity lies in the argument by which he endeavours to demonstrate the necessity of protection in the United States; it is the old argument of the aggravation of the cost of production by high wages, but presented in a new light.

According to Gunton, the idea of protection for young industries, so amply maintained in the United States in days gone by, and so generally accepted, is erroneous, and indeed in direct opposition to historical exigencies.

Protection is not necessary always, or for all nations; least of all is it needful for those of less advanced civilisation, or for inferior industries. It is rather the highly civilised countries that require a protective policy, since it is in them that wages are highest, and that the need is felt of warding off the competition of inferior countries, which tends to lower the level of their wages, and to undersell their products with products of less well-remunerated labour. In such circumstances free-trade, by introducing these products of inferior labour, will reduce the wages of the country to the same level, and will lead to a lessened consumption, and to a lower social life. The right economic basis for international competition is the standard of wages in the country where labour is dearest; and hence, to establish international trade on economic foundations, it is necessary that the country which has the highest wages should enforce a differential treatment against the products of countries where labour is less well remunerated. And the protective duties should be so adjusted as to compensate

[1] I say within certain bounds, for really, from one point of view, the isolation—less civilised though it be—of the agricultural state appears to be preferable to the horrible and inhuman agglomerations in certain modern industrial centres.

native industries for the whole difference between the local standard of wages and that of the inferior nations which export rival produce.

Social superiority, in fact, instead of rendering protection useless, makes it imperative; so that it becomes, so to speak, the historical commercial policy which distinguishes the more advanced from the less civilised nations.[1]

What can be said of such an economic paradox maintained with such singular audacity? In truth, we may point out to Gunton, that admitting, as has been demonstrated, that high wages are, in substance, an indication of greater productiveness in the larger number of industries, it is difficult to understand why these latter should fear foreign competition; still less how the standard of wages can be altered without any dislocation either in the demand or in the supply of labour. Foreign competition can injure only those trades which happen to be in a state of relative inferiority; and a gradual reduction of duties may be serviceable to them by enabling them to be transformed, or, as far as possible, the capital placed in them to be withdrawn; but this is another question, in no way germane to the subject; nor could it by any possibility affect wages.

The argument that the industrially strong countries should defend themselves against their weaker rivals is absurd; for in that case, the New England States ought to protect themselves against those of the south and the west, where manufactures are now spreading; and England, on account of her industrial superiority and the higher rate of wages received by her labourers, ought to guard her manufactures against Italian competition; whilst the United States ought to fear the latter more than English rivalry; and all the while it is exactly the reverse that takes place! It is sufficient to state these propositions to see clearly the consequences of Gunton's theory,[2] which arrives at the charming conclusion that as the

---

[1] *Vide* work mentioned, pp. 325, 329, 336, 341, etc.

[2] He endeavours to defend himself beforehand against the objection that might be made, that protection ought therefore to be less necessary against producers in England than against those in China, where labour is so much cheaper. But in China, says Gunton, there are no machines, which make labour so much more efficacious, and the United States have that advantage over China, which more than compensates them for their higher wages, but this is not the

United States is the country in which social progress has reached its zenith, it should maintain a rigorous protection against Europe, whilst the latter should hasten to throw open all her doors to American products!

We must do Gunton the justice, however, to admit that he does not shrink from the logical conclusions of his singular theory. One of them is to demand a general protection for all industries, whether manufacturing or agricultural; and this is implicitly admitted by Gunton when he says that industries ought to be fully compensated for the whole difference between the rate of wages in America and abroad,[1] since wages are higher in all industries in the United States than they are in Europe; this compensation will have to be granted in all cases—even in those of industries which do not require it, and have not so much as asked for it.[2]

Gunton is discreet in limiting the amount of support to the difference between the wages, but his theory implies general protection. And if we have dwelt upon it here, anticipating a study of the theories, which will occupy us later on, it is because it prepares us to understand—let us rather say, to expound—for certain extravagancies cannot be understood—the theory of absolute protection or prohibition; the theory of those whom Professor Walker wittily calls, " the Chinese Wall Men "!

43. In fact, as the reasons which in former times were alleged in favour of protection—the necessity of giving an impulse to industries indispensable for the defence of the country, of supporting young industries, of co-ordinating agriculture and manufactures—all implied temporary protection, when once the specific objects aimed at had been obtained, it was natural to suppose that the fetters placed on international trade should be removed. Nor is it difficult to

---

case with regard to England, which is well provided with machinery (vide p. 341). But in Italy also machinery is employed in the factories, and wages are lower; therefore England ought to protect her steel and woollen industries against those of Italy !

[1] It would be necessary, therefore, to set up as many different tariffs as there are countries having a different standard of wages from that of the United States, and at every rise or fall of wages these tariffs would have to be altered.

[2] As, for example, in the cotton trade, which, it is admitted by almost all, no longer requires protection, and yet in which wages are very high.

understand that protectionists should never have been willing to admit that that moment had arrived, when we take in consideration all the vested interests that have grown round this artificial system, and all the detrimental dislocation consequent on a change of commercial policy; but this in no way controverts the fact that, up to the time of the Civil War, resort had only been had to the protection of certain industries, and protectionism had not been advocated as a general and permanent system. But, on the other hand, when protection is based on the considerations which we have just been reviewing, when it is claimed as the bulwark of an advanced and progressive civilisation against the inroads of—to a certain extent—inferior influences, when it is founded on the higher rate of wages in America than elsewhere; then it can no longer be invoked as a temporary remedy, but it must be judged as a permanent system in perfect affinity with the natural character of American civilisation. For, even if the actual progress is continued, in all probability there will remain the same differences as at present between the degrees of civilisation of various nations; and, besides, Americans would look with horror to a time when they would not need protection, since—to follow logically this paradoxical theory to its conclusion—that would signify that the United States would have been unhorsed in the great tournament of nations.

Thus it is that the form in which protectionism is most frequently presented to the American people nowadays is that of the "home market"; it is a system that looks upon foreign competition as altogether harmful, and aims at its suppression by means of exceedingly high and prohibitive duties, and reserves for native producers the absolutely undivided market claimed by the numerous "home-market clubs" recently formed in the country.[1]

The actual protectionist theory of the United States maintains as good and useful a permanent system of protection, and the restriction of foreign trade even in normal circumstances; and it must be admitted that if we grant its premises, it is strictly logical.

Ideas such as these were not merely the isolated aberrations

[1] *Vide* Walker, article quoted, and George, chap. xi.

of a small school of economists; they became the fundamental policy of a great people.[1]

Now we have seen in the course of this study that this idea of economic independence is by no means new to the American people; it is one which we encounter at the very beginning of her national history, and which is, in a certain way, the economic application of the Monroe doctrine. And this idea, and its development, may partly be explained as resulting from the successive expansions of American territory which, as it may, on account of its extent, variety, and wealth, place the United States under conditions very different, so far as commerce is concerned, from those of nations with limited territories and resources, it enables us to understand the desire of Americans to derive the greatest amount of profit from their inexhaustible resources, and to make themselves independent of other countries, not only in regard to the more essential requirements of life, but with respect to many other things besides.

Perfect free-trade prevails within the boundaries of the immense American commonwealth, the population of which is ever spreading and augmenting; it is impossible to compare such a country either to Italy or to England, with their limited areas, nor can we fail to see that international trade is of less importance to the new republic than it is to the old European States; because in the former, trade, as a consequence of the division of labour, finds a vast and varied field, for the very reason that the principle of the division of labour finds there its most general application.

And so the conception of a relative economic independence in the United States can, up to a certain point, be both understood and justified. But this relative independence must be the result of the most complete and useful exploitation of the resources of the land, and not of an artificial endeavour to utilise others that would be better left in reserve, or that would bear better fruit if left to mature unforced.

But this doctrine of relative independence has nothing to do with the rude and absurd system of absolute isolation which regards all international trade as injurious, or with Gunton's contradictory idea, which almost seems borrowed from the old

[1] *Vide* Taussig, p. 174.

mercantilists, that the United States ought to raise their customs-barriers, whilst the European countries should lower theirs; just as if it were possible for any one to sell without receiving something in exchange from others. The whole thing is as fantastic as the old mercantile theory of always selling but never buying!

These are absurdities that need no further refutation; and yet they are, in fact, the last theoretical products of modern American protectionism. And to conclude our analysis, which has been drawn out to undue lengths, we must confess that the study of the motives generally brought forward in favour of protectionism by American writers of to-day, and of the more recent characteristics of the movement, has furnished us with information interesting indeed, but little apt to throw light on the causes of this singular and striking phenomenon. The arguments employed are unsound, and they are far weaker than those relied on in preceding periods; they reveal a desperate effort on the part of the writers to justify that which is not justifiable; they are the offspring of a literature that lends itself to the fabrication of sophisms whose only object it is to delude the people and to hide the truth from them by concealing the real and true reasons why one class of the community demands protection against the others. And if, to a certain small extent, the direction taken by American protectionism of to-day is justifiable, on the whole, when pushed as it is to its logical extreme, it is a social absurdity which reveals an abnormal and diseased state of things.

For the real motives of the movement we must turn directly to the economic and social conditions of the country.

44. The commercial policy during the first ten years of the period in question will not require, after the explanation we gave of it at the beginning of the present chapter, any very lengthy consideration.

The Civil War, with its financial requirements and the necessity of compensating for the heavy internal taxation levied on production, brought about a rise of tariffs, and the protectionists who were in power seized the occasion for enforcing their views. Thus the country was dragged into a strongly protective policy, which it would certainly not otherwise have adopted, because it did not answer to the requirements of its industries. But notable changes were brought about in the conditions of trade by the war, and afterwards by its cessation.

Now, although the national industries were heavily burdened by the multiplicity of war-taxes which ruined some and left others in a precarious state, owing to their frequent changes; although serious undertakings suffered, whilst speculation flourished and often resulted in enormous gains, to the detriment of the state, nevertheless American industries generally profited rather than otherwise from the war, because it gave them a great impulse.

This impulse came especially from the great demand for products of all kinds to supply the wants of the troops; from the rise in prices brought about by this largely increased demand; from the excessive emission of paper money; and also from a relative fall of wages, the increase in which had not been in proportion to the rise in prices. Wells calculates that in groceries and food generally, the rise in prices was from 90 to 100 per cent; in clothes and articles of domestic use, 86 per cent; in materials for heating and lighting, 50 to 60 per cent; in house rents, 90 to 100 per cent; in salt, 100 to 150 per cent; in butter, 100 per cent; in sugar, 70 to 100 per cent; in soap, 80 to 90 per cent; in cotton goods, 170 per cent; in woollen goods, 53 per cent.[1]

Even the agio on gold, which was light at the beginning of the war, but which rapidly increased until it reached a maximum of 185 in June 1864,[2] contributed to the productive impulse by favouring exportation, which could be effected at a far cheaper rate than was the case at home, as foreigners paid in gold.

One of the most curious effects of the war, Wells remarks, was the impulse given to the invention and employment of machines designed to economise human labour; from 3340 patents granted in 1861, the number rose to 6220 in 1865; and production increased immensely, in spite of the fact that

[1] *Vide* Wells, "The Recent Financial, Industrial, and Commercial Experiences of the U.S.," *Cobden Club Essays.*
[2] *Vide* Stringher, *Sulla abolizione del corso forzoso agli Stati Uniti*, Roma, Botta, 1879, p. 44.

a million and a half of labourers left the fields and the workshops to take up arms.[1]

But the war over, this state of things suddenly changed; the great demand for products ceased the very moment the soldier-citizens laid down their arms and returned to their usual occupations; the agio on gold declined; there was a great disturbance in prices.

The general wealth of the country, which had been able to maintain without flinching the vicissitudes of a war which, Wells calculates, must have cost altogether more than a million of men and more than 9000 millions of dollars; and the condition of the southern States, in need of every kind of manufacture and ready to take them immediately in exchange for the enormous· quantity of cotton which had accumulated in their warehouses; these causes combined to mitigate the effects of this inevitable crisis. For all that, the industrial situation could not be otherwise than most grave.

"The manufactures that had been set going on the spur of the artificial rise of prices could not be abandoned on the return of peace and the fall of prices which ensued."[2] No wonder then that at this moment when, there being no financial need for them, the war-taxes were being speedily removed, there was a strong disinclination to meddle with a tariff which (internal taxes being abolished) efficaciously protected the national industries; and indeed, this crisis offering a favourable opportunity, heavier duties were levied on many products.

What requires a more attentive study is the tariff policy which subsequently prevailed up to our own times. We have seen that a few years afterwards, in 1872, a general reduction of 10 per cent had been effected in the tariff; but that this had lasted a short time only, because the war-tariff was re-established during the crisis in 1873. Now for a few years after the conclusion of hostilities, the maintenance of the protective policy can be explained by the effects of the war upon the various industries, and by the subsequent crisis produced by the violent speculation which followed the keen industrial revival that came after the war;[3] but these effects

[1] *Vide* work mentioned.
[2] Jannet, *Les États Unis contemporains*, Paris, Plon, 1889, vol. ii. p. 156.
[3] Stringher, p. 71.

could not be prolonged indefinitely, the less so in a country like the United States, whose abundant resources would speedily make good (as in fact they did) all the damage done by war.

We cannot agree with Professor Taussig's opinion that the origin of the present system of protection in the United States must be attributed to the Civil War, and that it was accidental, the country drifting into it little by little, owing to the war, without which protection would not have attained its actual proportions.[1]

This explanation does not, indeed, go far enough. That the war was the accidental cause of the return to protection is evident; that for a portion of the period under consideration, for ten years or even more, its effects continued to react on the tariff policy of the country, that, too, is easy to understand; the more so if we bear in mind that the Civil War marked the triumph of the industrial capitalism of the north over the agricultural capitalism of the south. But this war, which lasted from 1861 to 1865, cannot be made to serve as a *deus ex machina* for the interpretation of a period of thirty years in the history of the tariff policy of a country like the United States. The persistence and strength of the present American protectionism demand a less superficial explanation.

45. The economic and industrial progress of the United States during the epoch in question is more than notable—it is positively marvellous, and can be easily pictured by means of a few eloquent statistics. In spite of the war, in the ten years from 1860 to 1870, although the population had only increased by 22·62 per cent, the wealth of the country augmented by 86 per cent; and from 1870 to 1885, whilst the population increased by 48 per cent, the production of corn was greater by 85 per cent, the consumption of cotton by 86 per cent, that of wool by 88 per cent, the production of cotton by 108 per cent, that of iron by 143 per cent; insurance of property against fire rose by 160 per cent, and the railways by 168 per cent.[2]

From a report presented by Mills to the House of Representatives in 1888, we can extract some comparative figures

[1] *Vide* "La tariffa MacKinley," in the *Giornale degli Econ.* Jan. 1891.
[2] *Vide* Atkinson, *The Industrial Progress of the Nation*, New York, Putnam, 1890, p. 68.

regarding the production and the consumption of national manufactures, and the importation of foreign goods during the years 1850, 1860, 1870, and 1880, which not only show clearly the astonishing progress made by American manufactures, but reveal also the fact that, if the United States give no sign of any large export of their manufactures, their industries, on the other hand, have during these thirty years shown a most pronounced tendency to take possession of the home market, since, in 1880, foreign manufactures constituted hardly 7·42 per cent of the total consumption of manufactured articles. Whether this be, on the whole, a good or an evil, whether it is more or less the effect of a protective system—these are not the questions which we propose to investigate at present ; but certainly the facts indicated bear witness to an extraordinary development of American manufactures, which are now quite capable of providing for the entire needs of the country.

From Mills' Report to the House of Representatives in 1888.

Years.	Production of National Manufactures.	Exportation of National Manufactures.	Importation of Foreign Manufactures.	Total Consumption of Manufactures in the United States.	Consumption of National Manufactures.	Consumption of Foreign Manufactures.	National Manufactures consumed at home.	National Manufactures exported.
	Dollars.	Dollars.	Dollars.	Dollars.	P. Ct.	P Ct.	P. Ct.	P. Ct.
1850	1,019,106,616	22,903,888	130,838,280	1,127,041,008	88·39	11·61	97·75	2·25
1860	1,885,861,676	45,658,873	261,264,810	2,101,467,113	87·57	12·43	97·58	2·42
1870	4,232,325,442	47,921,154	308,363,496	4,492,767,784	93·14	6·36	98·87	1·13
1880	5,369,579,191	79,510,447	423,699,010	5,713,767,754	92·58	7·42	98·52	1·48

And this progress appears even more evident and striking in the last ten years, from the returns of the eleventh census, both with regard to certain industries and the general trade of the country taken as a whole.

In the iron industries the United States have advanced with gigantic strides : till within these last few years they occupied the second place among civilised nations, England being their only superior ; but in 1890 they succeeded in wresting from her the place of honour, by producing a larger quantity of pig-iron.[1] And not only are the United States

[1] *Vide* Census Bulletin, No. 9, Washington, August 20, 1890.

now quite independent of foreign supplies of this product, but such is the progress of their own iron industries, that it is to be foreseen that, before long, England will have reason to fear American competition in the markets of the world.

Immense, too, is the progress which the United States have made in the textile industries; and the statistical tables which we reprint from the census bulletins, and which refer either to the textile fabrics or to the whole of the American manufactures generally, require no comment, and demonstrate, not merely the ever-increasing importance of these native industries in the bulk, but the growing magnitude of single enterprises.

Marvellous beyond measure is the growth of the American railways, which have now no rivals in the world. Out of a total railway mileage for the world of 370,281 miles, the United States had in 1890 no less than 163,597 miles, or 44·18 per cent of the whole; and the railway mileage of the United States exceeds by 3942 miles the entire mileage of the Old World. The census of 1860 showed the mileage to be 28,919·08 miles; that of 1880 placed the figures at 87,724·08 miles; while the eleventh census figures, as has been shown, give the astonishing total of 163,597 miles.[1]

Finally, another census bulletin gives us the figures of the evaluation of the real and personal property of the United States; and these figures, which we resume in the accompanying tables, bear eloquent witness to the economic power and to the widespread well-being of the great republic.

The Textile Industries of the United States.[2]

Years.	Number of establishments.[3]	Capital invested (dollars).	Hands employed.	Wages paid (dollars).	Cost of all materials (dollars).	Value of products (dollars).
1850	2804	103,842,616	135,586	—	62,100,020	111,540,810
1860	3336	141,008,286	185,466	37,580,191	104,749,928	198,436,114
1870	4498	270,381,508	260,563	81,352,653	253,700,110	407,249,327
1880	5827	386,407,515	367,553	98,576,302	280,045,500	500,376,068
1890	8865	701,522,861	491,630	165,830,332	408,328,226	603,043,702

[1] Extra Census Bulletin, No. 24, Washington, October 10, 1892.
[2] *Vide* Census Bulletin, No. 242, Washington, October 15, 1892.
[3] This table only embraces active establishments which reported goods manufactured to the amount of 500 dollars or over.

The Manufactures of the United States.
1880-1890.[1]

Years.	Number of establishments reporting.[2]	Capital (dollars).	Number of employés.	Total wages (dollars).	Cost of materials used (dollars).	Value of products (dollars).
1880	253,502	2,780,766,895	2,700,732	930,462,252	3,394,925,123	5,349,101,458
1890	322,624	6,138,716,604	4,476,094	2,171,396,019	5,018,277,608	9,054,435,337
Percentage of increase	27·27	120·76	65·74	131·13	47·77	69·27

Valuation of all real and personal Property in the United States.[3]

(a) 1850-1890.

Years.	Amount (dollars).	Per capita.	Increase per cent.
1850	7,135,780,228	308	—
1860	16,159,616,068	514	126·46
1870	30,068,518,507	780	85·07
1880	43,642,000,000	870	45·14
1890	65,037,091,197	1039	49·02

(b) 1890.

Real estates with personal improvements thereon . . . $39,544,544,333
Live stock on farms and ranges, farm implements and machinery 2,703,015,040
Mines and quarries, including product on hand . . . 1,291,291,579
Gold and silver, coin and bullion 1,198,774,948
Machinery on mills and product on hand, raw and manufactured 3,058,593,441
Railroads and equipments, including street railroads . . 8,685,407,323
Telegraphs, telephones, shippings, and canals 701,755,712
Miscellaneous 7,893,708,821

Total . . . $65,037,091,197

[1] Vide Extra Census Bulletin, No. 67, Washington, March 15, 1894.
[2] This table only embraces active establishments which reported goods manufactured to the amount of 500 dollars or over. The data for 1890 do not include some industries omitted at the census of 1880.
[3] Vide Census Bulletin, No. 379, Washington, March 19, 1894.

Bryce, the distinguished English writer, who has recently depicted the United States in an admirable work [1]—which finds a counterpart only in De Tocqueville's classical pages, with which, indeed, it need not fear comparison—describes with enthusiasm and in glowing colours the general well-being which prevails in the country, and draws a touching picture of the contrast between the condition of the poor classes in America and in Europe: he finds in the United States a general state of comfort, only interrupted here and there by pauperism, which is beginning to glide into a few of the larger cities; and he lauds the free and easy life of the farmers of the west.

"The life of the new emigrant in the further west has its privations in the first years, but it is brightened by hope, and has a singular charm of freedom and simplicity. The impression made by this comfort and plenty is heightened by the brilliance and keenness of the air, by the look of freshness and cleanness which even the cities wear, all of them except the poorest parts in a very few. The fog and soot-flakes of an English town, as well as its squalor, are wanting; you are in a new world, and a world which knows the sun. It is impossible not to feel warmed, cheered, invigorated by the sense of such material well-being all around one, impossible not to be infected by the buoyancy and hopefulness of the people." [2]

And yet we are not altogether in a bed of roses, even in this new and fortunate world, and if well-being is more general and life easier, preoccupations and anxieties are not wanting. And not only the anxiety regarding the future—perhaps not so far distant—when the whole land shall have been occupied, when the cities will no longer have an outlet for the superabundant population, and the chronic evils of old Europe will have settled down upon and brutalised the new world also; for indeed the United States have been already made acquainted with these chronic ills, and present troubles are more pressing than those looming in the future. Here, as in Europe, has been inoculated for some time past that all-pervading economic disease of our times—industrial

[1] *The American Commonwealth*, London, Macmillan, 1888.
[2] Bryce, work mentioned, 1888, vol. iii. p. 609.

depression, and this fact, the importance of which cannot be over-rated, demands all our attention.

46. In place of the famines of days gone by and of the temporary crises which characterised later times, we have been suffering for the last twenty years from a permanent ill-ease which seems to have become chronic. Its principal symptoms are a general fall in prices and profits, in conjunction with a systematic excess of production out of all proportion to the consuming capacity of the population, and a continual increase of the accumulation of capital and of the bulk of trade. And thus, whilst economic and industrial activity goes on augmenting, the advantage accruing to the various classes from their labours gets less and less; hence a fierce struggle among them to wrest from one another the scanty gains, and an increase of friction and discontent in the general discomfort. Industrial depression began to show itself simultaneously in Germany and in the United States in 1873, and has spread since then to England and to other European countries; there was an intermission for a few years, specially in America, then in 1885-1886 it reappeared in an aggravated form, and has continued, with a few interruptions, to the present day.[1]

For the depression in America it will be sufficient to refer to Wright's work,[2] which throws much light on its characteristics, and particularly the fall in prices and profits, over-production, and under-consumption; whilst more recent publications bear witness to the fact that of late years these salient features have not changed, and that, in spite of their great resources, the United States have been profoundly disturbed.

Many and varied are the explanations that have been offered of so grave a phenomenon. Insufficient, even if partially true, are those which attribute the depression to various local causes, bad harvests, destruction of capital, strikes, taxes, and other occurrences; and that, not merely because these facts have manifested themselves in diverse ways in the different countries in which depression has prevailed, but because the countries which have suffered

---

[1] Wells, *Recent Economic Changes*, London, Longmans, 1891.
[2] *Industrial Depressions*, Washington, 1886.

most are those which show no sign of penury, and where, on the contrary, all desirable productions and commodities have been—as Wells observes [1]—rapidly accumulating from year to year.

No less unsatisfactory are the theories which attribute the depression to the facts which form its most characteristic features, such as over-production, fall in prices, and protective legislation. Such explanations, indeed, do but substitute the effects and symptoms for the causes, the difficulty is merely evaded, and the reasons remain to be shown why there should be such a permanent excess of production, or such a fall in prices, or why a protective policy exists in the majority of states.

More convincing seems to us to be the interpretation put forward by Wells, who, in the work we have quoted, attributes the depression to the great transformations that have been brought about by new inventions and new systems of production and transport, which have resulted in a supply far larger than the remunerative demand, and hence the fall in prices.

Not even this, however, is in our opinion the true explanation; the actual depression appears to us too deep-rooted and general to have had its origin in transitory changes. More probably is it the beginning of the general crisis affecting the capitalistic system, which has now accomplished its historical cycle, and is struggling desperately for self-preservation. The technical transformations of industry are merely the effects of more general and deep-seated causes, and in their turn they bring about the inevitable changes in the capitalistic system of to-day.

The industrial depression that characterises our epoch, writes Loria, manifests itself when the land rent has for the first time permanently and generally reduced to a minimum the profits of productive capital, and hence the partial destruction of capital—in other words, a crisis—is followed by a chronic destruction, namely, depression.[2]

The actual depression is, in fact, the reflection of the chronic condition of capitalistic industry which is vainly

[1] *Recent Economic Changes*, p. 25.
[2] *Analisi della proprietà capitalista*, vol. ii. p. 361.

struggling to retain the profits that are escaping its grasp, and that will seize every means that may give it momentary relief.

But the struggle is a hopeless one; the remedies are ineffectual; the endeavours to realise a profit by continually increasing the production, and thus reducing general expenses, result in overproduction and fierce competition, and the attempt to give temporary relief to trade by means of protection leads to the multiplicity of evils which this system inflicts upon the various industries, and to the far more serious injury which it does to the whole country.

This way of looking at the question seems to us to be far nearer the truth, because it is broader, and because it affords us an explanation of all the graver phenomena characteristic of our times—times replete with singular and painful economic contradictions. For it not only explains the crisis in the production and circulation of wealth, but also that in its distribution, with its fierce antagonism between capital and labour, which is so much more deplorable owing to the fact that—as it is not merely a question of distribution, but goes to the very source and system of production—the capitalistic industries show themselves, in a crisis, quite unable to remedy it, and to effectually improve the condition of the poor classes. Thus we see how the general discontent, the dolorous agony of capitalism, leads, as a last resource, in various countries to an economic struggle, to vain endeavours to overcome one another; efforts that naturally paralyse one another, and hasten on the general ruin. Thus we see how the battle between capitalists is transformed into a fight between nations, each one trying to throw off the results of the crisis on its neighbour; and how—side by side of the economic struggle, the last and most significant manifestations of which are the ever-spreading, mutually-destructive excesses of protectionism—there is being waged a political warfare which shows itself in the present strange and contradictory state of the European nations; whilst declaring their desire for peace, they are ever hastening on preparations for war, which has been expected for a long while, with grievous anxiety almost worse than its realisation; and to avoid the calamities of war they maintain an armed peace which prostrates and ruins them.

All this characterises a situation in which a general economic and social reorganisation is felt to be inevitable, and gives a rational explanation of the complex and contradictory phenomena of our times. And these considerations will help us, as we shall see, to a better understanding of the present protectionism.

But we are being carried too far; it is sufficient for the moment to state one fact, the reality and importance of which cannot be doubted, and that is that the economic depression, permanent and spread as it is over the whole civilised world, and its foremost industrial countries in particular, rules, and has ruled for the last years, with varying intensity over the United States of America.

47. Another important fact which characterises the industrial circumstances of our times, and which is intimately connected, as we shall shortly see, with depression and protectionism, is the existence of trusts and other forms of industrial coalitions. The free competition laid down by economists as a positive law, has never been anything but an historical form of economic evolution, and a form the significance of which has been greatly exaggerated. And as it was preceded by forms that differed widely from it, so nowadays it is showing signs of a complete transformation; and an indication of the coming change is the formation of trusts, which endeavour to substitute a good understanding, and even monopoly, for the desperate life struggle, and which constitute a new and most important element in the serious problems of the day.

Many and varied are the forms assumed by these combinations in different countries where they adapt themselves to the industrial circumstances; and their evolution, which still continues, has already been studied by many writers.[1]

In them we observe three types especially, which represent three successive phases in their evolution: that which is a simple agreement limiting prices or production, and which leaves entire freedom of action to the individual producer;

[1] In the 'Italian edition of this volume we have treated this question at considerable length, making use of the numerous works dealing with it. Here we will content ourselves with a summary notice of these researches, in so far as they refer strictly to our subject.

that in which the sales and benefits are divided among the associates according to pre-determined rules; and, finally, that in which the individual enterprises have been completely fused into a single vast enterprise, of which they merely remain the branches. It is, above all, in the last-named form, that, under the name of "trusts," these unions have had a large and important development in the United States. The basis of the organisation of these trusts is that the majority or entirety of the shareholders of a certain number of corporations carrying on the same trade, entrust the management of their affairs to a committee of trustees, in whose hands is placed the supreme direction of all the various undertakings, which are united in one administration.[1] The English-speaking public are already too well acquainted with the "Standard Oil Trust," the "Sugar Trust," the "Whisky Trust," and all the other colossal American trusts, for it to be necessary for us to follow at any length in the footsteps of the numerous authors who have dealt with them. Thanks to these organisations, many industries have become unique and gigantic enterprises, which dominate the market, and give to production a new and unusual form, which has aroused much grave anxiety. It is certain that by eliminating or partly paralysing competition these trusts have sometimes provoked a rise, and more often prevented or retarded the fall of prices, as alarm has likewise been awakened by the agreements made by some of the great trusts with the railway companies, and by the dangers which such combinations present, not only to consumers, but also to workmen. Whilst the immense influence brought to bear by these trusts on the social, economic, and political life of the country has caused public opinion in the United States to rise up against them, so that a large number of States, and Congress itself, have drafted laws for the purpose of limiting their powers, and the judicial bench has shown much severity in dealing with them. For all that, in spite of their many disadvantages, the trusts really confer indisputable benefits. It cannot be denied, in fact, that the concentration of pro-

[1] This form of trusts (Professor Taussig writes us) is already a matter of the past in the United States. Events have moved quickly during recent years. The fact, however, still remains.

duction in powerful organisations renders it much more economical and advantageous by making possible notable savings in the costs of production and transport, so much so as to render plausible the declaration of the supporters of trusts that their great gains are not irreconcilable with the interests of consumers, and by no means imply their impoverishment. Thus it is that these trusts have found favour, from a scientific point of view, in the eyes of many writers, of whom some, such as Gunton,[1] confine themselves to point out how groundless are the fears that they might constitute monopolies detrimental to consumers; whilst others, among them Brentano,[2] discover in them, not a temporary expedient to protect producers in the actual crisis, but indeed a remedy for the social question, a new and general economic system, destined to take the place of the present order of things, and that would be the prelude, in fact, to a collective organisation of all industries.

On the other hand, a group of writers, having regard to the difficulties experienced by many sorts of these organisations in constituting and maintaining themselves, to the obstacles they frequently meet with in attempting to dominate the markets, and bearing in mind that they sprang into existence owing to temporary commercial adversity, assign to them far less importance, and maintain that they are only of a transitory nature.

Now there seems to us to be no great difficulty in solving the question, if we consider the origin and characteristics of these institutions. They have a twofold origin, the one in the actual depression, which may be looked upon as temporary, not in the sense that it will come to an end and things be as they were before, but that it cannot continue indefinitely, and must find a remedy in some new economic and social development; the other source is in the tendency to concentration which constitutes an organic need in a large number of industries, and which is paving the way for a new form of competition. Thus it is that these associations appear to us at the present moment bearing the marks both of permanence and of transitoriness: of permanence in

[1] Vide *Principles of Social Economics*, New York, Putnam, 1891.
[2] Vide *Die Ursachen der heutigen socialen Noth*, Leipzig, Dunker, 1889.

as much as they seem undoubtedly to be indications of a new and higher type of industrial organisation; of transitoriness in so far as they merely throw out hints of new forms not yet perfected, full of defects and dangers, and not yet adapted to the circumstances of the various industries, and that will not assume a definite shape till after a long evolution.

48. The question of the trusts is connected with that of protective policy, and it is for that reason that we have been induced to speak of them. Some writers indeed believe them to be intimately bound up together, and have come to the conclusion that coalitions and trusts are a product of protectionism. These organisations would, in fact, appear to be a complement of protection and a reaction against such of its indirect effects as tend to render its provisions nugatory. For the aim of protection is to ensure a home market for national industries and to raise the price of commodities, but this rise in prices greatly stimulates native competition, producing overproduction, which in its turn lowers prices. It is at this point that coalitions intervene, which tend to repress the excessive development given artificially to native production by means of protection, and to enable the protected producers to reap the benefit which would otherwise escape them.[1]

Bonham remarks that this fact is manifest throughout the United States: the state, by means of protection, has limited the area of markets, artificially stimulating protected manufactures and hence creating an excess of production; and protectionists endeavour to secure the fruits of this system, and at the same time to keep industrial development within bounds by means of coalitions. Thus protection serves the interests of manufacturers and ensures them a reward, but, instead of promoting the growth of industries, it becomes indirectly a bar to their progress, and favours monopolies.[2]

And not only, according to the upholders of this thesis, do coalitions find their *raison d'être* in protectionism, but it is the latter which makes them possible, by paralysing foreign

---

[1] *Vide* Raffalovich, *Les coalitions des producteurs et le protectionnisme*, Paris, Guillaumin, 1889, pp. 12, 13, 18. *Vide* also Bonham, *Industrial Liberty*, New York, Putnam, 1888, p. 142.

[2] Work quoted, pp. 231-234.

competition, which would prevent the formation of any internal monopoly. And both Raffalovich [1] and Jannet [2] remark that coalitions have been more prevalent and have exercised a more alarming influence in Germany and in the United States, where protectionism flourishes, than in free-trade countries, where indeed they are neither numerous nor dangerous.[3]

But this theory appears to us to be inaccurate. It does not explain the existence of trusts regarding products for which foreign competition is unimportant (as, for example, the notorious "Standard Oil Trust"), and of numerous international coalitions, nor does it account for the tendency to industrial concentration, which is an indisputable fact; whilst it looks upon protectionism as the cause of a fall of prices and depression, whereas it is on the contrary the effect of it.[4]

All this is understood by certain writers who have seriously studied the question of trusts, and who, without denying the connection between them and protectionism, do not admit that the latter is either the sole or the principal cause of their existence. And among these writers is Professor Dalla Volta, the author of an important essay on the subject,[5] who, wishing to establish an unbroken chain of cause and effect between protection and industrial coalitions, recognises that the latter owe their origin also to industrial depression and the tendency to industrial concentration.

Leaving aside for the present the permanent and organic part played by trusts in the tendency to industrial concentration, and examining its origin in connection with protectionism, it seems to us an error to consider that those two

[1] *Bulletin de la Soc. d'écon. pol.* Séance du 5 Jan. 1889.
[2] *Le capital, la spéculation*, etc., p. 317.
[3] Jannet, however, states inaccurately that free-trade England is exempt from coalitions, whilst Raffalovich (in the work quoted, pp. 7-9) mentions nine in that country, affecting salt, coal, iron, paper, flour, etc.
[4] It is not out of place to observe (in order that the connection between these facts may be evident) that the spread of trusts and rings, particularly in Germany and the United States, began in the very same years as the depression, namely, after 1873.
[5] "Le coalizioni industriali," in the *Giornale degli Economisti*, March to June 1889, and January to April 1890.

phenomena are bound together as cause and effect. The link between them is not of this nature; it is not a necessary nor essential connection, although a very close one. There is between them the natural affinity which knits together two children of the same birth. For the actual industrial depression is, in our opinion, the parent both of protectionism and of these trade coalitions, all phenomena characteristic of the present day. These two manifestations, having a common origin, are so intimately allied that they mutually support one another.

Protection, as a matter of fact, by limiting international competition, smooths the way for the establishment and maintenance of these industrial conditions; whilst they, in their turn, by restricting home competition, lend a ready hand to protective practices. And it is a result of the fatal co-operation of these two forces, both emanating from modern capitalism, that the most dangerous monopolies have arisen, and that the concentration of capital, which might be so advantageous to all, becomes a power of evil, which, to serve the desperate ends of capitalism, threatens to crush beneath its giant weight consumers as well as workmen.

49. The review of all these facts enables us to offer an explanation of the ever-increasing recrudescence of American protectionism during the last twenty years. It will not be a simple, nor yet a complete explanation: not simple, because it deals with complicated phenomena resulting from different factors, interwoven by a series of actions and reactions; and not complete, because it is not possible to determine all the factors with precision, nor always to make clear relations that are often deep and obscure. But it will be, we trust, a reasonable explanation, and one that will, in its general scope, bear criticism; whilst, as we have already pointed out, that is not a reasonable solution which attributes the whole of the American protective movement, or at least its continuous progress, during all this period, to the Civil War.[1]

---

[1] Professor Bastable explains the actual spread of protectionism, specially in the United States, by attributing it to the following causes : (*a*) the interested motives of particular classes of producers, who, exclusively preoccupied with their own immediate benefit, insist on protection ; (*b*) economic errors which

Among the factors of protectionism in the last period we find in the very first place industrial depression, which was most serious in the United States, and was especially aggravated during the last ten years, which corresponded with the increase in protective duties.[1]

The industrial depression resolved itself, for the capitalist, into a melancholy and persistent reduction of profits, against which he struggled daily. And in this desperate conflict he had recourse, in order to raise his profits, to various expedients, among which trade coalitions and protectionism figure prominently. By means of trusts the capitalist takes advantage of the actual tendency to industrial concentration, and tries to turn it, to his own advantage, into a monopoly, with a view to the recovery—regardless of the injury to consumers and work-people—of that profit which the land rent, the competition, and other circumstances of the present day will no longer allow him to derive from his investment.

By means of protection, too, the capitalist endeavours to maintain his profit; and it is for us to investigate if and how this can be done, and with what results to the capitalists as well as to all other classes of the community.

There are various ways in which protectionism can attempt to stave off the depression of profits, and many likewise in which capitalists can hope to obtain a similar result: some of them are superficial, others founded on deep considerations. Let us begin with the latter.

In the first place we must find out whether protectionism can act in this last period in the same characteristic manner as, we have repeatedly seen, it was wont to do in the first

have been popularly diffused, and on which protectionism is based ; (c) the sentiment of nationality invoked by protectionists. These observations, says Bastable, seem adequately to explain the persistence of a policy which is altogether opposed not only to the conclusions of scientific investigation, but also to the plainest dictates of common sense. (Vide *The Theory of International Trade*, Dublin, Hodges, 1887, pp. 149-153.) But to us these observations appear inadequate to explain the persistence of so grave a phenomenon—one requiring far profounder investigations.

[1] Professor Taussig remarks that in the electoral campaigns of 1876 and 1880 protection was not strongly insisted upon, and that the rigid enforcement of that policy has only been adopted by the Republicans during the last ten years. (See "La tariffa MacKinley," in the *Giornale degli Econ.* Jan. 1891).

epoch of capitalism; that is to say, whether it can maintain profits in the new capitalistic industries by lowering the condition of the workpeople, by keeping them off the free lands and forcing them to work for hire, or, if they are already doing so, to reduce their wages.

At first sight, such a question would seem to demand an assuredly negative answer, especially when we bear in mind the tendency of the present time to the disappearance of free land and the reduction of wages to a minimum.

Jannet, in fact, observes in picturesque language that in the United States the west seems to get ever farther and farther away; by which he means that in order to find free public land it becomes every day necessary to travel farther, to harder climates, and to less fertile regions, and that, although land may be had there almost gratuitously, a greater expenditure of capital and labour is now needful to turn it to account than was the case in the past.[1]

Besides this, the early colonisation of the west was effected by the descendants of old American families having some capital, or by European immigrants who had first of all made a little money in the country districts or cities of the east. But the unskilled labourers of to-day are altogether unprovided with this capital necessary to make the acquisition profitable.[2]

The condition of American workmen at the present time, although on the whole far superior to that of Europeans, has undergone great changes in the last fifty years. In spite of much disagreement as to whether their wages have really risen or fallen during this period (we cannot enter into this most difficult question, because it would be too great a digression from our argument, and its solution here is by no means necessary), yet, to believe those who admit that there has been an increase, the average condition of factory hands has fallen, because, owing to perfected machinery, less skill and capacity is now required.[3] No longer to be found are those simple and happy peasant girls working at Lowell, those gentle characters of the olden times so graphically described

---

[1] *Les États Unis contemporains*, vol. ii. p. 168.
[2] *Ibid.* p. 169.
[3] Wright, *Comparative Wages*, etc., p. 35.

by Dickens, who left their humble though comfortable homes in order to earn, in some distant factory, a sum on which they might marry. There, although working industriously, they lived a socially, intellectually, and morally elevated life; they had schools, libraries, and they even kept a journal; and, what is more, after a few years they returned to their families, and with their savings they bought a plot of land and built a modest cottage.[1] Such an idyll and that golden age of the workpeople seem to us nowadays to be creations of fancy.

The disappearance of free land and the lowering of the workman's status would therefore seem to point to the conclusion that it was no longer necessary, or, at all events, no longer useful, for the capitalist to adopt artificial means for debasing the condition of labourers, with a view to excluding them from the free land.

But if this is partly true—and if the capitalist's efforts to maintain profits must consequently be directed to other channels—it is not, however, the whole truth; so that that element which is of primary importance in the first period of protectionism still survives, though of considerably less weight, in later times.

A characteristic phenomenon of these last years is the division of workmen into two distinct classes, the "skilled" and the "unskilled," who seem to have a different fate in store for them; for while a notable improvement is observable in the circumstances of the former, the moral and economic standard of the latter is constantly sinking.[2] The first class, which is intelligent and flourishing, maintains its power by trade-unions; the second appears to be precluded from every means of betterment, even that offered by community of interests, since the skilled labourers, who might assist their less qualified brethren, tend to form themselves into an aristocracy of labour, pursuing different objects from them.

[1] Dickens, *American Notes;* Wright and H. Robinson, *Early Factory Labour in New England*, Boston, 1889; Chevalier, *Lettres sur l'Amérique du Nord*, vol. ii. pp. 395 *et seq.*

[2] *Vide*, among other essays dealing with this subject, Ricca Salerno's important contribution to the *Nuova Antologia* (Rome) of the 1st of May 1891, on the reduction of hours of labour in England.

R

This movement in the working classes is very manifest and accentuated in the United States, according to authors worthy of the highest credit—such as Jannet, Wright, and Atkinson;[1] and this disparity in the condition of the workmen also explains how, by taking a one-sided view of the subject only, so many contradictory opinions have been given. Thus it is that, whilst Jannet rightly declares, as we have seen, that free land is now beyond the reach of unskilled labourers, Wright, on the contrary, states that "the increase in aggregate earnings, with its complement the savings-bank system, has enabled the operative class gradually *to amass sufficient capital for the acquisition of land*, or for other profitable uses."[2] And this last-born class of labourers, who in the melancholy circumstances of the present day are yet able to better themselves, and, powerful through their trades-unions, exact higher wages, effect savings, and aspire to the possession of the far-distant fragments of free land which are still available, and which improved means of transport have rendered accessible—this new class, though numerically small, is yet strong enough to cause anxiety to the capitalists, who, in the desperate struggle for profits, do all they can to neutralise their courageous endeavours. For this class, the free lands, although they have become more distant and difficult of access, are less so, however, than they were to all the working-men of the last decennial periods; and although this is not, we repeat, the most important aspect of the question, it nevertheless enables us to conceive protectionism as an instrument for the depression of this category of labourers.

50. The American land policy confirms these observations. We have already seen how in the past it served the ends of the manufacturing and agricultural capitalists by excluding labourers from the land and forcing them to work for hire; and how, later on, when industrial capitalism no longer required this policy, it lent itself to the interests of agricultural capitalism. In spite of the ever-increasing protests of the people, the land laws keeping labourers off the soil lasted till the year 1862, when, by means of the Homestead Act, the occupation of the land by the cultivators was encouraged—

---

[1] *The Industrial Progress of the Nation*, New York, Putnam, 1890.
[2] Work quoted, p. 35.

lots to the extent of 160 acres each being granted to the settlers on very easy terms. Loria remarks on this point that this only occurred when the sterility of what remained of the free land, requiring a large capital outlay to render it productive, and the reduction of wages, rendered useless all efforts to keep the land away from those who worked for hire.[1] And if this observation is to a certain extent exaggerated, it none the less contains a profound element of truth. Certain it is, as we have already seen, that the majority of the labourers altogether lacked the necessary means of fixing themselves on the land, nor did the laws assist them in any way. And besides this, the best soil was already occupied. "We look at the figures showing acres and acres as still remaining, and forget that the productive land is gone. Long miles of mountains and sandy plains and cactus desert remain, without soil, rain, or water."[2] The capitalists could, therefore, now indulge in the luxury of liberal land legislation, without feeling too much anxiety. But anyhow, if anxiety it did cause them, if they took umbrage at the facilities granted to would-be landowners, the other provisions regarding the land and the very application of the Homestead Law freed them from all serious apprehension. For whilst, on the one hand, the soil was distributed in small allotments among cultivators, on the other, it was conceded in vast areas to railway companies, to private individuals and to associations, who speculated in it, and for whom it constituted huge capitalistic investments. And even the Homestead and Exemption Law was violated in those clauses which designed to reserve the land for the cultivators, inasmuch as capitalists caused the ground to be purchased in small lots, according to the provisions of the Act, but united them afterwards into one large domain.[3] And so immense territorial properties and the system of land leases rapidly developed in the United States.

It has been laid down, says Phillips, that the land ought to be reserved for the cultivators; but this has been carried out by no law, speculative and landed interests being too

---

[1] *Analisi*, vol. ii. pp. 251-252.
[2] Phillips, *Land, Labour, and Law*, New York, Scribners, 1886, p. 344.
[3] Sering, work quoted, p. 125.

strongly opposed to it. "Our whole land system has been nothing more than a piece of carelessly put-together machinery, adapted to further the ends of land speculation."[1]

51. But to return to protectionism. We have already adverted incidentally to another direction in which its influence was profoundly felt, and another method by which it endeavoured to overcome the fatal crisis through which capitalism was passing.

We have touched upon the close connection that exists at the present day between protectionism and trusts and monopolies, which have spread so widely and assumed such importance in the United States. With these, protectionism— which is itself essentially a monopoly—has aims and, to a certain extent, results in common. These trade coalitions have been formed, as we have seen, for the purpose of limiting production in order to raise prices, and they do effectually restrict production. But at the same time they tend to reduce wages, either by directly making themselves masters of the labour market, or else indirectly by limiting production and the demand for labour.

Similar are the tendencies of protectionism: it, too, restricts production and the natural development of productive forces ; as such, it may in some ways serve to ward off the causes of crises, by destroying or preventing the accumulation of wealth, which might be employed in an unproductive and fatal manner, and give rise to disasters.

As we have already pointed out, Loria, looking upon protectionism as a limitation of accumulation, labours, with great acumen, to justify protection during what he calls the "systematic period of capitalism" (which nearly corresponds to that which we designated its "first phase," that is to say, during the formation of the great industries); and he observes that this process is unconscious and involuntary on the part of

[1] Phillips, work mentioned, p. 355. Professor Taussig, who has kindly read through the proof-sheets of this volume, does not agree with the interpretation which we have in several places, and here especially, put upon the American land laws. He remarks that "historically there is little ground for saying that the United States land laws and land policy have been manipulated by the capitalist class." Although we do not feel able to modify the conclusions suggested by facts which have come to our knowledge, we hope nevertheless that the matter will be more deeply studied.

capitalists, to whom indeed protectionism appears as a method of increasing profits.[1] Whilst he maintains that later, on the contrary, profits having become automatic, such a method is no longer necessary, because there is no need to maintain them by setting artificial bounds to production; and hence, that free-trade should become more and more general. But it seems to us that such a view of the question does not altogether tally with facts, at least as they appear in the United States—and elsewhere also, although for other countries a more profound investigation would have to be made.

It appears to us that, both in the United States and in other countries that have attained the first rank in modern civilisation, there is manifest this twofold tendency—to protectionism and to an energetic restriction of production. And this tendency of the day follows two periods, which in the United States are quite clearly defined, in the first of which, with the formation of the great capitalist industries, protectionism was developed, and in the second, the industries being consolidated, relative free-trade ensued. The present American protectionism can therefore be regarded as an ulterior form that follows upon free-trade, and that, in the general fall of profits, tends to co-operate, especially by limiting production, in maintaining prices.

At this point we cannot refrain from alluding to certain remarks made by Ricca Salerno in the excellent articles which we have more than once quoted, and which, although we cannot now follow them in all their conclusions, contain many pregnant suggestions of which we have largely availed ourselves. After having developed certain perfectly truthful views on the causes of protectionism in new countries—to which we have repeatedly had recourse for the interpretation of the facts under consideration—he observes that, at a later period of capitalism, high wages being the rule (but no longer caused by free land, but rather by the high cost of the necessaries of life, on account of the increase of population, augmented rent, etc.), the capitalist, in order to lower these wages and maintain his profits, must lessen the price of commodities, and this is effected by means of free-trade, which consequently takes the place of protection.

[1] *Analisi*, vol. i. pp. 605, 606.

In this period, therefore, the interests of capitalists and landed proprietors are in opposition, since free-trade aids the former in reducing the price of provisions, and hence in reducing also the land rent accruing to the latter.[1]

These observations apply to old countries, and above all to Europe, where protectionism is chiefly agricultural, and where the protection of manufactures is therefore more difficult to explain, if it is not looked upon as a compensation granted to manufacturers for agrarian protection. In fact, free-trade must be—and has been in several countries for some time past —strenuously resisted by the landowners, whose interests it injures; and then the capitalists, whose condition becomes ever more critical with the enhancement of returns and the ceaseless diminution of profits owing to industrial depression, and who, moreover, are adversely affected by agricultural protection, grasp at industrial protection as an *ultima ratio*, for, by limiting production and accumulation, it tends, as we have already pointed out, to raise a last buttress against the fall of profits.

In the United States, however, especially in the first part of the last period with which we are concerned, circumstances are somewhat different, provisions being cheap and produced in sufficient abundance to be exported; so that the advantage which capitalists might derive from free-trade as a means for reducing prices would be most doubtful, and most doubtful likewise the harm that would accrue to landowners through foreign importations.

If, therefore, the preceding observations do not apply, in the United States, up to the most recent date, they none the less help us to explain the partial existence of American agricultural protectionism (as we have seen the duties on wool were of great weight in the tariff until 1894), and the fact that, recently, the importance of exports having diminished, whilst that of the home market for agricultural produce has increased, agrarian protection has largely developed in the United States as a compensation for the protection granted to manufactures. Beneath this apparent conciliation of landowners and capitalists, their interests are, even in America, strongly opposed, a

[1] "Protezionismo e libero scambio," etc., in the *Giorn. degli Econ.* April-May 1891.

fact brought out into bold relief by Ricca Salerno, as we shall more clearly see presently.

52. But even without attempting to sound the dark and uncertain depths of economic phenomena, a superficial investigation gives us several reasons for the actual protectionist revival, reasons, either of general application to the leading nations, or specially to the United States. We will begin with the more general. The widespread depression of industry and capitalism during the past twenty years is sufficient to explain, superficially at all events, the attempt—unreasonable though it be, and unsatisfactory in its results—to bring about a reaction by means of protection. The one significant fact is that whilst the United States from the year 1832, and Europe generally from 1846, were ever more inclined to free-trade, Europe from 1878 (Austria and Italy in 1878, Germany in 1879, France in 1881, etc.)—that is to say, a few years after depression had set in—returned to a rapid and uninterrupted system of protection ; while the same thing having occurred earlier in the United States, owing to an accidental cause—the war,—even after it was over protectionism remained and was more in favour than ever.

The economist is naturally led to ask how it is that protectionism, which restricts production, the accumulation of wealth and social well-being, and if injurious to the community in these ways, is unable on the other hand to raise the general standard of profits, because they, unlike land rent, cannot be increased by methods which lessen production—he is led to ask, we say, how it is that protectionism should be so ardently cherished by business men as the great remedy for all their ills ; and he is generally led to the conclusion that they are the victims of a fatal delusion. Now it appears to us that if delusion there be—and the permanence of such a delusion would require, at all events, some explanation—there is beneath it a substratum of truth. We will not return to what has been said above regarding the efficacy of protection in limiting production—which is what the present crisis chiefly needs—or in arresting the fall of profits. Without investigating such recondite effects, we may remark, in the first place, that in the present grave perturbations of trade, when so many industries are in a critical condition, and have even continued for a long while to produce without profits, or even at a loss, every remedy, or to speak more accurately, every palliative, is hailed with enthusiasm and confidence, just as a hopeless patient trusts in morphia to mitigate his sufferings. Protection, by means of the rise in prices, which is the immediate effect of higher import duties, can give this momentary relief. It will be brief: competition at home, sometimes a wrong direction given to production and other causes will quickly neutralise its effects; but it will, in the meantime, have given a stimulus to those moribund industries; it will temporarily raise profits, spur on speculations, and rekindle hope. And when, later on, the crisis sets in again with all its former severity, those undertakings, animated by a delusion, will be able to resist all the longer. Often, indeed, in the circumstances of the present day, may an element which tends to postpone a disastrous liquidation be looked upon as advantageous, at all events for the moment—for profitless production is not unfrequently preferable to winding-up a business.

This is not all, however, for in another way, too, can protectionism ensure a short-lived benefit to capitalists. Our century has witnessed not only radical transformations in the technical modes of production, but from the moment of their introduction they have constantly been undergoing rapid improvement by means of new inventions that show no signs of exhaustion. And it is worthy of note that whilst the exigencies of technical progress demand incessant transformations in the capital of an industrial enterprise, the investment of this capital in machinery and other fixtures renders it every day less adaptable to sudden changes. Hence frequently arises great embarrassment to investors, who suffer not only from the want of more capital, but also from the difficulty of transferring what they already have from one use to another, either by new investments, or merely by the purchase of more perfected machinery.

Wells, in the work which we have already quoted,[1] attributes the actual crisis directly to these changes and to the displacements which they have caused: but without going so far as that, their importance and influence on industry is unquestioned.

[1] *Recent Economic Changes*, London, Longmans, 1891.

Now protectionism can be a temporary help to business men in such circumstances. Economists have observed, and rightly, too, that it often produces results altogether opposed to those which it apparently aimed at, since, instead of giving an impulse to industrial progress, it seems—by limiting competition—to favour trade-stagnation. By doing this protection evidently injures a country, putting a drag on industrial development and making consumers pay more dearly for all commodities; and it must ultimately injure manufacturers, for it debars them from the advantages of new technical processes. But it cannot be denied that it sometimes stands them in good stead, in that it gives them a temporary relief by exempting them from, or at all events delaying the necessity of, technical changes which might heavily burden the undertaking or even prove altogether disproportionate to the means at its disposal.

53. It has been shown that the most salient and serious characteristic of the actual depression is overproduction, or rather an indiscriminate production, which finds no outlet, because it often fails to meet the particular demand, but more often on account of the diminished acquiring-capacity of the population.

This state of affairs is aggravated by the recent dislocations of international trade. Social and industrial progress has greatly reduced the line of demarcation which formerly existed between new countries, exporters of raw materials, and old countries, exporters of manufactures: the former have started manufacturing industries and are doing their utmost to consolidate them; as a consequence the exportation of such products from the older nations tends to diminish.[1] Hence follows the lessened importance of international trade; a fact which greatly aggravates the crisis in those countries whose prosperity largely depends on this trade. From this results the twofold tendency of modern states, to colonial expansion— by means of which it is endeavoured to substitute new markets for those that are closed—and to raise import duties in order to at all events secure the home markets entirely for national products. It would seem as though the nations, in the urgency

[1] On this point, see Professor Emilio Cossa's weighty considerations in his article on the Reduction of Hours of Labour, Milan, Vallardi, 1892.

of the crisis, had not been able to understand the radical absurdity of such a system, which though it may occasionally be of some temporary and delusive advantage, leads logically to economic isolation and to retaliation.

The political and economic condition of Europe in the present day is so singular that we seem almost to be harking back to a former period: the desperate struggle of capitalism for the maintenance of profits—characteristic of the days we live in—forces the nations, oppressed one and all by the crisis, to a political and economic antagonism similar to that which a few centuries ago formed the basis of the mercantile system. But the struggle then was fruitful—destined to lead to the organisation of strong and vital individualities, both political and economic, and the foundation of a system of economy pregnant with great results; now, on the contrary, it is a barren struggle, which is kept up to arrest the fatal dissolution of capitalism, and which, in order to galvanise its corpse into the semblance of life, threatens to destroy the very source of the wealth and prosperity of nations.

Nor must we lose sight of the way in which protectionism is influenced by the tendency of the present day to make the action of the state felt in the whole field of economy; an intervention—more or less efficacious and advantageous according to circumstances—which can always be tried experimentally in support of one or other of the social classes. And owing to the predominance of capitalistic interests, and in order to obtain an often quite delusive and always temporary and partial benefit for the capitalist class, ever fighting for the retention of profits, the action of the state ends by depressing the working classes and injuring the mass of consumers.

54. It may be asked, at this point, why the phenomenon of protectionism is not to be found in all the countries afflicted by depression, and how it is that, although both are suffering equally from it, the United States are altogether given over to protection, whilst England is entirely free from it?

Strictly speaking we might evade an answer to this question, on the ground that our study extends only to the United States, and only so far as that country is concerned have we collected the necessary data; but as in the preceding paragraphs we have somewhat overstepped our boundaries by allusions to Europe, a further digression may be permissible. A distinguished economist, Fawcett,[1] intent, above all, on investigating the effects of protectionism, observes that in Great Britain, for the very reason that free-trade prevails there, depression has been less serious than in the United States, where protectionism reigns supreme. It appears to us —and all our inquiries lead to this conclusion—that it would be possible, without any logical inconsistency, to invert the terms, and instead of saying that the United Kingdom has suffered less because it has remained faithful to free-trade, to say that it has remained faithful to free-trade *because* it has suffered less from depression. In our opinion, commercial policy, for all the influence it may have on the economy of a country, is much more important as an *effect* than as the *cause* of its economic condition.

If we admit, therefore, that protectionism is the *effect* and not the *cause* of industrial depression, it may be added that this depression has not everywhere assumed the same characteristics; and that, according to the dissimilarity of the circumstances in which it is developed, the same fact may produce very different effects.

Applying the argument, which we do not wish to press too far, to England, it is easy to understand how the spread of protectionism should encounter more obstacles than in any other part of the world. For in that country international trade is of vital importance; British industries are mainly export industries; the limited extent of the native islands, compared to their manufacturing capacity, offers but a small market for a prodigious output; and these industries, the first in the world, have no need whatever of any kind of encouragement—all they want is a cheap supply of raw materials. For England, therefore, a large exportation of her manufactured goods, and a large importation of raw materials are absolute necessities. And Fawcett, in the book quoted, in combating the "fair-trade" theory, shows how ruinous it would be for his country—an importer almost exclusively of raw materials—to impose customs duties in order to retaliate on protectionist nations, and to endeavour to force them to make better bargains. It may be said, in fact, that if free-trade is anywhere

[1] *Free Trade and Protection*, London, Macmillan, 1885.

advantageous, it is more so than anywhere else in the British Isles; and that if protection is hurtful, it would be more hurtful there than elsewhere. And though unable to ward off the very great injury done to their country by the protectionism of other nations, British statesmen have not hitherto shown any great anxiety to aggravate the situation by protectionism of their own. But the raging of the protectionist tempest is such at the present day that it is to be feared—especially in view of some fresh symptoms and the outbreak of "fair-trade" opinions—that England will not be able to resist the general tendency much longer.

55. If in Great Britain, however, we find causes which prevent, and have prevented, the adoption of protection, in the United States, on the other hand, we can put our finger on a series of particular causes of its more recent development. First of all, a long tradition; for, as we have seen, it was not free-trade that prevailed after 1832, but merely a slow preparation for it, during which protection was gradually mitigated, but never altogether abolished. And together with tradition may be bracketed the general conviction that the principles of protectionism are enjoined in a document which is looked upon by Americans with almost sacred awe—the Federal constitution.

This long tradition united in the protectionist cause vast and powerful interests which, the very moment that industrial depression and other causes rendered a protective reaction possible, spared no efforts to fan the flames and supply the rekindling movement with fuel. And the rumour that in 1888 the funds placed at the disposal of the Republican party by a large group of American manufacturers had contributed in no small degree to the success of that party in the electoral campaign, and that their reward, arranged beforehand, was the MacKinley tariff, seems by no means to have been inspired by mere party spite—to be classed with the accusations brought against Wells of being in the pay of English manufacturers, —for the suggestion is repeated by serious writers.

The prevalence of such shameful corruption must be partly laid at the doors of protectionism, which has given birth to artificial industries and speculations which must be kept alive at any price; but it is chiefly owing to the capitalistic crisis, which in its convulsive efforts, not only profoundly disturbs the economic life of the country, but corrupts and vitiates its moral and political existence as well.

The Civil War, if not the principal cause, was by no means an uninfluential factor in the protective movement of the last twenty years. As at the beginning of the century, European wars and the then condition of the United States constituted a sort of spontaneous protection, which prepared the way for—and indeed was far more efficacious than —the tariff protection adopted later on; so the Civil War by its financial exigencies gave rise in the last period to protection, which had smoothed the path for its future development, when industrial depression once more cleared the way.

But protectionism was fostered in the United States by another and more organic cause, which ensured its triumph. Here a state of things was being actively generated, altogether opposed to that which characterised England. Whilst in that country colonial and international trade was becoming day by day more important, it was the internal commerce of the United States that was daily gaining ground. Immense territories were being populated; new states were, one after the other, being formed out of them; and in the course of the present century, from being a mere strip on the shore of the Atlantic, the American commonwealth has become a vast continent, equal in size to the whole of Europe. It would be useless to tell a twice-told tale; of greater moment is it to confirm facts. Statistics show the unimportant part which international commerce plays in the affairs of the United States.[1] According to data furnished by the census of 1880, completed by subsequent additions, Nimmo calculates the value of the entire production of the United States at about 10,000 million dollars, to which manufactures contribute about half, and agriculture over 3000 millions. The returns of the last quinquennial period enable us to estimate the value of the exported portion of this total produce at only 794 millions of dollars; whilst importations from abroad amounted to 635 millions. Of relatively small importance are the exports and imports of manufactures generally; of little or no conse-

[1] *Vide* p. 226.

quence are those of coal, iron, steel, leather, wool, and woollen and cotton goods.

The paucity of the export trade of goods manufactured in the United States must be attributed, according to Nimmo, to the high cost of labour, to the distance between the raw materials and the factories, etc., but above all to the vast market for the sale and consumption of produce within the frontiers of the Union, whilst other nations are obliged to find an outlet for their exuberant products beyond their own boundaries, as they are compelled to import many articles in which they are wanting.

And the exportation of agricultural produce from the United States, though greater than that of any other country, constitutes barely 16 per cent of its total production; whilst the home demand for cotton, cereals, flour, and other eatables is increasing more rapidly than the foreign demand.[1]

[1] At one time the tariff question divided the Union; the agricultural States of the south were in favour of free-trade, the manufacturing ones of the north in favour of protection; a terrible war was the outcome. At present antagonism of this kind exists to a certain extent, and discontent with the protectionist policy is spreading in the west. But the complaints of agriculturists have been partly silenced by means of agrarian protection, which is now keeping pace in the United States with that of manufactures. We have already noticed the important part played in the American system by the duty on raw wool. But recently agricultural protection has been extended to many other products, chiefly to counteract Canadian competition.

We also noticed the fact that, in the last phase of capitalism in old countries which do not export agricultural produce, protectionism serves the interests of the landed classes, because, by raising the price of provisions, it enhances the returns. But it is difficult to conceive such a state of things in a country which exports agricultural produce, for in it the restrictions placed upon international trade by protection necessarily tend to diminish exports, and hence, from this standpoint, to injure agrarian proprietors and labourers. The phenomenon, however, is readily understood, if we bear in mind the absolute predominance which the internal market of the United States tends to assume over the foreign demand for goods. Protection secures to the cultivators of the soil an ample outlet for their produce, and increases the price of provisions; and thus in the long run, whilst affording capitalists a temporary and often delusive advantage, by tending to arrest the fall of profits, it materially benefits landowners by enhancing rents.

(These lines were written with reference to the agricultural duties of the MacKinley Act. Now the last phase presented by the American tariff and the Act of 1894 does not, through the abolition of the duties on raw wool, affect our observations, but some supplementary remarks are required. The desperate efforts of capitalism to sustain itself by protection and monopolies have excited popular aversion to such an extent that a reduction of tariffs is

All this, if it does not justify, at all events explains the development and excesses of American protectionism. As we pointed out further back, in this country the idea of autonomy —or, to call things by their right names, economic isolation —appears much less unreasonable—much less absurd, if we may be pardoned the expression—than elsewhere; for we must take into consideration the variety and extent of the territory over which civilisation is advancing with giant strides and the halo of patriotism surrounding the doctrine, which acts as a veil to its more egotistical provisions. And we may say of the United States the exact reverse of what we said regarding England, that for them less than for any other country in the world are the advantages of free-trade obvious, and less serious the harm done by protection.

56. If we wish, in the last instance, to say something of the effects of protection during the last thirty years, we shall find ourselves in greater difficulties than ever, for as we proceed on our work, the complexity of facts increases, and all the elements which perturb a scientific analysis—party-feelings, prejudices, etc., become more manifest. The opinions of the writers who have discussed the subject are most divergent, and few of them support one another.

Cairnes, founding his observations on data supplied by Wells, reports (in his *Leading Principles*) an economic depression in the United States from 1860 to 1870, as compared with the preceding decennial period; a fall in wages, in tonnage, and in the increase of foreign commerce; he remarks that this diminution is not sufficiently explained by the

imperative. In this reduction, moreover, capitalists, probably observing how agricultural protection paralyses industrial protection, have abolished the duties upon wool. This, as we have already observed, breaks the compromise between the interests of the two dominant classes. If by raising the rent agricultural protection becomes advantageous to the American agriculturists, it is not, however, necessary to them ; whilst the manufacturing protection is evidently very injurious to them ; so that it would seem probable that they would not insist on having a greater protection than that which would neutralise the advantages of the manufacturing protection, nor is there much doubt but that manufacturing capitalists, left only to combat against popular aversion, would little by little have to adapt themselves to a progressive reduction of the tariffs.

But, as we have already observed, the frequent vicissitudes of American policy, result of so many complex factors, make it impossible to foretell anything, as recent events have shown.)

abnormal circumstances brought about by the war, if we consider the vast resources of the country. And he concludes that the slower rate of progress, the decrease of wages, etc., must be attributed to protection, which forces on the nation more costly modes of production.

But, whilst freely admitting the injury done by protection, we cannot agree with an argument which, in dealing with the causes of the crisis which a country has been undergoing for a period of ten years, gives but secondary importance to a fact of the utmost magnitude, which for the greater part of that very period occasioned a disturbance of vast proportions and far-reaching consequences. If, on the other hand, these observations were well-founded, further progress ought to have been arrested, since protection continued and became stricter. But on the contrary, in spite of the depression, of which, we maintain, protection is not the cause but the effect—the production and economic development of the United States advanced by leaps and bounds in the two decennial periods that followed.

The protectionists, whose statements are as highly coloured as those of Cairnes, attribute this progress to the benefits conferred by the protective *régime* established in 1860 and subsequently. It is natural, however, that a young country, richly endowed by nature, extending over immense regions which were being rapidly populated, should with the spread of industry quickly increase in wealth and productiveness.

In our opinion protection does not deserve either all the praise nor yet all the blame that falls to its share; its effects are and have been of much less consequence than has been imagined; it was not the cause of the crisis that followed the war, neither was it the cause of the development of production. And on the whole, the thirty years of continuous protection that the United States have undergone, has conferred very few benefits, which have been more than outweighed by the injuries which it has, and which it must have, done to the country.

Inquiries of this kind are difficult—and as regards recent years and the last legislative enactments—quite impossible to answer; and we do not pretend to have arrived at any very certain conclusions; for all that, some observations on individual industries, as well as on trade in general, may be recorded.

So far as the woollen manufactures are concerned, although duties have been very high, the effects of protection have not been very appreciable: at one time prices went up for a while, and profits rose simultaneously; but soon competition, having rapidly developed at home, altogether neutralised these results. On the other hand the action of the tariff upon woollen manufactures was paralysed by the duty on wool, which greatly increased the manufacturers' outlay on raw material.

The last tariff has put excessive duties on finer fabrics, although the country is but little adapted to their production, and thus an altogether artificial direction is given to industry. In the manufacture of steel, also, if protection has occasionally raised prices and profits, competition has quickly brought them down again to their former level, or even below it.[1]

It is no wonder, therefore, that even allowing for some temporary benefits conferred upon certain industries—which accounts for their constantly clamouring for protection—that system has proved no remedy for so long a depression as the one under consideration; a depression alleviated in the United States much more by the great natural resources of the country than by the artificial palliative of protection.

But whilst its advantages have been scant and fugitive, on the other hand the evils which it has caused and the character which it has assumed are such, that, in the interests of this great nation, one cannot but hope that it may, little by little, find means of extricating itself from the python's folds in which it is so unfortunately involved. We do but touch on the subject, as we shall have to return to it in the last chapter.

All that protection can do is to mitigate now and then the sufferings of capitalists. Now, if the depression of industry and profits was merely transitory, such a remedy, though a costly one, might, to a certain extent, be justified. But, as we have seen, we are concerned with a permanent depression, and the movement which is ever reducing profits being one against which it is vain to fight, protection would, therefore, have to assume a permanent character—nor is this all; for as it is

[1] On these points, *vide* works of Taussig, Schoenhof, Bolles, Wells, George, etc., before mentioned.

only by the successive increase of duties that native industries derive momentary relief, it would be necessary to go on raising the tariffs until absolute prohibition had been attained; after which, in consequence of the usual development of internal competition, matters would be on the same footing as before, and without any apparent remedy.

It would all result in giving from time to time a flash of vitality to an economic organisation destined to undergo transformation: it would only arrest for a moment the fatal fall of profits and here and there secure, for a short period, unjust gains to certain capitalists; nor could it ever have as a result that which justifies protection in the first capitalistic epoch, namely, the vigorous impulse given to industries in their capitalistic development.

In the meanwhile, to attain such poor ends, really important and general interests have been sacrificed: production restricted and rendered costly; workmen oppressed, and all the while—supreme mockery!—they are told that protection, the instrument of their degradation, serves to keep their wages at a high level; and all consumers suffer. And not only this, but a breach is made in that chief, though imperfect, rampart of our actual organisation—competition; the basis of exchange is altered, with regard to labour as well as to goods; monopolies are created; much is sacrificed without obtaining anything in exchange. And from this point of view, protection is far more hurtful than trusts, for the latter have, at all events, a vital and organic foundation in the tendency to industrial concentration, and it may be foreseen that, in some future and glorious metamorphosis, something of them may survive: whilst nothing of the kind can be said of protectionism. It is only one of the last, petty, useless bulwarks of capitalistic despotism, behind which profits are fighting their last battle; and to demolish it is the task of the labouring classes, who do but claim their rights, protesting against the egotism of capitalists, who to gain paltry advantages do them and their country grave injuries. It is only in the triumph of these new classes, and in a new social and economic departure, that the final discomfiture of protectionism can be expected.

CHAPTER VII

SYNTHESIS

FREE TRADE AND PROTECTION IN THE HISTORY OF THE
UNITED STATES OF AMERICA

57. If, at times in the course of this study, we have been carried away by our argument, and led to make observations of a general character not strictly relevant to the facts under consideration, now, as we are about to furl our sails after this long voyage across the seas of American commercial policy, we feel the imperative need of casting anchor and firmly binding ourselves to our method of investigation, beyond which there can be, in our opinion, no scientific safety; and therefore, although the eloquence of certain facts may excite us to draw from them broader conclusions, in resuming our inquiry, which has been confined to the history of the United States, we do not propose to travel beyond those boundaries: for we are convinced that to do so, it would be necessary to extend the same method of investigation to other countries, and that, anyhow, the conclusions at which we might arrive would not be everywhere identical.

But even within these limits, the results of researches, which we have endeavoured to make as complete as possible, and which, if they have no other merit, have certainly that of being objective and absolutely free from prejudice of any kind—would appear to us of no slight importance.

Free-trade and protection, in the history of the United States, follow one another, turn by turn, as the products of the various economic stages through which the country is passing, in which a profound analysis of the facts discovers the organic causes of commercial policy, at one time responding to the general interests, at another to that of a particular class, which has succeeded in obtaining political and economic predominance. To the various periods in the American economic history correspond a different commercial policy, which owes its existence to the condition of the country and which is only modified when this condition undergoes a radical change.[1]

Twice has free-trade and twice has protectionism prevailed in the economic history of the United States: free-trade in the first period of primitive and domestic economy, when colonial conditions still existed, and in the third period, when the factory system was flourishing and consolidating itself; protectionism in the second and fourth periods at the inauguration, in the first instance, and subsequently during the crisis and dissolution of capitalistic industry. Now to recapitulate and synthetise what we have gathered in the course of our investigations, we will set forth what, in our opinion, is the reason of this alternation, corresponding to the historical phases of American economy to which we have alluded.

58. We will consider the first period in the history of the United States and examine its economy in its agricultural, manufacturing, and commercial elements, beginning with the last named. In the economy of nations it seems that, so far as trade is concerned, three phases may be observed: the first, in which no true division of labour having yet been effected, exchange and commerce have but slight importance; the second, in which foreign trade is developed for the supply of commodities which native industries, owing to the imperfect division of labour and to the difficulties of internal transit, are unable to furnish; and the third, when, the economic activity of the country having been developed, arts and industries multiplied, and means of transport by land—so

---

[1] "There are profound causes, in the historical evolution of society, which make protectionism necessary at one time and free-trade at another; and they are the same causes that determine the phases and vicissitudes of economy. . . . There is no absolute line of demarcation between these two great phases of capitalism, either in order of time or of space; but there is an alternate succession, and a predominance which inclines first one way and then the other, according to the different degrees of the decreasing productive power of the earth."—See Ricca Salerno, art. quoted.

much more difficult than by sea—perfected, internal exchange flourishes.[1]

In the first of these essays it was shown that the American colonies under English domination were in the first of these periods; trade, whether internal or international, was of no great importance to them: hence the fact that British commercial restrictions were but little felt by the colonists, who only began to murmur at them when an impetus had been given to transatlantic commerce.

We have also seen that prohibitions to manufactures were, up to the revolution, practicable, and were disliked by the colonists rather for political than for economic considerations; and this because nature itself prevented the colonists from giving themselves up to manufactures which, owing to the imperfect division of labour, were almost entirely in a domestic condition; so that production took place chiefly with a view to direct consumption, and internal commerce was of very slight moment.

The economic activity of the colony was then principally, almost exclusively in fact, directed to agriculture, of which domestic manufactures was an appurtenance.

Now, from the outbreak of the revolution to about the first ten years of this century, the industrial condition of the country remained practically unaltered. Although there may have been some slight progress, the industrial production was quite primitive, of a domestic nature, and closely connected with agriculture; most of the inhabitants led rural and isolated lives; and slight indeed was the extent of internal exchange. But foreign trade, in obedience to the tendency which was becoming more and more marked towards the close of the colonial period, underwent a great development during the whole of this epoch; it seemed to be the result of natural evolution and to be stimulated by the accidental causes into which we have already entered.

Freedom is the soul of international commerce; and the mere fact that this commerce flourishes in a country, whether the causes be natural or artificial, is sufficient to create an absolute need of a free-trade policy, and this necessity and the

[1] See Roscher's observations, to which we alluded on pages 29-30 of this volume.

impossibility of any other system arising at that moment are demonstrated by the very organisation of American economy, in this first stage of national existence.

The general interests of the country and those of the most numerous and preponderating classes were united in the requirement of free-trade.

The growth of population and production had given an impulse to foreign trade and had made the country not only a producer but also an exporter to a large extent of agricultural produce. The inhabitants, who were spreading over the land, required manufactured articles which the country was hardly fitted to produce; there can be no doubt, therefore, that the general interests demanded free-trade. It was needed by that large commercial class which the development of sea-trade, by means of the political circumstances of the times, had brought into existence. The interests, too, of the great class of agricultural producers was entirely on the side of free-trade. In fact, not only were these, the exporters of provisions and consumers of wares, capitally interested in an unfettered trade system, but there was no particular reason whatever which could indirectly turn them from this path. Such a reason might, as we have seen, be found in an organisation based upon hired service, in which the suppression of free-trade might depress workmen and hence benefit capitalists; but no such argument could apply to the period under discussion. At that time, indeed, it may be said that, so far as agriculture was concerned, wage-earning labourers did not exist; production was the work partly of independent settlers and partly of slaves.

Now Ricca Salerno, in the work which we have so often quoted,[1] makes this observation with regard to independent producers, that the advantages of free trade are all reaped by the same and only class of producers, who represent the interests of capital and labour in combination; and where slavery exists, the quantity of wealth which goes to make up the cost of labour being fixed and adjusted according to the irreducible needs of the slaves, whilst the value of this wealth is variable, it follows that free-trade, by lowering the price of provisions, necessarily benefits capitalists.

[1] *Vide* pp. 130-131 of this volume.

Therefore the interests of independent agriculturists as well as of the slave-owning farmers were for free-trade.

As to manufactured products, they were, as we have seen, to a large extent domestic—the work of the farm-labourers themselves; and there being but little trade in them, international commerce was of little consequence. There was, indeed, a sufficiently numerous class of independent artisans, who supplied the wants of the tillers of the soil; but their products were precisely those that it was not desirable to introduce from abroad, and for which, therefore, there was no fear of foreign competition;[1] and, anyhow, the remarks made above perfectly apply to their condition.

Finally, there was a small, newly-formed group of producers, on whom the effects of free-trade might be injurious; and these were the new capitalist-manufacturers; they were the first champions of the capitalistic system, at that moment in the bud. But theirs was the voice of the future, as yet too weak and distant, for its note of discord and of class-warfare to find an echo in that modest but harmonious and happy epoch in the existence of a people who had just secured their liberty, and the only blot on whose proud escutcheon was that revolting anachronism, negro slavery.

59. In this state of things, the interests of the various classes coincided with those of the nation at large, and free-trade, whilst hurting no one, could benefit the country in many evident ways.

The fundamental *raison d'être* of international trade lies in a difference of comparative cost, whereby every country finds its advantage to buy from others those goods which cost them the dearest to produce themselves, and give in exchange commodities which can be produced at a cheaper rate. This interchange not only effects a saving, but renders a larger production possible, because in the land where products are supplied at a lower cost there remains a certain surplus of labour available for further production; and consequently every hindrance to the free development of international trade increases the price of goods which, by means of international exchange, might be obtained on cheaper terms; and, moreover, it restricts industrial activity and limits production.

[1] *Vide* p. 131.

There is no flaw in this theory if we only take into consideration the general good of the country in the abstract; and when, as in the case in point, there is no conflict between it and the interests of the various social classes, its application presents no difficulty. But, on the other hand, it cannot easily be put into practice when these interests greatly diverge; in which case the theory does not seem to justify facts which at times appear contradictory to it.

We have already alluded, in the course of this study, to Ricca Salerno's profound observation,[1] that the theory of international trade, as it is expounded by economists, presumes an identity of interests among producers which is far from being the case in reality; it presumes that there merely are "producers," without any distinction between workmen and capitalists, without regard to the relation between capital and labour, a relation that varies in different economic periods, and which greatly influences commerce.

To this may be added that the theory presumes also a perfect identity in the interests of producers and those of the community as a whole—and such identity does not always exist; that it does not take other class distinctions into account, such as those between agriculturists and manufacturers, between landowners and industrial capitalists. It may likewise be pointed out that the theory of free-trade takes no heed of the difficulties often arising on the transference of capital from one investment to another, nor of the necessity of preventing the destruction of capital and industries; and, moreover, that it concerns itself exclusively with the interests of the moment, regardless of the future.

Now, as long as there is no class-division among producers, their interests will be identical and will coincide with those of the country at large; and that is the case illustrated above. But when producers are divided into workmen and capitalists, things are changed; the interests of these two classes are different, and circumstances may occur in which, owing to this divergence of interests, the capitalists may derive benefits from trade-restrictions which give them an advantage over the workmen. The latter will certainly suffer from these restrictions; but they will none the less be enforced if the

[1] *Protezionismo e libero scambio*, etc.

capitalists gain the day. It must be admitted that on the whole they will injure the country, and assuredly so if they artificially sustain and endow barely productive industries; but there may be cases in which they may either directly or indirectly benefit the community. This may occur to a certain limited extent when there is a question of preventing the collapse of some industry which, owing to particular and temporary circumstances, is threatened with ruin; and, on a larger scale, when these trade-restrictions are designed—even though with immediate ill-effects on workmen and on the nation—to forward the development of an industrial organisation ensuring the greater production which is necessary for the growing wants of the population. And this last case is the one which we must now take into consideration. It may happen, on the other hand, that these commercial restrictions, enforced by the interests, often merely momentary, of a single class, and opposed to those of others, may be both at the outset and afterwards hurtful to the community; yet the predominance of this one class may be such that the measures are carried in spite of the interests of all the others; and this constitutes another case, which will be examined in due course.

60. The preceding observations apply to the second phase of American commercial policy. In the 1807-1830 period the industries of the United States underwent a transformation from the domestic to the great capitalistic state of industry, and this new development was being gradually consolidated. Hence producers were divided into two classes having divergent interests, namely, capitalists and workmen, and the former were benefited by all kinds of restrictions on international trade that weakened the relative position of the labourers. Such commercial limitations (which strengthened the hands of the capitalist in other ways also) were fraught with harm for the working classes; the system of protection adopted from 1816 to 1832 undoubtedly injured the country by raising the price of provisions and diminishing production; but in the long run this injury proved a benefit, since in this way was originated and developed a more efficient method of production—the factory system—a method required by the wants which the growth of population had created.

It is for this reason that the capitalist class—to whom we are indebted for this system of production—succeeded in establishing protection in spite of the opposition of the landowners and rural classes, who were in favour of free-trade; for all such opposition must needs give way before the requirements of the population and of progress.

We shall see now how the demonstration of this theory naturally follows from the facts which we have gathered in our researches.

Let us begin by examining the situation of the manufacturing industries. As we have seen, they were, at the time of which we are speaking, in a state of transition: from an entirely domestic condition—that is, having no trade purposes in view—or when not strictly domestic, then of exceedingly limited proportions, and exercised almost exclusively by independent artisans, they were passing into a more important state, in which there was a distinction between workmen and capitalists, and machinery was being brought into use. The class of enterprising capitalists, which up to that time had hardly existed, was in course of formation, and was tending to assume a dominating industrial position.

This class found itself face to face with great difficulties: the scarcity of labourers, consequent on a scant population; their reluctance to work for hire, considering the quantity of free land easily accessible to them and offering a vast field for independent production; the high standard of wages resulting from this state of things.

Besides the impediments caused by the labour question, many other serious obstacles stood in the way of the new capitalistic industries, and chief among them was the cheapness of manufactured goods imported from old countries, such as England, where factories had flourished for a long time past; the inexperience of Americans in this new form of industry, which required competent and practical managers and workmen, also machinery; the scarcity of capital, and the excessive caution of those who possessed it.

In these circumstances the interests of the new class of enterprising capitalists required every effort on their part, in order to throw difficulties in the way of labourers and compel them to work for hire, to lower wages, and thus reduce the cost of production, as well as to raise prices. Now all these ends were reconciled in demanding protection. In new countries, Ricca Salerno observes in his oft-quoted work, free-trade is fatal to the manufacturing industries, owing to the influence of low prices and high wages; the one due to the importation of goods from abroad, the other to the effect of free-trade in cheapening provisions, facilitating their production, rendering the exploitation of industries easier, and fostering the culture of the soil by independent labourers—hence the scarcity of wage-earning hands.

Protection, on the contrary, promotes a more costly and difficult system of production, adds to the price of the articles used by the labouring classes either as provisions or raw material, and in this way fetters workmen in their endeavours to settle down to independent trades, and to the cultivation of the free land, forces them to work for hire, or, depreciating their condition in the labour market, lowers wages.

Thus protection, although undoubtedly prejudicial to labourers, renders capitalistic industries practicable by means of a profit which could not be otherwise obtained, either at all, or else of too scant a nature to permit of capitalistic production.

But the capitalist class, which in the historical evolution of the country was being gradually formed, found itself, when organising new undertakings, face to face with difficulties of other kinds, proceeding, as we have seen, from the scarcity of capital, the lack of machinery, and the want of skill and experience, and from foreign competition, which became most severe after 1815; for the time being, in fact, the great industries that were arising were less productive than the smaller ones already existing in the country, and less productive, too, than the foreign industries, and that being the case they would have furnished capitalists with no adequate returns. Now, in such circumstances, it does not seem to us to be going too far to admit that protection must be serviceable, not merely in supplying capitalistic industry with a profit by depreciating the labour market, but also (by increasing prices) in raising such profit to the level normal in agriculture and the temporarily more-productive smaller industries.

But, it may be objected, the capitalists might have derived greater benefit from a more productive investment of their money, and thus, without having recourse to protection, they might at one and the same time have forwarded their own interests and those of the nation at large. And, on the other hand, the lowness of profits being common to all industries, protection would have been no remedy—nay, by lessening the productiveness of labour it would still further have lowered profits.

These objections, however, do not appear to us to be sufficiently serious. American capital, which was gradually falling into the hands of one class—the capitalist class—and which had recently been diverted by political causes from maritime trade, found its best investment in manufactures. The decrease of foreign imports, the dearness of manufactured articles, and the wants of the country—these were the causes of the capitalistic system of production inaugurated in the years 1807-1815 (see this volume, p. 149 *et seq.*) To manufactures immediately flowed all the money which was lying idle owing to the interruption of foreign trade, and it was natural that capitalists should devote themselves energetically to the production of goods which they had hitherto imported, and of which the country stood in urgent need. Nor was it possible for any but a vast industry to absorb the capital that was lying fallow; agriculture, at that time in a very primitive and stagnant condition, by no means lent itself to the task; nor did the smaller industries, which demanded labour rather than capital.

This combination of circumstances gave rise to the first development of the great capitalistic industries, which were placed for the time being in a situation so extremely favourable as to be able to overcome the disadvantages which, as we have pointed out, their novelty naturally entailed upon them. But when after 1815 the aspect of things was completely altered (see pp. 153-4), and foreign competition brought down prices, these disadvantages were immediately and seriously felt; profits diminished or disappeared, and for the preservation both of the funds invested and of the new industrial system protection was invoked.

Let it be noted also that these great capitalistic enterprises which had just been launched, and which demanded protection, did not constitute the whole of the productive industries of the country, but only a part of them; and that, if it is inadmissible that protection can raise the profits of all industries, it is nevertheless possible for it to raise the profits of some of them. Finally, we must not forget that the exigencies of progress required the development of the great industries, whilst the difficulties which they encountered and their points of inferiority were merely temporary.

A production of this kind was evidently more costly, and if it had lasted for any length of time it would, in the long run, not only have done no permanent good to the capitalists who had been sufficiently ill-advised to sink their money in industries which were productive only owing to artificial stimulants, instead of placing it in those more adapted to local circumstances, but it would assuredly have become an unbearable burden on the country.

But the truth is that, speaking generally, this inferiority was merely momentary, and for a large number of industries was the no very distant forerunner of a real superiority and that greater power of production which was absolutely necessary for the increasing wants of the country.

This temporary inferiority was owing to the difficulties encountered at its outset by the new capitalistic *régime* of industry in the conditions of labour and capital; the future superiority of all those productions—and they were many—which found in the country circumstances favourable to their natural development (such as raw materials, fuel, etc.), was certain, owing to the more efficient methods of production which the new system could bring into operation.

And it was the growing requirements of the population that necessitated the adoption of these new methods.

Loria graphically describes the state of affairs that brought about these technical changes and protection in Europe in the seventeenth and eighteenth centuries; and his instance seems to us to be partly applicable to our own case. Protectionism, he says, arises in Europe when a growing population and the decreasing productiveness of the soil necessitate an agricultural and industrial transformation, which is marked by the absorption of small independent farms and mills into vast agricultural and industrial organisations. In order to supply the wants of an improved system of agriculture and of an increasing population, the invention of new technical processes is stimulated; and this technical revolution is the death-warrant of the small industries. But agrarian reforms are slow and the state has no means of hastening their development. Hence it is needful, in order to meet the requirements of the population, to give an impulse to manufactures by the expedient of protection.[1]

It is easy to see the difference between the industrial conditions of Europe and America at the epoch in question. In Europe protection was a means for obtaining agricultural produce at a low price: not so in America—here there was no importation of such produce—nor would it have been advantageous. But protection whilst inflicting an immediate injury, secured a distant though direct benefit by favouring the development of a more productive industrial system, which allowed of the natural resources of the country being turned to account, opened out a wide field for the employment of the population, and directly and securely provided the manufactured articles (no less needed than provisions), for the production of which the country was eminently fitted and would ever have striven.

The pressure of population makes a technical transformation inevitable, which, in its turn, can only occur with a parallel transformation in the economic organisation of industry, that is, with the establishment of a capitalistic system of economy.

It is natural that this system should, at the outset, meet in a new country with difficulties which can only be overcome by temporary sacrifices. Success may be more or less easy; but efforts should only be made on behalf of such industries as are unfavourably situated in the country; and it is evident that in such circumstances the interests of the capitalist classes and those of the nation at large are not in absolute conflict. Protection at such an epoch assumes a temporary character, and temporary too is the sacrifice imposed on the country. The interests, however, that are really sacrificed, are those of the labourers, whose condition is depressed to admit of the establishment of capitalism, which, having become a necessity

[1] Loria, *Analisi della proprietà capitalista*, vol. ii. p. 220.

for social progress, must accomplish its historical cycle, even if beset by ruin and maledictions.

61. Up to the present moment we have considered manufacturing industries only; but it is important not to lose sight of agriculture and the interests of the landowners. In what condition were they placed in the United States by capitalistic protectionism ? It appears to us that the interests of the landowners and the capitalists were opposed. The agriculturists were, in the south, almost exclusively either independent landowners who tilled the soil with their families, or slave-owners. Few indeed were the hired labourers where so many slaves were employed and where there was as yet no sign of that great change which was coming over the manufacturing industries. Now in such circumstances the effect of protection, which reduces wages and consequently the expenses of production, would prove of small benefit; whilst, on the other hand, Ricca Salerno has shown us how advantageous free-trade is to independent agriculturists and slave-owners. It is true that protection, by promoting manufactures, creates an inland market for the raw products of agriculture ; but of far greater importance than this home market (which would indeed have greatly influenced a more intensive and differentiated system of cultivation than was then the case in America) was the foreign export trade : and agriculturists were fully aware of the benefit conferred upon them in this respect by unfettered commerce.

And besides this, the interests of the landowners, who depended on rents, were favoured by free-trade, which in a country exporting raw materials gives an impulse to production, and by stimulating the cultivation of the less fertile lands, and raising the price of products, enhances rents and benefits the landowners;[1] whilst protection, by arresting the importation of manufactured goods, and transferring capital from agriculture to manufactures, causes the less fertile land to be neglected, and thus lowers the rent.[2]

It is clear, therefore, that at the period under consideration—the period of the foundation of the factory system in

[1] Bastable, *The Theory of International Trade*, Dublin, Hodges, 1887, p. 104.
[2] *Vide* Loria, in the *Journal of the Statistical Society*, June 1887.

the United States—there must necessarily have existed an antagonism between the interests of the manufacturing capitalists and those of the landowners.

Now such antagonism did really exist between the manufacturing states of New England and the agricultural ones of the south; and we have dwelt upon it in our account of the long controversies occasioned by the tariff question. Strange controversies, in very truth, in which the standard of liberty was hoisted by the owners of slaves, whilst the manufacturers, representatives of technical progress, put international commerce in chains!

But although protection was necessarily annoying, and temporarily at all events a burden on the country, there was very little doubt as to the course the nation would follow, nor indeed had they much free-will in the matter. Agriculture dependent on slaves represented barbarism and a scant and insufficient production; the factory system meant progress, even though it was purchased by some momentary sacrifices and by the depression of free labour.

The requirements of the growing population demanded technical improvements and ensured the inevitable triumph of the capitalist class.

62. More easy is the interpretation of the period from 1833 to 1861, during which protection gradually diminished in intensity—with a brief exception from 1842 to 1846—and ended by giving place to a system of international trade that was almost completely free.

As we have already seen, the foundation and consolidation of capitalism (due more to the spontaneous protection which it enjoyed from the beginning than to the tariffs afterwards enforced) was succeeded by a period of prosperity and progress so far as the great capitalistic industries were concerned; little by little all the difficulties which beset them in the beginning had vanished; they were now strong and productive. Technical improvements and experience had done much to arm them against foreign competition. The increase of population, the disappearance of free land, which day by day seemed to recede further to an inaccessible distance, the ever-growing complexity of trade, requiring a large amount of capital, all contributed to the uprising of a large class of hired workmen—for whom all other modes of life were difficult or impossible, and whose wages tended to fall.

There was no longer any reason, therefore, why capitalists should consider protection necessary: indeed, it may be said that free-trade would benefit them even, inasmuch as it would usefully purge out the unacclimatised industries, and concentrate capital in those most adapted to the circumstances of the country; whilst, on the contrary, protection would have been most injurious, for it would have breathed an artificial life into those industries which were not naturally fitted for the situation in which they were placed. The existence of a certain number of such industries explains that opposition to the reduction of duties which made itself felt amid the general assent of the capitalists.

But such insignificant and isolated cases of opposition were powerless when confronted with the general interests of the country and of the agricultural classes.

The interests of the latter had for long been neglected until the needs of the growing population had necessitated the establishment and consolidation of capitalism: but the time was now at hand for them to receive some satisfaction. And the adoption of free-trade at this period can be explained as compensation granted to the agrarian interests as well as a hearkening to the general feeling of the country, for both concurred in demanding the abolition of a system which was no longer necessary for the capitalist class.

For agriculturists, in fact, free-trade continued to be useful and opportune. No very substantial changes had yet taken place in agriculture: slavery still existed, and independent cultivators were still very numerous: the country continued chiefly to export agricultural produce, and this export trade was for agriculturists of greater importance than the home market—although the latter was beginning, thanks to the development of manufactures and the increase of population, to assume considerable proportions. Nor had agriculturists any grounds yet for apprehending the importation of provisions from abroad.

Now, although in an old country that imports its breadstuffs, protection may serve the purposes of landowners in increasing their rents by means of a rise in prices; in a new

T

country, on the contrary, as we have already shown, it is freetrade that favours land rent and hence the landlords.

But the land rent could not yet have attained in the United States such proportions as to threaten the profits of the capitalists (especially in the flourishing situation in which the latter were placed during the period in question), and thus between these two dominant classes, the capitalists and the landowners, who were so often at loggerheads, a *modus vivendi* was arrived at; and upon this basis free-trade gradually reared itself.

It must not be supposed, however, that the labourers profited by this understanding; it was founded, in fact, upon their subjection: slaves were they under the proprietors of the soil — hirelings without hope of betterment under the capitalists!

63. We now come to the last period, which extends from 1860 to our own days. It has already been subjected to so long and minute an analysis in the preceding chapter, that we should but weary the reader by recapitulating, however briefly, the ideas there developed, or enumerating, purely as a catalogue, the multiplicity of causes to which, in our opinion, the rise, maintenance, and aggravation of protectionism in the United States during the last thirty years is due. We must confine ourselves to considerations of a purely synthetical character, and above all to an examination—a matter of no secondary importance—of the relations at that time existing between the interests of the two dominating classes—the industrial capitalists and the agricultural proprietors.

Although the original impulse to energetic protection was, as we have seen, accidentally given by the financial measures necessitated by the war, yet, even before it broke out, some tendency to protectionism had manifested itself, and the protectionists did not let slip the first favourable opportunity to secure the adoption of their system, and to keep it in force as long as possible. The Civil War is generally regarded not only as the struggle for the abolition of slavery, but also as the outcome of the antagonism between the agricultural and free-trade States of the south and the manufacturing and protectionist ones of the north: and this is substantially the case, but requires some explanation.

Even if in the north protectionism still had traditions and followers, and could serve the purposes of certain industrial groups, it was none the less understood that on the whole American manufactures no longer needed state support. Therefore, although we can believe that certain interested groups should have turned the war to account, we cannot look upon it as a struggle for the establishment of a protective system which was no longer wanted by the mass of American capitalists: and, on the other hand, all those circumstances (such as trade depression), which subsequently strengthened the hands of the protectionists, did not then exist.

But it is easier to explain this conflict as a desperate effort on the part of the capitalists to subdue free-trade and slavery, that increased the land rent, which in its rapid development began to undermine the profits of capital.

We have already seen that, especially in a *régime* of slavery, free-trade was advantageous to landowners and augmented their rents. Now for a certain time this could not hurt the capitalists; but after a while, with the increase of the rent, it could not be otherwise than prejudicial to their interests. Hence the contest against slavery, which, by means of free-trade, increased the rent: hence also the opposition to free-trade, which was but the means to an end; and the struggle was naturally purposely inflamed by those groups of capitalists who, either because the industries in which they were engaged were but slightly productive, and they could not easily withdraw their capital, or else for other reasons, were interested in the establishment of protection.

This appears to us to be the most probable cause of the war—which was undoubtedly an economic one—and of the protectionism which followed from it, and which was fostered for several years afterwards by the financial and other effects of the great fight.

When hostilities were concluded with the abolition of slavery and the establishment of protection, matters underwent a complete change. When slavery no longer existed, observes Ricca Salerno, even the Southern States embraced protectionism.[1] The fact was that free-trade could no longer benefit the landowners by reducing the expenses of mainten-

[1] *Vide* the article quoted.

ance of the slaves; and, on the other hand, protection was advantageous to them, so far as labour was concerned, inasmuch as it threw difficulties in the way of labourers and emancipated slaves becoming independent cultivators, by raising the price of implements and all things needful for the pursuit of agriculture; thus compelling them to work for hire and lowering their wages. The capitalists, in the meantime, were intent on crippling the land rent, on which protection—which was then almost exclusively industrial—could exercise no elevating influence.

The agriculture of the United States, however, was at the conclusion of the war of secession still largely an exporting industry; and if the landowners gained something on the one hand from protection, on the other, the obstacles thrown in the way of international trade must necessarily have interfered with their export business: so that it was easy to foresee that any aggravation of protection would ultimately meet with uncompromising opposition from them.

In the meanwhile, coming to the last twenty years, that complex condition of American industrial economy was being evolved which we have discussed at length in the preceding chapter; there was great industrial progress, but there was at the same time a notable decline of profits, which determined a desperate rally to more intense protection (an attempt that was encouraged by the large development of the home market). This policy, which was strongly marked in these last years, necessarily encountered an energetic resistance on the part of the agriculturists, especially of the west, and of the independent cultivators, who felt the increased cost of implements and manufactured goods and the difficulties thrown in the way of exportation. This resistance, however, though vigorous, was not general, and was met by a compromise. To understand it, we must not lose sight of the fact, to which we have more than once drawn attention, that latterly the great extension of the territory of the United States, the multiplication of the population, the development of the home market, the growth of manufactures, the improvements in means of transport, have all contributed to a vast transformation of American trade; international trade has lost much of its importance, whilst inland commerce has enormously increased. At the present moment the agriculturists of the United States are more interested in the distribution of their products at home than in their exportation. It may be added that for some time past in the American market native agriculturists have been closely run by the competition of agricultural produce and raw materials from newer countries, and particularly from Canada. In this state of affairs, the opposition of the landed interest to the aggravation of protection has been overcome by means of a compromise which extends the support of the State to agrarian as well as to manufacturing industries—a course that had long been foreshadowed.

It is a curious fact that while in Europe industrial protection is at present regarded more than anything else in the light of compensation (illusory perhaps) granted to manufacturers as an equivalent for the favour shown to agriculturists; in the United States, on the contrary, it is agrarian protection that appears as compensation for support bestowed to other industries. And it has, moreover, been said and repeated that it is merely a vain trick, a mystification, by means of which the protectionists succeeded in gaining over the landowners to their views; whilst this mask of equal treatment and equal protection of all the branches of national production throws a halo of equity and justice round the protective system. But, possibly, the matter is substantially different and of far weightier import.

Agricultural protection, recently united to that of the other industries in the United States, is in truth a phenomenon of greater gravity than it appears to be at first sight. By enhancing the price of raw materials, it to a large extent neutralises those benefits which—though of a purely temporary nature — protection confers on industries: what we have established regarding the duties on wool may be taken as proof of this. And besides, in consequence of the rapid growth of the American population, the time is perhaps not far distant in which agricultural protection, by making all provisions dearer, will deal a severe blow at capitalists by raising the cost of labour.

The natural economic evolution is, in fact, rapidly bringing the United States to a phase in which protection, hitherto embraced with increasing fervour by capitalists, will seriously menace their interests, whilst benefiting agriculturists by increasing the unearned increment, as a result of the higher price of provisions.

At this point it is impossible not to be profoundly impressed by this gigantic struggle between capitalism and landed property, between profits and land rent. As a matter of fact, protection, which at an early period is instrumental in founding and consolidating capitalism, becomes later on a desperate weapon in the hands of capital, when, snared by the rent increment,[1] lacerated by competition, rendered almost useless to the speculator by its very abundance, it endeavours in every way, fair or foul, by restricting production and almost running the risk of extinguishing wealth at its fountainhead, to retain the profits which elude its grasp, and to arrest, or at all events to delay that fatal evolution which must inevitably lead to the dissolution of capitalistic economy. But that last instrument which capitalism wields with its expiring energies, and in which it puts its ultimate hope and trust—protectionism—by conjuring up agricultural by the side of industrial protection (as was inevitable and in disregard of the interest of capitalists), deals a fatal blow at capitalism itself, and ends by stimulating the unearned increment—that alarming spectre which advances step by step, and threatens to seat itself on the ruins of capitalism.[2]

64. All this is less felt and less evident in the United

---

[1] As symptoms of the anxiety roused in the breasts of capitalists by this cause, see Patten's book, *The Economic Basis of Protection* (Philadelphia, Lippincott, 1890), which we shall examine elsewhere, and in which protection is invoked in the United States against land rent, whilst the writer is blind to the fact that it may in the end prove instrumental in aggravating it.

[2] The last phase of the American tariff policy, as shown by the Tariff Act of 1894 (before the passing of which this present volume was written), modifies but does not contradict our observations.

In fact, the industrial protection, rendered almost useless by the agricultural protection, and undermined by increasing popular aversion, shows signs of decrease; and the abolition of the duty on wool, breaking the compromise between the agriculturists and the manufacturers, gives a foresight, if such be possible, of a further reduction of the protective duties of these latter. Thus protection to manufactures works in a vicious circle; if associated with agricultural protection, its industrial effects are neutralised owing to the higher rents which it occasions; whilst if it is opposed by the landowners on the one side and by the people on the other, it must necessarily disappear.

States than elsewhere, because their natural resources and immense extent of territory partly neutralise the injurious effects of this conflict. But the phenomenon is, none the less, essentially the same, and the danger that hangs over a not very remote future no less grave.

In the meanwhile, among the numerous evils brought about by this state of things, and which we have discussed elsewhere, that which affects us most is the melancholy fate of the labourers—even when we bear in mind that in America the conditions of labour are, for natural causes, far superior to what they are in other countries. As a matter of fact, in the great question of international trade, in the terrible contest between landed property and capital, they are always destined to be the victims; and whichever way the victory inclines, whether free-trade prevails or protection, they merely change masters, and are ever despoiled with greater rapacity.

This fate, sorrowful though it be, may appear an inevitable result of progress in the first phases of capitalism, when on the depression of workmen is based a superior and progressive form of economy which is necessary to provide for the wants of the people. And on the other hand, if, in those early stages of capitalism, the working classes lost their liberty, the favourable circumstances in which they were placed as regards the demand for labour, at all events allowed of their earning their bread. But far sadder is their lot nowadays: nor has their destitution that barbarous historical justification which represents them as the innocent victims of the requirements of the population and of social progress.

Placed, indeed, as they are between the limitation of production and the crisis in capitalism on the one hand, which deprive them of occupation, and turn them into immense bands of unemployed and half-starved beings, and the ceaseless advance of the unearned increment, which enhances the cost of their painful existence, on the other, it is impossible for their pitiful condition not to excite our sympathy. But their sacrifice is useless. Protection, which is hypocritically invoked by some in order to raise wages, is, indeed, instrumental in lowering them and in giving employers greater facilities for resisting trade-unions; but, as we have seen, it is powerless to overcome industrial depression, or to arrest, in its fatal course, the diminution of profits and the dissolution of capitalistic economy; and whilst limiting production and wealth, it ends by destroying that which it aimed at preserving, by stimulating the anti-social and inhuman element of land rent.

But the progress of the population, with its growing requirements, must necessarily find a solution for this dolorous state of things, which seems almost hopeless. What it may be, we cannot tell: but that an issue out of these troubles will come, and that a new form of economy will succeed the present one, this is inevitable. And to this new status will be assigned the task of solving the secular problem of protectionism.

George observes that if protection is hurtful to the labouring class, free-trade is none the less insufficient for them, because until land can be free and labour can dispose of it, the condition of labourers cannot be seriously improved.[1] And Loria bases the whole of the system of social harmony, with which he boldly attempts to pry into futurity, upon the institution of free land. But even without going as far as this, and without indulging in such a distant forecast, our investigations seem at last to lead us to a conclusion regarding the argument which has occupied us so long.

The strange and mysterious antagonism between economic science and facts, between the scientific conception of free-trade and the paradoxical reality of protectionism, seems to us to be no longer wrapped in impenetrable darkness. In our present economic stage, protectionism and free-trade lead nearly to the same results. Protectionism, which is generally injurious, but which, at certain historical epochs may do a country good, owes its existence only to the interests of a social class: it matters little whether or not it harms the others. And free-trade, which would undoubtedly make for the welfare of society at large, when considered in the abstract only, likewise benefits only certain classes or groups, by becoming in their hands instrumental for the safe-guarding of their interests. We can, indeed, come to no other conclusion when we find free-trade forwarding the interests of slave-owners and of landlords. In neither case is it the general welfare that is taken into consideration, but the special interests of the classes that pre-

[1] See *Protection and Free Trade*, p. 378, and *passim*.

dominate for the time being; and if such interests happen occasionally to tally with those of the nation at large, it is purely accidental. And so protection and free-trade are, alternately, the servants of those who rule.

In these circumstances the question of the commercial policy loses much of its importance, since it is concerned rather with particular class interests than with the general well-being of a country or society, which in reality are but little affected by the adoption of one system or the other, for neither the one nor the other completely satisfies their needs. The fault, however, must not be attributed to commercial policy, but to the social and economic organisation of our times, which is based, not upon the solidarity, but upon the antagonism of interests.

The splendid and harmonious principle of free-trade is perfectly true only on the supposition of an ideal social state founded upon the identical interests of all classes—a very lofty human conception. But the history of mankind is a succession of conflicts, occasionally interrupted by an armistice; there is no record of a durable equilibrium. As long as antagonism exists between property and capital, between capital and labour, between production and consumption, so long will continue the see-saw between protection and free-trade, which alternately serve the ends now of one class, now of another, and are always the instruments of oppression, of despotism, and of injustice.

And only when our social evolution, in the fulness of its fated development, and forced by the requirements of the population, shall have rent the bonds which bind together our actual economic organisation, and freed itself once for all from these sorrowful antagonisms (which after all are but so many obstacles to the growth of production and the spread of wealth and welfare); only when our social evolution—after having led humanity through the strife of centuries, which we have almost come to regard as an eternal fatality—shall have found, if not perfect peace, at all events order and quietude in an organisation based on justice and a harmony of interests: then, and then only, complete free-trade, hand in hand with class-union, will definitively bring about the solidarity of nations.

APPENDIX

Imports into the United States from 1791 to 1893, and average "ad valorem" duties, deduced from the proportion between the sum of Imports and the Custom-House Revenues.

[From the *Statistical Abstracts of the United States* for 1888, 1891, 1893.]

Year.	Total Imports.	Net Imports (exclusive of re-exports of foreign goods imported).			Amount of Duties Collected.	Average ad valorem Duties on the Goods.	
		Free.	Dutiable.	Total.		Liable to Duty.	Liable to Duty and exempted.
	Dollars.	Dollars.	Dollars.	Dollars.	Dollars.	Percentage.	Percentage.
1791	29,200,000	—	—	28,687,959	6,494,225	—	22·24
1792	31,500,000	—	—	29,746,902	4,938,074	—	15·68
1793	31,100,000	—	—	28,990,428	6,598,445	—	21·22
1794	34,600,000	—	—	28,073,766	9,588,382	—	24·82
1795	69,756,268	—	—	61,266,796	9,738,455	—	13·96
1796	81,436,164	—	—	55,136,164	12,581,167	—	15·45
1797	75,379,406	—	—	48,379,406	12,866,984	—	17·07
1798	68,551,700	—	—	35,551,700	11,402,185	—	16·63
1799	79,069,148	—	—	33,546,148	15,251,952	—	19·29
1800	91,252,768	—	—	52,121,891	16,003,779	—	17·54
1801	111,363,511	—	—	64,720,790	20,594,396	—	26·57
1802	76,333,333	—	—	40,558,362	14,843,132	—	19·45
1803	64,666,666	—	—	51,072,594	14,265,346	—	22·06
1804	85,000,000	—	—	48,768,403	19,888,622	—	23·40
1805	120,600,000	—	—	67,420,981	22,299,968	—	18·49
1806	129,410,000	—	—	69,126,764	24,825,592	—	19·18
1807	138,500,000	—	—	78,856,442	25,530,989	—	18·43
1808	56,990,000	—	—	43,992,586	10,662,507	—	18·71
1809	59,400,000	—	—	38,602,469	10,845,756	—	18·26
1810	85,400,000	—	—	61,008,705	15,263,356	—	17·88
1811	53,400,000	—	—	37,377,210	9,880,868	—	18·50
1812	77,030,000	—	—	68,534,873	14,373,782	—	18·66
1813	22,005,000	—	—	19,157,135	7,200,583	—	32·72
1814	12,965,000	—	—	12,819,831	4,241,482	—	32·72
1815	113,041,274	—	—	106,457,924	38,050,760	—	33·66
1816	147,103,000	—	—	129,964,844	32,829,923	—	22·32
1817	99,250,000	—	—	79,891,931	22,134,078	—	22·30
1818	121,750,000	—	—	102,223,304	25,860,327	—	21·24

CAUSES OF THE COMMERCIAL POLICY

Year.	Total Imports.	Net Imports (exclusive of re-exports of foreign goods imported).			Amount of Duties Collected.	Average ad valorem Duties on the Goods.	
		Free.	Dutiable.	Total.		Liable to Duty.	Liable to Duty and exempted.
	Dollars.	*Dollars.*	*Dollars.*	*Dollars.*	*Dollars.*	*Percentage.*	*Percentage.*
1819	87,125,000	—	—	67,959,317	21,345,915	—	24·50
1820	74,450,000	—	—	56,441,971	16,591,215	—	22·29
1821	54,520,834	1,730,725	41,965,680	43,696,405	18,883,252	35·97	34·64
1822	79,871,695	3,554,146	64,841,523	68,395,673	24,095,336	31·73	30·17
1823	72,481,371	2,626,630	48,684,106	51,310,736	22,416,277	32·71	30·93
1824	72,169,172	3,083,408	50,763,159	53,846,567	25,516,966	37·53	35·36
1825	90,189,310	3,707,960	62,687,762	66,395,722	31,683,096	37·10	35·13
1826	78,093,511	4,650,373	53,002,204	57,652,577	26,108,254	36·06	33·43
1827	71,332,938	2,890,130	52,010,978	54,901,108	27,962,145	41·35	39·20
1828	81,020,083	4,011,196	62,963,309	66,975,505	29,966,472	39·36	36·99
1829	67,088,915	3,481,946	51,259,625	54,741,571	27,769,769	44·30	41·39
1830	62,720,956	3,511,586	46,063,513	49,575,099	28,417,055	48·88	45·31
1831	95,885,179	5,508,094	77,300,016	82,808,110	36,623,270	40·81	38·19
1832	95,121,762	6,996,732	68,330,956	75,327,688	29,356,056	33·83	30·86
1833	101,047,943	20,211,675	63,258,392	83,470,067	24,196,103	31·96	23·95
1834	108,609,700	39,724,515	47,248,632	86,973,147	18,987,952	32·67	17·48
1835	136,764,295	57,796,380	64,211,594	122,007,974	25,931,233	36·64	18·95
1836	176,579,154	70,120,705	88,690,687	158,811,392	30,991,510	31·65	17·55
1837	130,472,803	50,977,428	62,333,143	113,310,571	18,191,605	25·36	13·94
1838	95,970,288	38,161,583	48,391,015	86,552,598	19,998,861	37·84	20·84
1839	156,496,956	65,188,174	80,682,642	145,870,816	25,631,888	29·90	16·38
1840	98,258,706	42,110,829	44,139,506	86,250,335	15,178,975	30·37	15·45
1841	122,957,544	57,078,044	57,698,265	114,776,309	19,941,090	32·20	16·22
1842	96,075,071	23,346,171	64,650,147	87,996,318	16,686,341	24·00	17·37
1843	42,433,464	11,571,486	25,722,643	37,294,129	7,508,627	25·73	17·70
1844	102,004,606	16,684,902	79,705,646	96,390,548	29,395,762	35·13	28·65
1845	113,184,322	15,664,548	89,934,993	105,599,541	30,978,558	32·17	27·37
1846	117,914,065	18,647,378	91,401,481	110,048,859	30,484,716	31·45	25·85
1847	122,424,349	15,838,500	100,419,095	116,257,595	28,137,922	26·86	22·98
1848	148,638,644	14,946,012	125,705,826	140,651,838	33,034,306	24·97	22·22
1849	141,206,199	13,710,610	118,854,498	132,565,108	31,027,772	24·73	21·97
1850	173,509,526	15,982,458	148,051,575	164,034,033	40,181,813	25·85	23·16
1851	210,771,429	17,910,930	182,565,378	200,476,308	48,627,600	25·44	23·07
1852	207,440,398	21,649,731	173,737,583	195,387,314	47,577,633	25·96	22·94
1853	263,777,265	24,732,613	225,424,532	250,157,145	58,467,814	25·93	23·37
1854	297,803,794	22,552,835	253,535,495	276,088,330	64,931,607	25·61	23·52
1855	257,808,708	29,913,974	201,736,366	231,650,340	54,119,676	26·82	23·36
1856	310,432,310	49,603,470	246,047,468	295,650,938	64,083,400	26·05	21·68
1857	348,428,342	49,942,107	283,569,188	333,511,295	63,664,863	22·45	19·09
1858	263,338,654	55,292,929	187,385,484	242,678,413	42,046,722	22·44	17·33
1859	331,333,341	66,856,406	249,966,964	316,823,370	48,894,683	19·56	15·43
1860	353,616,119	68,391,038	267,891,447	336,282,485	52,692,121	19·67	15·67
1861	289,310,542	67,421,022	207,235,303	274,656,325	39,038,269	18·84	14·21
1862	189,356,677	49,842,974	128,487,253	178,330,200	46,509,214	36·19	26·09
1863	243,335,815	30,026,756	195,348,524	225,375,280	63,729,203	32·62	28·28
1864	316,447,283	38,162,565	262,950,757	301,113,322	96,465,957	36·69	32·03
1865	238,745,580	40,097,208	169,559,317	209,656,525	80,635,169	47·56	38·46
1866	434,812,066	57,121,369	366,349,277	423,470,646	177,056,523	48·33	41·81
1867	—	17,033,130	361,125,553	378,158,683	168,503,749	46·67	44·56

Year.	Total Imports.	NET IMPORTS (exclusive of re-exports of foreign goods imported).			Amount of Duties Collected.	Average ad valorem Duties on the Goods.	
		Free.	Dutiable.	Total.		Liable to Duty.	Liable to Duty and exempted.
	Dollars.	Dollars.	Dollars.	Dollars.	Dollars.	Percentage.	Percentage.
1868	—	15,147,618	329,661,302	344,808,920	160,532,778	48·63	46·49
1869	—	21,692,532	372,756,642	394,448,174	176,557,583	47·22	44·65
1870	—	20,214,105	406,131,905	426,346,010	191,513,974	47·08	42·23
1871	—	40,619,064	459,597,058	500,216,122	202,446,673	43·95	38·94
1872	—	47,683,747	512,735,287	560,419,034	212,619,105	41·35	37·00
1873	—	178,399,796	484,746,861	663,146,657	184,929,041	38·07	26·95
1874	—	151,694,834	415,748,693	567,443,527	160,522,284	38·53	26·38
1875	—	146,465,463	379,795,113	526,260,576	154,554,982	40·62	28·20
1876	—	140,561,381	324,024,926	464,586,307	145,178,602	44·74	30·19
1877	—	140,840,149	298,989,240	439,829,389	128,428,343	42·89	26·68
1878	—	141,339,059	297,083,409	438,422,468	127,195,158	42·75	27·13
1879	—	142,550,159	296,742,215	439,292,374	133,395,435	44·87	28·97
1880	—	208,049,180	419,506,091	627,555,271	182,747,653	43·48	29·07
1881	—	202,557,412	448,061,588	650,619,000	193,800,879	43·20	29·75
1882	—	210,721,981	505,491,967	716,213,948	216,138,916	42·66	30·11
1883	—	206,913,289	493,916,384	700,829,673	210,637,293	42·45	29·92
1884	—	211,280,265	456,295,124	667,575,389	190,282,835	41·61	28·44
1885	—	192,912,234	386,667,820	579,580,054	178,151,601	45·86	30·59
1886	—	211,530,759	413,778,055	625,308,814	189,410,448	45·55	30·13
1887	—	233,093,659	450,325,322	683,418,981	214,222,309	47·10	31·02
1888	—	244,104,852	468,143,774	712,248,626	216,042,256	45·63	29·99
1889	—	256,574,630	484,856,268	741,431,398	220,576,989	45·13	29·50
1890	—	266,103,048	507,571,764	773,674,812	226,540,036	44·41	29·12
1891	—	388,064,404	466,455,173	854,519,577	216,885,701	46·28	29·25
1892	—	458,074,604	355,526,741	813,601,345	174,124,270	48·71	21·26
1893	—	444,172,064	400,282,519	844,544,583	199,143,678	49·58	23·49

THIRD ESSAY

THE THEORY OF PROTECTIONISM IN THE UNITED STATES AND THE HISTORICAL CIRCUMSTANCES OF ITS DEVELOPMENT

CHAPTER I

ALEXANDER HAMILTON

1. In the preceding essay we have dealt at considerable length with the historical evolution of the commercial policy of the United States, and we have methodically investigated the causes which led at one time to the adoption of protectionism, and at another to that of free-trade.

But the importance assigned by this great nation to the protective system is such, that we deem it opportune to follow up the history of American commercial policy by a study of the protectionist theory that was developed side by side with it, and which, if it was not its most potent factor (for we think it may be stated generally that it is facts that give birth to theories, and not *vice versa*), yet it influenced it to no inconsiderable extent, and became its doctrinal commentary and support.

A complete account of the protectionist theory in the United States would have to be treated in no sparing manner, and would require a mass of materials only accessible to American writers. It is evident that a system of commercial policy that, with certain interruptions, has prevailed for a century in the history of a country, and has given rise, in practice, to such lively disputations and to such grave conflicts, must necessarily have occasioned not merely copious scientific research, but have also raised up, in the domain of theory, a host of warm supporters of the predominating interests and of the ideas on which these interests were founded, and a body of writers, no less numerous, who advocated the cause of those whose interests were disregarded by the party then in power.

But besides the fact that we have not the materials at

hand for a complete study of this kind, we think that possibly the results obtainable — although no doubt scientifically interesting—might not be equal to the time and labour which such an investigation would demand. As a matter of fact, in the crowd of American protectionist writers and their contradictors (and even with our limited opportunities the number of works we have perused is by no means small), rarely indeed is originality to be met with, and mere commonplace abounds; and in the advocates of protection, many are the errors which do not even need refutation, whilst their adversaries repeat *ad nauseam* the old theoretical arguments dogmatised by liberalism: and in general, both sides are so engrossed with the attack and defence of their respective positions and the interests depending on them, that it is vain to expect any impartial scientific conclusions from their labours.

Whilst the aspect of American liberalism, however, is marked by an almost complete want of originality, and forms no particular code of doctrines, originality is, on the other hand, to be found in some of the more eminent advocates of protection, and they have inspired, to a greater or less extent, all their contemporaries.

And it is natural enough that the country which has given to history a whole century of predominantly protectionist policy, and has made such practical application of the system, should likewise contribute largely to the theoretical development of it.

It will suffice, therefore, for our purpose, to study the theories of a few of the more important and original writers belonging to the various epochs of the economic and commercial history of the United States. Their theories summarise and, to a certain extent, personify the ideas which prevailed in their times, and are a reflection of the economic conditions in which their authors lived.

"Economic writers are almost always influenced, though in varying degrees, by the special conditions, ideas, and institutions of the country and the period to which they belong, or to which they have by preference turned their attention." So says Cossa;[1] and we shall have many opportunities in what follows to bear witness to the truth of this observation.

[1] *An Introduction to the Study of Political Economy* (English translation), London, Macmillan, 1893, p. 113.

And so, without renouncing a critical analysis of the theories, we propose above all to make clear their connection with the social and economic circumstances in which they were developed, and this study, which is much facilitated by the researches made in the previous essay into the American economic evolution, will serve, in our opinion, as a useful comment on the vicissitudes of the commercial policy, of which we have endeavoured to fathom the secret springs.

2. The first great figure we meet with in the history of American protectionism is that of Alexander Hamilton.

Alexander Hamilton was one of the most distinguished men—perhaps the most distinguished, after Washington—of the heroic epoch of the constitution of the United States. As a soldier he was noted for bravery in all the battles of the War of Independence; as minister of finance, he has left indelible records in the political, financial, and economic reorganisation of his country; and a yet more lasting memorial of him remains in the history of the protective theory, in his famous *Report on Manufactures*, which had so great an influence on the historical development of protectionism in the United States, and which, taking into consideration the period in which it was written, undoubtedly gives its author the first place among the American theoretical advocates of protection.

But although he reached an eminent position, and had been able by word and deed to exercise a precious influence on the fortunes of his country, Alexander Hamilton had the ill-luck to be incompletely understood by his contemporaries, and he has not been impartially judged by all the writers of our own time: and his popularity was far less than that which his brilliant gifts and great services to his native land deserved.

His political conceptions were too lofty and too far removed from those that prevailed—especially in the masses—at his time; his tendencies were not in harmony with those of the majority; and later on, either his political, or else his economic ideas, and particularly his protective thesis—which became the object of the most excessive praise and blame—has had such an unbounded effect on public opinion, as to amount to an apotheosis on the part of

U

his admirers, whilst but scant justice has been done to him by others.[1]

But among our contemporaries there are judges by no means suspected of partiality who have testified to his exceeding worth; and Bryce, who, among foreign writers on America, is perhaps the most profound student of her history and politics, says of him: "Equally apt for war and for civil government, with a profundity and amplitude of view rare in practical soldiers or statesmen, he stands in the front rank of a generation never surpassed in history, a generation which includes Burke and Fox and Pitt and Grattan, Stein and Hardenberg and William von Humboldt, Wellington and Napoleon. Talleyrand, who seems to have felt for him something as near affection as that cold heart could feel, said, after knowing all the famous men of the time, that only Fox and Napoleon were Hamilton's equals, and that he had divined Europe, having never seen it."[2]

3. To fully understand the financial work, and also the protectionist ideas of Alexander Hamilton, it is necessary to preface a few observations regarding the political opinions of which he was the chief exponent, and which he carried with him into the Government; for in them we shall find the primary cause and foundation of all his work. We have already seen in the previous essay (pp. 122-125) to what degree political motives influenced the tariff of 1789; how

[1] If his editor and biographer, Lodge, is perhaps too well disposed towards him, Professor Sumner, a free-trader, on the other hand, is not merely too severe, but absolutely unjust to him.

[2] Bryce, *American Commonwealth*, vol. ii. p. 328. It may be convenient to give here a few biographical notes of Alexander Hamilton. He was born in 1757 at Nevis, one of the small West India islands subject to Great Britain; he was a most precocious boy; the first years of his life were spent in a house of business; in 1772, when fifteen years of age, he went to Boston, and thence to New York, where he gave himself up to study. The ideas of independence were then fermenting in the colonies, and from 1774 Hamilton wrote letters and articles in favour of the movement. He took part in the war and distinguished himself so much in it, that in 1777 he was made Washington's adjutant, with the grade of lieutenant-colonel. When the war was over, he took to the study of the law, and investigated political and financial questions. In 1782 he proposed a new convention and a better union of the States; he made vain efforts to procure resources for the Central Government, that stood in great need of them. He was elected a member of the Continental Congress in 1782, at a time of great difficulties; when the Government of the Confederation was hardly exercis-

one of its fundamental objects was to secure revenue for the
Federal Government, and to strengthen the union; and how
the principal aim of Hamilton and his party was to give
energy to the Federal power, and to reinforce the sentiment of
nationality. And further back, in the early pages of the first
chapter of the same essay, some description was given of the
exceedingly sad political and financial state of the Confederation, brought about by the complete absence of authority of
any kind. National existence, created at the cost of a long
series of heroic efforts and of much bloodshed, was jeopardised
by the want of a strong Government; and it was chiefly
owing to a small band of men who had the courage to oppose
the prevalent feelings of individuals, that the country obtained
the constitution which gave it a firmly-established unity.
Hamilton was among them, a champion of the Federal
party, which tended to subordinate the several States to
the nation as a whole, to place extensive powers in the
hands of central Federal authority, to constitute a strong
Government; while opposed to him was Jefferson, leader of
the party since called republican, that opposed the principle
of democracy to that of nationality, and that desired to secure
the largest possible amount of freedom for individuals and of
independence for the separate States, and hence impeded the
formation of a powerful Federal Government. The Federal
party, that appealed to feelings of law and order, was not

ing its functions, and its finances were exhausted ; he energetically, but vainly,
urged the necessity of supporting the Government. He was returned as representative of New York to the Convention of Annapolis, in 1786, and subsequently
to that of Philadelphia (1787), for the formation of a constitution ; when this had
been accomplished—though not in the way he desired—Hamilton became its
chief advocate and commentator in the famous *Federalist*, which is its best
interpretation, and which did much to render the new constitution acceptable
to the individual States. Immediately on the formation of the department of
the treasury, in 1789, he was called to preside over it, and he retained the post
for six years, till 1795, when he gave it up voluntarily. We shall refer to his
ministerial work in the text. He died in 1804, killed in a duel by Aaron Burr.

Among the principal publications of recent date illustrating the life and
works of Alexander Hamilton which we have been able to consult, we may
refer to H. Cabot Lodge, *Alexander Hamilton*, Boston, 1890 ; Anson D. Morse,
"Alexander Hamilton," in the *Political Science Quarterly*, March, 1890 ; W. G.
Sumner, *Alexander Hamilton*, New York, 1890 ; A. Johnston, "Alexander
Hamilton," in the *Cyclopædia of Political Science*, etc., New York, 1888 ; A.
Bolles, *Financial History of the United States*, vol. ii., New York, 1885.
Hamilton's writings have been collected by Lodge in seven volumes.

popular. That was the privilege of their opponents, who looked to the masses, claiming decentralisation, and advocating individual and local liberty.

When once the constitution had been approved, the struggle between these two tendencies continued, respecting its interpretation, among the same members of the first Cabinet, Hamilton and Jefferson, both of them Washington's ministers, and "while the piercing intellect of Hamilton developed all those of its provisions which invested the Federal Congress and President with far-reaching powers, and sought to build up a system of institutions which should give to these provisions their full effect, Jefferson and his coadjutors appealed to the sentiment of individualism, strong in the masses of the people, and, without venturing to propose alterations in the text of the constitution, protested against all extensions of its letter, and against all the assumptions of Federal authority which such extensions could be made to justify." [1]

The Federal party, unpopular as it was, remained in office but few years; "but its administration," says an impartial critic, "gave the new republic time to throw out deep roots, so as to be able, later on, to tolerate without harm the rapid development of those doctrines which it had first of all combated." [2]

The Federal party was, in fact, the true founder of American nationality, and its energetically concentrating action was necessary and fruitful in the first period of the establishment of the United States Republic. With the ideas and aspirations of this party all Hamilton's efforts, whether political, economic, or financial, were co-ordinated; his work formed one logical whole from beginning to end, and it should be judged in its entirety.

It may not be out of place, however, to observe that as regards the social law, which makes economic phenomena the substratum and the foundation of political events, the political idea, both of the Federal party and that put in practice by Hamilton, had, in fact, an economic basis, which

[1] Bryce, work mentioned, vol. ii. p. 326.
[2] Tocqueville, *La Democrazia in America* (Italian translation), Torino, Unione Tip. 1884, p. 176.

helps us to understand certain arrangements, and which is connected, so far as Hamilton's protectionism is concerned, with that theory which we expounded at some length in an earlier chapter. The Federal party was, in truth, composed chiefly of business men, who desired a strong Government in view of their commercial interests, to whom were added a large and new class, recently formed, of creditors, of holders of public securities, and, in the south, of great landowners.

The opposite party, on the other hand, consisted of the mass of the people, agricultural, democratic, and individualistic in tendency.[1] Now Hamilton laid the foundations of his scheme on the commercial and capitalist classes, and to this he co-ordinated all his projects, conceiving that upon this basis American nationality and the Federal Government would enjoy a secure existence. In the proposed constitution which he presented to the Philadelphia Convention of 1787, the President and the Senators were, in fact, to be named for life by electors possessing real property; and all the provisions regarding the public debt—so favourable to the State creditors —which Hamilton afterwards proposed to Congress, were evidently designed to interest the moneyed classes in the Federal Government, and to enlist their support in its behalf during the straits through which it was passing;[2] so also were his suggestions regarding a single bank; just as the same spirit—co-ordinated with other ideas—inspired his theory of protection.

4. The more important financial measures with which Alexander Hamilton's name is associated in the first years of the independence of the United States are the reorganisation of the national debt, the establishment of a bank, the regulation of money, and the dispositions regarding internal taxes and customs tariffs. We may be allowed to touch very briefly on these measures before coming to the question that chiefly interests us—namely, Hamilton's protectionist theory.

All these measures, as we have said, were co-ordinated for one political purpose, which we have already mentioned, and which is underlaid by an economical element.

[1] A. Johnston, "Federal Party"; "Anti-Federal Party," etc., in Lalor's *Cyclopædia*.
[2] Lodge, work mentioned, pp. 91, 92; and Morse, article quoted.

Far too long and complicated would be an investigation of Hamilton's provisions regarding the public debt, which gave rise to such prolonged and acrimonious discussions; it would necessarily lead us to a consideration of the complex state of the American national debt at that period, and this is altogether outside our purpose.

From a practical point of view, it does not appear difficult to us to give a summary estimate of the value of Hamilton's work in this field. It is evident, in fact, that he did good work, inasmuch as the fusion and consolidation of the numberless debts did much to raise the securities and the credit of the Government, which had been so shaken during the Confederation; whilst the assumption on the part of the Federal Government of the debts of the various States—whose creditors ran the greatest possible danger—inaugurated a policy of public honesty in the administration of the national debt.[1]

It is more difficult, however, on this question to pronounce an opinion on Hamilton's ideas from a scientific standpoint; nor can such a judgment be as favourable to him as the preceding one; for all that, he must not be too severely blamed for sharing in the errors of his times.

Sumner, who deals by no means leniently with Hamilton, says that he had very confused ideas regarding credit, and he accuses him particularly of maintaining the error that the public debt was capital; he accuses him of having repeatedly affirmed that a national debt, when not excessive, was advantageous to a country; and, among various quotations which he makes from him, he underlines especially an extract from his *Vindication of Funding*, written in 1795, in which Hamilton justifies his assertion that the public debt is capital, observing that if a Government borrows 100 dollars it spends them, and that constitutes capital; whilst the bond may be sold, and that constitutes another capital, so that the Government credit produces a new capital of 100 dollars.[2]

In these thrusts made at Hamilton there is some truth, but, in our opinion, not all the truth. The existence of a national debt was not considered by Hamilton to be advan-

[1] Bolles, vol. ii. chap. ii. iii. iv.
[2] Sumner, work mentioned, pp. 149, 150.

tageous in itself, but merely so as a means of cementing the national unity.[1] So far from looking upon public debts as advantageous in themselves, remarks Ross, Hamilton again and again declared that American finance should ever be inspired with the fundamental maxim that the creation of debt ought always to be accompanied by provisions for its ultimate extinction.[2]

Certainly the above-quoted extract clearly expresses the idea that credit is capital; so much so that—if it did not lead us too far away from our subject—it would be most interesting to compare Hamilton's opinions with those of MacLeod, whose precursor he might, strictly speaking, be considered. In the pages, however, which refer to public credit in his famous *Report on Manufactures*, Hamilton is less explicit, and, up to a certain point, seems to see with sufficient exactness the function of credit, which he qualifies, not as capital, but as an instrument of industry and commerce, observing that a funded debt cannot be considered an effective increase of wealth or of capital.[3] But although he caught a momentary glimpse of this fact, he allowed himself to be led astray by contemporary writers, who exaggerated in the strangest way the utility of public loans, attributing to public credit those effects on industry which are in reality the effects of productive private credit in general, and upholding the curious doctrine that the easy and prompt convertibility of the funded debt into cash makes it equivalent to money, and so operates that the bonds of the public debt may be used as capital in industrial enterprises.[4]

A similar judgment must be pronounced on our author's ideas regarding the extinction of the national debt, for they were, to a large extent, allied to those which Pitt was at that very moment applying in England, and which, after having

[1] See the quotation which Sumner himself makes of Hamilton's words, on p. 149 : "A national debt, if it is not excessive, will be to us a national blessing. It will be a powerful cement to our union." And note that these words were written in 1781, that is, when the American nation was as yet unformed, and when a national debt would appear exactly suited to unite the material interests of the citizens of the various States.
[2] Ross, "Sinking Funds," Baltimore, *Am. Ec. Ass.* 1892 ; and also Bolles, passage quoted.
[3] *Report on Manufactures*, edition quoted, pp. 60, 61.
[4] *Ibid.* p. 55.

raised so much enthusiasm, courted such signal failure and such severe criticism.

5. Another of Hamilton's enactments was the establishment of the Bank of the United States. There existed three small banks, which did not fulfil the requirements of the country, at that time ill-provided with circulating medium ; nor were they capable, in case of need, of lending a hand to the Federal Government. Hamilton wished to found a strong institution which, by facilitating credit and increasing the circulating medium, should smooth the way for the development of trade and industry, and which should assist Federal finance by eventually providing for the monetary wants of the Government. The Bank of the United States, constituted in 1791, with a capital of ten millions of dollars, of which two millions were subscribed by Government, lasted till 1811.

In the meanwhile Hamilton was not neglecting the money question. The specie in use was scarce, and coins of various kinds circulated in the different States, giving rise to great confusion. During the confederation, the problem had been studied by Morris and by Jefferson, who had proposed a decimal system that should differ as little as possible from those of the various States; Hamilton, availing himself of their labours, had the good fortune to secure, in 1792, the adoption of a monetary enactment, founded on bimetallism, which remained intact till 1834, and the fundamental provisions of which are still in force. Most notable is the report with which, in 1791, Hamilton presented his Bill to Congress. In it he insisted on the importance of a uniform monetary system both for the State and for private individuals; he set forth the actual evils and the leading features of the reforms he proposed. But, whilst declaring that had it been necessary to decide in favour of a single metal, he would have preferred gold on account of its greater stability in value, and admitting the difficulty of maintaining a fixed relation between the values of the two metals, he advocated the adoption of the bimetallic system, in order to secure for the country, which stood in great need of it, a more abundant circulating medium. Since, he said, "to annul the use of either of the metals as money is to abridge the quantity of circulating medium, and

CHAP. I PROTECTIONISM IN THE UNITED STATES 297

is liable to all the objections which arise from a comparison of the benefits of a full with the evils of a scanty circulation." In fixing the relation between the values of the two metals, he took into account that which existed in other countries, in order to facilitate international exchange.¹

The revenue system, arranged by Hamilton, was essentially founded on the one hand upon import duties, and on the other upon a number of internal taxes on production and sale, especially designed to provide the Government with a source of revenue in case of war, when the customs-dues might fall off. We have had occasion more than once to point out the grave defects of the American system of Federal revenue based on customs duties; a system which binds too closely together two absolutely different objects, which often mutually paralyse and damage one another, and disorganise the national economy—the fiscal purpose and the protective purpose; for it frequently happens that financial needs impose such modifications on the customs tariffs as to change their character and economic effects.

The origin of this financial system, however, cannot be attributed to Hamilton, but rather to the circumstances of the Federal Government, whose existence and authority—energetically supported, as we have seen, by him—were continually combated by the petty jealousies and strivings for autonomy of the separate States. These latter would not recognise the right of the Federal Government to levy internal taxes, and indeed Hamilton's determined insistence upon a tax on the production of spirits—for the very purpose of affirming this right of taxation—provoked in 1794 a rebellion in Pennsylvania, which had to be suppressed by Federal troops, commanded in person by this great and singular man, who exchanged with such ease the portfolio of a minister for the sword of an officer.²

As to Hamilton's work with regard to the customs tariff, the practical part has been discussed at some length in the preceding essay, and we shall shortly speak of his theories.

In the meantime, to conclude these brief remarks on his

¹ Bolles, pp. 156-175.
² *Ibid.* pp. 103-127; and Johnston, "Whisky Insurrection," in Lalor's *Cyclopædia.*

political and financial achievements, we may observe that both the one and the other left enduring traces.

His political work did much to consolidate the national unity which was still vacillating in the first years of the republic; his financial work strengthened the Federal finance by substituting a solid organisation for the administrative chaos which had been bequeathed by the Confederation. It is true that all that Hamilton accomplished was not perfect, and much of it—done in the midst of difficulties and incessant hostility—was speedily undone or neutralised by his enemies; but his efforts bore the stamp of greatness. And if he be not that wonder-working magician of finance described in glowing language by Webster,[1] he is at all events a great financier—the greatest the United States have ever known.

6. The *Report on Manufactures*, which we must dwell upon, was presented by Hamilton on the 5th of December 1791 to the House of Representatives, which had, ever since the 15th of January 1790, requested his attention "to the subject of manufactures, and particularly to the means of promoting such as will tend to render the United States independent of foreign nations for military and other essential supplies."[2]

The importance of this document for the history of American protectionism cannot be exaggerated; and its importance is twofold; it is both practical and scientific. Of the first aspect we have already spoken, but we pointed out that it was Hamilton's theories that especially demanded the attention of students; and now we propose to investigate the subject in order to see what place appertains to Alexander Hamilton in the history of the theory of protectionism in the United States.

The *Report* is divided into two distinct parts; in the first, which is by far the more important, Hamilton sets forth the reasons for which he believes it to be necessary to encourage

---

[1] "He smote the rock of the national resources, and abundant streams gushed forth. He touched the dead corpse of the public credit, and it sprung upon its feet. The fabled birth of Minerva from the brain of Jove was hardly more sudden or more perfect than the financial system of the United States as it burst forth from the conception of Alexander Hamilton."—Webster, *Speeches*, i. 199.

[2] *Report*, edition quoted, p. 9.

the development of the manufacturing industries, and he analyses the various means to this end. In the second part he gives a summary account of the state of production of the country in his time, particularly of those industries which, in his opinion, needed protection; he shows how the country was disposed towards these industries, the abundance of raw materials and other favourable circumstances, the extent to which they had already been developed, and their importance to the nation generally: all this to prove that these trades deserved encouragement, and to justify the proposals which he makes for each class of them.

We have already made use of this portion of the *Report*, which occupies barely 28 out of the 134 pages of the edition now in our hands, to draw a picture of the economic and industrial condition of the United States in 1789. (See *supra*, p. 128.)

It will suffice here to observe that it is not only of small importance from a theoretical point of view, but that it fails also in the object which the author himself had before him. In fact, although precise statistics were not at hand in those times, the information which the *Report* does contain regarding the circumstances in which the production of many of the industries was effected, is beyond measure unsatisfactory; there are no figures regarding wages, prices, and other essential data necessary to make clear the conditions of American production compared with foreign competition, of which not a word is said; and most superficial are often the author's proofs that the industries of which he treats really found sufficiently favourable natural means of development in the country.

But it is of the first portion of the *Report*, which is entirely theoretical, that we must make an accurate analysis; and certainly it is worth the trouble.

7. It appears to us necessary to preface our examination by a brief, so to speak, external recapitulation of its contents.

Hamilton begins his *Report* by stating that the expediency of encouraging manufactures was then generally admitted in the United States—especially as a result of the damage done by the restrictions on foreign trade; and he repeats the arguments adduced against the opportuneness of such encouragement, namely, the importance of agriculture for the national welfare, the danger of giving industries an artificial stimulus, the lack of hands—an obstacle to the development of manufactures—the fear of benefiting a limited class whilst injuring the mass of consumers. He admits the reasonableness of these arguments, if universally applied; but he points out that there are always exceptions; and, whilst fully granting the great and even predominating importance of agriculture, says that it is not wise to give it exclusive preference, and that its real interests would by no means be sacrificed even if other industries were fostered. On this point he exposes the physiocratical ideas regarding the unproductiveness of manufacturing industry and the preference that should be given to agriculture, and refutes them in a series of considerations on which we shall enlarge in due course.

Satisfied as to the productiveness of manufactures, our author goes on to enumerate and analyse the principal reasons from which it follows that their establishment contributes essentially to increasing the wealth of the country. As a matter of fact, he remarks, manufactures allow a large application of the division of labour (of which, as we shall see, he makes manifest the advantages); they admit, to a far greater extent than agriculture does, of the use of machinery; they offer additional employment for classes not usually occupied in business; they stimulate emigration from foreign countries; furnish a vast field for the exercise of human ingenuity, and a wider and more various scope for enterprise; and above all, they in some cases create a new—and in all cases ensure a more certain and constant—demand for the surplus product of the soil, by providing for it a home market.

Our author then examines the question from the standpoint of the particular circumstances of the United States, and shows how they were justified in creating, through the manufactures, a home market for their agricultural produce, by restrictive legislation, adopted likewise in other countries, and he always admits the advantages of free-trade, provided only that it be universally applied. He observes that the difficulties which manufactures always encounter at the outset would effectually retard their development did they not receive some assistance from the state; he contradicts the assertions of those who maintained that manufactures were impracticable in the United States on account of the scarcity of hands, the great cost of labour, and the want of capital;[1] and his replies deal largely with experience; he enumerates no less than seventeen different industries which had already been developed in his time, besides the domestic manufactures that were universal throughout the country. He answers the objection that protection grants a monopoly to a particular class at the expense of the community at large, by stating that the rise in prices, which sometimes follows the adoption of protective measures, is merely temporary, and that the ultimate effect is even a fall of prices brought about by greater home competition.

After having in this way silenced all the objections of his opponents, our author adds several arguments in support of his contentions.

He maintains that the trade of a country, where both agriculture and manufactures flourish, is more lucrative and prosperous than that of a merely agricultural one; he adduces the political necessity of the American commonwealth producing the first necessaries of life for the sustenance of its population and for the defence of its territories; finally, he makes some special observations, to which we shall return later on, regarding the distance of the United States from Europe, and the effect of this distance upon her commerce; and he repudiates to the last the idea that there is any incompatibility between the interests of the manufacturing north and the agricultural south. Indeed, he maintains that the prosperity of agriculture and manufactures being closely connected, the protection of the manufactures established in the north and centre will prove beneficial to the agriculturists of the south by creating a great demand for their produce.

Having thus proved the opportuneness and the necessity of protecting manufacturing industries, Hamilton proceeds to examine the methods which other nations have already adopted for this purpose; he passes in review protective duties on imports, prohibition and prohibitive duties on imports, prohibition of export of raw materials, bounties, premiums, the exemption of raw materials from duty, drawbacks on raw

[1] It is here that he sets forth those considerations upon the public debt to which we alluded a little farther back.

materials, the manufactured products of which are exported, and other systems of secondary importance. He dwells at some length on the system of bounties, to which he gives a decided preference; and he then passes on to the second part, in which he describes the state of the various American industries, and suggests practical measures for their protection.

8. Let us take a preliminary survey of the most general and characteristic ideas ventilated by Hamilton in his *Report*.

He is not blind to the advantages of free-trade; on the contrary he admits and illustrates them more than once. If the system of perfect industrial and commercial liberty prevailed among the nations of the world, then, he says, the arguments which dissuade the United States from giving an impulse to their manufactures would undoubtedly acquire great force. In such a state of affairs each country would enjoy the full benefit of its special capacities, and this would compensate it for its deficiencies. If one nation was in such a condition as to be able to provide manufactured goods better than another nation, that other one might find ample compensation in a capacity to furnish superior agricultural products. And a free exchange of the goods which each of them was best able to produce could be established to the mutual benefit of both nations, and would maintain their particular industries in the highest activity.[1]

Hamilton has evidently a clear insight into the advantages of free-trade; but in practice he arrived at other conclusions, actuated by a twofold object—political and economic (and in all his writings we observe this union of the political with the economic ideas), namely, reprisals, chiefly against England, which country overcome, as we have seen, by force of arms, wished to compensate herself by economic warfare and reciprocity. The idea of reprisals to force the hand of England—popular in those days—is naturally rather implied in the official report of a statesman than clearly expressed in so many words; but on the other hand, the idea of reciprocity is declared and illustrated more than once. The *Report*, in fact, takes its origin from the foreign restrictive ordinances which limited the American exportation of agricultural pro-

[1] *Report*, p. 38.

duce.¹ Such legislation is deplored by our author, who, nevertheless observes that, as matters now stood, if the United States adopted free-trade, they would remain isolated, their agricultural products would not be accepted, and they would not know how to pay for the manufactured articles sent to them; and hence the best policy would be to create a home market for native agricultural produce, by giving an impulse to manufactures, and thus render it independent of foreign demand.

If the United States did not react against the restrictive foreign measures, they would not be able to "exchange with Europe on equal terms; and the want of reciprocity would render them the victim of a system which should induce them to confine their views to agriculture, and refrain from manufactures. A constant and increasing necessity on their part for the commodities of Europe, and only a partial and occasional demand for their own in return, could not but expose them to a state of impoverishment, compared with the opulence to which their political and natural advantages authorise them to aspire."²

The analogy between this view of the question and recent English "fair-trade" manifestations is striking; and it might also be pointed out that this idea of reciprocity is more justifiable in Hamilton than in writers of to-day; for not only had it, in his case, a political foundation, but it was impossible to bring against it one of the most powerful objections to the English "fair-trade" proposals, namely, that as imports into England consist chiefly of raw materials for her factories and of food-supplies, any extensive reprisals that England might wish to make would redound to her own disadvantage.

Certain it is that all goods have ultimately to be paid for with other goods, and that to counterbalance duties by duties is merely to add to the injury done by foreign tariffs that of enhancing the price of all things consumed in the country. But this is not the time or place for criticism.

Another characteristic of Hamilton's *Report* is, as we have seen, the great importance given to political considerations. They are not only united to the ideas which we have just expressed, but they pervade the whole work as part of

¹ *Report*, p. 11. ² *Ibid.* pp. 39, 40.

Hamilton's fundamental principle of strengthening the national unity and of ensuring a home supply of all provisions and commodities that might be required by military exigencies.

This last idea was expressed by the House of Representatives, which requested Hamilton to draw up this *Report*, and it is repeated in the *Report* itself, which observes that the want of many commodities and means of defence had been seriously felt by the United States during the War of Independence; and that the absence of a navy, which in case of war would protect American commerce abroad, rendered all the more imperative a native production of all that might be required in warfare.[1]

These characteristics of Hamilton's *Report* show us how moderate was the protection which he demanded, and how very different from that subsequently called the "American system," and which became more and more a "system of isolation."

The fundamental motives on which Hamilton's protectionism was based were considerations of opportunity, and hence they were largely relative: he certainly did not regard protection as an ideal, but as a necessity owing to the political circumstances of the United States, and consequently limited to the needs of the country. It is true that there lay, as a substratum beneath Hamilton's political opinions and those of his party, the economic interests of the capitalist class; but the latter, as we have seen in the preceding essay, did not yet require any energetic protection. Hence Hamilton's moderation.

9. But the importance and singularity of his *Report* lies in the fact that, although merely advocating moderate protection and that chiefly on political grounds, he did not confine himself to proving his theories by means of the arguments we have recapitulated above, but he reinforced them with others of a more strictly economical character; and these arguments, although evidently of secondary importance to Hamilton, are of such weight in the history of protectionism that they give to the *Report on Manufactures* an especial impress of historical value. In them, in fact, Alexander Hamilton traced the principal lines of the protectionist theory

[1] *Report*, pp. 71, 72.

as it was subsequently upheld by its chief supporters, who drew largely upon him, and who did not add materially to his demonstrations.

Let us therefore briefly examine these arguments. In his criticism of physiocratic theories there is one idea on which he dwells at considerable length, and that was made much use of by others after him. It is that of the utility of the simultaneous existence in a country of agriculture and manufactures, and of the necessity of the latter for ensuring a home market for the produce of the former. Even admitting the advantages of free-trade, he makes certain reservations, observing that purely agricultural nations would probably not enjoy so high a degree of prosperity as those which combined manufactures with agriculture.[1] And elsewhere he remarks that the trade of a country which is both industrial and agricultural is more lucrative and prosperous than that of a simply agricultural one, because a market that offers many products of different kinds attracts foreign consumers much more readily, presents a larger field to commercial enterprise, and suffers less from the trade-stagnation which at times affects certain industries.[2]

Then, as to the idea of ensuring a home market for the agricultural produce of the country, it is true that it was suggested to Hamilton chiefly by political exigencies, namely, the existence of foreign restrictive measures; but it was not prompted by these reasons alone.

The demand of foreign nations for agricultural produce is, he says, uncertain and intermittent—and hence not to be depended upon by the country furnishing the supplies—and this is brought about not merely by artificial, but also by natural causes.

"Independently likewise of the artificial impediments which are created by the policy in question, there are natural causes tending to render the external demand for the surplus of agricultural nations a precarious reliance. The differences of seasons in the countries which are the consumers make immense differences in the produce of their own soils in different years, and consequently in the degrees of their necessity for foreign supply. Plentiful harvests with them,

[1] *Report*, p. 38. [2] *Ibid.* pp. 67-69.

especially if similar ones occur at the same time in the countries which are the furnishers, occasion of course a glut in the market of the latter."[1] Here is an opportunity of relieving the country from this uncertainty occasioned by the vicissitudes of foreign demand by establishing a home market for the native produce; and this can be obtained by the diffusion of manufactures, which not only create a natural demand for agricultural products, but which likewise stimulate the demand for new commodities.[2]

Another idea, allied to the preceding one, but which can stand alone, and which plays an important part in the history of American protectionism, is that of the small remunerativeness of the trade of the United States with Europe, in consequence of the great distance between them, and the nature of their exportations.

The great distance at which we are from Europe, which is the principal market of manufactured goods, and the weight and volume of our agricultural produce, render, says Hamilton, their freight to Europe very costly; and this expense, in cases where the European countries compete with us in their own markets, will be borne principally by us; whilst, on the other hand, the cost of transporting European articles to the United States, where American manufactures do not compete with them, will likewise be laid upon us. Hence the expediency of encouraging manufactures which shall compete with foreign wares in American markets.[3]

Finally, in Hamilton's *Report*, we find the main argument for protectionism, that which was unanimously adopted by American protectionists for many a year, and which is the corner-stone of the system in other countries as well: the need of protection for "infant industries"—that is, for industries in the first stage of development.

To those who represented that without the necessity of any support American manufactures would have spontaneously grown into vigorous life, Hamilton rejoined by pointing out the obstacles to be encountered owing to the great influence of habit and the spirit of imitation; the intrinsic difficulties inherent in first attempts, undertaken in competition with those of people who had attained perfection in such arts; and

[1] *Report*, p. 35.   [2] *Ibid.* pp. 35, 36.   [3] *Ibid.* pp. 72, 73.

the premiums, bounties, and other forms of encouragement given by foreign nations to the development of their own industries.¹ So here, too, we see Hamilton's fundamental idea, which bases its protectionism on the existence of foreign restrictive measures, expressed in a predominant manner:² but even here it is surrounded with other arguments. Experience teaches, he says, that men are the creatures of habit, and that the simplest improvements are adopted with hesitation and reluctance; the spontaneous adoption of new methods in a country long accustomed to act differently meets with great difficulties and requires the encouragement and patronage of the Government. Capital is wayward and timid in lending itself to new undertakings, and the State ought to excite the confidence of capitalists, who are ever cautious and sagacious, by aiding them to overcome the obstacles that lie in the way of all experiments.³

10. The part of the *Report on Manufactures* which refers to bounties and premiums is most important and original, and, at the same time, it is the part that is the most neglected by writers: and therefore it truly deserves to be reviewed with care. It is a most notable fact that Hamilton, who so completely formulated a theory of protection which has left profound traces in the subsequent commercial policy of his country, should at the same time have so clearly expounded a system of protection, which, on the contrary, has since been almost entirely obliterated in theory and in practice; whilst, all the while, the latter (at least from a theoretical point of view) is much the more rational.

Hamilton says:⁴—that pecuniary bounties granted to manufactures are, not only one of the best means of encouraging them, but, from a certain standpoint the very best of all. They afford, in fact, a whole series of advantages: (1) They constitute a more direct and positive encouragement than any other, and they have a more immediate and stimulating tendency at the outset of new enterprises; (2) They obviate the inconvenience common to other systems (and especially customs duties) of producing a temporary rise of prices; (3) They likewise obviate the inconvenience inherent in protective

¹ *Report*, p. 42.   ² *Ibid.* p. 43.   ³ *Ibid.* pp. 42, 43.
⁴ *Ibid.* pp. 81-87.

dues, of tending to produce a lack of the articles protected. In fact, says Hamilton, a rise of prices does not immediately follow an increase of the duties, although it generally results from it in the end (unless it be paralysed by the progress of domestic manufactures), and in the interval between the imposition of the duty and the proportional rise of prices, importation may be checked; (4) Bounties are sometimes not merely the best, but indeed the only proper expedient fit for encouraging at one and the same time a new branch of agriculture and a new branch of manufactures. As a matter of fact, a duty on raw materials would injure manufactures, and hence agriculture, which would be affected by the falling off in the demand for such material. Nor would the duty do anything to promote exportation. But the two interests would be reconciled by levying an import duty on manufactures which it was desired to encourage at home, and applying the proceeds of this duty to subsidising either the production of the raw materials for these manufactures, or of the finished article itself, or both.

The system of bounties is, according to Hamilton, in most cases indispensable for the introduction of new branches of industry, and especially for those goods which foreigners have been accustomed to provide.

Connected with bounties, although distinct from them, are the premiums conferred on marked excellence of production, or on extraordinary commercial ability; they serve as a general stimulus, and excite personal emulation as well as interest.[1]

[1] The advantages of the system of bounties and premiums (which has been so unaccountably neglected — nay, disdainfully misrepresented by modern economic science) and the reasons for preferring it to that of protective dues, have been set forth by Professor Gide in a profound and brilliant article "La Protection sans droit protecteurs," in the *Revue d'Économie politique*, September-October, 1891. The writer gives five principal reasons for preferring premiums to import duties. (1) They stimulate the development of industries, instead of leaving them—as duties often do—in a stationary condition; (2) They may be proportioned to the wants of the producers, only those being helped that stand most in need of it, and have a higher cost of production; whilst duties, on the other hand, favour producers who are in better circumstances, and are frequently of little avail for others; (3) For this reason, duties, by giving unjust and unnecessary advantages to those who do not require them, are even more costly to the country than bounties granted to those who most need them; (4) Subsidies and premiums are no hindrance to international relations; (5)

These considerations of Hamilton are also remarkable in this respect, that whilst the great statesman points out the advantages of direct pecuniary subsidies, he severely criticises the system of import duties, which he himself proposed and which were subsequently adopted as the exclusive, or almost exclusive, means of protection.

To sum up, from these famous pages of the American protectionist we learn that protective duties temporarily augment prices;[1] that they tend to produce a scarcity of the goods protected, until the rise of prices has given an impulse to the native production of these goods; that duties place in opposition the interests of agriculturists, who desire the high price of raw materials, to those of manufacturers who wish them to be cheap;[2] and finally, that the duties which raise the price of manufactures do not tend to promote exportation.[3]

We may conclude, therefore, that Alexander Hamilton is a protectionist, and that he has contributed a powerful series of arguments in support of the protectionist doctrine; but he is a protectionist who admits almost unconditionally the advantages of free-trade when it is universally applied, and who advocates reciprocity of treatment between nations, rather than protection as a principle; he is a protectionist whose proposals are founded more on political than economic considerations; finally, he is a protectionist who severely criticises protective duties, and who suggests a very moderate scheme of protection.

What then is the place that belongs to Hamilton and to his admirable *Report* in the history of American protectionism? To answer this question, it is not sufficient to have analysed his work: it is necessary to have also studied it in conjunction with the theories of his contemporaries, and of those who came after him, and taking into consideration the influence and the circumstances of the times in which he lived. And this is what we propose briefly to do.

11. Sumner brings two grave accusations against Hamilton:

Finally, as their mode of application, and the burden which they impose on the country, are far more manifest than is the case with duties, they are less likely to lead to abuses.

[1] *Report*, p. 81.   [2] *Ibid.* p. 82.   [3] *Ibid.* p. 83.

of having reproduced in his *Report* the old English mercantile system, and adapted it to the circumstances of the United States,[1] and of not having read Adam Smith, for, he says, if he had read him, even without accepting all his conclusions, he would not have repeated the old mercantile notions without referring to the objections raised against them by the great economist.[2]

We think we can show that both these assertions are absolutely unfounded: Hamilton was not a mercantilist, much less a follower of the old mercantile system, and he did far more than merely reproduce its theory; and, in the second place, he was well acquainted with Adam Smith's work. And we are glad of the opportunity which these criticisms afford us of confronting Hamilton with the mercantilists and with Adam Smith.

Alexander Hamilton had certainly some points of contact with the old mercantile doctrines: his fundamental ideas, his political opinions, which prevail over his economic views, are analogous to those of the mercantilists. The latter were bent on no absolute progress; all they contemplated was the relative superiority of their own country over other nations; the economic question appeared to them from a political standpoint—that of the common hostility of nations.

Thus Hamilton's principal aim was the national unity of his country, and he strove to secure, if not its supremacy, at all events its independence and economic prosperity in the rivalry of nations, and especially in competition with Great Britain; and in this respect he might be said to be a mercantilist behind his time, a mercantilist whose system was justified by the fact that at a late period his country had risen to the dignity of a nation, and was struggling for its national independence, at a time when, among other peoples, the epoch of this struggle—which was supported by the mercantile system—had passed away.

"The gradual transformation of mercantilism into protectionism took place between 1700 and 1750. The balance of trade and the negotiability of bills of exchange are the burning questions no longer, being regarded not as causes, but as symptoms of a flourishing trade. Everybody is pre-occupied with the increase and density of population, the development

[1] Work mentioned, p. 175. [2] *Ibid.* p. 108.

of trade and of navigation, and, most particularly, the rise and progress of manufactures where unheard-of profits could be earned."[1]

Alexander Hamilton maintained the necessity of manufactures, and urged their protection as a direct object, to ensure the well-being and the economic and political independence of his country, and the balance of trade to which he now and then refers was for him certainly nothing more than a symptom.

Besides, as we have seen, he had a most clear insight into the advantages of free-trade, and he deplored the excesses of commercial restrictions. On this point there is a passage in his *Report* which makes it evident that he was opposed to the doctrines of the old mercantile school; namely, where he laments the injudicious extreme to which the spirit of monopoly had been carried,—manufacturing nations endeavouring to produce raw materials, and barring their importation. By doing this, observes Hamilton, they prevent agricultural nations from obtaining, by means of an interchange of commodities, the manufactured articles which they require, and force them to endeavour to make them for themselves: *and thus they sacrifice " the interests of a mutually beneficial intercourse to the vain project of selling everything and buying nothing."*[2]

There are certainly some mercantile reminiscences to be found in Hamilton's *Report* which cannot be glossed over by a conscientious writer: but if, on the one hand, the author must be charged with the responsibility of them, on the other hand, they are explained by the then condition of the United States.

The indictable passages are from pages 69 to 71 of our edition of the celebrated *Report*. Here Hamilton, after having remarked that the trade of a country which is at once industrial and agricultural is more lucrative than that of one which is merely agricultural, adds:—

"From these circumstances collectively, two important inferences are to be drawn; one, that there is always a higher

[1] Cossa, *An Introduction to the Study of Political Economy* (English translation), London, Macmillan, 1893, pp. 206, 207.
[2] *Report*, p. 34.

probability of a favourable balance of trade in regard to countries in which manufactures founded on the basis of a thriving agriculture flourish, than in regard to those which are confined wholly or almost wholly to agriculture; the other (which is also a consequence of the first) that countries of the former description are likely to possess more pecuniary wealth or money than those in the latter. Facts appear to correspond with this conclusion. The importations of manufactured supplies seem invariably to drain the merely agricultural people of their wealth. Let the situation of the manufacturing countries of Europe be compared in this particular with that of countries which only cultivate, and the disparity will be striking. Other causes, it is true, help to account for this disparity between some of them, and among these causes, the relative state of agriculture; but between others of them, the most prominent circumstance of dissimilitude arises from the comparative state of manufactures. In corroboration of the same idea, it ought not to escape remark, that the West India Islands, the soils of which are the most fertile, and the nation which in the greatest degree supplies the rest of the world with the precious metals, exchange to a loss with almost every other country.

"As far as experience at home may guide, it will lead to the same conclusion. Previous to the revolution, the quantity of coin, possessed by the colonies, which now compose the United States, appeared to be inadequate to their circulation; and their debt to Great Britain was progressive. Since the revolution, the States in which manufactures have most increased have recovered fastest from the injuries of the late war; and abound most in pecuniary resources.

"The uniform appearance of an abundance of specie, as the concomitant of a flourishing state of manufactures, and of the reverse where they do not prevail, afford a strong presumption of their favourable operation upon the wealth of a country." [1]

It cannot be denied that these passages contain mercantile reminiscences; [2] but it must be observed that Hamilton

[1] *Report*, pp. 69-71.
[2] Jenks also observes this, vide *Henry C. Carey als Nationalökonom*, Jena, Fischer, 1885, p. 140.

alludes to the abundance of money not as the end but as a symptom of national prosperity; and that such an opinion was justified by the condition of the United States at his time, when the scarcity of specie was so great that barter was frequent, and that both the Government and private individuals were put to sore straits in their dealings abroad.[1]

If, therefore, Hamilton's ideas had some analogy with the old mercantile system—and indeed it could not be otherwise —it cannot be truly stated that he applied its maxims to the actual circumstances of the United States. Indeed, he sealed the fate of the old theory, and there arose from its ruins the protective system, of which he was in theory the founder, as he was in practice the precursor.

12. Still less founded is Sumner's observation that Hamilton was unacquainted with Adam Smith. Sumner says that there was a tradition to the effect that Hamilton not only read, but, in 1783, wrote an accurate comment on the *Wealth of Nations*—a comment that has been lost—but that there is nothing in his writings to prove that he had ever read the chief work of the great English economist.[2] On the other hand Adams remarks that American writers of Hamilton's time frequently quote from Adam Smith, and there is reason to believe that there is a certain connection between Hamilton's criticism of physiocratical theories and that of Adam Smith;[3] but he gives no proof of this supposition; and Lodge also states that Hamilton was familiar with Adam Smith's works, which he admired and quoted; but Lodge, too, gives no further particulars.[4]

Now the truth regarding Adams' supposition and Lodge's statement can, we think, be cleared up by giving the subject a little attention. It is not merely the idea of the general utility of free-trade—if broadly applied—dwelt upon by Hamilton, that he has taken from Adam Smith; but that he had studied him is made evident by three distinct passages in the *Report*, in which his textual words are quoted at length, although he does not indicate the source. These three passages refer to the criticism of physiocratical doctrines, to the demonstration of

[1] *Bolles*, vol. ii.
[2] Sumner, work mentioned, p. 108.
[3] *Taxation in the United States*, 1789-1816, pp. 20, 21.
[4] Work mentioned, p. 109.

the advantages of the division of labour, and to those of the development of means of transport. It will not be waste of time—since the comparison has not hitherto been made by commentators—to give a detailed examination to the point.

The *Report on Manufactures*, as we have already seen, starts with a critical survey of the physiocratic theory of the sterility of manufacturing industry.

It is impossible to compare Hamilton's pages with the ninth chapter of the fourth book of the *Wealth of Nations*, in which the founder of political economy treats of the physiocratic system, without noticing the fact that, whilst Adam Smith studied the subject in its entirety from a scientific and theoretical point of view, Hamilton merely dealt with it for the purposes of the moment and with reference to manufactures, which he began by showing to be productive, and for which he ended by demanding state support.

Hamilton begins by expounding the physiocratic theory on this point; he refutes the idea of the sterility of manufactures; and then he shows that they are perhaps more, and certainly not less, productive than agriculture.

Those who maintain the exclusive productiveness of agriculture, says Hamilton, state that labour applied to the cultivation of the soil not only pays its expenses and provides for the labourers at work, but, after deducting the ordinary profit due to capital, yields a net surplus to the owner of the soil; whilst, on the contrary, labour applied to manufactures only produces enough to cover the outlay and give the ordinary profit on the capital, without any further equivalent to the land rent, and hence adds nothing to the total value of the whole annual produce of the soil and labour of the country. The additional value given to those products of the soil which are utilised by manufactures is counterbalanced by the value of the products that are consumed by the manufacturers; and they cannot, therefore, increase the social return in any way except by savings and parsimony, and not by means of the positive productiveness of their labour.[1]

Now the arguments brought by Hamilton to refute this physiocratic theory, divided under three headings, are evidently taken from the chapter we have quoted of the *Wealth of*

[1] *Report*, pp. 13, 14.

Nations, and they correspond precisely with the third and the fourth observation made by Adam Smith on the physiocratic system; indeed, they are merely a recapitulation in the very words of the original author.[1] Hamilton, in fact, remarks, as Adam Smith does, that it is not true that labour applied to manufactures is unproductive; for, even if it be admitted that the consumption of the produce of the soil by manufacturers was exactly equal to the value added by their labour to the raw materials, it would not follow that it would add nothing to the returns of the community or to the entire value of the annual production of the land and of labour. If the consumption for each stated period amounts to a fixed sum, and the increase in the value of the manufactured product amounts in the same period to the same sum, the total amount of the consumption and production during this period will be equal to two sums, and hence will be of twice the value of the agricultural produce consumed by the manufacturers.[2]

The statement that manufacturers can only augment the returns of the community by parsimony, says Hamilton, following in Adam Smith's footsteps, is perfectly applicable to agricultural producers.

"The annual produce of the land and labour of a country can only be increased in two ways—by some improvement in the productive powers of the useful labour which actually exists within it, or by some increase in the quantity of such labour. With regard to the first, the labour of artificers being capable of greater subdivision and simplicity of operation than that of cultivators, it is susceptible, in a proportionably greater degree, of improvement in its productive powers, whether to be derived from an accession of skill, or from the application of ingenious machinery; in which particular, therefore, the labour employed in the culture of land can pretend to no advantage over that engaged in manufactures. With regard to an augmentation of the quantity of useful labour, this, excluding adventitious circumstances, must depend essentially upon an increase of capital, which again must depend upon the savings made out of the revenues of those who furnish or manage that

---

[1] *Wealth of Nations*, book iv. chap. ix. vol. iii. pp. 23-26 of the above-mentioned edition.

[2] *Report*, pp. 14, 15; and Adam Smith, vol. iii. pp. 23, 24.

which is at any time employed, whether in agriculture or in manufactures, or in any other way."[1]

After having thus, following the lead of Adam Smith, affirmed the productiveness of manufactures, Hamilton passes on, now speaking on his own authority, to show that this productiveness is not inferior to that of agriculture. He points out, above all, that, on account of the vicissitudes of the weather, agricultural labour is necessarily intermittent, whilst that of manufactures is regular and constant, lasts the whole year, and is continued in some cases also by night, and at the same time offers a wider field than agriculture does for the exercise of ingenuity.[2] Thence he proceeds to combat the principal argument of the physiocrats, namely, that manufactures do not yield that surplus of produce which in agriculture goes to the owner as rent of the land. Here Hamilton's observations appear, when examined in the light of recent economic science and actual circumstances, to be absolutely at fault. He remarks that the distinction made by the physiocrats is purely formal, and that the substance is the same. The product that in agriculture is divided into two parts, one of which constitutes the "ordinary profit" accruing to the cultivator's capital, and the other the landowner's rent, is in manufactures united under the single denomination of ordinary profit of the undertaker. The soil is a capital lent by the landlord to the tenant, and the landlord's rent is merely the ordinary profit on this capital, which in the shape of land has been let to those who have made it productive by applying other capital to it, and in their turn drawing a profit from it. The landlord's rent and the farmer's profit are but the ordinary profit of two capitals belonging to different persons, and united in the cultivation of a farm; a profit perfectly equivalent to that yielded by manufactures.[3]

It is impossible at this stage not to point out the error into which Hamilton falls in considering the soil as capital, and the land rent as the profit due to it, without discriminating between the portion of the return accruing to the

[1] *Report*, pp. 15, 16 ; and Adam Smith, vol. iii. 25, 26. The words are almost identical ; only Adam Smith's text is somewhat more extended—Hamilton's being an abbreviation of it.
[2] *Report*, p. 17. [3] *Ibid.* pp. 18, 19.

landlord, which can indeed be looked upon as the interest on capital sunk in the ground, and the unearned increment, of which he has no idea. It would, however, be unjust to find fault with Alexander Hamilton for not having been able to reply to the physiocrats that the land rent is not a phenomenon of production, but one of the distribution of wealth; that it is not the fruit of liberality on the part of nature which increases the national patrimony at the same time as it does that of the landlord, but rather an effect of the limitation and different productiveness of the land, and of the pressure of population; and that, as it does not constitute any increase of production, but only takes away a portion of it to hand it over to the landowners, it can in no way augment, speaking generally, the wealth of the country. It would, in fact, be unjust to charge Hamilton with not having understood the nature of the "land rent," which was imperfectly appreciated even by Adam Smith, and was not thoroughly comprehended until Ricardo had made the subject clear.

And besides this, Hamilton can be justified historically by pointing out that, if he did not grasp the exact nature of the land rent, one reason is that, at that time, it had not been developed in America, because cultivation was still limited to the more fertile lands, and hence the produce of the soil then consisted solely of wages and profit, and there was no question of rent.

To go back to Hamilton's view, the land rent was a profit on capital, and the question to be solved was whether, with a similar outlay of capital and labour, the production of agriculture, when all expenses had been paid, was greater or less than that of manufactures. And his reasoning led him to the conclusion that the balance was probably in favour of manufactures, and that, at all events, there was no inferiority on their side.[1]

13. We also gather from an attentive examination of their works that Hamilton has borrowed from Adam Smith not merely the idea of the division of labour and the opinion that it finds a better application in manufactures than in agriculture, but also the enumeration and illustration of the advantages of the technical division of labour. In fact, the

[1] *Report*, pp. 20, 21.

three advantages which he puts forward[1] are a faithful recapitulation, in the same order, of Adam Smith's three famous advantages,[2] namely, the great skill acquired by the artisan, who is always occupied on the same task; the saving of time in passing from one operation to another; and the larger use of machinery, the invention of which is rendered easier by the division of labour.

Hence Hamilton deduces the utility of the division of labour between agriculturists and artisans, and the utility of manufactures to effect, by means of the division of labour, an increase of productive industry.[3]

We are able, finally, to find another parallel, and this an absolutely literal one, between the *Report on Manufactures* and the *Wealth of Nations*. Among the means of encouraging the development of manufactures, Alexander Hamilton alludes to the improvement of means of transport in the interior of the country by land and water; and he quotes a long passage, of which he does not indicate the source, and of which he says that "the following remarks are sufficiently judicious and pertinent to deserve a literal quotation." Now we have found that this quotation literally reproduces a passage in Adam Smith's great work, where he illustrates the advantages of the extension of means of transport in the interior of a country.[4]

If, therefore, one were disinclined to conclude, as to us appears evident, from the general spirit of his doctrines, that Hamilton was no follower of the old mercantile school, nor yet an absolute and excessive protectionist, but that he even bore traces of a partial assimilation to the ideas of Adam Smith; still the comparisons we have made establish irrefutably that he had read the *Wealth of Nations*, and that he drew from it more than one passage in his *Report*, which must consequently be shorn of some of its originality.[5]

---

[1] *Report*, pp. 26, 27.   [2] *Wealth of Nations*, book i. chap. i. pp. 12-15.
[3] *Report*, p. 27.
[4] *Ibid.* pp. 93, 94, and compare with *Wealth of Nations*, book i. chap. xi. pp. 228, 229, from the words, "good roads, canals," etc., to the words, "since that time."
[5] The Italian edition of this book was published in 1893. It is now with great satisfaction that we make mention of an article by Edward G. Bourne, "Alexander Hamilton and Adam Smith," published in the *Quarterly Journal*

CHAP. I *PROTECTIONISM IN THE UNITED STATES* 319

14. But on the other hand, Hamilton's originality in the field of protectionist theories will stand boldly forth if we compare the ideas advanced in his short *Report* with those contained in the writings of subsequent protectionists, who drew so largely from him.

Without anticipating what will appear at greater length in the following chapters, we may, to complete our study of Alexander Hamilton, briefly compare him with the two best-known protectionists, Frederick List and Henry C. Carey. List is certainly a writer of far greater weight than Hamilton: the basis of his theories is philosophical; his conception is an organic whole, developed in a logical and systematic fashion; and, above all, what gives List his great superiority is his profound historical sense, which invests his system with a rational character, however much he may err in his explanations.

If, however, we analyse the various opinions elaborated by List in his *National System*, we are led to the conclusion that their germs are to a great extent to be found in Hamilton's ideas, which List developed, reduced to a system.

Like Hamilton, he admitted free-trade theoretically, and as a final conclusion; and if the former did not explicitly treat protection as a temporary expedient, this was, nevertheless, the character which it implicitly assumed, when once he had justified it chiefly on account of foreign restrictive legislation and the necessity of giving an impulse to manufactures. The comparison between purely agricultural countries and those which are industrial as well, in order to show the superiority of the latter, which is made with so much acumen by List, is also to be found in the *Report on Manufactures*. List clearly formulates the idea that if protection sometimes increases the price of products, it tends in the long run to augment the productive forces of the country, although at a temporary sacrifice; but Hamilton too observes that duties or bounties constitute a momentary expense, which is more than compensated for by the increase in production and wealth.[1] The

of Economics (Boston), April 1894. In it Bourne fully recognises the exactness of the comparisons which we made between Adam Smith's great work and Alexander Hamilton's *Report*, and he adds on his own part several others, thus confirming, in his accurate analysis, the thesis upheld by us.

[1] *Report*, pp. 84, 85.

greater security of internal trade compared with foreign commerce is insisted on both by List and Hamilton; and both of them maintain that the existence of manufactures assures a home market for agricultural produce. Finally, Hamilton's *Report* clearly expresses the necessity, which is enlarged upon by List in his *National System*, of industrial education and assistance to young industries in their early struggles with foreign rivals.

If we compare Hamilton with Carey, even more light is shed upon the great importance of the former in the history of the protectionist theory. And if Hamilton, having furnished List with the greater part of his arguments in favour of protection, yet remains vastly his inferior in the whole of his conception, he none the less a long way surpasses Carey, although the latter studied the question sixty years later, in very different circumstances, with far ampler materials, and when economic science had already largely developed the doctrines of international trade.

Carey, in fact, does not recognise, as Hamilton does, the general and final advantages of free-trade; he has no idea of that reciprocity which so largely attenuates the protectionism of the great American statesman; he has not List's historical perception, nor does he, like Hamilton, clearly indicate the temporary nature of protective legislation. On the other hand, the idea of the necessity of manufactures as a support for agriculture, which Carey has elaborated, had already been, as we have seen, amply dealt with by List, and, before him, by Hamilton; that of the heavy cost of transporting products, and especially agricultural produce, to long distances, and of the great advantages presented by home markets—the leading argument in Carey's theory—had already been sketched out in the *Report on Manufactures*; and that at a time when transport by sea was far more expensive and difficult than it was in Carey's days. Moreover, although Hamilton lauded the superiority of internal commerce over international trade, he never expresses for the latter that holy horror which characterises the declamations of the author of *The Principles of Social Science*. Hamilton's protectionism is far more moderate than Carey's, and after all, we think, it may be affirmed that the protectionist doctrine finds an ampler and more efficacious justification in the short *Report on Manufactures*, than in Carey's numerous and bulky volumes, in which are repeated *ad nauseam* the advantages of manufactures and of internal commerce, mingled with apostrophies against international trade.[1]

15. Before concluding this notice on Hamilton, we must show the relation of the protectionist theory, as we have analysed it in these pages, to the political and economic situation of the United States in his times, which we treated at length in the previous essay.

The fundamental characteristics of Hamilton's protectionism are the following: his theory is essentially based on political considerations, but it is corroborated by economic arguments, in which he has laid the principal foundations of the doctrine of protection; on the other hand, he recognises the advantages of free-trade, he criticises import duties and advocates moderate protection.

The position, therefore, of this founder of theoretical protectionism is somewhat singular and contradictory in his work, in which the economic arguments in favour of protection have a secondary importance, and the concrete demands for protection are so modest and different from those of the protectionists who came after him. But this singular and contradictory position of our author can be perfectly explained by the circumstances of his country at the time when he lived.

As a matter of fact the United States had only just emerged from a cruel war, which, though concluded in the field of arms, still raged in that of commerce, in which England still hoped to obtain practical revenge; and at the same time they were carrying on an internal struggle for the consolidation of that national unity, which, as yet barely cemented, was constantly threatened by the particularist tendencies of these States. It may be said that the United States were then in a condition analagous to that which, in other times, had given rise to the mercantile system in Europe; and in this way can be explained the somewhat distant resemblance which Hamilton's ideas had to these

[1] For a comparison between Carey and Hamilton, see J. W. Jenks, *H. C. Carey als Nationalökonom*, Jena, Fischer, 1885, pp. 140-143.

doctrines; and to this must be attributed, also, the reminiscences of them which yet lingered in a country where money was so very scarce.

On the other hand, as we have seen, the interests of an — as yet limited — capitalist class, began to assert and strengthen themselves by taking the political situation of the country as a pretext for claiming that protection which was to serve for the depression of the very large class of independent labourers and artisans, for increasing the number of those who worked for hire, and for creating the new capitalistic industries. In this capitalist class, Alexander Hamilton imagined a support for the new Federal Government, whose interests and whose existence he wished to bind closely to it; knowing perhaps by intuition that the capitalist class had a great mission to fulfil, a mission to produce and concentrate wealth —inseparable indeed from inequalities and injustice—but with which, none the less, the political and economic greatness of his country was intimately associated. Thus Hamilton, in reorganising the public debt, consolidated the Federal credit, and advanced at the same time the interests of the capitalist creditors; and so, by establishing a great bank, he provided for the wants of the Government as well as of the capitalists engaged in trade and manufactures; and also, by means of protective tariffs, he aimed at assuring a revenue for the Federal finances, and promoting the interests of the capitalist class, whose importance, in fact, he wished vastly to augment by means of industrial development, for he looked upon them as the foundation and mainstay of the national existence.

From this combination of political and economic circumstances Hamilton's protectionist theory was naturally evolved.

But, on the other hand, the general economic interests of the country were opposed to industrial protection, and would not anyhow have tolerated high protective duties.

As we have seen in the preceding essay, free-trade was then necessary for the country, the staple production of which was raw materials and commodities which ought to be exported, and all those manufactured goods retained in exchange which the United States were not yet capable of producing, and which were, nevertheless, indispensable. High import duties would have occasioned a scarcity of articles required for immediate and general use, and would consequently have caused inconvenience and discomfort.

Finally, by the side of the limited class of capitalists who would have been benefited by protection, there was the great mass of population, the immense army of independent labourers and artisans, scattered over the length and breadth of the land, who, if not conscious of the fact that protection would have been the means of their impoverishment, and have ended their economic liberty, must, for all that, have felt the direct and immediate advantages of foreign importations. The interests and wants of this great majority of the American people were advocated by the party since called Republican, which opposed the Federalists tooth and nail, and which was destined soon to overcome them.

Now this state of affairs, which constituted the reverse of the medal, could not fail to be appreciated by a mind like Hamilton's, even though he contemplated the question from the opposite point of view, and this explains how he came to accept in principle Adam Smith's theory of free-trade—the practical advantages of which were evident to him; whilst the political situation, the interests of capitalism, the restrictive legislation of other nations, induced him to carry out measures of a different stamp. It explains his criticism of high import duties; for he clearly saw the danger to the country of stopping the current of imported manufactures, which were required for immediate use; and it explains, too, his preference for bounties and premiums, which offered none of the objections of duties, but which the exhausted Federal treasury would not have been able to grant to any adequate extent.

And thus, placed as he was between political exigencies and the interests of the new capitalism, which tended towards industrial protectionism on the one hand, and the general welfare of the country and its most numerous class, which demanded free-trade in lieu of protection on the other, Hamilton's peculiar situation can be seen at a glance, and the discrepancy between the bold premises and modest conclusions of his report will be readily understood.

Besides, as we have already pointed out, the prevalence of

political over economic motives, and the predominance of the interests of the great mass of the population over those of a class still somewhat limited and weak, had for effect that the conclusions of Congress were even more modest than Hamilton's, and that industrial protection was for the time-being relegated to the letter of a law, not effectually applied in the commercial policy of the country.

Later on matters changed: the political motives of protectionism disappeared, and the economic ones took their place, as a result of the prevailing interests of the capitalist class, which had increased in wealth and power. Then Alexander Hamilton's ideas were destined to triumph, together with that class which he designed to be the basis of the political constitution; then the *Report on Manufactures*, but slightly appreciated in his own times, was bound to receive all honour; and in it—the gospel of American protectionism, the palladium of the capitalistic interests, merged into those of the nation at large—all business men, writers, and statesmen, will find their arguments.

CHAPTER II

FREDERICK LIST

16. An entire chapter on Frederick List, in this study of American protectionism, might at first sight appear out of place. We do not propose, however, to enter into a complete dissertation on the practical and theoretical work of this great German, who shared with Alexander Hamilton the unhappy lot of not having been sufficiently appreciated during his lifetime, nor impartially judged since his death. There is no need for it, since literature is richly provided with works on List—and we may honourably distinguish, among many others, the glowing pages which Roscher devotes to him in his celebrated history,[1] and the more complete, though perhaps less original and suggestive essay prefixed by Eheberg to the last edition of the *National System*;[2] nor, indeed, does our purpose require any lengthy dissertation.

But, on the other hand, the part played by Frederick List in the history of protectionism appears to us so important, and so greatly was he influenced by the United States, where he lived several years, and by the system of commercial policy adopted there, that we think it necessary to speak of him briefly, especially from this point of view.

Frederick List was certainly a man of superior mental power; in many economic and political questions he was, as Roscher excellently observes, a prophet: he undoubtedly was

---

[1] *Geschichte der National-Oekonomik in Deutschland*, Munchen, Oldenbourg, 1874, pp. 970-991.

[2] Frederick List, *Das nationale System der politischen Oekonomie*, siebente Auflage, mit einer historischen und kritischen Einleitung von K. Th. Eheberg, Stuttgart, Cotta, 1883.

one so far as the *Zollverein* was concerned, which, if put into practical shape by Nebenius, was nevertheless conceived by List, and rendered popular by him by means of an efficacious propaganda; he was a prophet too, as regards railways, having been one of the first to understand their economic importance, and to urge their construction all over Germany; finally, he was a prophet in matters of economic science, as he was the first to apply to it the historical method, and to utilise for economic researches historical materials, which had hitherto been made use of rarely and indiscriminately, but which were afterwards turned to valuable account.

And if he was not the originator of modern protectionism, he was certainly the first, and the only one who raised it to an organic and scientific system; a system which, if altogether one-sided, excessive, and often faulty, is none the less one that not only possesses the elements of truth, but leaves an unmistakably deep furrow in the field of economic research.

We shall endeavour here to condense this system into a few pages, to reduce it to its fundamental principles, as a preface to the study we must make of it in reference to the American circumstances.

17. As is the case with the old mercantilists, and, generally too, with the modern protectionists, Frederick List intimately binds up with the economic view of the question a political bias, which pervades the whole of his system. He finds fault with Adam Smith and with all those whom he calls, in frequently pungent and passionate language, "the school," for having always upheld an abstract economy by no means conversant with matters of fact, a cosmopolitan economy regarding the interests of humanity as a whole. Now, says he, the solidarity of human interests, humanity, in a word, is not merely an ideal, but, in very truth, a form of association, to which we must necessarily come: but it is the last of all, the very last step in the evolution of society. To reach this supreme ideal we must perforce pass through an inferior stage, that of separate nationalities—the stage, in fact, which we are at present traversing: hence the necessity of counteracting the "cosmopolitan" economy of the future by a "national" economy fitted to actual circumstances.

And now we shall see what was List's conception of this "national economy."

Before passing on to a system of cosmopolitan economy, it is necessary, he maintains, to have a complete political development of national economies; otherwise we should inevitably have the predominance of one nation over the other, and consequently an imperfect development of civilisation. To preserve, to develop, to make perfect its nationality, must be the principal object of the efforts of a nation, and it is, at the same time, the natural preparation for the universal association, which will only be possible and profitable when all nations shall have attained the same degree of culture and of power.[1]

The temperate countries, which are the only ones in which a complete development of civilisation is possible, pass through a long historical evolution, which our author divides into five great periods, the savage, the pastoral, the agricultural (in which agriculture is benefited by the importation of foreign manufactures, and by the exportation of native produce), the agricultural-manufacturing (in which the native manufactures provide for all the wants of the country), and finally, the agricultural-manufacturing-commercial (in which these three departments of industrial activity are all developed and manufactures are exported, whilst raw materials and agricultural produce are imported). In order that its political and economic individuality may be completely developed, and constitute an autonomous entity, every nation must pass through all these stages, and establish manufacturing industries on a large scale: and it will only be after this has been accomplished, that any efficient political and economic co-operation of nations will become possible. For the progress of a nation, for its political and economic existence even, it is absolutely necessary that there should be a large development of manufactures, which alone enable it to turn all its natural resources to account, give an impulse to progress, and ensure a state of prosperity and independence, which never would have been reached under a purely agricultural régime. All the nations of the temperate zone must, therefore, do their utmost to hasten on such a manufacturing development,

[1] *Das nationale System*, etc., edition quoted, p. 10.

in order to attain the highest degree of their evolution, and at the same time to consolidate their individuality and autonomy. But in their endeavours to reach this goal nations may meet with obstacles: progress is not equally rapid with all of them; some advance by leaps and bounds, others more slowly; and so it may happen that those who are ahead may hinder the development of those who lag behind and prevent them from fulfilling their natural evolution: and this according to List should be absolutely avoided.

And it is here, at a given period in the historical evolution of nations, in view of their different degrees of development, that the intervention of the state is advisable: it is here that List invokes protection as a means of industrial education for the people. For him, therefore, protection is but an historical transition, rendered temporarily necessary by the exigencies of the national evolution and the different degrees of the economic progress of countries; it is an historical system only to be justified within certain limits of time and space.

Protection should serve to complete the division of national labour by educating the country in manufacturing industries: it should be adopted for this alone, and not for agriculture, for the latter can only be usefully encouraged by the existence of manufactures, whilst the exclusion of raw materials and of foreign agricultural produce only hinders the development of native manufactures:[1] protection should cease as soon as this industrial education is complete.

In the first periods of national evolution protection is not necessary; when a people is still backward in intelligence and culture, and the country thinly populated, its economic education is best secured by free-trade and communications with more advanced nations; and when, under a free commercial *régime*, economic, intellectual, and political education shall have made such progress that the importation of foreign manufactures and the want of outlets are a bar to further development, then, and then only, can protective measures be justified.[2]

Protection must certainly not attempt to raise up industries which are contrary to the nature of the country;

[1] Work mentioned, p. 16. [2] *Ibid.* p. 16.

but, on the other hand, all its natural resources and capacities should be brought into play.

Commercial restrictions, which are designed to create and support manufactures, can only be legitimate in nations that possess all the qualities, all the moral and material requisites for the development of manufacturing industries, and through them, for the attainment of the highest degree of civilisation, prosperity, and political power, but whose progress would be arrested by the competition of foreign industries already in a highly perfected condition; protective legislation can only be justified with a view to strengthening native industries up to the point of no longer dreading their foreign rivals; and whilst this is in progress it should be resorted to only to the extent absolutely necessary to ensure the stability of native industries.[1]

List recognises the truth of the free-trade theory; he admits that, from the standpoint of general economy, protection necessarily implies a loss; he admits that it may temporarily burden a nation, which must produce at a higher cost those things which it might have acquired more cheaply from foreign countries; but he accuses the economists of materialism and improvidence. The loss which protection occasions to-day in the shape of "exchange values," will, he says, be recuperated to-morrow, and with interest, in the shape of "productive force"—a force pregnant with future wealth and prosperity—which will have been engendered in the country by protection. Whilst free-trade would have resulted in a certain momentary gain, to be followed by a much more sensible loss.

Nations must, therefore, submit to this necessary sacrifice in order to attain their complete individuality and political and economic autonomy, and to fit themselves to reap, later on, in an intimate union of nationalities, where all will be equal, the advantages of solidarity and free-trade.

18. What is the genesis of these ideas, in which we see for the first time modern protectionism issuing from a fragmentary and empirical state and assuming the form and organisation of a logical and complete system? It must be searched for first of all in the situation of Germany in the beginning of the century, and afterwards in that of the

[1] Work mentioned, p. 156.

United States, where Frederick List lived in exile from 1825 to 1830.

Upon List—who, to use Roscher's happy expression, was no bookworm, but, on the contrary, a practical man endowed in the highest degree with the aptitude of learning by observation—the circumstances in which he was successively placed exercised the most profound influence, and he had ample opportunity of thoroughly studying these surroundings in the sad experiences of his adventurous life.[1]

The condition of Germany as regards customs was most peculiar at the beginning of the present century;[2] there existed a confused multiplicity of state custom-houses which, with no co-ordination among them, admitted foreign goods, whilst the prohibitive tariffs of foreign States prevented the exportation of German products. In Prussia alone there were no less than sixty-seven different and often contradictory tariffs, and when that kingdom reformed its customs regulations in 1818, the change only aggravated the condition of the other German States, twenty-eight of which bordering on Prussia found themselves, owing to the disposition of their frontiers, in the position of prisoners (to use De Pradt's expression), only

[1] We will give a rapid sketch of List's life. He was born at Reutlingen in 1789, his father being engaged in trade. He himself entered the service of the state in Wurtemberg. Protected by the minister Wangenheim, he was appointed professor of political economy at Tübingen in 1817. Two years later he abandoned the chair, devoted himself to the *Zollverein* propaganda, and he was elected a representative of his native city; but his advanced opinions brought persecution upon him; he was excluded from the chamber and condemned; then began his long life of exile. In 1825 he emigrated to the United States on the invitation of Lafayette : he studied there the question of protection, at that time a burning topic ; he embarked in enterprises which brought him in a competency. He returned to Europe in 1830 as United States consul, gave himself up to the great work of popularising railways in Germany, and rendered important services to his country, receiving in return but scant reward. In 1841 he published his *National System*, which had immense success, and gained for him great popularity and influence throughout the country. Having lost his money through a commercial crisis in America, he was reduced to earn his livelihood by writing, and he died in poverty at Kufstein in 1846. See Leser's Biography of List, in the *Allgemeine Deutsche Biographie*, Leipsig, Dunker, vol. xviii. 1883 ; and that by Häusser in the (incomplete) collection of his works : Fr. List, *Gesammelte Schriften*, Stuttgart, 1850.

[2] We draw the following facts chiefly from Roscher's work, which we have quoted, in that part of it which deals with the establishment of the *Zollverein* (pp. 948 to 1004) ; and from Eheberg, *Historische und kritische Einleitung*, etc., chap. i.

able to communicate with one another through an iron railing. This was the state of things in which, as Roscher observes,[1] they had all the inconveniences of free-trade, together with all those of protection, without any of the advantages of either, when there supervened Napoleon's famous continental blockade, in which all the German States were included. This necessarily affected their industries, as it had affected those of other countries; and if some of them suffered owing to the interruption of trade, others, on the contrary, were efficaciously stimulated, thanks to the protection it offered them against English competition.[2] List, in his *Outlines of American Political Economy*, which we shall discuss farther on, magnifies the effects of the blockade on German industries. These industries, although only partially aided by it—since it protected them only against English and not French competition, whilst the markets of France were closed to them by prohibitive tariffs—made marvellous progress in these years, both as regards manufactures and agriculture, notwithstanding the war. Every kind of product was in demand at a high price; everything was worth more; wages, rents, interests, the value of land and of every other kind of property had gone up.[3]

But after the fall of Napoleon and the conclusion of peace in 1815, the aspect of affairs changed with the abandonment of the continental blockade; there was a great revival of British industrial activity, and English products, the importation of which into many countries was prevented by prohibitive tariffs, were directed to Germany, whose innumerable customhouses offered obstacles to internal trade, but none to foreign imports; whilst, on the other hand, the English corn-laws, which were almost prohibitory, impeded the natural exchange of British manufactures introduced into Germany with German agricultural produce.[4]

The consequence was a general crisis, which lasted a long time, and which affected both agriculture and manufactures. The latter, mostly of recent formation, or in course of transformation (industrial liberty had been introduced in Prussia in

[1] Work mentioned, p. 952. [2] Eheberg, work mentioned, p. 6.
[3] *Outlines*, etc., pp. 13-14.
[4] Roscher, work mentioned, p. 952; Eheberg, work mentioned, p. 7; and List, as quoted above.

1810, without, however, occasioning any great alterations in the condition of the industries), found themselves suddenly thrown on their own resources and confronted with the rivalry of industrial veterans; to agricultural produce all markets were closed. And the crisis was aggravated by the fact that unfavourable as were all the conditions of international commerce to Germany, she was precluded from finding compensation in domestic trade by her innumerable subdivisions into separate States, each with their own customs jurisdiction.

Hence arose complaints against foreign competition and against internal barriers; from which sprang the idea, which made way little by little, of forming a commercial union of all the German States, in order to facilitate the exchange of home products, and at the same time to strengthen the commercial and industrial interests of the whole of Germany, in view of foreign competition. This idea, which included two essential principles—the freedom of internal commerce, and a united customs administration, with a protective policy as a subordinate and occasional expedient to turn the flank of foreign rivalry—this idea met at first with innumerable difficulties in the legislatures of the various States, and it had a long gestation; but it was finally carried into effect in 1828 by the formation of the *Zollverein*, a customs association of the German States, which was gradually extended and consolidated.

19. It is impossible not to be at once struck with the analogy offered by these events to the vicissitudes of American economic history, from the independence of the United States to about the end of the second decennial period of the present century. They, too, went through an epoch of commercial disorder, similar in all respects to that undergone by Germany—the epoch from the declaration of independence to the establishment of the constitution; but the new country, full of energy and promptitude, found a quick issue out of all its difficulties, solving at one and the same time the political and the commercial problems, by means of the Federal Constitution, which gave to the country that economic as well as political unity which the German States had to wait for so much longer, and which the *Zollverein* merely foreshadowed.

In both countries there arose by the side of the question

of commercial unity that of protection, although the circumstances were somewhat different. In the first years of independence, the demand for protection in the United States was, as we have seen, altogether premature, and in fact freetrade prevailed for a while. When, in Germany, the idea of the *Zollverein* began to be agitated, about 1830, there really existed reasons, in the industrial crisis, for a cry of protection, and there undoubtedly was a protective bias in the intentions of its promoters; it was not realised, however, for some time, and we find the battle between free-trade and protectionism raging in Germany ten years later, in 1840.

There is another striking analogy to be observed in the conditions of German and American industries at the epoch with which we are dealing.

Whilst up to the year 1815 German industries were receiving a great impetus from the continental blockade, American manufactures, from 1807 to 1815, were undergoing a rapid, and, to a certain extent, premature development, owing to the combination of political events, which we have narrated elsewhere,[1] that destroyed the foreign commerce of the United States, arrested importations, and diverted to manufactures all that American capital which was at first intended for international trade. And whilst the European peace of 1815 caused Germany to be flooded with English manufactures, the very same thing happened in the United States in consequence of the termination, that very year, of hostilities with England.

Although the United States and Germany were in many ways very differently circumstanced, America being a new country with an immense expanse of free land, yet the industrial condition of the two countries presented, at that time, striking similarities; in the United States capitalistic enterprises were in course of formation, so in Germany the transformation and the freeing of industries and the diffusion of great undertakings was just beginning to bear fruit—urged on, perhaps prematurely, by political events; and both nations had to face the competition of a country far more advanced in the ways of industry, namely, England. Hence in both of them there was a demand for protection, made by the capitalist

[1] *Vide* p. 149 and following, in this volume.

class, on the twofold plea of the support of industries threatened by changed political circumstances, and of the consolidation of the new capitalistic phase through which industry was passing.

But, whilst in the United States, where the problem of political and commercial unity had been solved some time ago, the torrent of protectionism burst forth with violence, and the triumph of capitalism lasted long; in Germany, on the other hand, the question that absorbed public attention and energy for many a long day was that of a commercial union, and the advantages of securing an internal market took the edge off the discussions on foreign trade.

20. We can now understand the influence successively exercised on Frederick List's mind by the conditions of Germany and of the United States.

From 1819 to 1825, the years that preceded his visit to America, the salient point in his life was his active participation in the *Zollverein* propaganda. We have already seen that the constituent elements of this great movement were the liberty of internal trade and protection against foreign importations, and that the former was the predominant consideration. Nebenius, the great Baden statesman, who was the first to formulate a clear idea of the *Zollverein*, although a follower of Adam Smith's doctrines, was none the less a warm advocate of protective tariffs; he admitted the absolute truth of free-trade principles, but, at the same time, he maintained that, on account of the commercial barriers set up by most foreign countries, Germany was placed in an altogether exceptional situation, because her manufactures had not flourished to the same extent as agriculture, and therefore required remedies which would have been injurious in a normal state of things; hence he claimed for Germany internal freedom of trade and protective tariffs on her frontiers.[1]

In List, on the contrary, the protectionist bias was from the very beginning far less marked. He opens his campaign in favour of the *Zollverein*, inspired in part by free-trade ideas, and bent not so much on creating a general German customhouse, as on doing away with the petty customs jurisdictions

[1] Roscher, work mentioned, p. 961.

into which the country was then subdivided.[1] It is true that before long he began to throw doubts on Adam Smith's free-trade theory, observing that it holds good in a world where we could suppose no artificial barriers hindering the material course of industries; but that it would be dangerous to apply it in the actual state of Germany. She stands with open doors, he says, whilst other countries are closed to German products; and it would be opportune for her to endeavour, by means of retaliatory duties, to obtain better treatment from other States.[2] But these opinions cannot, strictly speaking, be regarded as protectionist, for Adam Smith himself admits the right of nations to impose retaliatory duties with the view of inducing foreign countries to alter their tariff policy.

What was in List's mind during the first years of the *Zollverein* propaganda and before his departure for America is made perfectly clear by the first pages of the preface to the first edition of his *National System*, though we must not lose sight of a certain natural anxiety on the author's part to show a thorough agreement between his early and his subsequent opinions.

Here List relates how, having in 1818 to prepare a course of political economy, he accepted in general the principle of free-trade, but how the recent example of the prodigious results of the continental system and the disasters consequent on its suppression convinced him that it was true only when applied to all nations. His thoughts were then led to the idea of nationality, to the different degrees of development of the various countries, to the distinction between cosmopolitan economy and political economy, and to the conclusion that Germany ought to do away with her provincial tariffs, and then, by a system common to the whole fatherland, endeavour to attain that degree of industrial and commercial expansion already enjoyed by other nations.[3]

But he did not merely investigate the subject in theoretical studies, he tried to test its soundness by practical application; he formed, in 1819, an association of manufacturers and merchants, for the purpose of "obtaining the suppression of provincial custom-houses and the adoption of a national com-

[1] Leser, work mentioned, pp. 762, 763; and Eheberg, work mentioned, p. 120.
[2] Eheberg, work mentioned, p. 121. [3] Work mentioned, pp. iii. iv.

mercial system"; an association that greatly influenced the establishment of the customs union.[1]

This association was rent by conflicting opinions; most of its members merely demanded the abolition of internal customs without protection against foreign competition; the others—few in number—claimed measures of retaliation, especially against England. List says that he was obliged to adapt himself to circumstances and work for the abolition of the provincial zones and the formation of a national custom-house —which was the immediate object in view—and he hoped that the other reforms would follow in due course.[2]

From these data we think we may conclude that, if at that time List had in his mind any germs of disagreement with the free-trade theory, he had certainly no very clear conception of an organised system of protection: and that, if the condition of Germany at that period filled him with doubts regarding doctrines of orthodox economics, the question that chiefly preoccupied him and his contemporaries was that of the unification of the German customs and internal freedom of trade.

21. Frederick List went to the United States in 1825, and remained there four years. There he found himself in the "golden age" of the American system, at the triumph of protectionism, at the very moment when it, having succoured the new manufactures against excessive foreign competition, was lending a hand to the foundation of capitalist industries and consolidating new and more efficient modes of production, in the interest more especially, as we have seen, of the capitalists, but also, as it ultimately proved, in that of the country at large.

List, in whose mind grave doubts had already arisen regarding the absolute principle of free-trade, in consequence of the state of his own country, was suddenly placed in new, but somewhat analogous surroundings, where protectionism was not only in the height of its popularity, but was to a large extent really justifiable.

He, who was, as we have pointed out, no bookworm, but a man endowed with the greatest capacity of learning by observation, was much impressed by this new world in which

[1] Work mentioned, pp. iv.-vi.   [2] *Ibid.* pp. viii. ix.

he could watch, side by side, all the various degrees of civilisation from primeval forests to overgrown cities,[1] in which economic phenomena were developed with greater simplicity than elsewhere; he was struck, above all, by the great fact of protectionism that appeared here as a logical result of the economic history of the country, and was all the more likely to impress a mind keenly alive to historical sense.

It is natural that, in such circumstances, the germs of heresy which already existed in List's thoughts should rapidly have developed, and that in the letters written by him at that time should be found the essential basis of that theory, which, laid aside for the moment by a man who in the new world was engaged in the struggle for life, was afterwards elaborated by him when he had returned to his native land. He himself bears witness to the great influence exercised on him by his American surroundings, in his preface to *The National System*. It was in the United States, he says, that, throwing aside all books, I studied actual life and formed an exact idea of the gradual development of national economy, a development proceeding far more rapidly in that country than in Europe. Progress, which in the old world has required centuries for its accomplishment, is there made under our very eyes: we see society passing on from a savage to a pastoral state, from that to an agricultural one, and then again to an industrial and commercial condition.

There the commonest farm-labourer knows how to make agriculture flourish and augment his returns better than the most far-sighted scientists of the old world; he does his utmost to attract manufacturers to his neighbourhood. There the contrast between agricultural and manufacturing districts is most clearly marked, and occasions the most violent disturbances. Nowhere else are facilities of communication so highly appreciated and their influence on the physical and moral life of communities so well understood. This living book List says he has read with eagerness and assiduity, and he has endeavoured to co-ordinate the lessons which it has taught him with the results of his previous studies, experience, and reflections. From all this has issued a system which, though it may still appear defective, is at all events not based

---
[1] Vide *Roscher*, passage quoted.

upon a vague cosmopolitanism, but upon the nature of things, the teachings of history, and the wants of nations.[1]

22. The letters, in fact, which List wrote to Ingersoll, Vice-President of the Pennsylvanian Society for the Promotion of Manufactures, in 1827, when the United States were more than ever aglow with protectionist fervour, contain, in our opinion, the essential foundations of the general theory which he elaborated later on in his *National System*.

We think it well to give some details of these letters, not only on account of their importance in the sense to which we have just alluded, but also because, in spite of their great success in the United States, which led to their reproduction in the newspapers, they were never republished, nor have they been printed in Europe, even in the collection of List's writings, edited by Häusser.

Roscher barely touches on them; Leser and Eheberg give a summary of them in the works we have quoted, drawing from them, however, perfectly opposite conclusions; Leser maintaining that the ideas expressed in them contained nothing new, and merely put in a synthetic form those already advanced by the American protectionists,[2] whilst Eheberg declares that in these letters is to be found much that was subsequently incorporated in *The National System*, of which they formed the basis.[3]

We are indebted to the courtesy of that learned economist, Professor Edwin R. A. Seligman of New York (whose well-filled library contains so many valuable documents regarding the history of American tariffs), for the privilege of having read the little volume—now a rare bibliographical treasure—containing List's American letters; and we will avail ourselves of this piece of good fortune to give our readers a sufficiently explicit summary of them.[4]

[1] Work mentioned, pp. x. xi. [2] P. 766. [3] Pp. 100 and 127.
[4] The work in question, of 40 octavo pages, is entitled, "*Outlines of American Political Economy*, in a series of letters addressed by Frederick List, Esq., late Professor of Political Economy of the University of Tübingen, in Germany, to Charles I. Ingersoll, Vice-President of the Pennsylvania Society for the Promotion of the Manufactures and the Mechanical Arts. To which is added the celebrated letters of Mr. Jefferson to Benjamin Austin, and of Mr. Madison to the editors of the *Lynchburg Virginian*." Philadelphia, printed by Samuel Parker, No. 48 Market Street, 1827.

The volume contains eight letters, dated successively from the 10th to the

In the first letter, the writer begins by declaring that he will confine himself to refuting the theory of Adam Smith and his followers, which is founded, in his opinion, upon errors that are not sufficiently understood, and which includes many castles in the air that pass for solid and well-founded edifices;[1] and he proposes to lead the assault under the flying colours of the " American system."

To Adam Smith's economy, List opposes the historical conception of national economy. There are, he says, three systems of economy : that of individuals, that of nations, and that of humanity; Adam Smith concerns himself only with the first and the last, teaching us how an individual creates, augments, and consumes wealth in a community of other individuals, and how the industry and riches of mankind influence the industry and wealth of the individual. But he has entirely overlooked, observes List, that which the title of his book, *The Wealth of Nations*, promised to elucidate, since he does not take into account the different situations of the various nationalities, and merely studies the question as if the human race were not divided into nations, but united under a general law and with an equal degree of culture.[2]

Could we grant this hypothesis, Adam Smith's conclusions would be true, and free-trade would be natural and beneficial, and so it undoubtedly will be in some distant future; but for the time being such a state of things does not tally with reality ;[3] and between individual economy and the economy of mankind it is necessary to interpose " national economy," that shall teach us the means by which a nation, in the particular circumstances in which it is placed, can best direct and regulate the economy of individuals, and modify the economy of humanity at large, either to prevent foreign limitations and influence, or else to increase its own productive forces ; that shall teach us, in fact, how, in the absence of one sole state

25th of July 1827, and they are preceded by a letter from Lafayette to List, and by another from Ingersoll to the editor of the *National Gazette*.

These eight letters were followed by an appendix containing three other ones, also published in 1827, under the title of *Appendix to the Outlines of American Political Economy;* but unfortunately we have not been able to peruse them.

[1] Work mentioned, p. 5.   [2] *Ibid.* p. 7.   [3] *Ibid.* p. 7.

embracing the entire globe, a separate world may be created, that shall be developed in the most complete way possible.[1]

In the second letter the conception of a national economy is completed from a political point of view, and the historical idea of protection, which had previously been shadowed forth, is more fully developed. The object of national economy, according to List, is not merely wealth, but also political power with which it is closely united; a nation must be able to defend its citizens, it must foresee wars, and be capable of producing all articles of first necessity, that is to say, must be independent of foreign resources.[2] Power and wealth are both promoted by the harmonious union of agriculture, manufactures, and commerce in a country; a state that is simply agricultural is necessarily dependent on foreign supplies, and always remains poor. Now the state must interfere to bring about this harmonious co-operation, because it is its duty to initiate or encourage everything that augments the wealth and power of the nation, whenever that cannot be done by private individuals.[3]

As to the opportuneness and efficacy of protective measures, that must depend upon the circumstances of the country. As long as a nation is in its infancy, it is best suited to free-trade and the exchange of raw materials for manufactured goods. The United States, after having passed from the condition of a colony to that of an independent country, did well to remain, at first, in a state of economic vassalage. But when once they had acquired the strength of a man, it was time to put away childish things.[4] The natural resources of America are immense, and the effects of the people's efforts to raise manufactures will be without a parallel in history: other nations may remain in a state of economic dependence, but this is impossible for this strong, rich, and well-educated people: and to become truly independent they must combine manufactures with agriculture and commerce.[5]

The third letter is of less theoretical importance: in it List tells us how he was at first a follower of Adam Smith, but changed his mind after having observed the effect in Germany of the continental blockade, and afterwards that of

[1] Work mentioned, p. 8.   [2] *Ibid.* p. 10.   [3] *Ibid.* p. 10.
[4] *Ibid.* pp. 10, 11.   [5] *Ibid.* p. 12.

its suspension;[1] and then comes a long digression regarding the commercial relations between France and England.

In the fourth letter is set forth, at considerable length, the theory of "productive forces," which plays such an important part in the "national system." The writer maintains that it is not the object of national economy to gain mere "matter" by exchanging goods for goods, as in the economy of a merchant, or in cosmopolitan economy, but rather to gain productive and political power. The error into which Adam Smith and Say fell, is that of not having taken this fact into account.[2] According to them, if the United States have greater capacities for producing cotton than for manufacturing it, they ought to send their cotton to England and take the manufactured article in exchange. This is right, says List, from the standpoint of strictly commercial interests, but not from a patriotic point of view, for by acting in this way the United States would place themselves in a position of dependence and limit their productive power, whilst by developing their manufactures they would, on the contrary, largely increase that power.[3] The abundance of raw materials and of provisions, the spirit of enterprise, the security of property, and a vast market, all combine to place the United States in the situation requisite for a great development of manufactures.[4] And such a development is necessary, otherwise too great a scattering of the population — if it were exclusively agricultural—over such a vast territory would be prejudicial to progress.[5]

It is incumbent on the state, therefore, to sacrifice the immediate profit to be obtained by exchanges, with a view to the acquisition of future productive power: the only question is whether that, in a given country, is possible; and it is evidently possible, says List, in the United States.

In the letters that follow the writer returns for the most part to the ideas which he has already set forth, amplifying and illustrating them; logical order not being the most meritorious characteristic of this polemical and occasional publication.

[1] *Vide* what we have said a few pages back.
[2] Work mentioned, pp. 18, 19.   [3] *Ibid.* p. 19.
[4] *Ibid.* p. 21.   [5] *Ibid.* pp. 23, 24.

In fact, List, in his fifth letter, returns to the historical idea of protection, observing that every nation has its particular economy, and that protection is not opportune in all countries, since it is essential for the development of manufactures that liberty, security, and instruction should have reached a certain standard.[1] Nor would it be reasonable to afford equal support to all industries; only those should receive aid which employ a certain number of workmen, consume a large quantity of raw materials, lend themselves to machinery, and which cannot obtain a large home market; and the commoner articles should alone be protected, not the finer goods or those administering to luxury.[2]

In the sixth letter, returning to the distinctions between the three economies, the individual, the national, and the cosmopolitan, he compares the first two and points out that they may come into conflict, that national economy ought to concern itself not merely with the present but also with the future, and that the principle of *laissez-faire* would only be true if individual and national interests never came into collision, which is far from being the case.[3]

And thus, in the seventh letter, alluding once more to the difference between national and cosmopolitan economy, List observes that, as a matter of fact, political as well as economic contests do occur between nations, and they are sometimes useful; and that a nation would be ill-advised indeed that endeavoured to promote the general welfare of the whole human race to the detriment of its own well-being and strength and independence. It is possible to conceive for the future a universal free-trade *régime;* but for the moment the laws of self-preservation render it incumbent on each nation to increase its own power to the utmost extent possible; and this should be done by promoting its industrial capacity.[4] This gives our author the opportunity of unfolding his views on the protection of young industries. He points out that in order to acquire industrial power, much experience and time are needed: speculators are unwilling to embark in new enterprises in which much risk is necessarily run owing to want of practice and skill. All this makes the outset of new

[1] Work mentioned, pp. 24, 25.   [2] *Ibid.* p. 25.
[3] *Ibid.* p. 27.   [4] *Ibid.* pp. 30-31.

undertakings most difficult; the promoters are shackled by the unskilfulness of their work-people, by the heavy outlay on installation, by the high price of labour, for, in a new country where manufactures are in the bud, wages are higher for inefficient workmen than they are for skilled artisans in an old manufacturing country. And to all this must be added, on the part of the employers, the want of knowledge of the best sources for raw materials, the difficulty of forming a business connection, and the consumers' prejudice in favour of foreign goods. It cannot be expected that these things should encourage manufacturers in their early trials; and, therefore, in a new country the state should encourage them by means of protection.[1]

Finally, in his eighth letter, List enumerates the advantages incidental, in his opinion, to a protective tariff; they are four in number—(1) that of securing the home market for national industries, thereby making them independent of the fluctuations in prices and political vicissitudes of foreign countries; (2) that of placing native industries in a more favourable position than those of nations that have adopted free-trade, and do not, therefore, defend their own industries by means of protective tariffs; (3) that of rendering the inland consumption of manufactures dependent, not on the exportation of native agricultural produce, but on its production at home—a production which, for the United States, is almost inexhaustible; (4) and, finally, that of giving ballast to the market, to labour, and to enterprise — an essential condition of industrial prosperity.[2]

23. Now the reader who compares this *résumé* of the contents of *Outlines of American Political Economy*, published by List in America in 1827, with the synthesis which we have already given of the theory set forth in the *National System* which the same author published in Germany in 1841, will not fail to observe that the short letters addressed to Ingersoll contain in substance almost all the ideas developed by List later on in his principal work; ideas which he only entertained before landing in America in the shape of vague doubts regarding Adam Smith's doctrine, and which were suggested, partly at all events, by the new surrounding which his capa-

[1] Work mentioned, pp. 31-32.   [2] *Ibid.* pp. 33-36.

cious and practical mind soon succeeded in fully understanding. In fact, the conception of a national economy as opposed to the cosmopolitan system of the economists; the historical idea of its development in distinction to general and absolute views; the notion that the general theory of free-trade is as applicable to the earlier as well as to the last forms of social evolution, but does not answer to the temporary requirements of a given historical epoch; the historical idea of protection which follows from it; the necessity of manufactures for progress, and the preference that should be given to a future increase of productive forces over momentary advantages — all these principles, which we find more or less fully developed in the *Outlines*, form to a great extent the foundation of the "national system," in which they are enlarged upon.

Whether they are all equally new and original is another question which regards not merely the *Outlines* but the entire system of Frederick List. Leser[1] says that the ideas contained in that publication did but recapitulate those already expressed by American writers; but this opinion appears to us to be absolutely at fault the moment we admit that they constitute the basis of the "national system," to which, as we shall see even more plainly later on, it is impossible to deny an impress of genuine originality.

It was natural that as List was in touch with the circumstances in which he was placed, and drew from them his economic theory, so was he necessarily familiar with the predominant ideas. We have alluded in the preceding chapter to the close connection which exists between List's ideas and those contained in Alexander Hamilton's *Report*;[2] nor, on

---

[1] *Vide* quotation.
[2] On this point, Eheberg (work quoted, p. 149) maintains that List could not have drawn his ideas from Hamilton's *Report*, because he had already adopted these views before coming to America; because what is expressed in his American letters differs from the contents of the famous *Report*; and finally, because what influenced his mind much more than any writings was the economic condition of the United States. Ingram observes, on the contrary, that there is some reason to believe that Hamilton's work really produced some effect on List.

Now there can be no doubt about this—that what primarily moved List to elaborate a system of which at first he had only thrown out sketches, was his American surroundings; on the other hand, it seems to us difficult to deny the influence exercised upon him by Hamilton. Even disregarding the fact

the other hand, can it be denied that List assimilated some of the protectionist theories which were more generally popular at that time, and especially that of protection to young industries, which was then the leading argument of American protectionists. But whilst that in no way detracts from the originality of List's other ideas, it none the less confirms the opinion that his system was partly a product of the American historical environment in which it originated; as indeed is clearly shown by the title affixed by List to his letters to Ingersoll—" Outlines of American Political Economy"— which was intended to show that the system evolved was designed for the country in which the letters were written.

24. Although this brief survey of List's work only enters incidentally into our argument, yet such is the importance we attach to his system, that we do not think it will be waste of time to give at this point a brief synthesis—under the guidance of the best critics—of his principal merits and defects, which we will follow up by a general estimate of his work.

The essential merits of Frederick List's system are to be found on two distinct points—economic science generally, and the particular question of protection.

Putting aside for the moment his exaggerations, his unjust attacks, his polemics, which at times are absolutely wanting in scientific serenity, List's vigorous opposition to the school of orthodox economy is in its main features of great value as a reaction against the abuse of abstractions, against a method which depends entirely on abstract reasoning that leaves the realities of life out of account. List's attacks on the "school" remind theoretic economists that side by side of their abstractions there is the real man, and there are the historical forms

(which is well-nigh incredible) that in 1827 List, who had already been two years in the United States, and was studying the customs question, should have paid no heed to Hamilton's *Report*, which had been reprinted in Philadelphia in 1824 by the same society for the encouragement of manufactures that three years later published the *Outlines*, even we say if this could be granted, the profound analogy between the ideas briefly thrown off by the great American statesman, and those amply and systematically developed by the German protectionist, as we have pointed out in the preceding chapter, appears incontrovertible. But this analogy, even if it adds to the value of Alexander Hamilton's work which preceded it, certainly does not detract from List's merits, for he, as we have seen, raised fragmentary ideas into an original and historical system.

of social evolution, which cannot be overlooked in the pursuit of abstract entities.[1]

He reproaches the "school," says Roscher, with three errors particularly—a boundless cosmopolitanism, which neither recognises the nature of nationalities, nor takes into consideration the satisfaction of their interests; a lifeless materialism, which over-regards the exchange-value of commodities without heeding the spiritual and political needs, either present or future, or the productive forces of the nation; and an ill-organised individualism, which contemplates all things from the merchant's point of view, so that Adam Smith's work is, in reality, merely a system of private economy of all individuals, just what we might expect if there were no such things as states, or constitutions, or nations, or national interests. And who could maintain, adds the illustrious founder of the historical school, that these objections are altogether groundless?[2]

In combating the abstractions of the economists, List is naturally led to associate political with purely economic judgment. It is true enough that, once launched on this course to oppose the "school" which exclusively considers the abstract economic view of social phenomena, he runs the risk of falling into the other extreme, that of the mercantilists, who concerned themselves wholly or principally with the political aspect. But, whilst mercantilism was dead and buried, the reaction against the one-sidedness of the new scientific movement was useful and practical.

And List, although, as Eheberg points out, he was not the first to discern the relation between economy and national existence,[3] has the credit of having copiously illustrated it, and of having drawn attention to the political side of economic phenomena.

But List's greatest merit—one intimately connected with those to which we have just alluded, but which is none the less a merit *per se*, giving him a high standing among the economists of our times—is that of having inaugurated and warmly defended the historical method in economic science.

If his reaction against the abstract school had merely been critical and negative, the value of his work would cer-

---
[1] Eheberg, work mentioned, pp. 159-161.
[2] Work mentioned, p. 975. [3] Work mentioned, p. 156.

tainly not have stood high; but List substitutes the inductive and historical method for the abstract method of scientific research, drawing his arguments chiefly from copious and well-ordered investigations into the historical evolution of the various countries; and his general idea of social economy and his general conclusions are historical and relative. His inductions may not always be correct, his investigations may, at times, be too coloured by prejudices for him to attain perfectly certain and scientific results; but this is evidently the fault of the application of the method, and not of the method itself; and to List is undoubtedly due the great honour of having been among the first to systematically apply historical research to economic studies, and to found that historical school which obtained subsequently, especially in Germany, so large a following, and which supplied modern science with such rich and abundant materials for examination.

Coming now to the special theory of protection, the importance and originality of List's system lie principally in the historical idea which inspires it. On many points he has largely drawn from opinions previously expressed by others: this may be said of the idea of the necessity of the correlative development of manufactures and agriculture, of the poverty and dependence on foreign supplies which mark exclusively agricultural countries, and, as we have already indicated, of protection for young industries.

But the historical foundation, which was already laid in this last idea, he not only copiously illustrated, seizing the whole measure of its importance, but he has broadened it and raised it to a system which, although imperfectly developed and applied by the author in details, is none the less of the utmost value as regards its fundamental idea, which may be reduced to this: to conceive protection as the appropriate form of a certain phase in the historical evolution of national economy, or, even more generally, as a form which answers to the exigencies of certain historical conditions of the life of a nation.

This conception is of great importance, and, as Lexis also observes,[1] has given a truly scientific basis to the protective

[1] *Vide* Lex s, "Handel," in the *Handbuch der Politischen Oekonomie*, by Schönberg.

theory, and this, in our opinion, not merely because in this way protectionism assumes a relative character, and one exceptional to the general rule of free-trade, but also, and chiefly, because on this basis all absolute judgment and all prejudice being banished, the door is open for a positive research into facts, to ascertain the causes which in the various countries and at the various historical epochs have really determined the adoption of protection or free-trade, and from these facts to deduce, under the guidance of experience, whether and in what cases and historical circumstances protectionism may be justified.

25. The salient defects of Frederick List's system may be summed up in four words—exaggeration, one-sidedness, imperfection, and uncertainty.

Exaggeration is an evident and constant fault in List; it occurs in his criticisms, in his history, and in his theories; his attacks on what he terms the "school" are overdone; his historical judgment is often overdrawn, as, for instance, when he says that in a short space of time Russia gained prosperity by means of the prohibitive system, or when he declares that it would be better for Americans to return to English domination than to give up protection. Overcoloured is his economic conception of nationality; he develops beyond all measure an idea which in itself is just and true; so, too, does he exceed the bounds of reason when, on writing the apology of manufactures, he leaves out of account the evils, especially those of a social character, which accompany them.[1] But above all is his exaggeration manifest in that he gives everywhere in his system an undue and excessive importance to the question of international trade; and to the principle of protection he likewise assigns, throughout, a weight which throws his own essentially historical theory out of equilibrium.

And it is the one-sidedness of List's standpoint that so often leads him to these exaggerations. Thus, whilst reproaching orthodox economists for having considered alone the abstract economic life of mankind, he falls into the opposite error of attaching too much importance to economic policy and too little to general economy, forgetting that

[1] Lexis, work mentioned. It is quite true that at List's time such evils were less felt than they are nowadays.

economic science, even while dealing with matters of fact, cannot restrict itself to theories concerning the state of a given country, but must rise to more general considerations.[1] In all his arguments, the defect of one-sidedness occurs frequently and vitiates many observations which otherwise contain elements of truth. Roscher remarks that the parallel which List draws between the slow, isolated, unimproving *routine* of agriculture, and the free, progressive, and many-formed activity of other industries, is certainly one of the most ingenious contributions to the new school of national economy; but that it is spoilt by the one-sidedness which everywhere confuses industrial energy with the highest economic culture.[2] The theory of the " productive forces " likewise contains a great element of truth, inasmuch as it lays down that the wealth of nations does not only depend on the quantity of their momentary possessions of exchangeable values, but also on their distribution in space and time; not only on present advantages, but on those secured for the future as well. The argument, however, is exaggerated and one-sided in so far as it does not recognise the importance of trade, and goes to the length of opposing forces to values, throwing a veil over the relations between cause and effect which bind them together, by means of which exchangeable goods contain or sustain productive forces, and these, in their turn, are transformed into exchangeable merchandise.[3]

And most undoubtedly are there elements of truth in List's theory of the dangers that may sometimes lurk in too great an international division of labour, in which commercial profits may be differently divided among the trading nations, for an economic inequality may supervene and one country obtain a superiority over another.[4] But it is also evident that the division of labour is not a purely national concern, that every country has special aptitudes due to the nature of its soil and its inhabitants, and that it is absurd to impose an excessive and unnatural division of native labour, when, by means of international commerce, the various countries can

[1] Eheberg, work mentioned, p. 163.
[2] Work mentioned, pp. 979, 980.
[3] Eheberg, work mentioned, p. 177 ; and Roscher, work mentioned, p. 984.
[4] Eheberg, work mentioned, pp. 199-201.

supply one another's wants. Now, though such reservations are at times present in List's mind, at other times he is quite oblivious of them in his enthusiasm for manufactures.

No less grave are the imperfections, gaps, and above all the uncertainties which we meet with in the positive part of List's system.

There is not much justice, perhaps, in the reproach directed by Carlo Cattaneo[1] against List, that he had inexactly defined the idea of nationality, by denying, in opposition to history, the character of nations to those not possessing unity of language, and those of limited extent devoid of seaboard; not because the criticism is wanting in truth, but because even in constitutional law the definition of nationality—which is essentially relative and historical—is not laid down in rigorously exact terms.

With greater justice, however, does the same critic observe that the distinction between hot and temperate countries—which plays so important a part in List's system—is not as absolute as the author supposes, and that if we adhere to his theory (which aims at isolating civilised nations from one another and bringing them into contact with the savages of the tropics), England, for instance, ought not to buy the wines and oil of France and Italy, nor those countries English manufactures, as they are all of them situated in the temperate zone. Roscher likewise points out List's mistake in having included Spain among the tropical countries unfit for manufactures.

And then, however much we may appreciate List's attempt to trace on broad lines the historical evolution of national economy, by mapping it out into various periods, such as savage, pastoral, agricultural, as we have already explained, yet for all that we cannot help acknowledging that he succeeds but indifferently well, for, founded as it is on a superficial and one-sided study of history, it does not, generally speaking, answer to the truth.

In fact, that evolution, although true as regards some peoples, is by no means so as regards others, presenting numerous variations of substance and time and many intermediate periods. And on this point Eheberg observes

[1] See his ' Opere" quoted, vol. v. p. 192.

that List's periods do not correspond to the economic evolution of England, where the development of commerce occurred independently of that of manufactures, which preceded it, and profited by communications with Flanders, a country that was industrially ahead of England.[1]

Moreover, in formulating the historical periods of economic evolution, List is often uncertain, inaccurate, and does not always express himself in the same way; and this uncertainty, which is one of the gravest faults of his system, is especially manifest in the historical limits which he sets to protection—limits which he by no means accurately defines. He seems to claim protection in the fourth period of his economic evolution, in the agricultural-manufacturing period, when native factories already partly supply the wants of the nation; and the question is how to aid the development of the infant industries. List's idea is therefore quite different from that of Stuart Mill, which we examined in the previous essay; and the protection which he demands is not, properly speaking, protection to manufactures at their outset, but rather protection to consolidated industries—protection in the capitalistic sense. This is the rational system of protection which we saw inaugurated in the United States at the time of the foundation of capitalistic industry, and of which List was, in reality, the theoretical advocate.

But this idea is not expressed by List with any degree of certainty; and although it may be generally deduced from his system as a whole, we find here and there in his writings passages which point to another theory—that of protection at the outset, or tentative establishment of manufactures; as, for example, in the *Outlines*, when he speaks of the grave difficulties encountered at the beginning of every new undertaking, and demands protection for a country in which industries had only just started;[2] and when he laments the inadequacy of protection in the United States in the first years of the century[3]—a time when the foundation of the capitalistic industries had not yet been laid. And the uncertainty of List's protective idea does not merely lie in the fact that he does not declare unhesitatingly and explicitly

[1] Work mentioned, p. 168.   [2] Work mentioned, p. 31.
[3] *Das nationale System* etc., p. 93.

whether protection should be resorted to at the very starting-point of manufactures or somewhat later on, but also in that, as we have already seen, with reference to the adoption of protection, he sometimes makes large and rational reservations regarding the moral, social, and economic conditions necessary for the development of manufactures—conditions without which protection would be useless; and thus he admits that a country of limited extent and few resources could not derive any great benefit from a protective policy; whilst elsewhere he applies too absolutely the principle of the division of national labour, and seems to advocate its complete development in all the countries of the temperate zone.

These uncertainties of List, and especially that regarding the period of the national economic evolution in which protection ought to be applied, probably depend on the fact that our author, although he had considered the historical character of protectionism and the relation between commercial policy and the historical evolution of nations, was not successful in sounding the depths of this relation, and did not arrive at the conception of protection as a direct instrument in the hands of capitalists at the epoch of the foundation of the great manufactures.

It is true that List has a reverence for manufactures and for the aristocracy of money and factories;[1] that he identifies the progress of manufactures with the general progress of economy and civilisation, and restricts protection to manufactures—excluding agriculture. Notable above all is his aversion to the distribution of the population over the western territories and to the cultivation of those immense and distant regions[2]—which would evidently have an injurious effect on the capitalists, both because the west was the free land which it was their interest to keep as much in the background as possible, and its colonisation implied an emigration of capital and labour from the eastern States, and hence a rise of wages; and because the tilling of a new soil, if it is less fertile than that previously in cultivation, tends to lower the standard of profit to the advantage of land rent. But although these are indications in favour of the supposi-

---

[1] Roscher, work mentioned, p. 976.
[2] *Das nationale System*, p. 97, and *Outlines*, pp. 23, 24.

tion that at the bottom of List's protectionist theory lies the capitalistic idea, we can, nevertheless, find no positive trace of this in any of his writings.

26. But the serious defects that are to be met with in Frederick List's system must not make us forget the merits which entitle it to so important a place in the history of the theory and policy of international trade.

His exaggerations and one-sidedness can be chiefly explained by the fact that he was powerfully influenced by his environment; and although this was beneficial in as much as it induced him to take into account facts as they really are, and to base his theories upon them, yet by engrossing him too much with what was close at hand, it led to disproportionate and unscientific views, prevented him from completing his system by rendering it truly historical, and presenting a profound and perfect interpretation of the historical forms of economy.

Both Adam Smith and List, Eheberg justly remarks, were one-sided, for they allowed themselves to be too greatly influenced by the special conditions of England and of Germany in their own times. As Adam Smith had deduced the whole of his economic system from the principles of egoism and of commercial liberty, because free-trade was better adapted to the condition of England when he lived, so List, mindful of the errors which the principle of liberty had borne with it, taking into consideration the situation of Germany at the beginning of the century, and endeavouring to find a theoretical explanation of it (and, we may add, having in mind the features of American life such as he had studied them whilst living in the United States), came to the conclusion that protection of manufactures should rank as a fundamental principle. No one, adds Eheberg, can make himself independent of the influence of his times; and when we think of the state of Germany (and all the more so, that of the United States) at the beginning of this century, and of the influence which a well-directed commercial policy exercised there by means of a moderately protective tariff, it is easy to understand how he was led to exaggerate, from a one-sided standpoint, the importance of national restriction and of a moderate tariff protection.[1]

[1] Work mentioned, p. 244.

But the one-sidedness and the exaggeration—which so frequently characterise the work of those who strike out in a new direction and raise a courageous protest against received opinions, and which are so easily incurred when the intricate and difficult ways of social phenomena are substituted for the beaten paths of abstract reasoning—these faults, as well as those of imperfection and uncertainty, which likewise are necessarily inherent in studies which break fresh ground, on which light is shed, ray by ray, from the midst of a canopy of clouds, so that its first streaks are barely visible; these faults, we say, cannot detract from the great value of Frederick List's work, which placed the study of commercial politics on a truly scientific basis, and which, although it does not include all the arcana of protectionism, nor is able exactly to interpret it, nevertheless laid the foundation of this interpretation in the historical evolution of nations, where, at given moments, protection may answer the particular requirements of a predominating class, or even of the whole country.

If this path—upon which List has poured such a flood of light, notwithstanding all his exaggerations and uncertainties—had been followed up, and the question of protectionism had been studied on rigorously historical lines in the economic history of the various peoples, the theory of international commerce would have taken a very different direction. But, while on the one hand protectionists enveloped themselves more or less in a narrow empiricism, or had recourse to ingenious sophisms in order to forward the interests of the capitalist class, and to try and hypocritically lull to sleep by clever artifices the great mass of consumers and work-people; economists, on the other hand, mostly continued to take refuge in theoretical formulæ, which, although carried to a marvellous perfection of logical architecture, offer, none the less, a striking contrast to the reality of things.

CHAPTER III

HENRY C. CAREY

27. Very different from that of Hamilton and of List has been the fate of Henry C. Carey. To the two first—the true founders of the protectionist theory—posterity, after a life torn by struggles and embittered by the enmity and injustice of the men and the circumstances of their times, gave little attention, less popularity, and frequently but scant justice. But Carey, on the contrary—who in our opinion is so much inferior to them—was judged so favourably, even in his lifetime, that he was by some compared to the great masters of political economy, to Adam Smith and to Ricardo; he had the satisfaction of seeing his works, crowned by the success of popularity, translated into various languages and distributed over the world, and he did not fail to exercise much influence upon the concerns of his country. Time and science, however, in the long run are honest; and whilst Hamilton and List are little by little advancing into the rank which is their due in the history of economic theories, Carey, who lived so much later than they did, has already been removed—by the operation of serious and severe criticism—from the pedestal on which he had been too hastily placed.

Anyhow, the success which Carey enjoyed in his own country and abroad, the extent of his work, the philosophical and economic system which he unfolded, all combine to make him—if not the most eminent American economist—at all events the best-known and the most discussed, and consequently the most popular protectionist of the United States.

The chief characteristics of Carey's system are optimism and protectionism — two traits which at first sight appear contradictory, but which he has ingeniously found means of reconciling, if not quite satisfactorily, at all events formally. And it is perhaps to the mingling of these two utterly distinct currents that the great success of his system was due, for it enabled him to appeal to the sympathy of the two opposing parties: to that of the optimistic free-traders, who, rejecting his protectionism as a partial mental aberration,[1] set great store on the theory of the economic harmonies which permeates his system; and to the protectionists, who never expected to see the protectionism, which Carey so fervently advocated, clothed in such attractive garb.

Carey is not a protectionist in all his works. He begins by being distinctly in favour of free-trade: in his first writings, and above all in his *Principles of Political Economy* (1837-1840), not only is there no trace of protectionism, but every obstacle in the way of free-trade is vigorously combated; import duties are called " violations of the rights of property," and the desire is expressed for the most complete establishment of free-trade in the United States.

But later on the author's views undergo a radical change; in his book, *The Past, the Present, and the Future* (1848), he combats the principal theories of the classic English school, and invokes protection in order to place manufactures by the side of agriculture. But Carey's sympathies for freedom have not yet entirely vanished, either in this work, or in another on the *Harmony of Interests* (1850), and there are hints to the effect that protection may be a means to attain complete freedom of exchange, which would be for the general good. In his last writings, however, and notably in his chief work, *Principles of Social Science*, Carey throws off all restraint and becomes, as we shall see, the advocate of a system of absolute protection, without limitations of time or other reservations, and he gives to protection the predominance over all other questions.

This great change is explained by Carey in the preface to the French edition of his *Principles of Social Science*, written

---

[1] *Vide*, for example, Ferrara, introduction to Carey's " Principles of Political Economy " (Italian edition), in the *Biblioteca degli Economisti*, series I. vol. xiii. p. 73.

in 1860,[1] where he says that at the time of the publication of his first works, he had had little opportunity of studying the effects of free-trade and of protection in the United States, and that subsequent study had convinced him, by the evidence of facts, of the erroneousness of the free-trade theory; whilst, later on, his investigations into the theories of rent and population assured him that the great tendency of the American people to dispersion and isolation was due to the gradual exhaustion of the soil caused by the exportation of agricultural produce, which ought not to find its way into foreign markets, but for which a home market should be created, and at the same time manufactures encouraged by means of protection.

What naturally interests us above all in Carey is his view of protectionism, and we shall devote time to its consideration; but we cannot refrain from alluding to the other points in his system, both because they are intimately connected with the question of protection, and because the whole of his theory reveals an interesting study on the influence of environment.[2]

28. The predominant idea in Carey's system is the optimistic conception of the existence of a perfect harmony and unity in all natural, physical, organic, and social laws; a conception, which developed in his last work, *The Unity of Law*,[3] from the general philosophical point of view, is treated in the preceding ones with regard especially to its bearings on economic phenomena. These he regards as the outcome of natural providential laws, which bring about a perfect harmony

[1] We do not find this preface in the American edition in 3 volumes (1858-1859) which we possess.
[2] A very few notes are all that is needed regarding the writer's life. Henry Charles Carey was born at Philadelphia in 1793, and died in 1879. He was the son of Matthew Carey, a well-known publisher and economist. He occupied himself with the book-trade till 1838, and then devoted himself altogether to study. He was an exceedingly prolific writer—too prolific indeed. Jenks (in his *Henry C. Carey als Nationalökonom*, Jena, Fischer, 1885), gives a complete account of his literary works, which include eight books (of which two are in 3 volumes each) and fifty-seven pamphlets, most of them referring to the question of protection, of which he was practically an agitator. We have already alluded to his more important works in the text: the chief one in which his whole system is fully developed is *Principles of Social Science*, published in 3 volumes at Philadelphia in 1858-1859. For further particulars regarding Carey's writings, see Jenks, a most diligent critic, mentioned above, and Cossa's *Introduction to the Study of Political Economy*.
[3] Philadelphia, H. Carey Baird, 1873.

of interests, that leads with the uninterrupted accumulation of wealth to general prosperity. A harmony of interests exists between all, between owners and tenants, between capitalists and labourers, even between masters and slaves. The interests of all men are perfectly identical, and social evolution makes for universal felicity.

We shall not pause long to consider Carey's much discussed theory of value. According to it the cause of value is labour, whilst the cost of reproduction is its measure. It is the application of labour to the soil and to other natural agents which constitutes their value. The value of capital and of products tends constantly to diminish in comparison with that of labour. From these ideas Carey deduces his theory of wages, which, completed by a criticism, or rather by a negation of the theories of population and land rent, forms his optimistic system of the distribution of wealth.

Every increase in the balance between capital and population is accompanied, says Carey, by an increase of the proportion in which the remuneration of labour stands to that of capital, and workmen are thus enabled to retain an ever larger quota of the produce of their labour, whilst leaving an ever proportionally lessening one in the hands of the landowner or capitalist. The share of the workmen increases both absolutely and relatively, whilst that of the capitalists augments in absolute, but diminishes in relative amount. Thus, although no antagonism exists between workmen and capitalists, the progress of production tends to benefit the former more than the latter, tends to a necessary and continuous improvement in the condition of the workmen at a more rapid rate than is the case with regard to the capitalists, and hence tends in the long run to a diminution in the distance between these classes, and an equalisation of social conditions.

This optimistic theory is, as we have said, completed by the author by the denial of the Malthusian doctrine of population, and of Ricardo's theory of rent. Carey denies the law put forward by Malthus; such a law would, says the American writer, be in contradiction to divine wisdom! Scarcity of food is, in his opinion, characteristic of the less advanced and not of the more progressive countries, for the latter have succeeded in overcoming the evil. The advancement of knowledge and of its applications, by making possible an extension of agriculture, ensure the well-being of labourers and the welfare of landowners. A development of accumulated wealth accompanies that of population in such a way that in proportion as the latter increases, there increases with it the means of applying labour more productively, and of thus augmenting production and consequently food. And if this does not always occur in reality, the fault is not to be put down to a natural law, but to some false and insane system of economic policy which has been adopted by the United States.[1]

And Carey likewise denies the other fundamental principle of classical economy, that of land rent, for he considers the rent derived from land a legitimate compensation for the capital sunk in it, and he maintains that with the increase of population there follows an ever more productive cultivation of land. The phenomenon of the gradual exhaustion of the soil, which is evident even in America, did not escape him; but instead of attributing it, with Ricardo, to the natural law of decreasing productiveness, he puts it down, likewise, to an artificial cause, to an error in economic policy, to the absolute predominance of agriculture, which impoverishes the soil by the exportation of its products and their consumption far away from the place of production.[2]

29. It is easy now to see the correspondence of these ideas to the theory of international commerce—that is, the protectionist system—put forward by Carey. Although this system is expounded at considerable length in many volumes, so great in reality is its simplicity and so great the exuberance of verbosity of its author, that it is no difficult task to sum up its leading features in a few pages. The cause of social ill-being does not lie, we repeat, according to Carey, in any natural or absolute law, but simply in an error of economic policy, an error that may be remedied by means of good legislation; in a word, by protection.

The error consists in not securing the correlative development of agriculture and of manufactures, by bringing together consumers and producers into an association where life and

[1] *Principles of Social Science*, Philadelphia, Lippincott, 1858, vol. i. p. 288.
[2] Work mentioned, *passim*, and specially pp. 210, 287, etc.

labour would be concentrated, and which would result in that progressive increase of production and well-being that natural laws tend to promote, but that require co-operation on the part of man.

Purely agricultural countries are necessarily poor. The exclusion of all arts except the cultivation of the soil leads to its exhaustion and to the depopulation and impoverishment of the land. Weakness and poverty are found in all communities in which agriculture has not been allowed to strengthen itself by means of the natural alliance between the plough and the loom, the hammer and the harrow.[1]

The reason of this is that the country cannot turn all its resources to account, and must be dependent on foreign nations for the exportation of its agricultural produce and the importation of manufactures: facts that cause a series of far-reaching evils.

We have already alluded to Carey's law of the succession of cultivations. According to it, man begins everywhere by tilling the poorest lands, which are those which need no disforesting, nor draining, nor other heavy labours, and are consequently the easiest of access and culture: and only at a later date does he succeed in cultivating the more fertile and less amenable regions. But the latter, to which an intensive system of culture is applied, are not turned to account until there has been established in the country an extensive home market offering an immediate outlet for the many products of the soil, such as meat, milk, and dairy produce, etc., which cannot be transported to a distance. To bring this about, it is necessary that there should exist vast and flourishing manufactories, the work-people in which would consume the agricultural produce in the neighbourhood of its origin.

Instead of that, as long as agriculture is pursued alone, and its products must be to a large extent exported, there is a tendency for cultivation to spread even more over the less fertile ground, and to remain in a scattered state, in order to produce such articles as can be easily transported to distant markets.[2]

[1] Work mentioned, vol. i. p. 317.
[2] *The Past, the Present, and the Future*, London, Trübner, 1856, pp. 118, 119.

Thus it is that the country is hindered from profiting—through the cultivation of its more fertile land—by its greatest natural resources.

The necessity experienced by purely agricultural nations of exporting the greater part of their products is fatal to them, according to Carey, for several reasons, and above all because it places them in a state of permanent dependence on foreign markets, because it tends to exhaust the fertility of their soil, and because it burdens them with the entire cost of transport of these products.

In dealing with an essentially exporting country, foreign merchants not only determine the prices of that portion of the produce which is exported, but they influence also, owing to the variations in their demand, the prices of all the rest of the produce which is consumed in the land of origin. On the other hand, the foreign nations inundate the agricultural countries with their manufactures; and thus they are enabled, in both ways, to get the better of them.

The exportation of agricultural produce deprives the soil of the benefit of that transformation of matter, by means of which the products of the earth reinvest it with a fertilising power in the shape of manure. When the consumers are close at hand, when there are great industrial communities adjoining the land under cultivation, the detritus of their consumption goes to fecundate that land, and the productive capacity of the soil continually increases and becomes more and more able to maintain a growing population. When, on the contrary, agricultural produce is exported to a distance, the ground, deprived of its fertilising elements, gradually loses its power, and its productiveness is ever on the wane.[1]

Finally, according to the author of the *Principles of Social Science*, agriculture pursued alone is unremunerative, and the export of its products is injurious, because the cost of their transport is entirely thrown upon the exporting country. The conveyance of goods to a distance is most expensive; it is the heaviest tax paid by producers, and it ought to be diminished as much as possible by bringing the consumers near to them. Agricultural products and raw materials are the

---

[1] See, for example, *Principles of Social Science*, vol. ii. pp. 65, 66 ; and *The Past, Present*, etc., p. 307.

goods the carriage of which costs dearest; and their producers, who are obliged to send them to a distance and to pay for their transport, suffer a serious loss.[1]

To remedy all these ills and to restore to society the beneficent harmony of natural laws, recourse must be had to an opportune economic policy. Such a policy must reinvest inland trade with all the true importance that was not denied to it by Adam Smith, whom Carey is so fond of quoting. It must endeavour to curb international commerce, which is detrimental to inland traffic, and not lose sight of the enormous loss of labour that is entailed by the exportation of cotton, wool, and other natural products in their raw condition, in order to import them subsequently in the shape of tissues and other manufactures.

Internal commerce creates towns by stimulating an infinite local demand for labour, and gives stability to economical life. International trade ruins villages and creates great centres, agglomerations of misery and speculation. A fatal deterioration is the lot of all those countries that sacrifice local commerce to international trade.

A good economic policy ought, therefore, to assign the first place to internal commerce by encouraging the association and concentration of labour with a co-ordinate development of agriculture and of manufactures, by the instrumentality of which producers and consumers are placed side by side. Manufactures as well as agriculture are necessary for a country; and those nations which are either exclusively agricultural or else exclusively manufacturing cannot be prosperous and happy. The economic policy can, however, ensure such a state of prosperity and happiness by promoting, by means of customs protection, agriculture as well as manufactures, by encouraging that complex economical co-operation which fosters the progressive growth of means of production and economic forces, and hence ensures the general well-being.[2]

And thus we arrive at protection, which is the final word of all Carey's system. Absolute, complete, continual protection, which makes no distinction between one country and another, one period and another, or between manufactures and agriculture, a protection which becomes a kind of *Deus ex machina*

[1] *Principles of Social Science, passim.*   [2] Work mentioned, *passim.*

for setting in motion that supreme and sublime law of natural harmony which, according to Carey, is the mainspring of all social phenomena.

30. But the whole of this harmonious edifice, so pompously reared by Carey in his voluminous treatises, trembles and vanishes, for the most part, at the lightest breath of criticism, which may be directed against it, either from the standpoint of general views or from that of the particular position of the United States, of which Carey is apparently the theorist.

The harmony of interests, which gave such satisfaction to the optimists, is, in very truth, but a beautiful dream which the American economist has fashioned into a system by denying, on no critical grounds, some of the received economic theories, and substituting for them hypotheses and even assertions that are quite gratuitous, whilst what little truth that there is in them in no way warrants the conclusions which he draws from them.

Carey's theory of value, which assumes labour to be its only cause, is partial inasmuch as it altogether loses sight of utility; and the providential tendency which he discovers in the value of capital and of products to diminish in comparison with that of labour, if true at times, is only partially so, because the absolute and relative limitations of quantity must be taken into consideration, which cause an increase in the value of mineral and agricultural products. And the theory of the cost of reproduction as a measure of value throws no appreciable light on this complex phenomenon, as it merely postpones the question, in that it determines labour by virtue of the cost of another product; whilst it really adds nothing new to Ricardo's theory. In fact, as Lexis justly remarks,[1] Ricardo assumed implicitly that the conditions of production would remain unaltered; and it is evident that should they improve, value will be determined on the basis of the actual and not the past cost. While Ricardo has considered society at a static moment, Carey has looked upon it in a dynamic state, and has, moreover, supposed that all social modifications are for the best.[2] So that when we thoroughly understand

[1] See "H. C. Carey," in the *Handwörterbuch der Staatwissenschaften*, Jena.
[2] Held, *Carey's Socialwissenschaft und das Mercantilsystem*, Würzburg, Stuber, 1866, p. 91.

Ricardo's theory, we see that Carey adds nothing new to it, except this last somewhat inaccurate hypothesis.

Carey's theory of distribution betrays a great confusion of thought, and is founded on gratuitous assertions which are not amenable to the most elementary criticism. The American economist confounds interest, profit, and land rent; looks upon the last as a compensation for capital; confuses capital with money by making the rate of interest depend upon the quantity of specie; nor does he distinguish between interest and profit, and he expounds a doctrine which he calls the theory of interest—but which ought rather to be called the theory of profit—and which, as Böhm Bawerk has demonstrated, is a tissue of vulgar errors![1]

Carey's theory of wages, which we have explained, and which some critics have deemed the best part of his system of economy, is entirely based upon the hypothesis that, as production increases and the value of products diminish, wages rise in a larger proportion than does the return on capital.

But Carey, who treats this grave question in the most superficial way, has given no proof of his supposed law, and he has based it on purely abstract considerations, without taking into account any of those matters of fact which might modify it. And even if we admit for a moment that the tendency of interest and of profits to a relative fall is sure and continuous, and leave out of consideration the opposite phenomenon of land rent, which Carey denies, how are we, even then, to shut our eyes to the circumstances of labour-competition, circumstances such that, in the capitalistic system of to-day, labour is a commodity the vendors of which find themselves normally in a state of inferiority as compared with the purchasers? Nor is it possible, as Jenks observes, that the depression of prices, which follows in the wake of increased production, should so work that the benefit of this state of things should redound entirely to consumers, without in any way augmenting profits or wages.[2]

Carey's law has in it an element of abstract truth, in that the interests of workmen and capitalists are not necessarily in absolute antagonism, since, if there be an increase of products,

[1] *Kapital und Kapitalzins*, vol. i., Innsbruck, 1884, pp. 179-189.
[2] Work mentioned, p. 85.

the benefit may be shared by all. But not only is the fact uncorroborated, but it is altogether false, that the part which in our actual social state tends to augment, is that which falls to the workman; and, moreover, to deny the existence of an antagonism of interests is to shut our eyes to the light, either because at any given moment the quantity of the product being determined, a conflict arises to decide who shall obtain the larger share, or else because, even when products increase, competition always steps in (generally, in existing circumstances, to the disadvantage of workmen) to settle who shall reap the whole profit, or between whom and in what proportions it shall be divided.

But Carey's theory of distribution is founded, as we have said, on a denial of the principles of population and of rent, as well as on the hypothetical law of wages, which we have just criticised. As to population, he does not advance any serious argument against the Malthusian theory, nor does he furnish any proof of his asserted law of accumulation, which ought to proceed at the same rate as the growth of population, satisfying all its wants. And only from a certain point of view is it discernible that his opposition to Malthus has in it a glimmering of truth, in that he attributes the actual excess of population to social and not natural causes. Only that instead of discovering such causes in a bad method of wealth-distribution, Carey falls foul of the system of circulation and commercial policy. Besides this, his criticism of Ricardo's theory is based upon a misconception of the theory itself, and, even if Carey's law of the succession of cultivation be true, and true likewise that cultivation ever tends to pass from scantily productive lands to those of greater fertility, which may perhaps be the case sometimes in new countries at the outset of agriculture, but certainly does not occur, or only very exceptionally, in old ones—even then Ricardo's law in no way affects the question, for it is founded not on a successive transition to land of greater fertility, but on the necessity of simultaneously tilling soils of different degrees of productiveness, whereby the owners of the richer lands benefit more largely than their neighbours. Thus it is that the whole of Carey's harmonious system, even though containing some scintillas of truth (which, indeed, is the case with every theory, however erroneous), falls to pieces at the first touch of criticism, and can certainly not be used as a basis for further deductions.

31. From what we have already said, it is evident without further observations, which would only lead us far beyond our set purpose, that Carey's fundamental ideas that social ill-being is the result of an error in economic policy, and that the remedy is to be sought for in a reform of commercial policy, are altogether faulty.

The very starting-points, therefore, of the American economist's theory of international trade are wanting. But even if, disregarding this, we come to consider the theory itself, we shall find that, although here too occasional grains of truth are not wanting, it cannot stand fair criticism.

That the co-existence and co-operation of agriculture and manufactures is useful; that by this means a concentration of life is ensured which favours progress, and that agriculture alone makes for isolation and a slower advance of civilisation and also of wealth in a country—all these are ideas which contain the element of truth, and, indeed, much of it; so much so that they have been expressed by many writers both for and against protection, long before Carey's time, and he cannot in any way lay claim to their paternity.

But from these premises to Carey's deduction, which is without any distinctions or reservations to the effect that the remedy for existing ills lies in a system of protection that encourages manufactures as well as agriculture, there is a great gap.

As a matter of fact, the simply agricultural phase is one through which nearly all nations must pass; and the other productive industries are subsequently developed in proportion to local fitness. Now, nothing tells us that such a gradual development may not occur of itself spontaneously; whilst of one thing we may be certain, and that is that it will take place differently in different countries, and that according to their nature some will remain exclusively or predominantly agricultural, whilst others will in their development balance the culture of the soil with the other industrial arts.

In order to accept Carey's thesis, it would be necessary, putting all other considerations aside, to demonstrate that a spontaneous development of manufactures side by side with agriculture would not be possible, but that it would be feasible by means of protection, and equally so in all countries, for Carey makes no distinctions; and, finally, that the results obtained by every nation would compensate them for the evils that would inevitably be wrought by the violation and suppression of their natural aptitudes. It may be added that Carey says nothing as to the moment when protection should intervene to produce these wonderful results, or when its operation should be suspended.

In fact, protection, which within certain defined limits of time and space, and in certain historical situations, may be reasonable, becomes, when presented in this fashion, simply irrational and absolutely absurd.

One merit must not be denied to Carey: it is that of having recognised the importance of agriculture, which he places on a level with that of manufactures, and of having copiously illustrated the significance of inland commerce as compared with foreign trade. The first of these points is frequently forgotten by protectionists, the second by free-traders; and yet it is essential that the latter question especially should not be lost sight of, as the error of attributing to international trade a much greater importance than it really possesses, is exceedingly common and damaging.

We must not, however, exaggerate on the other side; and the undue prominence given by Carey to domestic commerce leads him, as we shall presently see, to the absurdity of complete isolation.

We have seen how he tries to draw an inference in favour of protection from his law of the succession of cultivations, a law which he tells us, leads necessarily to protectionism.

Now let us for a moment admit that the more fertile land is cultivated last, and let us also grant that its products (meat, garden and dairy produce), are more difficult to transport to distant countries than the cereals raised on less productive soil. We may remark in parenthesis that the improvements in means of transport now allow of fresh meat being brought to England from Australia, and oranges to the United States from Sicily, whilst even milk, by being condensed, may be taken immense distances without losing its chief qualities. But even if we disregard this, it seems evident that an intensive culture — which is in reality what Carey means—naturally follows a large growth of population, which concentrates itself, and from which industries spontaneously spring with more or less alacrity and profusion. For this to occur there is no need of industrial protection, for an intensive system of agriculture, with a rational method of cattle-rearing, with specialised and perfected cultures, naturally develops itself in proportion to the population, and keeps pace with its requirements, however vast and complex they may be. Whether there be a more or less numerous class of artisans in the country is, from this point of view, of secondary importance: the main thing is the growth of population and the increase of and variety in the requirements of the inhabitants.

The dependence of nations which export agricultural produce upon foreign markets, which Carey has observed, is true; but can it be said that it is not reciprocal, or, indeed, that it is not more often of greater risk to the importing than to the exporting countries? Then the danger that one nation by flooding another with its manufactures might arrest its industrial development and acquire a certain supremacy over it, is to a certain extent real, as we have seen elsewhere, in particular circumstances; but when it is assumed generally and absolutely, as Carey does, it loses all seriousness; for if we are dealing with countries similarly situated, or with industries that are truly adapted to the territory, it is not possible that their development could be hindered for any length of time by foreign competition, or that one people should establish a lasting supremacy over the other.

But Carey's most characteristic ideas—and one of them is sufficiently original — are those regarding the exhaustion of the soil in consequence of the exportation of its products, and concerning the loss undergone by exporting countries in the transport of their commodities to distant lands.

The idea that an exporting agriculture exhausts the fertility of the soil because it does not restore to it its vital energies by means of the detritus of consumption effected close to the place of production, has in it some element of truth, but not sufficient to justify Carey's thesis.

CHAP. III *PROTECTIONISM IN THE UNITED STATES* 369

Even in the countries where the population is most densely concentrated, the sewage of the great cities, which would be of such great use for manuring purposes, is much neglected; and no satisfactory solution has yet been found for the problem.

On the other hand, the progress of agricultural chemistry enables us largely to counteract the exhaustive tendencies of land cultivation by means of artificial manures. But, even if we admit that the evil effects of these tendencies were acutely felt, and that protection, by encouraging manufacturing centralisation, could remedy them, would it not be questionable whether the benefit would not be altogether neutralised by the greater cost of the national manufactures as compared with the imports for which they have been substituted?

No less ill-founded is Carey's opinion on the cost of transport. That it is a burden on the consumer, and that the production ought consequently to be effected as near as possible to the place of consumption, appears to us evident; but it is equally evident that when the cheapness of production outweighs the expense of transport, or when the productive forces of a country can be more profitably directed to other industries, then importation would prove advantageous. Carey seems unable to persuade himself that it could be useful to export raw cotton in order to bring it back again in a manufactured condition; and yet it is clear that it is beneficial whenever such manufactures cost less than it would have cost to produce them in the country, or when this country could more greatly benefit by the production of other goods.

And besides, if the expenses of transport were so very heavy, they alone would exercise a protective influence, by promoting the home production of goods, which would be able to undersell their foreign rivals handicapped by heavier freightage.[1]

Carey makes none of those distinctions or previsions for the future which are to be found in other writers, and which make the doctrine of protection reasonable; and, consequently, his views are inadmissible.

And, moreover, it is a purely arbitrary assertion that, because the cost of transporting agricultural produce is for its bulk higher than that of manufactures, therefore all this cost

[1] John Stuart Mill, *Principles of Political Economy*, book. v. chap. x. § 1.

2 B

should be borne by the exporting country. In order for that to occur, it would be necessary for the latter to be in an inferior position to the importing one. Now Jenks observes[1] that as far as England and the United States are concerned, this supposition is false, since Great Britain stands in greater need of raw materials and of agricultural produce than do the United States of manufactured articles. The manufacturer is as anxious to sell his wares as the farmer is.

But the most notable feature, and at the same time the greatest defect in Carey's system, is the absolute value which he attaches to protection, and the constant and universal character which he assigns to it.

In fact, as we have already pointed out in another chapter, and as we shall see yet more clearly, the arguments brought to bear on protectionism by Carey had already been more or less fully developed, and he adds little to their variety, and merely repeats them with greater emphasis and at greater length.

But his true originality lies in this last point; and it may really be said that he was the first to formulate the absolute theory of protectionism, and can lay the flattering unction to his soul of having been the forerunner of the so-called "Chinese Wall Men."

After having at first warmly defended free-trade, and then guardedly advocated protection, referring to it as a means of ultimately attaining commercial liberty, Carey, in his last works, and notably in his *Principles of Social Science*, throws all reservations to the winds and declares himself the henchman of absolute and unrestricted protectionism. Freedom of trade ceases to be an ideal, however remote: his ideal now is association and concentration through the co-existence of industry and agriculture, and the approximation of producers to consumers; and the means to attain this is for all and in all conceivable circumstances a most complete protective system. Free-trade always brings about ruin; protection general well-being; and, if on some exceedingly rare occasion he—with his frequent contradictions—hints at the possibility of free-trade ultimately taking the place of protection, he never for all that recommends moderate duties as a step in

[1] Work mentioned, p. 121.

that direction, and indeed he consistently inveighs against them for all countries. He regards protection as a lasting system, a constant principle, an infallible instrument placed in man's hands in order to attain social harmony.

We have seen in the second essay how certain circumstances, peculiar to the United States, may perhaps not justify, but explain the growth, in that country, of the strange theory of economic isolation; and we shall return to the question farther on in connection with Carey. But from the general theoretic point of view, abstraction being made of matters of fact, which may give rise to exceptions, and which may, as we have seen, justify a protective policy at given moments in the life of a nation; when, we say, we are dealing with abstract theory, there can be no room for hesitation, and to this egotistical system of isolation, falling so short of the social harmony dreamed of by Carey, we cannot do otherwise than contrast the free-trade system of solidarity and progress, which triumphs over it by the logic of its deductions, and by its harmonies which, at all events in theory, are perfectly logical.

32. Criticism of Carey's theories is completed by comparing them to mercantilism—which has been excellently done by Held, and also alluded to by Jenks, Lexis, and others.

And in truth, it is singular how much affinity there is between the old mercantilism and Carey's conception of money. He attributes no small importance to specie, looking upon it as a force that promotes production and that fulfils for society the same function that fuel does for a steam-engine. Increase of money he considers to be ever a good, and the necessary foundation for economic progress; there can never be too great a quantity of the precious metals in a country, and their abundance does not raise, but rather lowers the price of commodities, because it augments the intensity and the productiveness of economic energy. "The more abundant the supply of those (precious) metals, the more instant become the exchanges of society, the greater is the economy of mental and physical force, and the greater the power to produce commodities to be given in exchange for further supplies of these great instruments of association and combination."[1]

And even more singular is a passage in which Carey com-

[1] Carey, *Principles of Social Science*, vol. ii. p. 306.

pares capital employed in specie with capital employed in a ship or factory, and draws the conclusion that money renders to society, as a method of economising force, a much greater service than manufactures or commerce! (perhaps because it circulates faster).[1] A little farther back we alluded to Carey's false idea of interest, which he considers to be the price of money and depending on its amount. It is upon this assumption that Carey invokes protection in order to increase the quantity of specie in the country and to diminish the rate of interest.

Such ideas stand so little in need of criticism that Held's learned pages on the subject appear to us to be entirely wasted; and the only fact worthy of record is that a writer in the second half of the nineteenth century, alarmed as Carey apparently is by the consequences of a temporary scarcity of money, should confuse specie with capital, and reproduce old theories that have been exploded a couple of centuries ago: for, as Held justly remarks, and as we too have pointed out,[2] even the later mercantilists had become more clear-sighted, and recognised that an unlimited increase of money could not be good.[3]

These strange errors concerning money logically reduce Carey to the old idea of the balance of trade. He maintains, in fact, that to endow the precious metals with that stability of value which they need for their monetary functions, it is requisite that there should be in the country a prompt and regular balance in favour of trade, payable in coin.[4] Now every country that exports raw materials, exports, according to Carey, money as well, and has an unfavourable balance; and a favourable one can only be secured by nations that export manufactures and import raw materials.[5] And opposing the relative free-trade that existed in the United States at the time when he wrote (1858), he declared that although they possessed the richest gold mines, their commercial policy was impoverishing them, and creating an unfavourable balance against them.

[1] Work mentioned, vol. ii. p. 298.   [2] See this volume, pp. 33-34.
[3] Held, *Carey's Socialwissenschaft*, etc., pp. 196, 197.
[4] *Principles of Social Science*, vol. ii. p. 435.
[5] Vol. mentioned, pp. 316-322.

Now it is difficult to understand, observes Held, why a country that exports agricultural produce could not have a favourable monetary balance:[1] unless, indeed, we connect this idea with the one which we have already shown to be faulty, by which countries that export agricultural products would be necessarily obliged, in international trade, to bear the expenses of their transport. Nor is there any need to point out what an anachronism and how groundless it is to fear that an unfavourable balance might permanently deprive the country of the metals necessary as a circulating medium. Many other facts, such as, for example, a bad paper currency, may cause the disappearance of metallic money by replacing it with an inferior medium; and it is indeed singular that Carey, who invests the question with so much importance, should have been so favourable to a forced currency and have resisted its abolition! This is one of his many contradictions which makes it all the more curious that he should have believed in the balance of trade, which, necessarily implying an antagonism between nations, is a false note in his optimistic system of social harmony. Nor is it beside the mark to observe that, even in what concerns the balance of trade, Carey adopts the principles of the most uncompromising protectionism, since the later mercantilists had considerably modified their original ideas.

From Held's interesting comparisons it would appear that Carey's theory is but a reduced mercantile system; and such is the case not only with regard to details and to the particular doctrines which we have touched upon, but likewise in its general spirit. It is quite true that the American economist combats the idea of the industrial and commercial ascendency of one nation over another; but, as Held remarks,[2] some of the mercantilists had already transformed that idea into one of national industrial autonomy. This in reality is the key-note of Carey's system; this the practical issue of the association of agriculture with manufactures, and of the approximation of producers to consumers.

If, therefore, after criticising Carey's system from a theoretical point of view, we consider it from the standpoint of the history of economic doctrines, we shall arrive at the con-

[1] Work mentioned, pp. 199, 200. [2] Work mentioned, p. 163.

clusion that it constitutes a retrograde movement of notable importance.

33. Copious and interesting are the researches made by Lange[1] and by Jenks[2] into the method adopted by Carey, and they complete its critical analysis from the theoretical point of view. From these investigations we draw a conclusion which alone is sufficient to account for the scant value of Carey's scientific production; he is wanting in method, we might almost say that he had no very precise idea of what method meant. In fact, as Jenks acutely remarks, he begins by praising Ricardo's method, and then says that the only true method in dealing with social science is that of induction; he argues against John Stuart Mill's political economy, saying that it is founded on hypotheses, and then adduces in proof of his theories of value and of wages what Robinson Crusoe would have done in his island. From the life of Robinson Crusoe, however, Carey often passes on to history and to facts in confirmation of his views; but in what way does he apply the inductive method to which he frequently condescends? His volumes will tell. He chooses, without any orderly research, those facts and those statistics which tally with his theories, leaving all others aside; he does not quote the sources of his information, nor give any clues for referring to them; he often adduces inaccurate facts and false data. Then without any analysis or investigation whatever, he attributes all the facts he has arrayed to one preconceived cause, namely, commercial policy, and never so much as troubles to observe whether these given effects could not, in the complexity of social phenomena, be assigned to any other causes. Thus he applies, on foundations that are often defective, that faulty method of reasoning which is commonly expressed by the Latin saying: *post hoc ergo propter hoc.*

It is hardly necessary to say that such a mode of applying the inductive method is false and erroneous, and renders valueless the investigations which depend on it; but we may point out that it serves to discredit inductive reasoning by artificially adapting facts to any preconceived theory. It is sufficient to take in hand one of Carey's volumes, especially of the *Prin-*

---
[1] *Mill's Ansichten über die sociale Frage*, Duisburg, 1866.
[2] Work mentioned, pp. 143-154.

ciples of Social Science, to see at once that this is the plan which he follows in his researches, when he does not prefer— in order to give a greater scientific weight to his opinions— to refer to the fable of Robinson Crusoe and his man Friday.

Such a system naturally falls to pieces of itself, not only on account of its untruthfulness, but chiefly in consequence of the strange contradictions into which the ingenuous author is constantly falling. To these contradictions we have had occasion more than once to refer in dealing with his theories, but no less singular are those to be met with in the facts which he quotes and the judgments which he pronounces, as, for instance, when in many passages of *Principles of Social Science* he hurls his thunderbolts against England, accusing her of having, by her fatal commercial policy, brought ruin upon other countries and upon herself,—whilst elsewhere he calls England the richest country in the world, and invites other nations to follow her example.

34. We may appear to deal too severely with Carey, and to take too little into consideration the environment in which he lived and which might perhaps explain and justify his views. But we do not think that even this investigation, which we are about to make, can modify to any appreciable extent the general opinion which we have formed of this American economist. If it could really be said that his system reflected the surroundings in which it was evolved, and was the theoretical expression of those circumstances; if it had its origin in the historical condition of the United States in his own times, and was true to it, its theoretical value would certainly be far greater, and Carey could merely be reproached for having generalised that which was true only of his own country and his own time. The influence of his American surroundings upon Carey's ideas are evident enough; but the strange thing is that this influence seems to affect him against the grain, so to speak, and causes him to formulate theories which, even if partly and momentarily true, seemed no longer to be so when he proclaims them with so much emphasis. Carey lived more than eighty years, his life may be said to have included all the stages through which the great American nation passed in its social-economic evolution, from its foundation to the most recent times (he died in 1879); his

scientific activity lasted more than forty years, from 1835 to 1879. During this period the economic history of the United States shows the greatest transformations, a whole evolution, in fact, from which the country emerged in a totally different condition; the last phase alone—that of industrial depression —is posterior to Carey, only having set in during the last years of his life.

Now the evolution of Carey's ideas does not proceed hand in hand with that of his American environment, and partly indeed it goes in an absolutely contrary direction. For if the situation of the United States could in the beginning justify an optimistic social system, that, as we shall see, was no longer possible at a later date; but Carey maintains to the very end his system of economic and social harmonies, based upon facts which, if true at a given period, had long since ceased to be so. And, on the contrary, whilst in his first works, beginning from 1835, he is a perfect free-trader, at an epoch when the then condition of the United States offered some justification for protection (which, though already out of date, would have responded to a state of affairs by no means remote); later on Carey became a protectionist in the 1850-1860 period, just when protection lost all *raison d'être* and fulfilled none of the requirements of the country.

It might perhaps be said that Carey proved to be a prophet, since he imagined a system of absolute protection which later on enjoyed great popularity throughout the land; but if there is some truth in this (and we shall see presently what merit appertains to it), it in no way alters our judgment, that, on the whole, Carey's system is an anachronism, and while altogether false as a general conception, it is not even adapted to the historical circumstances in which it was conceived.

This is what we now propose to demonstrate at somewhat greater length.

35. The justification most frequently given of the optimism of Carey's system is that it naturally arises in the contemplation of a young and progressive nation furnished with abundant resources and boundless future prospects.[1] There is undoubtedly much truth in this explanation, and it is natural

[1] Ingram, *History*, etc., p. 172.

that in a new country possessing a vast extent of free land and a multiplicity of rich natural resources, a country still scantily inhabited, where the great industries had not yet been developed, nor any of those phenomena which result from the pressure of population, the exhaustion of the soil, etc., had yet manifested themselves, general ill-being and social friction should not show itself, and that consequently a rose-coloured picture of the economic and social outlook should be drawn. But at Carey's time, and particularly at the beginning of the latter half of the century, this was by no means a correct view of the United States. It is true that then as now the immense riches of the American territory and the ceaseless energy of its people spread over it a general well-being far greater than is the case in Europe, and which partly affects even the labourers; but this relative well-being does not exclude hardships endured by large numbers, nor does it in any way prevent those antagonisms and social struggles which in the United States, as elsewhere, are becoming every day more acute.

Towards the middle of the century the free land that was easily accessible in the United States was far from being as plentiful as it was at first; the decline in the productiveness of the soil began to show itself, and whilst it reduced profits, it tended at the same time to lower wages, and this downward tendency became much more sensible about 1870, and was accompanied by a remarkable depression of the working classes.[1]

Jenks observes that if in his theory of value, Carey asserts the tendency of the price of products to fall constantly without heeding the great exception of agricultural produce, it is owing to the fact that he has in his mind's eye the United States, where, on account of the vast extent of free and fertile land, the cost of production of agricultural produce was still very low.[2] Wright's statistical researches, however, show us how considerable was the rise in the prices of American agricultural produce from 1830 to 1860; to mention a few instances only, the price of corn increased by 21·4 per cent, that of flour by 26, that of rice by 36, that of butter by 40, that of beef by 65·8, that of fuel by 55, and that of candles by 68 per cent.[3]

[1] See Loria, *Analisi*, vol. ii. pp. 253, 254.   [2] Work mentioned, pp. 30, 31.
[3] See *Comparative Wages*, etc., in the accompanying tables.

In the same way does Held justify, at all events partly, Carey's optimistic law of wages, remarking that it represents the happy, though transitory, state of America; but Wright's accurate figures tell us, on the contrary, that although wages rose in the United States from 1830 to 1880, the general condition of the factory hands deteriorated.[1]

In the circumstances of his times, too, there is to be found some excuse for Carey's denial of the laws of population and of rent, but no complete justification of his views. America was certainly not yet oppressed by over-population;[2] and, as to the theory of rent, that too may to a certain extent be justified, if we take Ingram's view that Carey, recollecting the traditions of the colonisation of his country, and seeing with his own eyes the rapid settlement on American land, and the grave difficulties to which it gave rise, exaggerated the importance given to the labour involved, and attributed to it, and hence to a legitimate return on capital invested, the whole of the rent, in opposition to Ricardo's theory.[3]

It is probable that about the middle of the century the phenomenon of land rent was less widespread, and certainly less important socially, in the United States than in European countries; but its significance was being more appreciated day by day, so that if Carey had really understood the question, he could not have failed to be struck with its importance. The reasons which, as we saw, justified Hamilton, are not applicable to Carey, and it is his own works, indeed, that accuse him of having criticised Ricardo without understanding him. As a matter of fact, the phenomenon of the diminishing return of the soil was, as we have already noted, so evident, even in America, that Carey could not deny it; but, unable in the least degree to grasp its true cause and bearings, he referred it to the dispersion of agriculture and to the exhaustive tendency of the exportation of land-produce.

If, therefore, Carey's optimistic theory might at the outset find some justification in his environment, such a justification was ever losing force, whilst he, on the contrary, persisted in a system, the optimism of which, far from being true to nature, offers a striking contrast to the accumulating

[1] Work mentioned, pp. 32-35.   [2] See Roscher, *Geschichte*, etc., p. 1013.
[3] Work mentioned, pp. 173-174.

social difficulties with which the United States bristle, and must be regarded, even in his own time, as a strange anachronism.[1]

36. But the lack of agreement between Carey's system and the surroundings in which it was evolved 'is even more manifest when we consider its fundamental theory, that regarding international trade and protection. This theory was principally developed in Carey's two leading works, *The Past, the Present and the Future*, and *Principles of Social Science*, published, the first in 1848, the other in 1858-1859.

To convince ourselves of the fact that, at this era, Carey's theory is an anachronism, it is only necessary to refer to what we have said in the fifth chapter of the second essay in this volume. Carey describes the ruin of exclusively agricultural countries, maintains the necessity of associating manufactures with agriculture, and accuses the relatively free-trade system, which at that time prevailed in his country, of undermining its prosperity by neglecting to ensure this association. But we have clearly seen that this could by no means be said of the United States, where, between 1840 and 1850, manufacturing industries had been established on solid foundations and had greatly flourished and multiplied, whilst between 1850 and 1860 manufactures had progressed with giant strides, and had brought about a veritable golden age.[2]

During the preceding years it was easy to understand the necessity for the development of manufactures and the opportuneness of protection for this end; but at the time of which we are now speaking this development was proceeding rapidly and without assistance. Carey's insistence, in demanding the association of manufactures with agriculture, and the bringing together of producers and consumers, can only be explained, therefore, by supposing that he desired these things universally,

---

[1] Jenks (see work quoted, pp. 103, 104) adroitly compares Carey to George. Carey lived in the eastern States, where wealth accumulated rapidly, chiefly owing to manufactures, and speculation on land was neglected. George, on the contrary, was brought up amid the great land speculations of California. Hence the all-importance given by the latter to the question of rent, and its scant consideration at Carey's hands.

[2] The golden age of manufactures and capitalism; not that of the labourers, whose condition, though better at first, was beginning to be affected by the entire occupation of accessible free land.

and that, in spite of the difference of climate, of soil, and of habits, manufactures should be developed, and that immediately, in all the States of the American union, in the southern ones as well as in those of the north. And this is clearly what he means when he invites South Carolina, Virginia, and the other States to follow the example of Massachusetts—the manufacturing district *par excellence*. It would be loss of time to refute such an argument.

But this is not all. Who could find fault with List, the great apostle of railways, for not having sufficiently prognosticated the revolutionary effects of steam navigation upon the transport of goods? But who, on the other hand, can excuse Carey for having, at a period little remote from our own times, so greatly exaggerated the importance of the cost of transport between America and Europe?

And thus, strange as is the anachronism of Carey's resuscitation in our days of the doctrines of old mercantilism, no less strange and out of place is it that he should so energetically preach protection between 1850 and 1860, when that idea was no longer popular, and when the capitalistic manufactures, now consolidated and strong, required no further aid from the state.

Nor is it easy in Carey's time to justify his aversion to the settlement of the far west. From the capitalistic point of view, it was, as we have seen, perfectly explicable in List's days; but Carey systematically opposes it at a period when to work for hire was the normal condition of the American labourer, and free land was far away and required considerable capital for its cultivation.

And besides this, Carey's views are still less justifiable on other grounds. As he denied the land rent and maintained that the land last cultivated was the best, he could not have been actuated by the fear that the tilling of less fertile soil would increase the rent, to the detriment of capitalists.

From every point of view, therefore, Carey's system is unadapted to the circumstances of his times, and besides being based on false theories, it appears to us as an anachronism as well.

37. A few remarks may, however, be admitted which tell in Carey's favour. Although he published his prin-

cipal works on protection at an epoch when the country stood in no need of such legislation, shortly afterwards, at the conclusion of the War of Secession, the great period of protectionist reaction set in; and, moreover, as we have already seen, he advocated a system of absolute protection, similar to that of its most recent American partisans. It may also be observed that in attributing supreme importance to home markets, and disregarding international trade, he may perhaps have foreseen those circumstances which in the United States could alone have explained such uncompromising protectionism.

But these remarks can only give a very partial historical justification to Carey's system, and in no way invalidate our preceding judgments.

We have seen that the first causes of the protectionist revival which followed the war were purely accidental, and were the consequences of the war itself; whilst the maintenance and aggravation of protection was due to facts of later occurrence, to the capitalistic crisis, and to industrial depression. Now all this has nothing to do with Carey and his system; since he could neither have foreseen the accidental protectionist effects of a war which broke out two years after the publication of *Principles of Social Science,* nor have guessed the advent of that industrial depression, which is so characteristic of the last twenty years and plays so large a part in the protectionism of to-day.

In one matter only was Carey perhaps in advance of his times—he understood the ever-increasing importance accruing to the inland market of the vast American territory; he felt that if there was a country in the world where economic autonomy was conceivable, it was the United States. And although even this idea did not originate with him, for, as we have pointed out more than once in the preceding essay, it had been elaborated during the whole of the century, it nevertheless was capable, if not of historical justification, at all events of adequate explanation. And while all the rest of Carey's system was a reflection on times past and gone for ever, this idea concerned the future even more than the present, and a future by no means in accordance with his own aspirations; a future in which the colonisation of the far west having been fully accomplished—against which he was so strongly prejudiced—the American Union would be able to offer some substantial justification for its inhumanitarian endeavour to "stand alone," thanks to the variety of its natural resources, which should be drawn together by a perfect network of roads and railways, from the cold regions of the north, the temperate zones, and the fertile fields of the tropics—in a word, from the Atlantic to the Pacific shores.

38. And now it is easy to come to a conclusion. Henry C. Carey certainly does not deserve even the ephemeral success which his writings obtained at the hands of international opinion; and modest indeed is the place to be assigned to him in the history of economic science.

We say nothing of the enthusiasm of his followers, for it is some time since it has evaporated; but we cannot really understand what the important services were which, according even to impartial writers, he is said to have rendered to science. He assuredly did not render them by his method of research, not by his strange and paradoxical coupling of optimism and protectionism, to which, however, a large part of his good fortune was due, nor yet by the originality of his theories, for it would be hard to say what merit and utility accrue to the originality of theories that are substantially false, often based on mere uncorroborated assertions, and not infrequently reproduced, even without novelty of form, from old doctrines, now of historical interest only.

If Carey's services consist of having refurbished the old ideas of mercantilism, we are indeed unable to grant him any great praise.

But even if there be some merit in the general conception of Carey's system, which we greatly doubt, of slight value indeed is his theory of protection.

We do not now wish to renew the comparisons which we have repeatedly made, and which naturally suggest themselves from our criticisms of the theories of Hamilton, List, and Carey. The conclusion which we draw from them is that Carey's protectionist theory is lacking in originality, since the arguments on which it is founded had all been more or less previously enunciated by those two great and true founders of protectionism; and had, moreover, been put forward at a time when they found no little justification in the historical circumstances of the country, whilst Carey's system, on the contrary, in no way responds to its environment. But Carey disassociates himself from his predecessors on one point especially: they, and List in particular, do not deny the theory of free-trade, and were only bent on making a great exception by means of protection, and on investing the latter with historical attributes and placing its *raison d'être* on rational and scientific bases. Nothing of the kind is to be met with in Carey, whose system of absolute protection, which has been completely refuted by economic science, marks a step backwards in the theory of protectionism, and turns it aside from that new and luminous path to which Frederick List had directed it, whilst it finds but an inadequate justification in American surroundings. In this respect, perhaps Carey was unconsciously the theorist of the future for the United States, but in all other ways he was the theorist of the past; and we cannot consider as otherwise than just the severe judgment passed upon him by Held, to the effect that instead of being, as was claimed for him, the leading economist of his own epoch, he was only a reminiscence of centuries gone by.[1]

The most just, however, and at the same time the most severe sentence on Carey, is that which time has pronounced. In fact, he almost outlived his fame; his system answered so little to the requirements of his own country, that his most numerous followers were to be found in Europe; nor was it long before here, too, his star had set. In the United States most of the contemporary economists followed other paths; few, and of no great weight, were these led on by Carey; the best of them, Thompson, did but faithfully re-edit his leader's ideas, without adding anything new or supporting them with fresh arguments.[2] And the protectionists of to-day no longer speak of Carey or draw inspirations from his works; a sign that even that adaptability of his theories to recent times, to which we alluded, is but apparent, and that his system, which even thirty years ago was deficient in vitality, is more so now than ever.

[1] Work mentioned, p. 213.
[2] *Vide* Robert Ellis Thompson, *Political Economy*, Philadelphia, Porter, 1882.

CHAPTER IV

SIMON N. PATTEN

39. Among the American economists of the present day, Professor Simon N. Patten is certainly one of the boldest and most prolific; and he is undoubtedly one of the very few in the large army of living protectionist writers in the United States who treat the question of international trade from a scientific standpoint, and almost the only one among them who displays any real originality.[1]

Indeed, in his numerous and varied works Patten always shows the questions in a new light, and original ideas are frequently to be met with; but it must be observed that the impatient and painstaking effort for novelty, which is perhaps the author's principal characteristic, often mars the clearness of his conceptions, in which the freshness of form and diction does not always reveal a corresponding originality of scientific matter. This fault, by no means a small one, is frequently a distinguishing trait of the numerous followers of the Austrian school, whose so-called scientific conquests have more often proved to be merely nominal; nor is it surprising to meet with it in Patten, who is directly attached to this school by his tendencies and his method, though he departs from it in some particulars.

Mr. Patten is professor of political economy in the Wharton School of Finance and Economy in the University of Philadelphia—that almost legendary school of protectionism, of which so much has been spoken. But we do not wish to enter here into a question which it would be useless to discuss;

[1] Of Gunton, another American protectionist of to-day, whose writings deserve attention, we spoke in the sixth chapter of the second essay of this volume.

it is our business to judge of theories and nothing else. That the ideas which inspired the beneficent founder of this school were purely protectionist does not appear to us to admit of doubt, and that he should have desired that these principles should be taught seems to be expressed clearly enough in the syllabus of instruction drawn up by him, and to which, in its general features, the administrators of the University of Philadelphia are bound to conform.[1] It is laid down, in fact, by Wharton in the guiding rules for the education which he planned for the school which he had founded, that, among other things, it should be taught: "How a great nation should be, as far as possible, self-sufficient, maintaining a proper balance between agriculture, mining, and manufactures, and supplying its own wants . . . how by suitable tariff legislation a nation may keep its productive industry active, cheapen the cost of commodities, and oblige foreigners to sell to it at low prices, while contributing largely toward defraying the expenses of its government; and lastly, the necessity for each nation to care for its own, and to maintain by all suitable means its industrial and financial independence, the right and duty of national self-protection must be firmly asserted and demonstrated."[2]

If the origin of the Wharton School, therefore, is somewhat open to suspicion, and calculated at first sight to raise doubts regarding the scientific character of the education imparted; on the other hand, its records up to the present date, the names on its professorial staff, its numerous scientific publications, and above all Patten's writings and the works of his disciples, go a long way to allay these misgivings. Anyhow, the very fact that Patten's ideas took birth in a radically protectionist environment, together with the marked originality which characterises them, appear to us a sufficient justification for having selected him for detailed notice; and we do not think we are far from the truth in stating that Patten's works are the most notable theoretical products of American protectionism of the present day.

We do not propose to enter into at any length, or to

[1] The Wharton School was founded in 1881 by Joseph Wharton, a wealthy manufacturer, of protectionist tendencies, by means of a gift of 100,000 dollars, to which he added 25,000 for a library.

[2] J. Wharton, *Is a College Education advantageous to a Business Man?* Philadelphia, 1890, pp. 32-34.

criticise all the ideas expounded by Patten in his numerous writings, still less to follow him in his frequent abstract elucubrations, based on the utilitarian theory. Besides other reasons, the co-ordination of all these ideas would be no easy matter, for although they are often connected by a chain of reasoning, they do not really form an organised whole: the author has probably not yet elaborated a complete system in his mind, and his striving after novelty frequently leads, as we shall see, to contradictions.

We will confine ourselves to a brief examination of the points which seem to us of greater importance, and above all to the author's theory of protection.[1]

40. The most salient features in Professor Patten's writings are: the importance and the pre-eminence which among economic facts he assigns to consumption, and his theory of the transformation of diet; the distinction between static and dynamic economy, the opposition between these two types of economy, and his theory of prosperity; and, finally, the principles of protection which follow from these conceptions.

His particular theory of consumption, although chiefly expounded in his work on the *Consumption of Wealth*, holds a prominent place likewise in his other principal studies, of which they may indeed be said to form the groundwork; and it will be needful to give it a somewhat detailed examination.

Professor Patten considers the evolution of our requirements and consumption from an altogether novel point of view. He denies the unrestrictedly progressive tendency of human appetites, and maintains that the law of consumption establishes the fact that the appetites of men tend to diminish.

[1] The following appear to be Professor Patten's more important works:—(1) *The Premises of Political Economy*, Philadelphia, Lippincott, 1885; (2) *The Consumption of Wealth*, Philad., Univer. of Penn., 1889; (3) *The Economic Basis of Protection*, Philad., Lippincott, 1890; (4) *The Theory of Dynamic Economics*, Philad., Univer. of Penn., 1892. Besides these Professor Patten, who is evidently a hard worker, has published other writings, written in a very brief period of time, among them, *The Stability of Prices* (Am. Econ. Ass., 1889); *The Principles of Rational Taxation* (Philad., 1889); *Malthus and Ricardo* (Am. Ec. Ass., 1889); *The Educational Value of Political Economy* (Am. Ec. Ass., 1890), etc. We are indebted to Professor Patten's courtesy to have been able to take notes from these works, to some of which we should not otherwise have had ready access. Professor Patten too has been good enough to furnish us by letter with copious explanations regarding his theory, and although differing profoundly from him, we are sincerely obliged to him for his kindness.

He admits that in the first phases of civilisation the development of desires was a constant stimulant to progress; but he observes that this must have a limit, since there is a time-limit to man's work, given by its efficiency; beyond this limit the efficiency of the work diminishes, and farther additions to the hours of labour will be an injury. Now when the time-limit of highest efficiency of labour is reached, all growth of human desires that render greater labour necessary is harmful, and strong appetites, instead of constituting an element of strength and progress, become a source of weakness.[1]

Besides this, the spread of civilisation and the transformations effected in food, tend to decrease the sum total of man's bodily needs and the quantity of food necessary for satisfying them. An extended use of machinery which lessens the need of muscular exertion; well-constructed buildings, adequate clothing, and cheap fuel which reduce the supply of carbonaceous food required to keep our bodies warm; and above all the variety of food which ever increases with advancing civilisation, reduce the need for nourishment and the quantity of aliment necessary for keeping men in life.[2] In proportion to the increase in the variety of food, the quantity of edible substances that is required diminishes; large appetites are signs of inferior civilisation; the savage and the rustic, who know little variety of eatables, consume much larger quantities of them. The progress of civilisation makes therefore for a diminution of the amount of alimentary sustenance requisite for each man.

But human desires and consumption must undergo at the same time another and most important modification; men must ever adapt themselves better to the territories in which they live, so that by opportunely changing their diet they extract from the land those alimentary products which it is able to supply in the greatest abundance and most economically.

The land (says Patten) could give a greatly increased return if men were willing to produce and consume in such a way as to derive the greatest advantage from it.[3] But men are conservative in their habits; and thus Americans follow

[1] *Consumption of Wealth*, p. 29.   [2] Work mentioned, pp. 16, 17.
[3] Work mentioned, p. 63.

the customs which they brought with them from Europe centuries ago, and do not modify their food and their dress to suit the environment in which the people now exist. There are in the United States immense tracts of land which cannot be utilised, because there is no demand for the products to which these regions are best adapted; if a transformation of diet occurs and stimulates this produce, an entirely new civilisation will be developed in this part of the world.[1]

Thus with the progress of civilisation, whilst on the one hand human consumption tends to diminish, on the other there must necessarily be an increase of the advantage derived by mankind from the soil on which they live.

41. Most ingenious are the conclusions which our author has managed to draw from these premises.

Without altogether denying the theory of rent and of population, Patten substitutes for the pessimistic conclusions which usually follow from it, an optimistic result, by maintaining that rent and excess of population are due not to physical but to social causes, and more particularly to an imperfect adaptation of human food to existing circumstances and to an imperfect evolution of the consumption itself.[2] —

In proportion to the development of varieties of food and to the decrease in human appetites, will it become possible to meet the requirements of a larger population.[3] Besides this, the dearness of provisions is caused, not so much by the increase of population, as by men's customs regarding the consumption of wealth, and especially of food. Instead of preferring those commodities which are most abundant, they strive to augment the quantity of those that are rare: meat is demanded instead of vegetable food, wheat-bread instead of rye-bread, while corn is mainly used as animal food or for making whisky, and tobacco displaces other more useful crops.

If mankind adapted their habits to their environment, and forced the soil to yield those things for which it is best fitted; if, moreover, they did not occupy a large portion of the earth for the production of useless or hurtful commodities,

---

[1] *The Economic Basis of Protection*, pp. 103, 114, 117, 121. We shall return to this question later on when dealing with protection.
[2] *The Premises of Political Economy*, p. 11.
[3] Vide *Consumption of Wealth*, p. 45.

the price of food would be considerably lower. A high price of food is not the result of the pressure of population against the means of subsistence, but rather of the imperfect adaptation of the human race to the conditions of its territory.[1]

Thus land rent is the outcome of a state of things which, with the progress of civilisation, is destined to disappear. This progress, with the reduction of food and the better utilisation of the land, will necessarily diminish more and more the extent of soil needful for the maintenance of a family. Hunting communities require an immense area for keeping alive a scanty population. A primitive system of cultivation which is only occupied with raising wheat, likewise demands a considerable surface of territory. But when agriculture becomes more varied and more complex, when there is a greater variety of consumptions, and an ever-increasing adaptation of the latter to the conditions of the soil, each family will be able to live on the produce of a much more limited area. Rents increase because human appetites desire only a few limited products, and it is necessary to force the earth to obtain them: this is the only reason why the demand for food increases more rapidly than the supply, and prices rise, and with them rents.[2]

If we ate to live, instead of living to eat, and accustomed ourselves to food which could be produced at a cheaper rate, not only would it be possible for this globe to maintain a larger population, but it would diminish rents in this way also that, all land not being forced to produce the same crops, and each piece of ground being devoted to the products to which it was most suited, difference of fertility would become less marked.[3]

A decreasing productiveness and the pressure of population are, according to Patten, characteristic of a primitive stage of civilisation: the amelioration of agriculture and the transformation of diet by effecting a better adaptation of the inhabitants to their environment, must augment the productiveness of the earth and make it capable of nourishing a larger population.[4]

[1] *The Premises of Political Economy*, pp. 15, 48, 55, 62, 64.
[2] *The Consumption of Wealth*, pp. 53-55.
[3] *The Premises of Political Economy*, pp. 48, 49.
[4] Work mentioned, pp. 182, 183.

In order to develop their civilisation and to ensure a general state of well-being, the American people, therefore, must adapt themselves to the territories in which they live, modify their food to suit the productive capacities of the soil, accustom themselves to eat and drink new products, and to clothe themselves in a way better fitted to their surroundings, so as, by this means, to draw from the land its utmost available resources.[1]

In this evolution, however, the American people finds obstacles in the immigration of foreign workmen, who, accustomed to inferior food and ruled by fierce appetites, supplant American artisans and labourers of higher standing, or are at all events instrumental in bringing them down to their own level, thus impeding the transformation of diet, reducing by their inadequate wages the price of manufactures, and, on the other hand, raising, owing to their increasing numbers, the price of provisions and the rent. The immigration of these inferior work-people ought, for the security of American progress, to be checked.[2]

42. The other idea which pervades Patten's writings and which is chiefly developed in his last work,[3] is the distinction between static and dynamic economy. This idea, as we shall see better farther on when we come to criticise it, although it is to a large extent derived from his theory of consumption, is not formulated by Patten with sufficient clearness and precision, nor is it rendered more comprehensible and definite by the numerous abstractions of a utilitarian character with which he supports it, and which specially illustrate, in the book we have quoted, the theory of value.

Patten distinguishes and contrasts two types of economy; a non-progressive economy which he styles "static," and a progressive one which he calls "dynamic." In the first, nature dominates over mankind, whilst in the second there is a reciprocal action, man is affected by his environment, which, in his turn, he modifies: the first is characterised by a want of adaptability of man to his surroundings which prevents him from dominating them, whilst in the second this adaptation is

---

[1] *Consumption*, etc., Introduction, p. 6.
[2] Work mentioned, pp. 51, 62, 67.
[3] Vide *The Theory of Dynamic Economics*, Philadelphia, 1892.

ever becoming more complete. Static economy is the rule in the early phases of civilisation: in it, value is determined by the law of cost, and distribution by the law of rent, which represents the subjection of mankind to nature.

The change from one form of economy to the other is determined by transformation of diet from a simple, costly and inharmonious form, requiring products of which nature is less bountiful, to a more varied, harmonious, and less costly form. Just as an individual, by varying his food, draws from the same source higher final increments of pleasure—to use the expressions of the Austrian school—so a nation, by diversifying the articles which it consumes, can attain a greater degree of utility, and give to its products in general a value greater than that of the produce of countries whose consumable goods are less differentiated and less adapted to their circumstances.

Following, too, to a large extent, the teachings of the Austrian school, and entirely adopting its abstract and subjective method, Patten reforms its doctrine of value, and to the theory of final utility which he terms "static," opposes a "dynamic" theory, according to which, in a dynamic economy, subjective values tend to increase in consequence of the rise in value of the last increment of consumption and, at each successive stage of our social progress, the total value of commodities approaches more closely to the sum total of their utility.

We are not able to dilate—for it would take us too far out of our way—on Patten's abstract deductions regarding the theory of value, in which frequent obscurity of thought is often associated with the use of newly-coined words of which it is not easy to grasp the exact meaning intended by the author. There is one point, however, which we cannot pass over in silence, for it is of capital importance in Patten's theories, and he himself has pointed it out to us as the basis of his whole system and of his protectionist doctrines. We refer to his conception of progress and of the influence exercised upon it by prices. The progress of production is, he says, generally caused by the rise of prices. It is always good to have high prices. The fall of prices is a symptom of statical conditions and not a sign of prosperity, but rather an indication of a more unequal distribution of wealth, which gives a larger share to monopolies

The fall of prices in industries in which competition exists is accompanied by an increase of value of the products connected with landed or industrial monopolies; and thus nothing is gained by consumers. On the other hand, a rise of prices is not detrimental to the latter, for the burden of these high prices is not borne by them, but by those producers whose increase is the slowest—namely the monopolists. The consequences of this theory, so far as protection is concerned, are evident at a glance; we shall nevertheless return to the subject presently.

43. The protective system especially developed by Patten in his essay on the economic basis of protection, and which refers only to the particular conditions of the United States, may be summed up briefly. The American nation, as compared to the European States, is in a dynamic stage of far greater progressive activity; having within it the germs of a rapid development, it must give a free hand to the elements of progress which it contains, and turn to the best possible account all innate resources; and at the same time it must systematically curb all those static and retrogressive tendencies which bar the way to such progress, especially by means of the development of land rent, and which are encouraged by economic relations with Europe. A protective policy is, in Patten's opinion, the best means for the American people to attain this double end. Free-trade is an uncompromising theory, suited to a people in a static, inert condition; and when indiscriminately applied to stationary and to progressive countries, tends to place the latter on the same level as the former, by raising the returns of monopolies. As long as a community is dynamic and progressive, protection should always be resorted to, and this not temporarily and exceptionally, but as an established and normal instrument for supporting the progressive energies of the country.[1]

Like List, Patten denies the perpetual and cosmopolitan character of free-trade: he does not admit the solidarity of interests among nations, for he fears the contact of the less advanced with the more civilised, and would do all in his power to isolate the latter. He would wish to replace

[1] See on this point, *The Economic Basis of Protection, passim*, and particularly pp. 7, 11, 24, 51, 97, 98.

universal political economy by a particular economy adapted to a single country in a special stage of its development (an historical conception of the greatest wisdom if it could be logically carried out): for free-trade cosmopolitanism he would substitute a "dynamic nationalism," by means of which each nation, after undergoing a series of transformations tending to harmonise its social conditions with its economic environment, would develop and consolidate a peculiar national type, capable of utilising all national resources, and allowing the population to live on the soil and adapt to it their habits and their diet.[1] When this ideal has been reached, there will always remain room for international commerce in those special products which individual countries may supply in an absolutely superior manner.

Patten does not therefore demand, at all events formally, absolute protection, and he apparently gives his protective system an historical character; but it is a very different character to that of List: the period for which protection is necessary must be indeed a long one, if it is to be maintained, so long as the American people remain "dynamic," that is to say, progressive.

No wonder, therefore, that since an energetic protectionist régime has only existed in the United States for about thirty years, Patten is in no hurry to abandon it; indeed, he would like to reduce it to a true policy of commercial isolation from our poor plague-stricken Europe, which might contaminate the "dynamic" health of the great American republic with the dangerous contagion of our "static" diseases.[2]

But let us put comment aside for the present, and see by what arguments Patten supports his thesis. The principal point deserving examination is the task incumbent on protection, of stimulating the progressive tendencies of the country, and of clearing the way for the development of these tendencies.

44. His theory of consumption, which we have already explained, provides Patten with one of the foundations for his system of protection.

The people of the United States, being of European origin, have not yet completely adapted themselves to their American

[1] Work mentioned, pp. 21-24, 138. [2] *Ibid.* p. 140.

surroundings; and if they wish to advance, they will have to suit their diet and their habits to the land they live in; and as, for example, the United States are more fit for the production of cotton than that of wool, Americans will have to accustom themselves to wear cotton clothes which shall be so manufactured as to keep them as warm as woollen ones. And—pardon the comparison, it is not ours, but supplied by our bold Philadelphian economist—as the American pigs of the west have been used to feed exclusively on corn and have become different from the pigs of any other place, so must Americans accustom themselves to consume the produce of the soil and of the industries of their native land, and to regulate on them their lives and their tastes.[1]

The territory of the United States requires to be turned to better account; it needs cultivation in far more varied ways, for the law of agricultural industry is different from that of manufacturing industry, and whilst a factory is more productive if devoted to the preparation of a single product, the soil is best exploited by a variety of crops, and thus the exclusive culture of cotton and of tobacco in the southern States has impoverished the land.[2]

Now, according to Patten, free-trade is a bar to all this; it tends to restrict agriculture to one or to very few products —those which are the best able to be transported long distances, and hence it causes the exhaustion of the soil. When the western States were cultivated for export purposes only, their sole produce was wheat; and if this course had been pursued, the whole of the United States would have been divided into three great parallel zones, devoted exclusively to raising cotton, tobacco, and wheat.

But this logical consequence of Ricardo's law of comparative cost would have resulted in the ruin of the country; it would have hastened the exhaustion of the soil, whilst the development of home markets has brought about a varied agriculture, which has turned to far better account the resources of the American territory.[3]

Then elsewhere our author advances an argument which, in form at all events, is not wanting in originality; it is this, that whilst protection is generally reproached with

[1] Work mentioned, p. 119.   [2] *Ibid.* pp. 29-31.   [3] *Ibid.* pp. 41, 85-88.

giving an artificial direction to production, this is, on the contrary, the very effect of free-trade, which diverts the land from its best uses far more than protection does, for, as a great foreign demand for certain products is a premium on their production in a given country, it follows that, in that country, preference is given to these particular products, to the neglect of others which the land would be better fitted to supply, but which cannot be transported to great distances.[1]

Free-trade thus restricts the use of the soil to a few products, does not favour a variety of food, and hence limits the advantage to be taken from the land. Finally, free-trade is an impediment to progress and differentiation of consumption, for, in international trade, the greatest request will be for the products of that nation which, having lower wages and interests to pay, will be able to produce commodities at a cheap rate, and in which, consequently, there prevail inferior classes of work-people, living on simple, coarse, and little-varied food.[2]

It is therefore necessary to remove this retrogressive factor, this impediment to national progress, this obstacle to the evolution of consumption and the better utilisation of the soil; and instead of free-trade—(strangely enough, Patten often speaks as if the United States were a free-trading country, and it is difficult to understand what species of protection he requires, if even the MacKinley tariff does not satisfy him!)—instead of free-trade, it will be needful to adopt, together with all the other means for the greater development of national resources, a protective trade policy, opening up a home market for agricultural produce and creating a demand for that multiplicity of products which a varied and progressive culture will draw from the ground, by a better use, without any diminution of its fertility.[3]

45. But the most original part of Patten's protectionist theory consists of the relations which he discerns and illustrates between international trade and land rent. The theory of international commerce assumes an altogether different and singular aspect when we consider it in connection with rent and other natural monopolies; so that what may be true in

---

[1] *The Premises of Political Economy*, pp. 188-190.
[2] *Vide* work quoted, *passim*, and specially pp. 190, 191.
[3] *The Economic Basis*, etc., pp. 29-31, 41, etc.

circumstances in which such monopolies are of no consequence, is very far from being true when the reverse is the case.

In countries which produce provisions and raw materials, free-trade favours the development of land rent in two ways: by restricting the agricultural yield to a few products only, as we have already implicitly observed, and by impeding that greater and better utilisation of the land which a more varied cultivation would render possible; and also by increasing, through the agency of foreign demand, local agricultural production, and thus forcing the country, in order to meet this demand, to till inferior soil, with the result that a rise in the price of those products is effected. In this way, the landowner's rent is augmented, and at the same time the condition of capitalists and of labourers is depressed, for it is naturally lowered by competition, which reduces the value of manufactured goods, whilst, on the other hand, that of agricultural produce is constantly rising.

Every product which in a nation's progress becomes a natural monopoly (that is *rent*) acquires a greater value if it is exported than if it is merely used for home consumption. Free-trade, by giving an impulse to the exportation of such products, increases the returns of the owners of natural monopolies, and affects the distribution of the national wealth.

Protection, on the contrary, tends to raise the value of goods produced entirely by labour and capital (manufactures), and to lower that yielded by natural monopolies (agricultural produce).

But if, on the other hand, we consider a country that imports agricultural produce, the effects are exactly opposite, for in this case free-trade lowers the price of provisions, reduces rent, and raises wages and profits.

Considering the condition of the United States, Patten remarks that although the country is still young and rich, there is observable a great tendency to an increase of rent and of the returns of natural monopolies, and he concludes that free-trade would only aggravate this state of things, and produce the same effect as an increase of population. Protection, therefore, is needed for the United States in order that the land may be exploited to greater advantage, that a transformation of diet may be effected, that the exportation of agricultural produce may be checked, home consumption increased, rent lowered, and the economic forces of the country stimulated by higher wages and profits.[1] And this protection, which proves so beneficial to the progress of the nation, cannot in any way injure consumers, for the rise in prices which it begets and maintains does not tell upon them, but only on the landed and industrial monopolists.

46. We will now pass on to a brief critical examination of these doctrines of the Philadelphian professor, and especially of those which concern us more particularly.

In the first place we must touch on the method adopted in his investigations by Patten. He is decidedly in favour of the deductive process, which he invariably follows, remaining, however, in a purely abstract field of speculation; but he departs considerably from Ricardo, preferring the subjective analysis, characteristic of the modern Austrian school,[2] to the objective analysis on which the Ricardian laws, which are essentially objective, are based. Patten's abstract researches have, however, a peculiar character; whilst accepting, and even exclusively adopting the deductive method, he does not assign an absolute value to economic laws, and hence gives in a certain way an historical impress to his deductions. He denies the existence of a system of economy whose doctrines are equally true for all civilisations, and he entirely acquiesces in the conception of a national economy appropriate to a given country in a given phase of civilisation; but when the more important characteristics of a nation have been determined, which act as the economic mainspring at a given stage of its development, then he would like us to proceed deductively, and analyse abstractly the logical consequences of these historical premises, without ulterior recourse to the study of facts.[3]

Hence the peculiar character of Patten's deductions, which aim at having an historical value, and of a national theory of economy evolved out of abstract reasoning and having an essentially psychological foundation.

[1] Vide *The Economic Basis*, etc., *passim*, and specially pp. 13, 20, 37-40, 47-49; and *The Premises*, etc., pp. 193-195, 207.
[2] See particularly *The Theory of Dynamic Economics*, Introduction, pp. 6, 7, etc.
[3] *The Economic Basis*, etc., p. 10.

We cannot linger here, since it is not our purpose to criticise the methods of the Austrian school, to note the remarkable retrogression which, in economic science, has been brought about by the substitution of subjective reasoning for the objective Ricardian deduction, a change that is in the most complete opposition to the evolution of all the other sciences, progress in which has been attained by the very converse transition from subjective to objective reasoning; but we will only observe that the adoption of an exclusively, or almost exclusively subjective method, is not reconcilable with an historical conception that must necessarily take not man but his environment as its starting-point, since, although they without doubt mutually influence one another, the foundation must ever be in the surroundings.

Nor can we understand an historical method, or anyhow an historical conception which does not, in its investigations, assign a prominent part to inductive research; for, if any absolute reasoning is possible which is founded on a few premises of a general nature, as is the case with the classical school, researches, if they are to have an historical character, must evidently be built on an ample inductive basis, which shall set forth in all clearness the special characteristics of a given historical period.

Now the grave defect of Patten's method lies precisely in this, that he more frequently limits himself to investigations of a subjective character, which lead him on to that abuse of deduction and into that labyrinth of fruitless abstractions which mark the Austrian school: his work on dynamic economics is an instance in point, and, as we shall see presently, although it was the author's intention that it should lay the foundation of his whole system, yet to us it does not appear to contain the secure, much less the clear and intelligible basis of an economic theory. And when Patten, to conform to the historical character which he wishes to impart to his laws, endeavours to place them on an objective basis, as when he founds his protectionist theory on the particular historical circumstances of American life, his evident aversion to any kind of inductive research frequently renders his investigations insufficient. In fact, if some of his premises, founded on obvious facts—such, for example, as that the increase of population leads to the cultivation of inferior land — may be accepted without demur; with regard to others, relating to American conditions, facts are wanting or are insufficiently supported; so that the reader views with the greatest diffidence historical deductions which are neither seductive as absolute abstractions nor conclusive as evidence of concrete facts.

47. This defective method is observable above all in that idea upon which Patten, as we have seen, builds his whole theory, and which has not, in our opinion, a sufficient scientific foundation: that of the distinction between static and dynamic economy. In his writings, these two expressions of scientific appearance are constantly met with, but they do not lend much clearness to the subject, because the meaning which is so unmistakable in physics is not equally so in the author's mind; he speaks not only of static and dynamic economy, but also of static and dynamic theories, of static and dynamic classes, of static and dynamic elements, and in fact abuses the words to such an extent as to cause the utmost confusion. As long as our ingenious American economist distinguishes a static theory from a dynamic theory, pointing out that the error of the classical school is to consider economic laws as fixed and absolute, and that the truth is that there exists an economic evolution, the characteristics and laws of which are undergoing successive transformations, we shall entirely agree with him—noting the fact, for all that, that this is but the old idea of the historical school, to which are tacked on new expressions, which are of absolutely no use.

But, admitting this idea, the question is to trace the historical evolution, to find out what are the economic laws at the various historical epochs: what has, in fact, to be done is to complete that great historical research which has only just been commenced, and which the historical school has, upon an inductive basis, so courageously undertaken.

It is at this point that we find a great confusion in the ideas at which Patten has arrived by following the deductive method. He distinguishes, in fact, two economics, one static and the other dynamic, one stationary and the other progressive, and he compares the one with the other: and yet we do not clearly understand whether, in his mind, these are two separate and isolated forms, two different types of civilisation, or two historical forms which mark two distinct periods in the history of nations.

Judging from the whole of Patten's works, we should conclude that it is rather the second idea that he has in his mind; and this idea is indeed the only historical one, for we can only regard as quite exceptional cases of static civilisation, or better, arrested civilisation (such as savage races, China, etc. —it is not, however, to such people that he alludes, as he is always comparing the state of Europe with that of America).

Now assuming these two hypothetical forms of static and dynamic economy to be historical forms, what then is their law of historical succession, and how does time develop them? Here, too, we find a great confusion of thought. Patten constantly recurs to the idea that static economy is characteristic of primitive communities, of the early phases of civilisation: that it implies the resistance of nature, which little by little is overcome by civilised man, who, having once removed the natural barriers from his path, advances day by day in an ever more progressive and dynamic economy. The law of rent is considered by him, as we have seen, to be characteristic of a primitive state, and under the influence of progress, is destined to disappear. But then he adds—and this is one of the foundations for his protectionist theory—that America is in a far more dynamic condition than Europe, and he repeatedly contrasts the European type of static civilisation with the dynamic type of America, and fears for the latter any contact with the former.

But how are we to reconcile all this with the logic and reality of facts? If rent was peculiar to a primitive state and marked an economy regulated by nature, which tended to be eliminated by civilisation, we ought to find it prevalent in new countries, and to have become merely of secondary importance in old ones. If static precedes dynamic economy, the new nations ought to be static and the ancient States dynamic; America ought to be static, and Europe dynamic.

Our author gets involved in a series of inextricable contradictions, which reach a climax when after all this, after having qualified the law of rent as static and characteristic of primitive non-progressive conditions, and after having quoted the United States as a type of dynamic civilisation, he comments on the great development of rent and natural monopolies in that country, and upon it bases his most ingenious argument in favour of a protective policy!

The truth is that even if this abstract distinction between static and dynamic economy contains some element of truth, in that the conditions of progress are really different in different countries, yet the problem is not clear in the author's mind, nor, as far as we can understand it, does it tally with the reality of things; so that in order to apply his theory, Patten is constantly brought into contradiction with himself and with facts. We entirely fall in with the idea of the different historical importance of land rent and of the very great influence which social circumstances exercise on this phenomenon; but although we accept for the most part Loria's ideas, which are based on a profound study of the historical evolution of land rent, we cannot, on the other hand, agree to these confused ideas of Patten, whose endeavour to trace new laws of economic evolution does not seem to bear any useful fruit.

We must not, however, leave this distinction between static and dynamic economy without alluding to a singular conclusion at which Patten arrives regarding his protectionist theory. He accuses the doctrine of free-trade—and in our opinion he is fully justified in so doing—of being part and parcel of that old economic system which admitted the existence of absolute and perpetual laws of economy applicable to every nation in all stages of their development; and he observes that the historical method has rejected this erroneous idea, and has substituted a dynamic theory for the old static conception. Now it would seem that from these premises the conclusion should be arrived at that the question of international trade should be studied in connection with the conditions of the various countries, and that at certain given periods either protection or free-trade may be opportune. To this conclusion (which in substance is that come to by List, and for which consequently no great novelty can be claimed) Patten would seem to arrive, but—and here is the mischief—whilst all that is new and important lies in determining at what moments in the life of a people protection may be necessary, he, with his usual expressions, solves the problem in an unexpected way truly, but his conclusion is strangely discordant from his premises. He says, in fact, that free-trade, which is a static system, adapts itself to the circumstances of a static, non-progressive country, whilst protection, a dynamic system, lends itself to the state of a dynamic one.

Hence the conclusion that as long as such dynamic conditions last, so long must protection be maintained; and hence, we may add, as the time when the progress in civilisation of a nation may be arrested can neither be foreseen nor desired—(nor indeed does our author include it in his calculations, laying down, as he does, that the static precedes the dynamic phase, and his views being essentially optimistic)—protection must last for all eternity! Thus it is that starting with an historical premise and the denial of absolute laws, the writer, by means of this distinction between static and dynamic, which in this case resolves itself into a mere play upon words (since neither free-trade nor protection can be called dynamic, but the historical conception can be applied to both of them), thus, we say, the writer arrives at a conclusion quite as absolute and ten times as absurd as that reached by free-trade theorists.

48. As we have already pointed out, Patten's theory of consumption is certainly his most original idea, and the one that contains the greatest elements of truth.

Altogether just are his views of the better exploitation of the land, and of the adaptation to the environment of consumption; and although open to question, there is much originality in the idea of the diminution of the quantity of food needful for mankind, in consequence of a more varied diet and of the progress of civilisation. But all these premises, even if we accept them in their entirety, are not, in our opinion, sufficient to warrant the optimistic conclusions of our author, who fancies he has gone to the root of the sad phenomena of over-population and rent. That this over-population is, in actual circumstances, frequently artificial and not a result of natural laws, we firmly believe; and that an alteration of diet might do some good appears to us evident. But we also think that the social cause of the artificial excess of population in many countries at the present day lies not in their consumption or customs policy, but in the defective organisation of landed property, which is the principal hindrance to a more copious fructification of the soil; and only a radical reform in this quarter will provide an efficacious remedy.

On the other hand, while Patten's observations show how the gravity of the phenomenon of rent might perhaps be mitigated by means of a reform in diet and of the methods of cultivation, and the limits of a diminishing productiveness be thus pushed out of sight, yet do his remarks in no way bear on the phenomenon itself in its essential cause, the unequal fertility of different lands, and hence they do not sound the depths of the problem.

For example, the fact which he brings so ingeniously forward, that with the progress in diet, an ever relatively smaller quantity of ground will be needed for the sustenance of mankind, serves to demonstrate that the human race, under the increasing pressure of population, will endeavour to turn his surroundings to better account in order to meet the requirements of larger numbers, but leaves the essential feature of the rent phenomenon unaffected.

Nor do the conclusions which Patten draws in favour of protection from his theory of consumption appear to us very logical. As a matter of fact, the idea of adapting consumption to our environment with a view to the better exploitation of the land and the obtaining from it those things which it is best able to yield, is certainly not devoid of reasonableness; but to maintain that to effect this purpose men should completely transform themselves and imitate the insects which even assume the colour of the vegetation in which they live, appears to us extravagant, and instead of marking the supremacy of mankind over their surroundings, would establish the very contrary. If it is said that a country provided with many varied resources ought to utilise them to the largest extent possible for home consumption, this we can, up to a certain point, endorse; but to lay down that the inhabitants of a country should sustain themselves almost exclusively on the produce of their own soil, and give up the production of such things as could be usefully exported, and for which other articles could be obtained in exchange, seems to us to be utterly absurd. We admit the idea of a better cultivation of our native land and of our better adaptation to it; we admit that for certain countries of great and various resources, international trade must be less important than for other less-favoured nations, but we maintain that a large gap must be filled in to reconcile these propositions to the system of economic isolation, which is a necessary corollary to Patten's views.

49. These considerations clear the ground for a more particular examination of Patten's theory of protection. It is, as we have before remarked, most decidedly original—as indeed are all the ideas of this ingenious writer. We must not, however, let ourselves be carried away too far by this seductive originality, which is often only apparent. Patten's works have, among others, the defect of not unfrequently giving a new form or new expression to old ideas. For all that, it seems undeniable that traces of List and of Carey are discernible in some of his thoughts, although starting from different premises and clothed in different language. When, for example, in criticising the theory of comparative cost, he maintains that a progressive nation must not only secure profitable trade and industry for its actual population, but must also secure the gradual utilisation of the latent qualities in man and land,[1] he does but reproduce List's theory of reproductive forces; and he develops the same theory when he says that there is no need to concern oneself about a good market for products, the essential thing being the productive power of the country.[2] And in common with Carey, Patten holds the opinions that the plots of ground first tilled are not the best, and that protection should favour the cultivation of the more fertile land;[3] and that with the progress of society, general well-being tends to augment, and social inequalities tend to diminish; both writers associate optimism with protection, so that the latter is presented as instrumental to progress and to the elimination of social difficulties.

The historical conception of protectionism, even if it had been clearly set forth by Patten, would always be due to List; but we have already seen how Patten's protectionism is only historical in appearance, and how in a disguised form it is really of a permanent character.

[1] *The Economic Basis*, etc., p. 84.   [2] Work mentioned, p. 127.
[3] *Ibid.* pp. 56, 57.

On this point, however, Patten's ideas are not only wanting in clearness, but they appear to us contradictory; for whilst there can be no doubt that in his essay on the economic basis of protection, he assigns to it, in the United States, a permanent and not a transitory character,[1] in the last pages of his theory of dynamic economics, on the contrary, after having traced an exceedingly abstract and nebulous historical evolution of economy, in which, at various epochs there presented itself, in his opinion, a necessity for protection, he ends by observing that experience shows that the classes favoured by protection tend to become static, that protected industries tend to lose all progressive development, and that conflicting interests spring up and divide the social classes; and concludes that society will in time be dissatisfied with its present progress, which is obtained by indirect and costly means, and will have recourse to better and more efficient agents, such as the advancement of morality and social ideals.[2]

Others of Patten's opinions regarding protection are merely reproductions of old ideas in new forms, or else are not amenable to criticism. Thus he expounds in somewhat novel fashion the relation between protection and wages, by applying the doctrine of final utility to the theory of wages,[3] and maintaining that trade with less progressive countries tends to lower American wages, while protection tends to raise them. But we think we have sufficiently demonstrated the nugatory influence of customs protection upon wages, and that to benefit them what is needful is to hinder not the importation of foreign goods, but the immigration of inferior work-people. And thus the idea which is also expressed by Gunton, and constantly maintained by Patten, of the danger to more advanced countries of contact with their less developed neighbours, appears to us to be founded on an altogether unsubstantial basis, as indeed we have shown in the previous essay.

Finally, Patten's idea, to which we have so frequently alluded, that protection should serve to excite a reform of diet

[1] This is likewise observed by Adams in an article on that work in the *Political Science Quarterly*, December 1890.
[2] *The Theory of Dynamic Economics*, pp. 151, 152. Note that in the *Economic Basis of Protection*, p. 35, Patten maintains, on the contrary, that protection strengthens the spirit of enterprise which animates protected traders.
[3] *The Economic Basis*, etc., pp. 173-180.

and a complete utilisation of the national territory on behalf of its inhabitants, who should, in this way, make it directly provide for their wants; this idea, though exaggerating that of List's national economy, contains in fact, under a new disguise, the old idea of the preference that should be given to native trade and consumption when competing with foreign commerce. Now we have repeatedly pointed out how this view, which has been slowly elaborated in the history of the United States, contains, in the actual condition of the American territory, elements of truth which have been constantly increasing, and we are still of opinion that herein lies the best justification of American protectionism. But it is evident that this is no new contribution made by Patten to protective theories.

50. The most original part of his view of protection is, as we have seen, that regarding the relation between protection and rent.[1] The importance which he gives to the division of the social classes and to the land rent, in the theory of international trade, is perfectly justified, and opens out a fresh field for investigation; and very ingenious is his contention that in exporting countries free-trade tends to raise rents.

Professor Taussig has attempted to refute this argument.[2] He says that the rise in prices of provisions and in rent in countries which export food does not indicate that their commerce with other nations is hurtful to them, for if this were so, that commerce would cease of its own accord. The fact that it exists, means, according to Taussig, that in spite of recourse being had to inferior soil, it is of advantage to the country to export the produce of this soil, and to import manufactured articles in exchange, rather than itself produce such articles.

These observations, however, do not seem to shake Patten's position in the very least; for, even if we admit that from a strictly economic point of view such commerce is advantageous, the fact that, by raising rents it increases social inequalities and necessarily lowers profits and wages, renders it socially harmful.

[1] Original so far as Patten's explanation goes and the importance which he attaches to it, but not, properly speaking, new; since, as we have seen, these ideas had already been broached by Bastable and Loria.

[2] *Vide* "Recent Literature on Protection," in the *Quarterly Journal of Economics*, January 1893.

And however strange it may appear that the Philadelphian professor, who in his writings, and especially in his *Premises of Political Economy*, so violently attacks the theory of rent, and endeavours to attenuate its importance in every way, should base his strongest argument in favour of American protectionism on this very phenomenon, yet on this head his conclusions, from an abstract point of view, are in our opinion unassailable.

But if we look at the matter in its true light, and ask ourselves whether protection can really have, in the United States, the depreciative action on rent claimed for it by Patten, the answer is very different. The fact is that for more than thirty years the American republic has been subject to a protective *régime* of ever-increasing severity; and yet (the admission is made by Patten himself) land rents show an unmistakable and progressive tendency to rise. And this makes it clear enough that free-trade (which does not exist in America) is no more responsible for such a rise than a protective policy (which has been in operation for so long) is capable of modifying it.

But the most serious practical objection that can be urged against Patten's abstract theory is the one we have put forward in the last pages of the last chapter of the preceding essay.

The history of American protectionism during these last years clearly shows that in the United States industrial protection cannot be resorted to except by indemnifying the landowners, by means of agricultural protection, for the damage which it does them. Duties on manufactured goods cannot be maintained unless similar duties are levied on agricultural products. But in this way, the policy which, to believe Patten, tends to depress land rents by limiting the rise in price of agricultural produce, provoked by its exportation, co-operates, on the other hand, by means of agrarian protection, in raising that very price, and therefore conduces to higher rents. So the imagined efficacy of tariff protection proves to be a complete delusion.

But our professor invokes protection not only as a safeguard against land rent, but against industrial monopolies and trusts as well, maintaining that the burden of high prices, caused and kept up by protection, must also tend to check such monopolies.

The truth is that reason and facts unite to demolish this strange paradoxical theory, which apparently calls in the aid of protection to defend open competition! Reason tells us that trusts derive powerful support from protection, which renders it easier for them to make themselves masters of the home markets and to monopolise them; and facts show us, side by side in the United States, a system of protection which has been adhered to for more than thirty years with unflinching energy, and a colossal and overbearing organisation of industrial monopolies, unknown to any other country!

51. The connection between Patten's theories and the actual American situation is not, at first sight, very manifest. The Philadelphian professor is a follower, as we have seen, of the deductive method, and he takes great delight in abstractions, rarely condescending to touch realities and to clearly and accurately apply his theories to concrete facts. He is, moreover, to a large extent a follower of a new economic school, which has originated far from the United States, and which is founded chiefly on subjective analysis.

It is quite true that Patten, especially in his work on protection, says that he is concerned above all with American affairs, and that his theories are formulated only to meet the requirements of the United States; but taken on the whole, his investigations, though often deep and original, are none the less abstract and abstruse, so that it is no easy task to adapt them to actual circumstances and to determine their relation to the conditions of life in America.

If, however, we divest Patten's protectionist doctrine of all superfluous and unessential matter; if, for instance, we free it from that embarrassing and confused conception of dynamic economics, and attend only to the more concrete ideas, we shall see that they refer to two most important characteristics of the American situation, which the author has grappled with most effectually; only they are presented by him in so unusual a way, that we do not, at first sight, recognise the connection between the theory and actual facts.

The whole of his theory of consumption, with its protective applications, advocating a more complete and direct utilisation of the American soil by its inhabitants, is nothing in reality but the reflection of the fact to which we have more than once alluded, that the territory of the United States lends itself, owing to its extent and variety, to the most diverse forms of exploitation, and to the providing of all the various wants of a progressive population; so that although absolute isolation would be absurd, yet the dependence of this country upon other ones is only relative, its pretension to stand alone is to a large extent practicable, and the advantage of free-trade and disadvantage of protection—in a word, international trade—is of far less importance to the American nation than to any other nation in the world.

And the weight attached by our author to the phenomenon of land rent, with regard to protection, and his principal argument in favour of protective tariffs as a weapon against rent, refer indirectly to the actual crisis in American capitalism to which we gave a detailed analysis in the preceding essay, a crisis in which, as we have seen, capitalism seizes every possible means of reacting against the depression of profits, and as a last desperate resource beards her eternal but triumphant enemy land rent, now more powerful and strong than ever in the United States.

52. The question of protection and free-trade in the actual condition of that country presents itself, therefore, in the shape of a struggle between the two dominant classes, the landowners and the manufacturers, rent and profits. But let not the capitalists imagine that the victory will be theirs, nor the American people, nor even the labourers, fancy that they will reap any advantage from the success of one side or the other. Whether protection be as strictly maintained in the future as it is at present, or whether its provisions be modified, the advantage which capitalist manufacturers will draw from it will be slight indeed. In fact, as we have already set forth, protection cannot, in the most favourable circumstances, be other than an inorganic and temporary expedient to enable them to react against the depression of profits, an expedient that in no way removes the cause of this depression, and that can at the present moment only prove of transitory benefit.

But even such fleeting advantages are neutralised and effaced by the struggle between the two classes, between profits and rent. At other times, when capitalism was young and represented progress and the future, the interests of the capitalists, which were then the interests of the country at large, could for a while prevail; but the knell of capitalism has now sounded, and rent, stimulated by the social organisation and by the constitution of landed property of the present day, is everywhere triumphant, and it is impossible to imagine how profits can turn the scales against it in the conflict now raging.

The actual American protectionism is a concession by the landowners to the manufacturers, and is only maintained by flanking industrial protection, which tends to lower rents, with agricultural protection which tends to raise them.

Now the landowners either find in these higher rents a sufficient compensation for the evils of industrial protection, and in this case the latter is of no use whatever to capitalists; or else this compensation is inadequate, and then they will certainly insist on a reform of the tariff system. Such a reform may be effected either by broadening and aggravating agricultural protection, or else by passing from the actual state of almost prohibitive protection to a system of relative free-trade. In the first case, capitalists must not flatter themselves that any benefit will accrue to them, for what they might gain on the one side by the protection granted to industries they would lose on the other by that afforded to agriculture; in the second case, free-trade would set a seal on the victory of landed property and rent.

Taking into consideration the existing condition of the United States, it is possible, and even probable, that the latter may be the course chosen, and that the sun of protectionism is about to set. American free-traders will do well, however, to curb their enthusiasm at such a prospect; for, however much it may interest Europe, which would gain so largely by an invigorated trade with the United States, no great advantage could be derived from it by the American people. We do not certainly deny that something would be gained by the abolition of an artificial system, which causes no end of inconvenience and evil, and which is frequently an instrument of injustice and the means of enriching a privileged few, whilst, on the other hand, it does not, in existing circumstances, make for the lasting welfare of any class, still less for that of the nation at large; but for all that, the advantages to be secured would, in our opinion, be small, both because the question of international trade plays no very important part in the present state of the American republic, and because, as long as the actual system of the distribution of wealth is in existence, the victory of free-trade in the United States will be merely the victory of a single and a privileged class.

The great question of the future for America will not be the question of protection or free-trade; it will be the fundamental, fruitful, and all-important question of property in land and the social organisation of production.

These lines were written in the spring of 1893, that is, long before the passing of the last Tariff Act, which came into force 27th August 1894. There is, however, really nothing to add to our conclusions on the respective conditions of industrial and agricultural protection, upon the probable future of the American Commercial Policy, and on the probable effects of a great reduction of the tariffs. We note with great pleasure also that Professor Taussig, certainly one of the greatest authorities on the subject, in his article published in the December number of the *Economic Journal*, 1894 (which appeared during the revision of the proof-sheets of this work), expresses the opinion, already maintained by us in these pages, that the tariff question has actually in the United States a much less importance than appears at first sight; and that the social questions are much more deserving of prior consideration.

INDEX OF THE NAMES OF AUTHORS MENTIONED

ADAMS, 109, 118, 122, 123, 124, 125, 127, 142, 143, 182, 183, 313, 405
Anderson, 8, 38
Atkinson, 225, 242

BACON, 10
Bancroft, 6-9, 13, 14, 18-24, 50-55, 58, 65, 71, 81-85, 97, 102, 109, 129
Bastable, 238, 239, 271, 406
Beer, 5, 10, 12, 13, 21, 54, 57, 70, 85, 87
Bidermann, 27
Bishop, 18, 50, 52, 55, 57, 67, 69, 70, 73, 81, 98, 100-102, 105, 106, 119, 120, 122, 127, 128, 139-142, 144, 150, 153, 154, 156-158, 161, 162, 174, 184, 185, 188-190
Bodio, x.
Böhm-Bawerk, 364
Bolles, 6, 17, 19-21, 50, 53, 56, 67, 69, 70, 98, 99, 101, 103, 105, 106, 119, 122, 125, 134, 136, 149, 151-153, 155, 156, 196, 202-204, 257, 291, 294, 295, 297, 313
Bonham, 236
Botta, 23, 83, 84, 97
Bourne, 318
Brentano, 235
Bryce, 229, 290, 292

CAIRNES, xviii., 186, 214-216, 255, 256
Carey, H. C., xvii., xviii., xxi.-xxiv., 159, 172-176, 196, 199, 210, 216, 312, 319-321, 355-383, 404
Carey, M., 106, 357
Carnegie, 23
Cattaneo, 104, 122, 163, 350
Chevalier, 241
Child, 30, 35, 36, 38
Cognetti, 196
Cooley, 82
Cossa, E., 249
Cossa, L., x., 27, 33, 35, 36, 288, 311, 357

Cunningham, 5, 10-12, 14, 27, 28, 31, 42, 59

DALLA VOLTA, xix., 237
Davenant, 35, 36
Davis, 82
Dickens, 241

EDGEWORTH, x.
Eheberg, 145, 325, 330, 331, 335, 338, 344, 346, 349, 350, 353
Ellena, 201
Elliott, 107, 125
Ely, x., 122, 123, 142, 168, 174, 211
Eyma, 66, 97

FAWCETT, 251
Ferrara, 356
Ford, 117, 121, 185, 201
Franklin, xiv., 52, 66, 71-80, 83, 84, 102, 127, 132

GALLATIN, xvii., 149-152, 176
George, 211, 220, 257, 280, 379
Gibbins (De), 32, 61, 62
Gide, 139, 308
Gladstone, 24
Gobbi, 35
Goss, 51, 56, 57
Gunton, xviii., 210, 216-219, 221, 235, 384, 405

HAMILTON, xvi., xvii., xxi.-xxiii., 76, 81, 85, 120, 124, 126-128, 133, 135-139, 164, 165, 174, 176, 216, 289-324, 325, 344, 345, 355, 378, 382
Häusser, 330, 338
Held, 27, 33, 35, 36, 363, 371-373, 378, 383
Heyking (Von), 27, 34
Hildreth, 106
Hill, 99, 100, 107, 121, 125
Hoyt, 215

INGRAM, 35, 344, 376, 378
JANNASCH, 7
Jannet, 224, 237, 240, 242
Jefferson, 120, 124, 132, 140, 291, 292, 296, 338
Jenks, 312, 321, 357, 364, 370, 371, 374, 377, 379
Johnston, 108, 148, 291, 293, 297

LANGE, 374
Lecky, 89
Leroy Beaulieu, 49, 66, 81, 82
Leser, 330, 335, 338
Levi, 16, 62, 63, 66, 106, 121, 122, 142, 148
Lexis, 347, 348, 363, 371
List, xvii., xxi.-xxiv., 145, 165, 194, 320, 325-354, 355, 380, 382, 383, 392, 393, 401, 404, 406
Locke, 35
Lodge, 109, 290, 291, 293, 313
Loria, x., xvii., 51, 52, 63, 64, 71, 73, 88-90, 109, 131, 170-172, 178, 231, 243, 244, 270, 271, 280, 377, 401, 406

M'CULLOCH, 12, 14, 18, 62, 65, 105
M'Leod, 295
Malthus, 65, 74, 358, 365, 386
Mason, 98, 103, 106, 107, 109, 119, 210
Merivale, 87
Mill, Stuart, xvii., 165-168, 351, 369, 374
Mills, 225-226
Moireau, 206
Montefiore, 63
Morse, 291
Mun, 33-35

NEBENIUS, 326, 334
Niles, 153
Nimmo, 204, 253, 254
North, 35, 36

PATTEN, x., xxii., xxiv., 278, 384-408
Petty, 35
Phillips, 243, 244

RAFFALOVICH, 236, 237
Ramsay, 85
Ricardo, vii., xiv., 37, 42-44, 317, 355, 358, 359, 363-365, 374, 378, 394, 397
Ricca Salerno, x., xvii., xix., 131, 171-172, 174, 183, 212, 241, 245, 247, 260, 262, 264, 267, 271, 275
Robertson, 6-8, 14, 55
Robinson, 241
Rogers, 32, 33, 82
Roscher, 7, 8, 13, 21, 27, 29, 35, 44, 49, 55, 81, 261, 325, 330, 331, 334, 337, 338, 346, 349, 350, 252, 378
Ross, 295

SAY, 341
Schanz, 5, 11
Schoenhof, 214, 257
Schönberg, 347
Scobell, 13
Seeley, 89, 90
Seligman, x., 108, 122, 124, 186, 195, 202, 204
Sering, 177, 178, 243
Sismondi, 61
Smith, Adam, vii., xiv., xxi., 12, 14, 16, 17, 24, 25, 28, 37-42, 44-46, 56, 59, 76, 199, 310, 313-319, 323, 326, 334, 335, 339-341, 343, 346, 353, 355, 362.
Smith, Mayo, 108, 122, 124, 186, 195, 202, 204
Spofford, 135
Sterne, 96
Stringher, 223, 224.
Sumner, xxi., 85, 109, 117, 122, 132, 139, 154, 168, 178, 184, 185, 190, 196, 290, 291, 294, 295, 309, 313

TAUSSIG, x., xvii., xviii., 122, 123, 127, 151, 156, 162-164, 179-182, 185, 186, 196, 197, 199, 202, 204-206, 208, 221, 225, 234, 239, 244, 257, 406, 411
Temple, 35, 36
Thompson, R. E., 383
Thompson, R. W., 109, 119, 121, 122, 125, 145
Tocqueville (De), 229, 292
Tucker, 120
Twiss, 35

WAKEFIELD, xvii., 175
Walker, A., 167, 196
Walker, F. A., 167, 213, 219, 220.
Webster, 298
Wells, 10, 14, 55, 81, 118, 186, 190, 196, 201-203, 212-214, 223, 224, 230, 231, 248, 255, 257
Wharton, 385
Wright, x., 127, 129, 151, 152, 161, 162, 188, 196, 197, 230, 240-242, 377, 378.

THE END

Printed by R. & R. CLARK, LIMITED, *Edinburgh.*